New Issues and Paradigms in Research on Social Dilemmas

New Issues and Paradigms in Research on Social Dilemmas

Edited by

Anders Biel
Daniel Eek
Tommy Gärling
Mathias Gustafsson

all of
Psykologiska Institutionen
Göteborg University
Göteborg, Sweden

 Springer

Anders Biel
Psykologiska Institutionen
Göteborg University
Göteborg, Sweden

Daniel Eek
Psykologiska Institutionen
Göteborg University
Göteborg, Sweden

Tommy Gärling
Psykologiska Institutionen
Göteborg University
Göteborg, Sweden

Mathias Gustafsson
Psykologiska Institutionen
Göteborg University
Göteborg, Sweden

ISBN: 978-0-387-72595-6   e-ISBN: 978-0-387-72596-3

Library of Congress Control Number: 2007929478

Printed on acid-free paper.

9 8 7 6 5 4 3 2 1

springer.com

Contents

Contributors

Wing Tung Au, The Chinese University of Hong Kong, Hong Kong, China

Alicia F. Bembenek, University of Arkansas, Fayetteville, AR, U.S.A.

Anders Biel, Göteborg University, Göteborg, Sweden

Gary Bornstein, The Hebrew University of Jerusalem, Jerusalem, Israel

Robyn Dawes, Carnegie Mellon University, Pittsburgh, PA, U.S.A.

David De Cremer, Tilburg University, Tilburg, The Netherlands

Eric van Dijk, Leiden University, Leiden, The Netherlands

Daniel Eek, Göteborg University, Göteborg, Sweden

Ilan Fischer, University of Haifa, Haifa, Israel

Margaret Foddy, Carleton University, Ottawa, Ontario, Canada

Tommy Gärling, Göteborg University, Göteborg, Sweden

Robert Gifford, University of Victoria, Victoria, BC, Canada

Mathias Gustafsson, Göteborg University, Göteborg, Sweden

Ali Kazemi, University of Skövde, Skövde, Sweden

Kimberly M. Kinsey, University of Arkansas, Fayetteville, AR, U.S.A.

Shirli Kopelman, University of Michigan, Ann Arbor, MI, U.S.A.

Rie Mashima, Hokkaido University, Sapporo, Japan

Michael McGinnis, Indiana University, Bloomington, IN, U.S.A.

Holger Meinhardt, University of Karlsruhe, Karlsruhe, Germany

Laetitia B. Mulder, Tilburg University, Tilburg, The Netherlands

Chi Sing Ngan, The Chinese University of Hong Kong, Hong Kong, China

Axel Ostman, University of Saarland, Saarland, Germany

Elinor Ostrom, Indiana University, Bloomington, IN, U.S.A.

Yuval Samid, University of Haifa, Mount Carmel, Haifa, Israel

David A. Schroeder, University of Arkansas, Fayetteville, AR, U.S.A.

Mizuho Shinada, Hokkaido University, Sapporo, Japan

Julie E. Steel, Rhodes College, Memphis, TN, U.S.A.

Jeroen Stouten, University of Leuven, Leuven, Belgium

Ramzi Suleiman, University of Haifa, Haifa, Israel

Nobuyuki Takahashi, Hokkaido University, Sapporo, Japan

Andria J. Woodell, Central Oregon Community College, Bend, OR, U.S.A.

Toshio Yamagishi, Hokkaido University, Sapporo, Japan

Chapter 1
The Conceptual Framework
of Social Dilemmas

Anders Biel

Introduction

An important topic concerning human nature and motives directing human behavior has guided social dilemma research over the years. Is human nature, as many theorists assume, basically selfish and human behavior driven by egoistic incentives, or should a more truthful account also include that humans sometimes cooperate for the best of fellow humans? On theoretical as well as empirical grounds (e.g., Caporael et al., 1989; Dawes, 1980; Komorita & Parks, 1994), cooperative behavior in the absence of egoistic incentives was soon accepted within psychology. In recent years, economists have followed the path (e.g., Fehr et al., 2002; Frey, 1997). Hence, the battle over human motives has partly been settled. Still, situational factors can influence whether humans answer their selfish motives in the affirmative or cooperate to the benefit of the group or society at large. Earlier research on social dilemmas has advanced our knowledge of situational conditions that make a difference (e.g., Messick et al., 1983; Komorita & Parks, 1994; Ostrom et al., 2002). The present volume will hopefully make additional contributions.

Social dilemmas capture significant problems in society such as tax evasion, scarcity of natural resources, and human contributions to climate change. These problems are often adhered to in the research community, motivating the studies that are presented. As a consequence, those concerned with the problems, either as policy makers or as victims, may request that scientists have something to say about potential solutions to social dilemmas. To live up to expectations, properties of relevance for behavioral decisions in social dilemmas should be incorporated in the research design in that findings can be generalized to situations where the phenomenon under investigation naturally occurs. Contributions to this volume present research on new concepts and propose original methods in response to this request. They span from cooperative motives on the individual level to methods for studying aggregate-level consequences of individual-level processes.

A. Biel et al. (eds.), *New Issues and Paradigms in Research on Social Dilemmas.*
© Springer 2008

New Issues

The Individual

Earlier research has pinpointed several factors that may determine whether people cooperate or defect. Some of these reside within the individual, e.g., his or her value orientation (Messick & McClintock, 1968) or degree of interpersonal trust (Yamagishi, 1986). Within social dilemma research, social value orientation in particular has drawn attention. Individuals are assumed to differ in their disposition to cooperate or defect in social dilemmas. While some are assumed to be driven by a desire to maximize their absolute gains (individualists) and others desire to maximize their relative gains (competitors), a substantial body is believed to strive for the maximization of joint outcomes to self and to others (cooperators). Despite a substantial amount of research, the motive behind the last orientation still rests in doubt (e.g., van Lange, 1999). As Eek and Gärling (this volume) point out, decomposed games that have been used to measure social value orientation (e.g., van Lange et al., 1997) have not made a distinction between possible motives. Do cooperators seek to maximize joint outcomes or to minimize differences in outcomes, or rather, as Eek and Gärling investigate, to equalize outcomes? Imagine that you have to distribute valuable points between yourself and an unknown other. What would you prefer, 500 to each of you or 500 to yourself and 600 to the unknown other? The cooperators in Eek and Gärling preferred the first choice. Evidently, we don't want others to be more equal than ourselves. Imagine now that the options were 500 each or 600 to you and 500 to the other. Again, cooperators preferred the equal option. Apparently, we don't want to have an advantage than others either. Perhaps even more astonishingly, cooperators chose 400/400 rather than 600/500. Equality has a strong appeal among cooperators. However, it is not unconditional. When efficiency was made salient and points not distributed were destroyed, cooperators switched their preference. Eek & Gärling place these results in a wider theoretical framework and discuss their implications for behavior in social dilemmas.

The Group

As research on social dilemmas has accumulated, growing attention has focused on the fact that decision making in social dilemmas often is embedded. Not only do individuals decide whether to promote individual or collective interests, but they often take these decisions in a group context. This signifies that which kind of group people belong to may have a decisive influence on their decision. Sometimes people make decisions in social dilemmas as individuals, sometimes as members of unitary or cooperative groups, while now and then they decide as members of non-cooperative groups; decisions are taken independently without the possibility to make binding agreements. Bornstein pits these three types of agents against 4 types of opponents: the same 3 as above and nature, creating 12 different prototypical decision situations. While several of these combinations have been commonly studied—for example, individual versus nature (individual decision making), individual versus individual (prisoner's dilemma), and non-cooperative groups versus nature (social dilemma)—less regard has been paid to many of the other combinations. In his chapter, Bornstein makes it very clear that many interdependent decision-making situations involve conflicts of interest, and often between "asymmetric" parties; that is, different types of agents in his taxonomy. This aspect of decision making in social dilemmas has so far been almost totally neglected.

Another aspect of research on group decision making in social dilemmas that has been partly neglected is that in real life, groups often share a history. Members of a group know something about the behavior of the others, thereby reducing social uncertainty. In their chapter, van Dijk et al. review how group members react to feedback on past behavior of the group. They distinguish between explicit feedback, what the group has done in the past, and implicit feedback. The latter refers to information about certain characteristics of the dilemma that could be used to draw inferences about former behavior. If a reporting system has been introduced, it may signal that group members are not to be trusted. For example, my own university wishes to introduce a data system where each employee reports most of his or her doings to the central administration. Besides being inefficient, it signals that the administration does not trust that our inner motivation will support us in carrying out our duties. While previous research has mainly concentrated on explicit feedback, their review shows that effects of implicit feedback have been overlooked along with emotional reactions to feedback and their effects on judgment and behavior in social dilemmas.

In a similar vein, Foddy and Dawes scrutinize trust in a group context. In social dilemmas, a cooperative move can easily be exploited by others. A "rational" view on decision making prescribes that this is indeed what will happen, but reality tells a different story. People do business and become involved in joint ventures with strangers and still avoid exploitation, despite the fact that laws of contract or other mechanisms are not in place. An experimental parallel to joint ventures is the trust game. Here, a sender decides how much, if any, of an endowment to invest in a receiver. Any amount sent is tripled, and the receiver decides how much, if any, to send back. Thus, to enlarge the potential joint outcome, the sender must trust the receiver and the receiver may choose to reciprocate. Anonymity is preserved throughout in the one-shot game. In this game, exchange takes place indicating that the sender trusts the receiver. Furthermore, it is of mutual benefit since the receiver sends back more than the initial investment. Finally, a shared group membership between sender and receiver increases the mutual benefit.

In addition, decisions are embedded in a social context. This implies that the course of action is not only guided by considerations of potential consequences for oneself or for fellow beings. Rather, to do the right thing in line with rules or norms that guide behavior in the situation at hand becomes the lodestar. While earlier research on social dilemmas mainly has studied either contributions to public goods or "harvesting"/distribution of resources in common pool dilemmas, few studies have investigated the relationship between contribution and allocation. One possible explanation might be that once public goods are established, nobody can be excluded from their use, and the existence of a resource in common pool dilemmas is more or less taken for granted. However, it is not uncommon that groups of people are excluded from the access to public goods. In addition, people may have different views on a resource whose establishment or maintenance they have contributed to as compared to a resource that they inherit. In this context, Kazemi and Eek focus upon people's motivation to contribute to a public good under different rules of allocation. In particular, they emphasize fairness conceptions in both the input and output phases and how they relate to the goals that the group wishes to pursue (cf. Deutsch, 1975, 1985).

Although individuals have a propensity to cooperate, as pointed out above, they do not always follow this tendency. Cooperation is not unconditional. Compensatory and retributive actions are two means to bring defectors back on track. When these strategies fail, procedures may be revised and new structural solutions installed. In their chapter, Shinada and Yamagishi remind us that Thomas Hobbes postulated that people are conditional cooperators. Still, though a majority might prefer cooperation to defection, they may need assurance that defection is a strategy that people don't get away with. Shinada and Yamagishi review research on sanctioning systems and the effects of sanctioning behavior. In particular, they discuss under what conditions people are willing to contribute to a sanctioning system, despite costs to the punishing party. The authors convincingly show how present empirical research on sanctioning systems can illuminate insights offered by Thomas Hobbes 350 years ago and pave the way for interdisciplinary work.

Samid and Suleiman join a modern imitator of Hobbes on the regulation of common resources, Garret Hardin. Hardin had little trust in people's cooperation without swords and proposed coercion, but mutual coercion that is mutually agreed upon by the majority that is affected. Samid and Suleiman developed an n-person prisoner's dilemma game, or an "authority game," to mimic Hardin's proposal. Under various conditions, subjects could either keep their resources to themselves (defect), contribute to a common pool that is equally divided between all group members including non-contributors (cooperate), or support the authority. Supporters paid a fee to the authority, while the authority had the power to punish non-contributors by means of a fine. The fee to the authority varied between game conditions, as did the fine or the coercive power. One important question to settle is whether or not coercion has a positive effect on resource management. If it is the case, other significant inquiries concern the minimal effective coercion needed and if people will support institutions that exploit their contributions. Samid and Suleiman address these problems and show that designing an institution that balances these forces is a delicate challenge.

In their chapter on justice concerns in social dilemmas, Schroeder et al. link outcomes to procedures and draw our attention to the request for compensatory and retributive justice. While compensatory justice requires the transgressor to compensate those who have been harmed, retributive justice targets the transgressor and the desire to punish him or her. The authors highlight conditions that foster either compensation or retribution. They also describe similarities and divergences in the pattern of motives and justice concerns that support compensation and retribution, respectively. Their main point is to emphasize the rule of compensatory and restorative justice to uphold procedural justice systems. However, compensatory and retributive attempts may fail, and to avoid ruin in the commons a change in procedures may be prescribed, bringing us back to the first two chapters above. Together, these last three chapters give insight into how groups create and maintain structures to avoid exploitation and the ruin of public goods.

Society

The chapter by Mashima and Takahashi is also structured around norms in social dilemmas. In their case it is the widely recognized reciprocity norm that is of interest. However, it is not the direct exchange of favors that is investigated. Rather, the interest relates to generalized exchange or to helping non-kin without expectations of future interaction. What their analyses show is that individuals try to take into account the recipient's past behavior. In doing so, are they also prepared to help a recipient who has a reputation of being a free rider, or do they only help those who have cooperated in the past? Mashima and Takahashi show that generalized exchange is conditional. This implies that although behavior is norm-based, people do not act upon the norm unless they have good reasons to believe that others are also prepared to follow the norm.

Mashima and Takahashi also discuss the origin of generalized exchange and point out that settings activating generalized exchange may vary between cultures. Hence, dilemmas could be culturally embedded. What is regarded as proper behavior in a specific situation in one culture may not be seen as fitting in another culture. Whether cultures emphasize self-enhancement or self-transcendent goals (cf. Schwartz, 1992) may, for example, have an effect on people's disposition to cooperate. In her chapter, Kopelman explicitly addresses the issue of cultural influence. Among other things, earlier research shows that cultures may vary to the extent that independence or interdependence is emphasized (e.g., Fiske et al., 1998). Kopelman discusses how culture may influence the emergence of identity, the perception and interpretation of situations, and what rules, norms, or practices apply. To the extent that behavior in social dilemmas varies between cultures, such variations could be mediated by identity (e.g., self-construal), perception of the situation (is this an interdependent or independent decision situation?), and proper rules (what is the appropriate action here?). As an example, Kopelman shows how culture may influence whether an independent or an interdependent perspective is evoked in managerial decision making.

Another geographical aspect, besides culture, is that dilemmas could be locally or globally embedded. Sometimes decisions about cooperation or defection have local effects, for example, on the group present or in the local community. Other decisions have wider implications and may have effects worldwide, such as decisions in resource dilemmas where our climate could be at stake. Much of our current knowledge about decisions and behavior in social dilemmas comes from experiments and from research on local common pool resource dilemmas. An intriguing question is to what extent lessons learnt can be applied to large-scale, global social dilemmas such as climate change. McGinnis and Ostrom review design principles of robust common pool resource institutions (see Ostrom, 1990) and discuss under what conditions these principles can be generalized to a global scale. Despite substantial differences, for example, in the feasibility of face-to-face communication, the number of individuals involved, and their dependency on the resource, the authors are quite optimistic about the extension of local design principles to the global level. This does not imply that these principles can be implemented straight away. Rather, it takes ingenuity to reshape or set up new institutional arrangements to benefit by the principles. In this process, the authors stress institutional components outside the public sector.

New Paradigms

Taken together, there is now a wide array of potential factors guiding decisions in social dilemmas under study. As a response, new methods have been devised to incorporate these factors in the research design. Ngan and Au remind us that not only are there often numerous people making their decisions in a social dilemma, but, in many instances, they do it at different points in time. This includes that those who make their decisions early provide feedback to those who await, just as the information that many people not yet have made their decision could create social uncertainty about proper behavior. Ngan and Au report a step-level public-good dilemma, where participants in a group context could contribute to either a personal or a joint account. Decisions were made under four different conditions. In one condition, participants had no information about others' decisions. In two conditions, they were updated with partial information. In one of these two conditions, they knew the number of people who chose the joint account, but not the number who chose the private account, while in the other condition they knew the number who chose the private account, but not the number who chose the joint account. In the final condition, full information was provided. Compared with the no-information condition, participants in the other three conditions made their decisions later. The number of cooperators (contributing to the joint account) also varied among conditions. Ngan and Au provide accounts of these variations and also contribute to our understanding of how campaigns to solve social problems can benefit from feedback information.

Ostmann and Meinhardt apply a more formal analysis in their game-theoretical chapter. By relying on cooperative game theory, they show how inefficient solutions can be avoided in asymmetric dilemmas. Asymmetric dilemmas imply that group members have different interests in the good or that they differ in wealth. They further show how game theory can embrace ideas from negotiation and bargaining theory to better understand the positive effects of communication, resulting in non-binding agreements that increase the outcomes for rational players. Such solutions are assumed to coincide with fair solutions in that both rich and poor benefit.

The aforementioned chapters by Bornstein and by Samid and Suleiman also provide examples of new games to study decision making in social dilemmas. Bornstein emphasizes how the social context, and in particular the composition of types of players, affects interdependent decision making. Samid and Suleiman pick out Hardin's suggestion about coercion in social dilemmas and show how his principle can be dressed in an experimental game. Taken together, these four chapters show how important aspects of interdependent decision making can be modeled in strategic games.

A very different approach to studying social dilemmas is introduced by Fischer, who applies genetic algorithms to simulate social dilemmas on a societal level. In society, people carry out a lot of activities. Some of these contribute to the common good, while others are performed to promote individual benefits. Such patterns of activities are more or less stable across time. Habits, preferences, and social and cultural norms are among factors that contribute to a stabilized pattern. Hence, in simulations based on generic algorithms, these factors should be modeled. Imagine now that the government is not too happy about the existing activity pattern in society. People spend too much time on leisure activities at the expense of productive labor. In order to shift the balance, policy makers may reduce taxes to increase labor, also to be modeled in the simulations. Based on two sets of data, census data on the actual time that Britons spent on relevant activities and the satisfaction that individuals in Britain associate with these activities, simulations could be run to predict the effect of such a policy measure for different percentages. Fischer shows that simulation of social dilemmas based on genetic algorithms provides opportunities to study complex real-life social dilemmas.

A Theoretical Framework

An extension of research into novel domains and with fresh methods will increase our understanding of cooperation. At the same time, the research community of social dilemmas has so far not settled on a theory of framework to encompass all this variety. Two recent approaches could provide a point of departure. In 1998, Eleanor Ostrom presented what she called the "core relationships" of social dilemmas. This core consists of mutually reinforcing trust, reputation of trustworthiness, and reciprocation. People invest in trustworthy behavior, trust others with a reputation of being trustworthy, and reciprocate cooperation and avoid social exchange with persons who are believed to be untrustworthy. This framework primarily models social face-to-face interaction. A second approach was presented by David Messick in 1999, labeled the AIR hypothesis. Messick also emphasizes the social aspects of social dilemmas. The perceived appropriateness (A) in a situation and rules (R) that guide behavior are both social elements. Appropriateness is at the heart of this model. Is the situation perceived as a collective problem or as a personal problem? If the former is distinguished, it is more likely that social aspects of one's identity (I) are evoked, cooperation becomes an issue, and proper rules that guide behavior may be abided.

These approaches have in common that they underscore the importance of the social context and of norms and rules. Decision making in social dilemmas is not primarily driven by concern for consequences. At the same time, they differ somewhat in their accent. While Ostrom emphasizes the importance of social interaction for cooperation, Messick brings out the significance of the attribution process. Taken together, these two theoretical frameworks could promote knowledge of how social contexts influence intergroup decision making and behavior.

In the final chapter of the book, Gifford presents his version of a framework. In this framework, a number of factors that could determine decision making in social dilemmas are incorporated. The nature of the resource or geophysical influences, governance influences or rules and regulations, the relationship to other decision makers, and the decision maker's own characteristics and motives are all expected to determine the behavioral strategies that a decision maker adopts. They do so mediated via dilemma awareness. Hence, Gifford presents a wide variety of factors that settles the appropriateness of the situation. In addition, outcomes to the decision maker and to the environment provide feedback links to the other factors. Gifford shows how contributions from other authors in the book illuminate these links.

The chapters in this book give evidence to the sensitiveness for the rich contexts of our everyday social environments that social dilemmas are embedded in. For the future, let's hope for a lively discussion around concepts and models that social dilemma research is theoretically embedded in.

References

Caporael, L. R., Dawes, R. M., Orbell, J. M., van de Kragt, A. J. (1989). Selfishness examined: Cooperation in the absence of egoistic incentives. *Behavioral and Brain Sciences, 12*, 683–739.

Dawes, R. M. (1980). Social dilemmas. *Annual Review of Psychology, 31*, 169–193.

Deutsch, M. (1975). Equity, equality, and need: What determines which value will be used as the basis for distributive justice? *Journal of Social Issues, 31*, 137–149.

Deutsch, M. (1985). *Distributive Justice: A Social Psychological Perspective*. New Haven, CT: Yale University Press.

Fehr, E., Fischbacher, U., Gächter, S. (2002). Strong reciprocity, human cooperation and the enforcement of social norms. *Human Nature, 13*, 1–25.

Fiske, A. P., Kitayama, S., Markus, H. R., Nisbett, R. E. (1998). The cultural matrix of social psychology. In D. T. Gilbert, S. T. Fiske & G. Lindzey (eds.), *The Handbook of Social Psychology* (4th ed., Vol. 2, pp. 915–981). New York: McGraw-Hill.

Frey, B. S. (1997). *Not Just for the Money*. Cheltenham, UK: Edward Elgar.

Komorita, S. S., Parks, C. D. (1994). *Social Dilemmas*. Madison, WI: Brown & Benchmark.

Messick, D. M. (1999). Alternative logics for decision making in social settings. *Journal of Economic Behavior and Organization, 39*, 11–28.

Messick, D. M., McClintock, C. G. (1968). Motivational bases of choice in experimental games. *Journal of Experimental Psychology, 4*, 1–25.

Messick, D. M., Wilke, H., Brewer, M. B., Kramer, R. M., Zemke, P. E., Lui, L. (1983). Individual adaptations and structural change as solutions to social dilemmas. *Journal of Personality and Social Psychology, 44*, 294–309.

Ostrom, E. (1990). *Governing the Commons: The Evolution of Institutions for Collective Action.* New York: Cambridge University Press.

Ostrom, E. (1998). A behavioral approach to the rational choice theory of collective action. *American Political Science Review, 92*, 1–22.

Ostrom, E., Dietz, T., Dolsak, N., Stern, P. C., Stonich, S., Weber, E. U. (eds.) (2002). *The Drama of the Commons.* Washington, DC: National Academy Press.

Schwartz, S. H. (1992). Universals in the content and structure of values: Theory and empirical tests in 20 countries. In M. Zanna (ed.), *Advances in Experimental Social Psychology* (Vol. 25, pp. 1–65). New York: Academic Press.

Van Lange, P. A. M. (1999). The pursuit of joint outcomes and equality in outcomes: An integrative model of social value orientation. *Journal of Personality and Social Psychology, 77*, 337–349.

Van Lange, P. A. M., Otten, W., De Bruin, E. M. N., Joireman, J. A. (1997). Development of prosocial, individual and competitive orientation. Theory and primary evidence. *Journal of Personality and Social Psychology, 73*, 733–746.

Yamagishi, T. (1986). The provision of a sanctioning system as a public good. *Journal of Personality and Social Psychology, 51*, 110–116.

Chapter 2
A New Look at the Theory of Social Value Orientations: Prosocials Neither Maximize Joint Outcome nor Minimize Outcome Differences but Prefer Equal Outcomes

Daniel Eek and Tommy Gärling

Introduction

A friend of one of this chapter's authors once checked in at a conference hotel together with a colleague. The hotel was posh and expensive, but because the prices were heavily subsidized, both had made reservations for the best rooms ("class A"). However, something had gone wrong with the reservations. Only one of the best rooms was available, as well as one room with a somewhat lower standard, "class B," and a few rooms with a considerably lower standard, "class C." Given the subsidies, prices were the same irrespective of class, so there was clearly no incentive to choose anything but "class A." The question was, who should take "class A" and who "class B"? None of the colleagues was likely to turn hostile on the other, so more or less simultaneously they honestly said, "Pick whatever room you want." It was also clear that both wanted the nicer "class A." But it was equally clear that none wanted it at the other's expense. Hence, "class A" and "class B" lost their attraction, resulting in that both chose "class C."

Readers familiar with social value orientation theories know that irrespective of whether the friend and his colleague had an individualistic, a competitive, or a cooperative social value orientation, these theories would predict that they choose "class A" when given the opportunity and that no one chooses "class C." However, both chose "class C." Hence, current social value orientation theories cannot account for the outcome described.

The aim of this chapter is to present empirical evidence pointing out that current social value orientation theories need to be revised in order to better explain the behavior of cooperators, which both persons in the example above then and now consider themselves to be. The theoretical revision put forward herein emphasizes the importance of equality for prosocials. The choice of "class C" in the anecdotal example did not reflect a preference for a low standard, but for an *equal* standard.

A. Biel et al. (eds.), *New Issues and Paradigms in Research on Social Dilemmas.*
© Springer 2008

Theories of Social Value Orientations

Theories of social value orientations (SVOs) (e.g., Kuhlman & Marshello, 1975; McClintock et al., 1973; Messick & McClintock, 1968; Van Lange, 1999; Van Lange & Kuhlman, 1994) propose that when people distribute something valuable between themselves and another person, their SVO makes them weigh outcomes to self and the other differently and to distribute the resource accordingly. Although people can have one of many possible SVOs, only a cooperative, competitive, or individualistic SVO is typically identified: Cooperators maximize the joint outcome to self and the other; competitors maximize the difference in outcomes to self and the other (i.e., the relative advantage); and individualists maximize outcome to self with little or no regard for the outcome to the other.

SVO was introduced to explain individual differences in cooperation in prisoner's dilemmas (and later in social dilemmas), which are situations where people make decisions between acting in their own interest, called *defection*, or in the collective interest, called *cooperation*. Thus, previous research has shown that people with a cooperative SVO (usually referred to as *prosocials*) more frequently cooperate in social dilemmas than do individuals with individualistic or competitive SVOs (usually referred to as *proselfs*) (e.g., Allison & Messick, 1990; Kramer et al., 1986; Liebrand, 1984; Van Lange & Liebrand, 1989). It has also been shown that a prosocial SVO increases helping behavior (McClintock & Allison, 1989), public transport choices (Van Vugt et al., 1995), willingness to sacrifice in close relationships (Van Lange et al., 1997), and concerns for multiple goals in organizational settings (Nauta et al., 2002) and increases integrative negotiation outcomes as well as affects the cognitive processes engaged by negotiation (De Dreu & Boles, 1998; De Dreu & Van Lange, 1995).

Different methods have been developed to assess SVOs (e.g., Grzelak et al., 1988; Liebrand & McClintock, 1988). The most common method is so-called decomposed games. One such method that distinguishes among the cooperative, competitive, and individualistic SVOs is the triple-dominance measure of social values (TDMSV) (e.g., Kuhlman & Marshello, 1975; Van Lange et al., 1997). In the TDMSV, participants make nine choices among three alternative allocations of valuable points to themselves and another unknown person. The individualistic alternative maximizes own outcome (e.g., 560 to self and 300 to the other), the cooperative alternative maximizes joint outcome (e.g., 500 to self and 500 to the other), and the competitive alternative maximizes own outcome relative to the other's outcome (e.g., 500 to self and 100 points to the other). To evoke feelings of interdependence, participants are asked to imagine that the other person is also confronted with the same nine choices, so that the total number of points that each obtains is determined by the choices both made. Participants who at least six times (66.7% of the choices) choose the alternative consistent with one of the three SVOs are classified as having this SVO.

In a recent meta-analysis (Au & Kwong, 2004) based on all published studies since 1973 using decomposed games as the assessment method, 57.4% of the participants classified to any SVO chose the alternatives that maximize the joint outcome, 27.1% the alternatives that maximize their own outcome, and the remaining 15.5% the alternatives that maximize their own advantage relative to the other. The proportions of cooperators, individualists, and competitors can, to some extent, vary from study to study due to, for instance, cultural differences (see, e.g., Gärling, 1999, who observed a slightly different distribution in Sweden compared to the averaged distribution reported by Au & Kwong). Still, the distribution has been shown to be rather stable across different studies in multiple cultures (e.g., Van Lange & Kuhlman, 1994; Van Lange et al., 1997).

It seems uncontroversial that decomposed games assess individualists' and competitors' motives. However, since the TDMSV, used in the bulk of the previous research, fails to distinguish between the two motives of achieving equal outcomes and maximizing joint outcome, the relative stability of previous results does not rule out that prosocials' primary motive is the former rather than the latter.

An Alternative Equality Hypothesis

Little effort has been made to empirically investigate whether maximizing joint outcome or attaining equal outcomes to self and the other drives prosocials' choice of the cooperative alternative in decomposed games. In this vein, Van Lange (1999) noted that defining prosocials as individuals who maximize joint outcome may fail to explain their basic motive. Instead, he hypothesized that prosocials' motives are concerns for both joint outcome *and* equality. It is important to note that Van Lange (1999) regarded equality as synonymous to minimizing the difference in outcomes between self and the other. In contrast, we claim in this chapter that *equal outcomes* is prosocials' dominant, perhaps only, motive.

Our claim that prosocials' motive is equal outcomes is related to a recurrent finding in previous research that people prefer equal distributions of outcomes in interdependence situations (e.g., Allison & Messick, 1990; Messick, 1993, 1995; Messick & Schell, 1992). For instance, numerous studies on resource dilemmas show that people prefer to take equally much from common resources (e.g., Rapoport et al., 1992). Similarly, McClelland and Rohrbaugh (1978; cited in Messick, 1993) found that participants even preferred equal outcomes to larger, but unequally distributed, outcomes. In line with this previous research, it is concluded that the dominance of equal outcomes among prosocials may reflect an equality or fairness motive (e.g., Loewenstein et al., 1989; Van Dijk & Wilke, 1995) that is similar to the demonstration of a reciprocal motive (e.g., Gallucci & Perugini, 2000, 2003). Thus, in many situations, for instance, in social dilemmas (e.g., Eek & Biel, 2003) and in negotiations (Kristensen, 2000), people act in line with what they consider to be fair. Consequently, in circumstances either where there are no individual differences in abilities, efforts, or needs (e.g., Rapoport et al., 1992; Rutte et al., 1987), or when such differences are unknown (Van Dijk & Grodzka, 1992), equality is generally considered the fairest principle for outcome distributions (e.g., Messick & Sentis, 1979). This should be contrasted to some other research (e.g., Allison et al., 1992; Allison & Messick, 1990; Harris & Joyce, 1980; Messick & Schell, 1992) demonstrating that equality is a simplifying heuristic for distributing resources when there is a high degree of uncertainty.

The instructions to participants completing the TDMSV convey no information concerning, for instance, whether there are differences between self and the other. The research reviewed above then seems to predict that an equal-division rule is what most people would consider to be the fairest distribution. In addition, it is less plausible that prosocials maximize the joint outcome or merely minimize the difference in outcomes given that there is no other evidence in previous research suggesting that people hold such motives in interdependence situations.

In several studies (e.g., Eek & Gärling, 2006) that will be briefly reviewed below, we pitted the proposed equality hypothesis against the joint-outcome hypothesis. Generally, strong support was obtained for the former hypothesis. As a matter of fact, maximizing joint outcome was not even chosen as the second most preferred distribution by prosocials. Instead, maximizing own outcome (a clear proself motive) was the second best. Thus, these results contradict the argument by Van Lange (1999) that prosocials in the TDMSV are motivated both to maximize joint outcomes and to minimize the differences in outcomes. In an additional study reported in Eek and Gärling (2005), also reviewed below, the equality hypothesis was pitted against a minimizing-difference hypothesis. It is argued, and shown, that prosocials only want to minimize differences in outcomes when this leads to equal outcomes. If not, their choices will not differ from choices made by proselfs. Similar results were obtained by Cunha (1982; cited in Kuhlman et al., 1986), who found that prosocials in two-choice tasks preferred to maximize their own gain (e.g., 9 to self and 5 to the other) to minimizing outcome differences (e.g., 8 to self and 6 to the other). Note that the joint outcome was held constant by Cunha since the expectation was that joint-outcome maximization was the core motive for prosocials. Still, it was also noted that prosocials' behavior in other tasks than decomposed games (e.g., the prisoner's dilemma game) cannot be understood if their core motive is to maximize the joint outcome.

Empirical Evidence in Support of the Equality Hypothesis

Do Prosocials Maximize Joint Outcomes?

The SVO theory thus posits that proselfs' motives are either to maximize the outcome to self (individualists) or to maximize the relative advantage over the other (competitors). Similarly, prosocials' motive is twofold: first and foremost, a preference for maximizing the joint outcome (e.g., Messick & McClintock, 1968), and second, to minimize the differences in outcomes (e.g., Van Lange, 1999).

In Study 1 in Eek and Gärling (2006), a questionnaire was administered that consisted of an extended version of the TDMSV. Standard TDMSV instructions were given to the participants indicating that numbers to be distributed represented valuable points and that the other person was someone they had never met and did not expect to meet in the future. The extension consisted of increasing the number of choices from 9 to 12 and adding a fourth alternative to each choice set. The added alternative maximized the joint outcome for an unequal distribution between self and the other. An example is

	A	B	C	D
Own outcome	560	500	500	500
Other's outcome	300	100	500	800

Alternatives A, B, and C are adopted from the original TDMSV. A is the individualistic alternative, B the competitive alternative, and C the cooperative alternative. In the extended TDMSV, alternative D maximized the joint outcome.

Participants were instructed to rank-order the alternatives A, B, C, and D based on how attractive they found them. They were then classified as belonging to one of the SVOs if they consistently rank-ordered first one of the four alternatives in at least 8 of the 12 choices (66.7%). The same classification was used for participants' second, third, and fourth rank orders. Thus, the extended TDMSV allowed classification of participants' first, second, third, and fourth motives. The terms *equal-outcome prosocials* and *joint-outcome prosocials* were introduced to distinguish prosocials who preferred equality (alternative C in the example above) from those who preferred to maximize the joint outcome (alternative D).

If prosocials' motive is to maximize the joint outcome, as suggested by SVO theory, no participants should be classified as equal-outcome prosocials on the basis of their first rank orders. Instead, based on the meta-analysis by Au and Kwong (2004), between 55% and 60% of the participants should be classified as joint-outcome prosocials, between 25% and 30% as individualists, and between 10% and 20% as competitors. Furthermore, should the alternative conjecture be correct that prosocials have the two motives of maximizing joint outcome and minimizing outcome differences (Van Lange, 1999), participants classified as joint-outcome prosocials on the basis of their first rank orders should be classified as equal-outcome prosocials on the basis of their second rank orders, or vice versa.

The results for the 48 participants who produced consistent rank orders, allowing a classification into SVOs, showed strong support for the equality hypothesis. On the basis of their first rank orders, 40% of participants were classified as equal-outcome prosocials, 43% as individualists, and 17% as competitors. Since no participant was classified as a joint-outcome prosocial, the results suggested that prosocials assessed by the TDMSV primarily prefer equality to maximizing the joint outcome.

An important additional question asks whether participants' secondary SVO is predicted by the SVO theory. For individualists and competitors, this was clearly the case. Their rank orders were predicted by the assumption in SVO theory (e.g., Messick & McClintock, 1968; Van Lange, 1999) that they have a single motive.

Individualists were indifferent in their second, third, and fourth preferences, as should be expected since individualists only focus on the outcome to self, and alternatives B, C, and D render self the same number of points. According to the theory, competitors should be classified as individualists on the basis of their second preference, as equal-outcome prosocials on the basis of their third preference, and as joint-outcome prosocials on the basis of their fourth preference. All of the competitors rank-ordered the alternatives accordingly. However, the theory did not predict the second preference for prosocials in that only 21% of the equal-outcome prosocials were classified as joint-outcome prosocials on the basis of the second preference and the remaining 79% as individualists. In fact, more than half of the equal-outcome prosocials regarded maximizing joint outcome as the worst among the four alternatives.

The results of Study 1 clearly demonstrate that it is incorrect to regard prosocials' motive as a desire to maximize the joint outcome. However, one could object to this conclusion by arguing that prosocials did not want to receive less than the other and that they therefore preferred the alternative that provided both with equal outcomes instead of maximizing the joint outcome. Thus, prosocials may still prefer to maximize the joint outcome if they do not receive less than the other.

Study 2 in Eek and Gärling (2006) aimed at corroborating that prosocials' preference for equality is a convincing explanation of the results of Study 1. More specifically, three questions were addressed: (1) Would prosocials prefer to maximize the joint outcome if they did not receive less than the other? (2) Would prosocials still prefer equality if they themselves could receive more points without the other person's receiving less? (3) If so, would prosocials still prefer equality even though both self and the other could get higher but unequal outcomes?

Fifty-one participants' SVOs were first classified using the standard TDMSV. Subsequently, the participants were asked to complete some unrelated filler tasks before rank-ordering three alternative distributions of points between self and the other. In each of 24 tasks, two alternatives rendered equal outcomes to self and the other, and a third alternative maximized the joint outcome with unequal outcomes. An example is

	A	B	C
Own outcome	600	700/600	500
Other's outcome	600	600/700	500

For half of the tasks, self was in the advantageous position and received more points in the joint-outcome alternative (B). For the other half of the tasks, self was in the disadvantageous position. The hypothesis was that prosocials and proselfs would rank-order the three distributions differently. Proselfs were expected to maximize their own outcome and, therefore, in the example, rank-order alternative B first, alternative A second, and alternative C third. Prosocials would rank-order the alternatives in the same way as proselfs if they preferred to maximize the joint outcome. If, however, they preferred equality, in the example they would rank-order alternative A first, alternative C second, and alternative B third. It was thus not hypothesized that prosocials would be indifferent between alternatives A and C. They were also expected to prefer a larger to a lesser share, as long as it was distributed equally (cf. Van Lange, 1999).

When the outcomes in the joint-outcome alternative were reversed so that self was in the disadvantageous position, proselfs were expected to be indifferent between alternatives A and B but rank-order alternative C third. In contrast, according to the equality hypothesis, prosocials' rank orders were not expected to differ depending on whether self was in the advantageous or disadvantageous position.

The results were based on 23 participants who were classified as prosocials and 23 who were classified as proselfs (very few were classified as competitors, and since individualists alone were regarded as a sufficient comparison group to prosocials, only the results for individualists were analyzed). Table 2.1 shows participants' mean rank orders of the three distributions related to SVO and whether self or the other is in the advantageous position in the joint-outcome alternatives. Large numbers correspond to high attractiveness. As the results clearly show, prosocials did not prefer to maximize the joint outcome even when they received more than the other. In fact, they rank-ordered Equality-high (A) as more attractive than Joint-outcome (B), both when self and when the other was in the advantageous position. Furthermore, irrespective of whether self or the other was in the advantageous position, prosocials also rank-ordered Equality-low (C) as more attractive than

Table 2.1 Mean Rank Orders of Three Distributions Related to Advantageous Position and Social Value Orientation (1 = least attractive, 3 = most attractive)

Distribution[1]	Advantageous Position[2]	Social Value Orientation			
		Prosocial (*n* = 23)		Proself (*n* = 23)	
		M	*Sd*	*M*	*Sd*
Equality-high	Self	2.72	0.43	2.00	0.02
	Other	2.78	0.34	2.61	0.47
Equality-low	Self	1.71	0.44	1.01	0.03
	Other	1.69	0.40	1.61	0.50
Joint-outcome	Self	1.57	0.87	2.99	0.04
	Other	1.53	0.72	1.78	0.97

[1]Equality-high refers to alternatives that provide self and the other with most points distributed equally. Equality-low refers to alternatives that provide self and the other with least points distributed equally. Joint-outcome refers to alternatives that provide self and the other with most points distributed unequally.

[2]Self refers to joint-outcome alternatives where self receives more points than the other. Other refers to joint-outcome alternatives where the other receives more points than self.

Joint-outcome. Finally, prosocials rank-ordered Equality-high as more attractive than Equality-low. In contrast, proselfs clearly took advantageous position into account. When self was in this position, proselfs rank-ordered Joint-outcome as more attractive than Equality-high and Equality-high as more attractive than Equality-low. When the other was in the advantageous position, proselfs were not indifferent between Joint-outcome and Equality-high, but they rank-ordered Equality-high as more attractive than Equality-low.

In sum, the results of the two studies demonstrated that prosocials' motive is not to maximize the joint outcome. No participants were classified as joint-outcome prosocials in Study 1. Moreover, most of those classified as equal-outcome prosocials rank-ordered the joint-outcome alternatives as the worst alternative and were even more reluctant to choose to maximize the joint outcome than were individualists. This result contradicts the proposition that prosocials have two motives (Van Lange, 1999), instead suggesting that maximizing the joint outcome is not even potentially desirable to prosocials. More specifically, we believe that the first of the propositions made by SVO theory regarding prosocials' motive is false: The evidence does not support that prosocials maximize the joint outcome between self and the other.

Do Prosocials Minimize the Differences in Outcomes?

We argue that the dominance of equal outcomes among prosocials reflects an equality motive based on fairness considerations. This contrasts with other research in which equality has been considered a heuristic for distributing resources. Furthermore, we assume that prosocials' motive is to achieve equal outcomes, not to minimize the difference in outcomes to self and another person. Thus, if equality cannot be achieved, rather than minimizing the differences in outcomes, prosocials would choose another alternative.

A study reported in Eek and Gärling (2005) aimed at testing the validity of the SVO theory's second proposition that prosocials strive for minimizing the difference in outcomes between self and the other. According to the equality hypothesis, the striving for equal outcomes only holds when equality is possible to reach.

In nine allocation tasks, similar to those used in the TDMSV, we asked participants who had been classified into SVOs based on the TDMSV to choose between two alternative distributions of points between self and the other. The instructions were similar to those in the TDMSV. The number of points to self and the other was fixed in one of the distributions. In the other distribution, the number of points to self was fixed, but the number of points to the other was left open. If participants wanted to choose the open alternative, they were asked to fill in the number of points that they wanted the other to have in order to make this alternative more attractive than the fixed alternative. This had to be done within a given point interval that sometimes was below, sometimes above, and sometimes both below and above the number of points to self. The number of points to self was always fixed in both distributions. An example is

	A	B
Own outcome	400	300
Other's outcome	200	X ____ Y

Alternative A was fixed and always provided 100 more points to self than did alternative B. In alternative B, participants chose the other's outcome by filling in the number of points to the other within a fixed point interval. If participants wanted to choose A, they were asked to circle A and move on to the next task. If they wanted to choose B, they were asked to indicate the number of points within the point interval that they wanted the other to have in order for alternative B to be more attractive than alternative A. The point interval (X–Y) was either below (e.g., 100–200 in the example above), above (e.g., 400–500), or both below and above (100–500) the outcome to self. It is thus only the point interval both below and above that permits the choice of equal outcomes.

Since the number of points to self was higher in the fixed than in the open alternative, we hypothesized that proselfs (both individualists and competitors) should choose the fixed alternative. Given that prosocials prefer equal outcomes to self and the other, we hypothesized that prosocials should choose the open alternative only when the point interval permitted equal outcomes. In contrast, should prosocials be motivated to minimize the difference in outcomes, as posited in the SVO theory, they would choose the open alternative also when the point interval was below outcomes to self. Furthermore, were they motivated to maximize the joint outcome, they would choose the open alternative when the point interval was above outcomes to self and when it was both below and above outcomes to self.

One hundred and twelve undergraduates at Göteborg University were recruited for two samples. In Sample 1, a total of 139 participants was recruited in different classes and asked to volunteer without any payment in a study on decision making. They were guaranteed anonymity. Those who accepted to participate were asked after class to complete the TDMSV. Between three and six weeks later, they were invited via email to the laboratory. On different occasions, 58 of those participants showed up. Data from Sample 2 were obtained from 54 undergraduates prior to their taking part in unrelated experiments.

Participants had to complete a questionnaire consisting of different decision-making tasks. In order to check the consistency of the classification on the basis of TDMSV at different points in time for Sample 1, and to classify participants according to SVOs in Sample 2, the final task in the questionnaire, which was not immediately preceded by the main task described above, was to complete the standard TDMSV.

The results showed that of the 58 participants who showed up at the laboratory (Sample 1), 34 were classified as prosocials, 2 as competitors, 18 as individualists, and 4 unclassified due to inconsistent responses the first time they completed the TDMSV. Revealing that the classification was relatively stable, the second time the TDMSV was completed, 41 participants in Sample 1 were classified into the same SVO as on the first occasion. A measure of agreement between the two assessments of SVO revealed that the classifications were reliable, Cohen's $K = 0.448$, $p < 0.01$. The following analyses were based on participants' SVOs as measured on the second occasion. A χ^2 test revealed that the distribution of SVOs did not differ between the samples ($p > 0.65$). In total, 69 were classified as prosocials, 22 as individualists, and 11 as competitors. Individualists and competitors were collapsed into one group consisting of 33 proselfs. The remaining 10 participants were unclassified and discarded from further analyses.

In Table 2.2, absolute frequencies of prosocials' and proselfs' choices of the different distributions are presented for tasks where the point interval for the open alternative was either below, above, or both below and above outcome to self. Given that there were three tasks for each level of the point interval, there were in total 207 responses from prosocials ($n = 69$) and 99 responses from proselfs ($n = 33$). Some participants had responded incorrectly on one or a few of the tasks. In a vast majority of those cases, these incorrect responses were made by prosocials who had distributed the points according to equality, even though this was not permitted because the point interval was not both below and above outcome to self. The relative frequencies of choices that correspond with the different distributions adopted by participants, also given in the table, exclude incorrect responses.

Table 2.2 Absolute and Relative Frequencies of Choices of Distribution Related to Social Value Orientation

		Social Value Orientation			
		Prosocial ($n = 69$)		Proself ($n = 33$)	
Point interval[1]	Distribution[2]	f	%	f	%
Below	Fixed distribution	146	76.4	77	82.8
	Minimizing difference	36	18.9	8	8.6
	Total		*95.3*		*91.4*
Below and above	Fixed distribution	56	27.0	69	72.6
	Minimizing difference (Equality)	98	47.0	18	19.0
	Maximizing joint outcome	38	18.3	2	2.1
	Total		*92.3*		*93.7*
Above	Fixed distribution	124	66.7	87	92.6
	Minimizing difference	19	10.2	5	5.3
	Maximizing joint outcome	36	19.3	1	1.1
	Total		*96.2*		*99.0*

[1] Below refers to when the point interval in the open alternatives was below outcome to self. Below and above refers to when the point interval in the open alternatives was both below and above outcome to self, permitting equality. Above refers to when the point interval in the open alternatives was above outcome to self.

[2] Fixed distribution refers to choice of the fixed alternative. Other labels refer to the rules that coincide with the distributions chosen by participants by the open alternative.

As seen in Table 2.2, more than 90% of participants' choices were made of the fixed distribution, or a distribution that minimized the difference in outcomes, or a distribution that maximized the joint outcome. This was true for all levels of the point interval. The relative frequency of choices of the fixed distribution and a distribution that minimized outcome differences were submitted to a 2 (SVO: prosocials vs. proselfs) by 2 (distribution: fixed vs. minimizing outcome differences) by 3 (point interval: below vs. below and above vs. above) analysis of variance (ANOVA) with repeated measures on the two last factors. The main effect of distribution, $F(2, 200) = 56.42$, $p < 0.001$, was significant and indicated that the fixed distribution was chosen more often than minimizing outcome differences. Although the two-way interaction between SVO and distribution, $F(2, 200) = 15.28$, $p < 0.001$, and that between distribution and point interval, $F(2, 200) = 42.86$, $p < 0.001$, were significant, they were of little interest since the hypothesized three-way interaction among SVO, distribution, and point interval was also significant, $F(2, 200) = 15.28$, $p < 0.001$.

When the point interval was below outcome to self, both groups preferred the fixed distribution where the outcome difference was 200 points. For proselfs, this was predicted by the SVO theory. However, should prosocials' motive be to minimize outcome differences, a majority of their responses would give the other 100 points more and thereby reduce outcome differences by 50%. This was clearly not the case. Although this result could suggest that prosocials wanted to maximize the joint outcome that was confounded with maximizing their own outcome when the point interval was below outcomes to self, this is inconsistent with the results presented above (Eek & Gärling, 2006). In line with the equality hypothesis, separate Bonferroni-corrected t-tests at $p = 0.05$ showed that there was no difference between prosocials and proselfs in the percentage of choices of the fixed distribution or of choices of minimizing outcome differences.

When the point interval was above outcome to self, choices by proselfs were again as predicted by the SVO theory. Both motives that SVO theory regards as prosocial—maximizing joint outcome and minimizing outcome differences—were possible to follow when the point interval was above. Twice as many responses from prosocials preferred the former to the latter motive. Still, a clear majority of prosocials preferred the same distribution as was preferred by proselfs. Even though the post-hoc tests showed that there was a difference between prosocials and proselfs in the percentage of choices of the fixed distribution, the tests also indicated that both groups preferred the fixed distribution to minimizing outcome differences.

As predicted by the alternative equality hypothesis, it was only when the point interval was both below and above outcome to self that a majority of prosocials preferred the open to the fixed distribution. The post-hoc tests showed that proselfs preferred the fixed distribution more than did prosocials and that prosocials preferred minimizing outcome differences more than did proselfs. The results thus indicate that prosocials prefer equal outcomes, not to minimize outcome differences. If equal outcomes cannot be obtained, prosocials' choices do not differ from proselfs' choices.

Moderating Factors

Even though SVOs have been shown to be a rather stable person characteristic (e.g., Van Lange & Kuhlman, 1994; Van Lange et al., 1997), situational factors may still moderate people's choices in TDMSV. For instance, characteristics of the other person (e.g., likeability) would most likely affect the distribution of SVOs because both prosocials and proselfs give more points to a friend and less to an enemy. If both groups' choices are affected, whether a theoretical clarification is obtained by such a demonstration is, however, questionable. On the other hand, it is clearly relevant to investigate under what circumstances only one SVO group switches from one motive to another. It is in line with the focus of this chapter to investigate situational factors that make prosocials become more concerned about joint outcomes. This was the aim of an additional study (Eek & Gärling, 2000) that examined the possible moderating effect of concerns for efficiency on prosocials' motive in allocation tasks such as the TDMSV.

In the TDMSV, nothing is mentioned about what happens to points not distributed. We expected that prosocials more than proselfs would be more concerned about the joint outcome if they knew that points not distributed are wasted, thereby signaling inefficient resource use. In Wilke's (1991) GEF hypothesis, efficiency was explicitly introduced as one of three important motives explaining cooperation in social dilemmas: Although people are greedy (G) and therefore defect in social dilemmas, greed is constrained by a desire that the resource is utilized efficiently (E) and by a desire that the distribution of benefits between group members is fair (F). Thus, even though people want to defect out of greed, they sometimes realize that defection is either inefficient or unfair. As a consequence, they instead choose to cooperate.

As noted above, prosocials cooperate more than proselfs in social dilemmas. There are many possible reasons for this. We argue that some of the reasons highlighted by Kuhlman et al. (1986) are related to the GEF hypothesis. Kuhlman et al. proposed and showed (or referred to other studies showing this) that prosocials have a strong sense of moral obligation to cooperate and that they anticipate that others will also cooperate. We believe that such a moral obligation is closely related to the fairness component in the GEF hypothesis and that it may explain why prosocials hold the motive of equality in the TDMSV. Thus, prosocials prefer equal and fair outcomes. Kuhlman et al. (1986) also stated that "Prosocial persons have a time perspective on the commons which extends farther into the future than do Individualists. They have a better appreciation for the 'social trap' character of the commons" (p. 171). We believe that such a "time perspective" is equivalent to endorsing efficiency according to the GEF hypothesis. Therefore, we hypothesized that prosocials will switch from the motive of equality to the motive of maximizing the joint outcome when considerations for efficiency are evoked. In contrast, proselfs were expected to stick to their basic motive also when efficiency considerations are evoked.

Participants made choices among the four alternatives in the extended TDMSV employed by Eek and Gärling (2006). Replicating the previous results, more participants were expected to be classified as equal-outcome prosocials than joint-outcome prosocials. However, the reverse was expected when the instructions emphasized that the points would be destroyed if not allocated, implying inefficient resource utilization. No effect of the changed instructions was expected for those classified as individualists or competitors.

Participants were 100 undergraduate psychology students randomly assigned to one of two groups. They volunteered without any payment and were assured that their responses would be anonymous. Instead of rank-ordering the attractiveness of the four alternatives as in Eek and Gärling (2006) (see p. X), they were asked each time to choose the most attractive alternative.

Both groups of participants received the standard instructions in the questionnaire. One of the groups received additional instructions informing the participants that for each task there were 1,500 points to distribute and that points not distributed would be destroyed.

In Table 2.3, the classification of the participants to SVOs is displayed for each condition. As may be seen, under standard instructions, 5 of the participants were not possible to classify, while 10 were not possible to classify under efficiency instructions. Furthermore, none and two were classified as competitors in each condition, respectively. The numbers classified as individualists were almost the same (12 and 11). Consistent with the hypothesis, the added instructions reduced the number of participants classified as equal-outcome prosocials from 22 to 9, whereas the number classified as joint-outcome prosocials increased from 11 to 17, $\chi^2(4, n = 99) = 10.44$, $p < 0.05$. Partitioning the contingency table into four independent 2 by 2 subtables, additional analyses revealed that only the difference in the number of equal-outcome prosocials and joint-outcome prosocials was significant, $\chi^2(1, n = 99) = 5.91$, $p < 0.05$.

Thus, equality was preferred to a distribution that maximized the joint outcome when standard instructions were given. However, when the instructions made efficiency salient, more cooperators were classified as joint-outcome prosocials than equal-outcome prosocials, indicating that considerations for efficiency moderate the motive held by prosocials. The numbers of individualists and competitors were not affected by the efficiency instructions. In order for prosocials to pay attention to maximizing joint outcome, it seems as if something must be added that rationalizes this motive.

Table 2.3 Absolute and Relative Frequencies of Social Value Orientations Related to Standard vs. Efficiency Instructions

Social Value Orientation	Standard Instructions		Efficiency Instructions	
	f	%	f	%
Equal-outcome prosocials	22	44.0	9	18.4
Joint-outcome prosocials	11	22.0	17	34.7
Individualists	12	24.0	11	22.4
Competitors	0	0.0	2	4.1
Not classified	5	10.0	10	20.4

Discussion and Conclusions

The present research addressed a major question that for a long time has been unanswered but treated as if it had been answered: What motive guides prosocials' choices? First, the SVO theory assumed that the motive was to maximize the joint outcome (e.g., Kuhlman & Marshello, 1975). Later, Van Lange (1999) argued that a better understanding of prosocials' behavior is obtained by treating their motive as dependent on both maximizing the joint outcome and minimizing outcome differences.

It is difficult to investigate the effects of SVO and the underlying motives to people's choices by means of assessments based on the TDMSV. One reason is the imperfect test-retest reliability. Even though a significant number of people are classified into the same SVO from one time to another, quite a few are not. Van Lange's (1999) cautiousness in statements such as "social value orientation reflects dispositions that are at least somewhat stable yet open to modifications, particularly over a relatively longer period of time" (p. 343) appears warranted. The fact that some people are classified into different SVOs depending on when and where the assessment takes place indicates that for those people long-term effects of SVOs cannot be taken for granted. Still, many interesting and important studies of the effects of SVO on various behaviors, where studies by Van Lange and colleagues in the last decade constitute the core, are important since they show that responses to tests such as the TDMSV correlate reliably with various prosocial behaviors. Thus, responses to TDMSV that allow a classification of participants to different SVOs appear to capture important aspects of their behavior. Therefore, it is essential to reach a better understanding of the motives that lead to the different choices. Otherwise, one may make wrong inferences when interpreting behavioral differences between prosocials and proselfs.

In the present chapter, we did not intend to examine behavioral effects of SVO. Instead, our focus was the underlying motives for prosocials' choices in the TDMSV. Two studies by Eek and Gärling (2006) were reviewed that tested the alternative equality hypothesis, that prosocials want to obtain equal outcomes instead of maximizing the joint outcome. We conclude that the results were in strong favor of the equality hypothesis, particularly in Study 2, where it was shown that prosocials preferred worse outcomes to both parties as long as these outcomes were equal.

Another study by Eek and Gärling (2005) tested whether prosocials prefer to minimize outcome differences when equality of outcomes cannot be achieved. Again in support of the alternative equality hypothesis, the results indicated that prosocials' choices differ from proselfs' choices only when equality can be achieved. When outcome differences were merely decreased, prosocials preferred the alternative that maximized outcome to self exactly as proselfs did.

We argue that our research shows that prosocials are trying to obtain equal outcomes. However, we are not arguing that the results invalidate any of the different methods used to measure SVOs. Our argument is instead that the SVO theory (e.g., Messick & McClintock, 1968; Van Lange, 1999) needs to be revised. It should be noted that, even though effects of SVO nowadays are studied in very many different contexts (e.g., Au & Kwong, 2004), SVO was primarily introduced to explain individual differences in cooperation in the prisoner's dilemma game (e.g., Kuhlman & Marshello, 1975). Prosocials' higher degree of cooperation relative to proselfs' is believed to depend on a (prosocial) wish to maximize the joint outcome. This implies that prosocials are regarded as more rational than proselfs at a collective level. By providing information about the other's choice in a modified prisoner's dilemma game where the largest joint outcome is achieved when one player cooperates and the other defects, an additional study in Eek and Gärling (2006) actually directly tested and rectified what so far has been taken more or less for granted: Whereas the high cooperation rates among prosocials have been interpreted as a preference for maximizing the joint outcome, the results clearly demonstrated that prosocials cooperate because they prefer equal outcomes. Thus, rather than assuming that prosocials are rational at a collective level and that proselfs are rational at an individual level, we suggest that prosocials' willingness to be fair sometimes entraps them to be both collectively and individually irrational. However, we could also demonstrate in the last study reviewed in this chapter (Eek & Gärling, 2000) that prosocials but not proselfs can be induced to act rationally at a collective level. The three key components of the GEF hypothesis (Wilke, 1991) can be used to summarize the main points raised by the results reviewed in this chapter: In order to serve their own interests, proselfs are by default driven by greed. In contrast, prosocials are by default motivated to achieve fairness, which is served by equality. Thus, the efficiency component does not on its own affect either group's choices. Should, however, a concern for the resource be induced, choices by prosocials are also influenced by concerns for efficiency. We believe these arguments help to explain why choices made by prosocials and proselfs differ, with regard to both assessments of SVO and the behavioral responses predicted by SVO.

Acknowledgments This research was financially supported by Grant 421-2001-4697 to Daniel Eek from the Swedish Research Council. We thank Anders Biel for valuable comments and Karin Anckar Webner, Karl Gillholm, Ted Hedesström, and Tomas Karlsson for assistance in collecting data.

References

Allison, S. T., McQueen, L. R., Schaerfl, L. M. (1992). Social decision making processes and the equal partitionment of shared resources. *Journal of Experimental Social Psychology, 28,* 23–42.

Allison, S. T., Messick, D. M. (1990). Social decision heuristics in the use of shared resources. *Journal of Behavioral Decision Making, 3,* 195–204.

Au, W. T., Kwong, J. Y. Y. (2004). Measurements and effects of social-value orientation in social dilemmas: A review. In R. Suleiman, D. Budescu, I. Fischer & D. Messick (eds.), *Contemporary Psychological Research on Social Dilemmas* (pp. 71–98). Cambridge: Cambridge University Press.

De Dreu, C. K. W., Boles, T. L. (1998). Share and share alike or winner take all?: The influence of social value orientation upon choice and recall of negotiation heuristics. *Organizational Behavior and Human Decision Processes, 76,* 253–276.

De Dreu, C. K. W., Van Lange, P. A. M. (1995). The impact of social value orientations on nego-tiator cognition and behavior. *Personality and Social Psychology Bulletin, 21*, 1178–1188.

Eek, D., Biel, A. (2003). The interplay between greed, efficiency, and fairness in public-goods dilemmas. *Social Justice Research, 16*, 195–215.

Eek, D., Gärling, T. (2000). Effects of joint outcome, equality, and efficiency on assessments of social value orientations. (Göteborg Psychological Reports, 30, No. 4). Sweden: Göteborg University, Department of Psychology.

Eek, D., Gärling, T. (July 2005). *Only Equality Matters: Prosocials Don't Minimize Outcome Differences That Cannot Be Eliminated*. Paper presented at the 11th International Conference on Social Dilemmas, Krakow, Poland.

Eek, D., Gärling, T. (2006). Prosocials prefer equal outcomes to maximizing joint outcome. *British Journal of Social Psychology, 45*, 321–337.

Gallucci, M., Perugini, M. (2000). An experimental test of a game-theoretical model of reciprocity. *Journal of Behavioral Decision Making, 13*, 367–389.

Gallucci, M., Perugini, M. (2003). Information seeking and reciprocity: A transformational analysis. *European Journal of Social Psychology, 33*, 473–495.

Gärling, T. (1999). Value priorities, social value orientations and cooperation in social dilemmas. *British Journal of Social Psychology, 38*, 397–408.

Grzelak, J. L., Poppe, M., Czwartosz, Z., Nowak, A. (1988). "Numerical trap": A new look at outcome representation in studies on choice behaviour. *European Journal of Social Psychology, 18*, 143–159.

Harris, R. J., Joyce, M. A. (1980). What's fair? It depends on how you phrase the question. *Journal of Personality and Social Psychology, 38*, 165–179.

Kramer, R. M., McClintock, C. G., Messick, D. M. (1986). Social values and cooperative response to a simulated resource conservation crisis. *Journal of Personality, 54*, 576–592.

Kristensen, H. (2000). Does fairness matter in corporate takeovers? *Journal of Economic Psychology, 21*, 43–56.

Kuhlman, D., Marshello, A. (1975). Individual differences in game motivation as moderators of preprogrammed strategy effects in prisoner's dilemma. *Journal of Personality and Social Psychology, 32*, 922–931.

Kuhlman, D. M., Camac, C. R., Cuhna, D. A. (1986). Individual differences in social orientation. In H. A. M. Wilke, D. M. Messick & C. G. Rutte (eds.), *Experimental Social Dilemmas* (pp. 151–176). Frankfurt: Verlag Peter Lang.

Liebrand, W. B. G. (1984). The effect of social motives, communication and group size on behav-iour in an N-person multi-stage, mixed-motive game. *European Journal of Social Psychology, 14*, 239–264.

Liebrand, W. B. G., McClintock, C. (1988). The ring measure of social values: A computerized procedure for assessing individual differences in information processing and social value ori-entation. *European Journal of Personality, 2*, 217–230.

Loewenstein, G. F., Thompson, L., Bazerman, M. H. (1989). Social utility and decision making in interpersonal contexts. *Journal of Personality and Social Psychology, 57*, 426–441.

McClintock, C. G., Allison, S. T. (1989). Social value orientation and helping behavior. *Journal of Applied Social Psychology, 19*, 353–362.

McClintock, C. G., Messick, D. M., Kuhlman, D. M., Campos, F. T. (1973). Motivational bases of choice in three-choice decomposed games. *Journal of Experimental Social Psychology, 9*, 572–590.

Messick, D. M. (1993). Equality as a decision heuristic. In B. A. Mellers & J. Baron (eds.), *Psychological Perspectives on Justice: Theory and Applications* (pp. 11–31). Cambridge: Cambridge University Press.

Messick, D. M. (1995). Equality, fairness, and social conflict. *Social Justice Research, 8*, 153–173.

Messick, D. M., McClintock, C. G. (1968). Motivational bases of choice in experimental games. *Journal of Experimental Social Psychology, 4*, 1–25.

Messick, D. M., Sentis, K. (1979). Fairness and preference. *Journal of Experimental Social Psychology, 15*, 418–434.

Messick, D. M., Schell, T. (1992). Evidence for an equality heuristic in social decision making. *Acta Psychologica, 80*, 311–323.

Nauta, A., De Dreu, C. K. W., Van Der Vaart, T. (2002). Social value orientation, organizational goal concerns and interdepartmental problem-solving behavior. *Journal of Organizational Behavior, 23*, 199–213.

Rapoport, A., Budescu, D. V., Suleiman, R., Weg, E. (1992). Social dilemmas with uniformly distributed resources. In W. Liebrand, D. Messick & H. Wilke (eds.), *Social Dilemmas: Theoretical Issues and Research Findings* (pp. 43–57). Oxford: Pergamon.

Rutte, C. G., Wilke, H. A. M., Messick, D. (1987). Scarcity or abundance caused by people or the environment as determinants of behavior in the resource dilemma. *Journal of Experimental Social Psychology, 23*, 208–216.

Van Dijk, E., Grodzka, M. (1992). The influence of endowments asymmetry and information level on the contribution to a public step good. *Journal of Economic Psychology, 13*, 329–342.

Van Dijk, E., Wilke, H. A. M. (1995). Coordination rules in asymmetric social dilemmas: A comparison between public good dilemmas and resource dilemmas. *Journal of Experimental Social Psychology, 31*, 1–27.

Van Lange, P. A. M. (1999). The pursuit of joint outcomes and equality in outcomes: An integrative model of social value orientation. *Journal of Personality and Social Psychology, 77*, 337–349.

Van Lange, P. A. M., Agnew, C. R., Harinck, F., Steemers, G. E. M. (1997). From game theory to real life: How social value orientation affects willingness to sacrifice in ongoing close relationships. *Journal of Personality and Social Psychology, 73*, 1330–1344.

Van Lange, P. A. M., Kuhlman, D. M. (1994). Social value orientations and impressions of partner's honesty and intelligence: A test of the might versus morality effect. *Journal of Personality and Social Psychology, 67*, 126–141.

Van Lange, P. A. M., Liebrand, W. B. G. (1989). On perceiving morality and potency: Social values and the effects of person perception in a give-some dilemma. *European Journal of Personality, 3*, 209–225.

Van Lange, P. A. M., Otten, W., De Bruin, E. M. N., Joireman, J. A. (1997). Development of prosocial, individualistic and competitive orientations. Theory and primary evidence. *Journal of Personality and Social Psychology, 73*, 733–746.

Van Vugt, M., Meertens, R. M., Van Lange, P. A. M. (1995). Car versus public transportation? The role of social value orientations in a real-life social dilemma. *Journal of Applied Social Psychology, 25*, 258–278.

Wilke, H. A. M. (1991). Greed, efficiency and fairness in resource management situations. In W. Stroebe & M. Hewstone (eds.), *European Review of Social Psychology* (Vol. 2, pp. 165–187). New York: Wiley & Sons.

Chapter 3
A Classification of Games by Player Type

Gary Bornstein

Introduction

In this chapter, I lay out a classification of social situations—situations of interdependent decision making—based on the type of decision makers involved. Then, using this framework, I review the decision-making literature and point out the gaps that still exist in it. The classification of social situations, or games, builds on a distinction between three basic types of decision-making agents, or players: *individuals,* cooperative or *unitary groups*—groups whose members can reach a binding (and costless) agreement on a joint strategy—and *non-cooperative groups*—groups whose members act independently without being able to make a binding agreement. Pitting individuals (I), unitary groups (U), and non-cooperative groups (G) against one another, and adding nature as a potential "opponent," generates the 3 (type of agent) × 4 (type of opponent) matrix depicted in Table 3.1.

The I cell in the leftmost column of Table 3.1 represents the vast literature on individual decision making or one-person "games" against nature (e.g., Camerer, 1995; Kahneman et al., 1982). This cell is the only one in the matrix that does not involve interdependent or social decision making per se (although social factors play a major role in shaping individual decision making as well). The U cell represents the literature on decision making by unitary ("common purpose") groups in games against nature (e.g., Davis, 1992; Hastie & Kameda, 2005). There is also a substantial literature, particularly in social psychology (but recently also in economics, e.g., Blinder & Morgan, 2005), which compares group decision making with that of individuals in these types of games (e.g., Kerr et al., 1996; Hill, 1982). The G cell in the bottom of column 1 represents the literature on non-cooperative *n*-person games, in particular the social dilemma and public-good literature (e.g., Dawes & Messick, 2000; Hardin, 1982; Ledyard, 1995; Kollock, 1998) and the literature on coordination games (e.g., Van Huyck et al., 1990, Cooper, 1999). In the broader framework suggested here, these *n*-person games are seen as games of a non-cooperative group against nature.

The preparation of this paper was supported by grants from the Israeli Science Foundation (907/01 and 535/05) and the U.S.-Israel Binational Science Foundation (2003–299).

A. Biel et al. (eds.), *New Issues and Paradigms in Research on Social Dilemmas.*
© Springer 2008

Table 3.1 A Taxonomy of Games by Player Type

Opponent Player	Nature	Individual (I)	Unitary Team (U)	Non-cooperative Group (G)
Individual (I)	I	I-I	I-U	I-G
Unitary team (U)	U	U-I	U-U	U-G
Non-cooperative group (G)	G	G-I	G-U	G-G

Another cell that has received much attention is the I-I cell, which represents the literature on two-person games (e.g., Komorita & Parks, 1995).[1] Two-person games have played a pivotal role in the study of cooperation and competition in interpersonal relations (e.g., Kelley & Thibaut, 1978). However, a good deal of the interest in dyadic games has stemmed from issues of intergroup interactions, such as military confrontations, labor-management disputes, and competitions between organizations and interest groups, rather than interactions between two individuals (e.g., Axelrod, 1984; Brams, 1975; Deutsch, 1973). Two relatively recent lines of research have expanded the study of two-person games to the interaction between two groups. One has focused on competition between unitary groups, as in the U-U cell, while the other has investigated competition between non-cooperative groups, as in the G-G cell.

U-U vs. I-I: The "Discontinuity Effect"

In a series of experiments, Insko and his colleagues (Insko & Schopler, 1987; Schopler & Insko, 1992) compared the two-person prisoner's dilemma game played between two unitary groups (whose members conducted face-to-face discussion to decide, as a group, on whether to defect or cooperate) with the same game played between two individuals. They found that intergroup interaction is far more competitive than inter-individual interaction, and termed the observed difference between U-U and I-I interactions the *discontinuity* effect. Insko and Schopler (see, e.g., Wildschut et al., 2003) offer two explanations for the increased competitiveness of groups. The *social support for shared self-interest* hypothesis argues that groups are more competitive than individuals because group members provide one another with support for acting in a selfish, ingroup-oriented way. The *schema-based distrust* hypothesis postulates that group members compete because they expect the outgroup to act competitively and want to defend themselves against the possibility of being exploited. As a result of these processes, unitary groups are more selfish than individuals and also expect their opponents to behave more selfishly.

---

[1] The I-I cell can be seen as a special case of the G cell with $n = 2$. The difference between these two cells captures the common distinction between 2-person and n-person games (e.g., Colman, 1995) made in the literature.

Several studies have employed the U-U vs. I-I design in the context of other two-person games. Bornstein and Yaniv (1998) compared group and individual behavior in the one-shot Ultimatum game. In this game, player 1 has to propose a division of a sum of money between herself and player 2. If player 2 accepts the proposed division, both are paid accordingly; if player 2 rejects the proposal, both are paid nothing. In the U-U condition, the members of the allocating group conducted a face-to-face discussion to decide, as a group, on a proposed division, and the members of the recipient group held a discussion on whether to accept or reject the proposal. The game-theoretic solution for the Ultimatum game prescribes that player 2, as a rational, self-interest maximizer, should accept any proposal greater than zero, and therefore player 1, who is similarly motivated, should propose keeping all but a penny for herself. Bornstein and Yaniv (1998) found that, although neither individuals nor groups were fully rational in that sense, groups in the role of player 1 offered less than individuals, and groups in the role of player 2 were willing to accept less. Similar findings for the behavior of player 1 were reported by Robert and Carnevale (1997).

Luhan et al. (in press) compared individual and group decisions in the Dictator game (Kahneman et al., 1986). The Dictator game is a one-sided ultimatum game where player 1 has to divide a sum of money between itself and player 2, and player 2 must accept the division. Their experiment used a within-subject design where decisions were first made individually, then in a (three-person) group setting, and then individually again. Individuals were assigned to groups based on their decision in the initial stage, so that each group consisted of a relatively selfish member, a relatively other-regarding member, and a moderate one. Luhan et al. found that groups were less generous than individuals—the least generous group member exerts the most influence on the group's decision, and following a group decision individual allocations become more selfish as compared with the initial decisions.[2]

Kocher and Sutter (in press) studied individuals and groups in a one-shot gift-exchange game. This game models bargaining in the labor market, where the employer first determines the employee's wage, and the employee then chooses her effort level. Rationally, the employee should exert minimum effort regardless of her wage and, anticipating that, the employer should pay the lowest wage possible. Kocher and Sutter (2002) found that groups in the role of employers and employees chose lower wages and effort levels, respectively, than individuals.

Cox (2002) compared the trust game played between two individuals with the same game played between two unitary groups (of three individuals each). In the trust game (Berg et al., 1995), the *sender* receives an initial endowment, $X > 0$, and can transfer any part of it ($x \le X$) to a *responder*. The latter receives $3x$ and can return any amount $y \le 3x$ to the sender. The sender's choice of x is taken as a measure of trust—one's willingness to make oneself vulnerable to the actions of another agent (Coleman, 1990)—whereas the return y indicates the responder's trustworthiness.

---

[2] However, an earlier study by Cason and Mui (1997) found that (two-person) groups made somewhat more generous, other-regarding allocations in the Dictator game than individuals.

Cox's main findings were that individuals and groups did not differ in the amount sent, x, but groups in the role of responders return significantly smaller amounts, y.

Kugler et al. (in press) also compared the behavior of individuals and unitary groups in the trust game, but obtained different results. In their study, groups in the role of sender sent smaller amounts than individuals and expected lower returns. Groups and individuals in the role of responder return on average the same fraction of the amount sent. Hence, Kugler et al. concluded that groups are less trusting than individuals, but just as trustworthy. Obviously, more experimental work is needed to establish the difference between individual and group behavior in the trust game.

Bornstein et al. (2004) compared the centipede game (McKelvey & Palfrey, 1992) played by either two individuals or two unitary groups (see Figure 3.1). The two competitors in this game alternate in deciding whether to take the larger portion of an increasing pile of money, and as soon as one takes the money the game ends. The rational, game-theoretical solution is again based on the logic of backward induction. Assuming that player 2 is selfish and therefore will choose Take at the last decision node, player 1, who is similarly selfish, should choose Take at the next-to-last node. Applying the same logic to all moves up the game tree, player 1, the first mover, should choose to exit the game at the first decision node. Bornstein et al. (2004) found that, although neither individuals nor groups fully complied with this theoretical solution, groups did exit the centipede game significantly earlier than individuals.

Recent studies by Cooper and Kagel (2005) on signaling games, and by Kocher and Sutter (2005) on guessing ("beauty contest") games, where social (other-regarding) preferences play little role, show that unitary groups are better than individuals in reasoning from the point of view of the opposing player and, in particular, unitary groups learn much faster than individuals to play strategically.

Summary

The rapidly accumulating experimental literature on the I-I vs. U-U contrast shows quite clearly that groups and individuals make different decisions in two-person games. Groups, it seems, are more selfish and more sophisticated players than

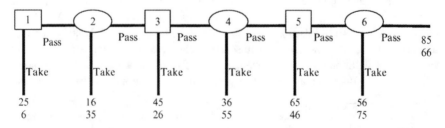

Figure 3.1 The centipede game

individuals, and, as a result, interactions between two unitary groups are closer to the rational, game-theoretical solution than interactions between two individuals.[3]

G-G vs. G: Intergroup vs. Single-Group Games

Competition between two non-cooperative groups (e.g., war, elections, rivalry between interest groups) is often associated with conflict of interest within each of the competing groups as well. The primary reason for the internal conflict is the fact that the benefits associated with the outcome of the external competition (e.g., territory, political power, status, pride) are public goods, which are equally available to all the members of a group, regardless of their contribution to their group's effort (Bornstein, 2003; Palfrey & Rosenthal, 1983; Rapoport & Bornstein, 1987). When contribution entails personal cost (e.g., time, money, physical effort, or risk of injury or death), rational group members have an incentive to *free-ride* on the contributions of others. Of course, as a result of free riding, the group might lose the competition, in which case the public good will not be provided or, worse yet, a public bad will be provided for contributors and non-contributors alike.

This intragroup problem of public-goods provision in the intergroup or G-G case is fundamentally different from that studied in the single-group or G case. In the case of a single group, the provision function (which relates the level of contribution to the amount of the public good provided) is determined by nature. Nature, while sometimes uncertain (e.g., Messick et al., 1988; Suleiman, 1997), never competes back. In contrast, the provision function in intergroup conflict is determined by comparing the levels of contribution made by the competing groups. The existence of another group whose choice also affects the outcome requires each group to make strategic considerations in selecting its own action. The group's choice of strategy and its success in carrying it out depend on its ability to mobilize contributions from its individual members, and its beliefs about the outgroup's ability to do the same. Several studies that contrasted a G-G game with a comparable G game illustrate the differences between the two social situations.

The Intergroup Prisoner's Dilemma (IPD) Game

The IPD game (Bornstein, 1992, 2003) provides a particularly suitable setting for comparing G-G and G situations. This game, as exemplified here, involves

---

[3] Unitary groups in the experiments reviewed in this chapter were operationalized as "natural" groups whose members can talk freely among themselves and share information and ideas. Unitary groups can, however, also be operationalized as nominal groups—groups whose members arrive at a group decision by some imposed public choice (i.e., voting) mechanism (e.g., majority rule, dictator choice) without an opportunity for face-to-face discussion (e.g., Bornstein et al., 2004; Allbitar et al., 2004).

competition between two groups of three members each. Each group member receives an endowment of two points and has to decide whether or not to contribute her endowment. Each contribution increases the payoff to each ingroup member (including the contributor) by one point and decreases the payoff to each outgroup member by one point. Since the individual loses one point by contributing, regardless of what the other (ingroup and outgroup) players do, a rational player should never contribute. However, since a two-point endowment generates a total of three points for the group, all ingroup members are better off if they all contribute their endowments. Thus, the intragroup payoff structure in the IPD team game (or two-level game; e.g., Putnam, 1988) is an n-person prisoner's dilemma, regardless of what the other group does (Dawes, 1980).

Bornstein and Ben-Yossef (1994) used this property of the IPD game to test whether a social dilemma game is played differently when embedded in an intergroup conflict than when played in an isolated single-group setting. We simply contrasted the IPD game with an identical three-person PD game. The only difference between the two games is that in the single-group PD contributing a two-point endowment generates a point for each group member without affecting the outgroup in any way.[4] The payoff matrix for the IPD game appears in Table 3.2 (a flat bonus of three points is added to prevent negative payoffs).

The results of the Bornstein and Ben-Yossef (1994) study show that individual group members are more likely to contribute in the intergroup IPD game than in the single-group PD game. Since the only difference between the two conditions is that in the IPD game the two groups were in competition against each other, while in the PD game each group was engaged in a separate (independent) game, this increased cooperation must reflect changes in the individuals' utility function due to the "real" conflict of interests between the groups. Evidently, the intergroup conflict induced individual group members to substitute group regard for egoism as the principle guiding their choices (Brewer & Kramer, 1986; Kramer & Brewer, 1984; Dawes & Messick, 2000; Hardin, 1995). The participants' self-reported motivations are consistent with this interpretation. The participants in the IPD condition viewed themselves as motivated less by self-interest and more by the collective group interest than those in the PD control condition. They also reported a higher motivation to maximize the ingroup's relative advantage over the outgroup (Turner et al., 1979).

Another experiment that employed the IPD vs. PD design was conducted by Baron (2001). Like Bornstein and Ben-Yossef (1994), Baron found that ingroup

Table 3.2 Individual Payoffs in the Intergroup Prisoner's Dilemma (IPD) Game

	Number of Ingroup Contributors – Number of Outgroup Contributors						
	3	2	1	0	−1	−2	−3
Contribute	6	5	4	3	2	1	—
Not contribute	—	7	6	5	4	3	2

---

[4] Also, to exclude the possibility that the classification of players into groups rather than the conflict of interests between the groups (Rabbie, 1982; Tajfel & Turner, 1979) is responsible for any potential effects, we included two groups in the PD (G) control condition as well.

cooperation was higher in the IPD than the PD condition. Baron attributes this "two-groups vs. one-group parochialism effect" to the "illusion of morality as self-interest" (Baron, 1997)—the tendency of people to believe that self-sacrificial behavior on behalf of one's group is, in fact, in one's self-interest. Baron hypothesized that this illusion is greater when the ingroup is in competition with an outgroup. Indeed, he found that participants in the IPD condition were more likely than those in the PD condition to believe that contribution would earn them more money, and their contribution decisions were strongly correlated with this belief.

Probst et al. (1999) also compared the IPD with the PD game. Probst et al. were interested in the relations between the players' values and their decision to cooperate or defect in these games. They found that vertical individualists—competitive people who want to do better than others—were less likely to cooperate in the single-group (PD) dilemma, where one's relative payoff is maximized by defection, and more likely to cooperate in the intergroup (IPD) dilemma, where winning is achieved by cooperating with one's own group to defeat the other group. In contrast, vertical collectivists—cooperative people who tend to sacrifice their own interest for the interests of the group—were more cooperative in the single-group dilemma, where contribution serves the collective interest, and less cooperative in the intergroup dilemma, where universal defection is collectively optimal.[5]

Summary

The experiments described above suggest that individuals make different decisions in the G-G than in the G version of the PD game. Specifically, they show that people are more likely to cooperate in intergroup conflict, where the ingroup's gain comes at the expense of the outgroup, than in an isolated single-group game, as hypothesized by the intergroup conflict–intragroup cooperation hypothesis (Stein, 1976; Campbell, 1965, 1972). In the IPD game, as in the social reality that it models, this greater willingness to sacrifice on behalf of the group is destructive from the perspective of the larger society (which includes all members of both groups). As observed by Campbell (1965), altruistic behavior, while collectively beneficial in single-group dilemmas, is often detrimental in intergroup conflicts (Campbell, 1965).

Intergroup competitions are not always destructive, however. In some cases, increasing individual contribution through competition between groups is beneficial for both the group and the society at large. Constructive competition regularly takes place between different organizations (e.g., firms, universities) as well as subgroups within the same organization (e.g., R&D teams, academic departments). These competitions are won by the groups whose members are more cooperative and better coordinated with one another than the members of the competing groups.

---

[5] Baron (2001) suggested that vertical individualists, who value both pursuit of self-interest and competition against others, are especially vulnerable to the illusion of self-interest. These participants are willing to sacrifice their self-interest on behalf of their group when in competition against another group since in this context they do not see what they are doing as self-sacrifice.

Several experiments (Erev et al., 1993; Bornstein & Erev, 1994; Bornstein et al., 2002; Nalbantian & Schotter, 1997; Rapoport & Amaldoss, 1999; Gunnthorsdottir & Rapoport, in press) have demonstrated that, by decreasing free riding and enhancing coordination within the competing groups, intergroup competition can improve overall performance as compared with the single-group case.

G-G vs. I-I: Intergroup vs. Inter-Individual Games

The use of two-person games to model conflicts between groups (e.g., Brams, 1975; Snidal, 1986) treats each group as a unitary, purposive player. However, as discussed above, the unitary-player assumption collapses when the benefits associated with the outcome of the intergroup conflict are public goods, and group members cannot make a binding (and costless) agreement to overcome the ensuing free-rider problem. To test how sensitive bilateral interactions are to the violation of the unitary-player assumption, this section reviews two experiments that contrasted I-I and G-G games. The first experiment involves the game of Chicken, while the second involves a price competition game (the Bertrand game).

The Game of Chicken

The game derives its name from the practice of two drivers racing toward each other on a narrow road. Each driver has the choice of swerving to avoid a head-on collision or continuing on a collision course. While the original contest involved individual drivers, much of the interest in this game was motivated by questions about competition between groups. The two-person Chicken game has been commonly used to model intergroup situations such as military confrontations and disputes between workers and employers where, as in the driver scenario, a failure of either side to yield leads to a collision (war, strike) that is disastrous for both.

Bornstein et al. (1997) compared the intergroup Chicken game with the two-person game. The games were played repeatedly, as our interest was in assessing the ability of the participants in the two games to use the opportunities provided by repeated interaction to cooperate in realizing their mutual interests. The intergroup (G-G) game in our experiment was operationalized as a competition between two teams of two members each.[6] Each player received an endowment and had to decide between keeping it or investing it. A reward (defined to be larger than the initial endowment) was given to each member of a group if the number of ingroup investors exceeded that in the outgroup. Members of the losing team received nothing. If there was an equal number of investors in both groups, the players received no

---

[6] Strictly speaking, the intergroup conflict in this experiment is an I-I vs. I-I game, but see footnote 2.

bonus. Regardless of the outcome of the game, players who did not invest their endowment kept it. In the two-person (I-I) game, each player received an endowment and had to decide whether to keep it or invest it. A reward was provided to a player who invested the endowment when the other player did not. If both or neither player invested the endowment, neither received a reward.

As predicted, the level of cooperation in the two-person Chicken game was much higher than that in the intergroup game. In the I-I game, more than two-thirds of the rounds resulted in the collectively optimal outcome of one player contributing, and turn-taking between the two players (which generates a fair as well as an efficient outcome) was rather common. Moreover, the level of efficiency, as reflected in the amounts of money earned, increased steadily as the game progressed. These results stand in sharp contrast to those observed in the G-G competition. In the intergroup competition, only about a quarter of the rounds resulted in the collectively optimal outcome of one player contributing; practically all the other rounds resulted in a higher, and therefore inefficient, rate of contribution, and, most notably, about 12% of the rounds ended up in a full-scale "collision" of all players contributing their endowments and all receiving a payoff of 0. There was also little indication of turn-taking within or between the groups, and no signs of improvement in collective efficiency over time.[7]

Price Competition

The second experiment by Bornstein et al. (in press) employed the G-G vs. I-I design to study price competition in a duopolistic market. For simplicity, the competing agents in economic markets are typically modeled as unitary players and are represented by individual subjects in experimental investigation of such markets. In reality, however, the agents operating in the market often consist of multiple players, and the possibility of conflicting interests within agents must be taken into account. This is obviously true when the competitors are alliances of firms (Amaldoss et al., 2000), but it is also true when the competitors are single firms.[8]

The two competitors were operationalized as either individuals or non-cooperative groups (with either two or three players in each group). The game was played repeatedly for many rounds with the same set of players. In each round, the players

---

[7] It can be argued that the differences between the two-person and the intergroup Chicken games is due to the fact that the intergroup game involves twice the number of players and thus entails a more intricate coordination problem. However, a comparison between the intergroup game and a four-person single-group (G) game of Chicken provides evidence against this possibility. The intergroup and the single-group games involve the same number of players and therefore present subjects with an identical coordination problem. Nonetheless, the coordination in the single-group game was much better than in the intergroup game.

[8] For example, principal-agent theory acknowledges the existence of conflicting interests within firms, but when firms are studied in strategic contexts of competition against other firms, these internal conflicts are typically ignored.

stated their asking price (an integer between 2 and 25) independently and simultaneously. The team whose total asking price was lower won the competition and was paid its price, whereas the losing team was paid nothing. In case of a tie, the teams split the asking price. Each group member was paid his or her asking price if the team won, and half that if the game was tied. This internal payoff structure provides each group member with an opportunity, indeed a temptation, to free-ride. That is, if the other players in her group settle for a low price, a player can demand a higher price and might yet win.[9]

Theoretically, if the two competitors meet only once, the prices should equal the marginal cost (2 in our experiment) regardless of whether the players are individuals or groups. However, when the game is played repeatedly, as in our experiment, tacit collusion between the two competitors becomes both theoretically possible and practically viable (Tirole, 1988). This is because repeated interaction forces the players to take into account not only current profits but also the potential long-term losses of a price war. These long-term considerations decrease the temptation to cut prices and may encourage the competitors to collude in order to sustain higher (even monopoly) prices (Chamberlin, 1929).

Nevertheless, Bornstein et al. (in press) found that asking (and winning) prices were much higher when the competitors were individuals than when they were (two- or three-person) non-cooperative groups. Moreover, in competitions between two individuals, prices increased with practice and, as the game progressed, the collusive outcome (where both sides are paid the highest, monopoly price) was achieved in a substantial number of cases, whereas in competitions between two groups prices remained stable, and there was little evidence of learning to collude. Clearly, price competition is highly sensitive to violations of the unitary-player assumption, and cooperation to keep prices high is much more likely when the competitors are individuals rather than multiplayer groups.

Summary

The results of the two studies reviewed in this section accentuate the importance of distinguishing between I-I and G-G games. Clearly, games between two non-cooperative groups are not played out in the same way as games between two unitary players. Rather, the conflicts of interests within the players intensified the conflict between them. If nothing else, this finding suggests that extrapolation from experiments that study interaction between two individuals to interactions between two non-cooperative groups (nations, strategic alliances, firms) could be seriously misleading, as it provides a prediction for the prospects of cooperation that is far too optimistic.

---

[9] For groups we also included a "shared profit" treatment in which a group's profit for winning or tying the game was divided equally among its members. This division rule eliminates the internal conflict of interest. However, team members still face the problem of coordinating a joint strategy without communicating.

Competition Between Different Types of Players

The experiments reviewed so far involved competition between two players of the same type. The discontinuity research has studied the U-U game, using the I-I game as a control. The team-game research has focused on the G-G game, using the G or the I-I game as a control. Little research has been done so far on asymmetric games, where the competition is between agents of different types (i.e., G-U, G-I, and U-I). Real-world examples of such asymmetric competition are abundant. A strike of an unorganized group of workers against an individual employer or a unitary board of directors, a standoff between a democratic state and a dictatorship, or a clash between a scattered group of demonstrators and a cohesive police force are only a few of the examples that come to mind. How does the asymmetry between the conflicting sides affect the course and outcome of their interaction? Which type of player, if any, has the advantage?

A few recent experiments provide some preliminary answers to these questions. Kugler and Bornstein (2005) examined repeated interaction between a non-cooperative group (of three members) and an individual player.[10] The two sides in this G-I game were symmetrical in that they had equal resources at their disposal. However, while the individual player had complete control over her resources, the group's resources were divided among its members. If the group ended up winning the competition, the ensuing reward was divided equally among its members regardless of whether or not they contributed to the group's success.

The fact that the group has to overcome a collective action problem to fully realize its potential power, whereas the individual player is free of internal problems, gives the individual an advantage. Kugler and Bornstein (2005) found that the size of this advantage depends on the strategic structure of the game. The individual's advantage over the group, as reflected in relative payoffs, was more decisive in the Chicken and Prisoner's Dilemma games and less decisive in the Assurance game.

Kugler et al.'s (in press) study of the trust game mentioned above included two asymmetric conditions, where a group sender played against an individual responder, and vice versa. These conditions were included to examine whether either individuals or groups behave differently toward other individuals and groups. Unfortunately, the results fall short of providing a definitive answer to this question. On the one hand, the average amount sent in the G-I condition was not significantly different from that in the G-G condition. On the other hand, groups sent nothing ($x = 0$) significantly more often to group responders than to individual responders.

Sutter (2005) studied the "beauty contest" game played by either individuals or three-person unitary groups. In this game, N decision makers simultaneously choose a real number between 0 and 100. The winner is the player whose number is closest to two-thirds of the mean of all the choices. The game is solved by a process of elimination of dominated strategies and thus provides a good setting for

---

[10] The G-I game was compared with the two symmetrical control conditions, namely, competition between two individuals (I-I) and competition between two non-cooperative groups (G-G).

estimating the players' depth of strategic reasoning. In the first, most naïve level, players assume that others will choose randomly, and therefore choose 33 (as two-thirds of a mean of 50). Assuming that others also think this way, the chosen number should be two-thirds of that (or 22), and this process continues until the equilibrium of 0 is reached. Sutter (2005) found that, while individuals and groups did not differ in their choices in the first round, from round 2 on, groups played much closer to the game's equilibrium than individuals, which indicates that they learn much faster to think strategically. Most relevant for this section is the finding that in a game involving both group and individual players, groups significantly outperformed individuals in term of payoffs.

Summary

In a competition with an individual player, a non-cooperative group is at a disadvantage. This is because, unlike the individual, the group has to overcome a collective action problem in order to realize its potential power. Although we did not study competition between a non-cooperative group and a unitary one, it seems safe to assume that non-cooperative groups would fare badly in such asymmetric competitions as well. In a competition between unitary groups and individuals, unitary groups seem to have the upper hand.

Concluding Comments

The taxonomy outlined here draws a clear-cut distinction between cooperative (i.e., unitary) and non-cooperative groups. This sharp distinction is obviously a simplification of the reality. In a more elaborated and realistic model, groups would be characterized by some continuous parameter to reflect their position on a dimension ranging from a fully cooperative or unitary group at one end to a fully non-cooperative one at the other. This parameter could take on many different but essentially equivalent meanings, such as group cohesion, group identification, group-based altruism, etc. The important thing is that the more cohesive the group, or the more patriotic its members, the lower the group's cost for mobilizing collective action. When group members identify with the group to the extent that its interest and the individual's interest become one, collective action is costless, and (not considering coordination costs) the group is a truly unitary one. When, on the other hand, group members are narrowly rational players who care only about their own interest, the group is a truly non-cooperative one. Real groups are always located somewhere in between these two hypothetical extremes. Moreover, as demonstrated by Bornstein and Ben-Yossef (1994), a group's location on this continuum is affected by the social context. Keeping the internal payoff structure constant, a group becomes more cooperative when facing another group than when playing against nature.

This taxonomy covers interactions between just two agents (although each agent can comprise many decision makers). By adding more dimensions to the matrix, the taxonomy can be expanded to n-agent games. When modeling competition between several firms (i.e., oligopoly), multiparty elections, or multilateral negotiations among nations, such an expansion is necessary. The "beauty contest" experiment by Sutter (2005), described in the previous section, is the only one I know of that compared the behavior of U and I players in a multi-agent game.

There are many other differences between groups (both unitary and non-cooperative) that have not been considered in this chapter. For example, groups differ from one another in size (Isaac & Walker, 1994; Ledyard, 1995),[11] in their internal payoff structure or profit-sharing rule (Rapoport & Amaldoss, 1999), in the ability of their members to communicate with and influence one another (e.g., Bornstein et al., 1989; Bornstein, 1992; Takacs, 2001), in the voting rule used for arriving at a group decision (e.g., Elbittar et al., 2004), in the symmetry of the players within and between groups (e.g., Budescu et al., 1990; Rapoport et al., 1989), and the like. Nevertheless, the classification outlined here captures the most fundamental situations that humans (and non-humans as well, e.g., Conradt & Roper, 2003; Heinsohn, 1997; Velicer, 2003; Wilson et al., 2001) have encountered throughout their evolution. People, either alone or as part of a group, have to make decisions vis-à-vis nature and vis-à-vis other individuals and groups.

References

Amaldoss, W., Meyer, R., Raju, J., Rapoport, A. (2000). Collaborating to compete. *Marketing Science, 19*, 105–126.

Axelrod, R. (1984). *The Evolution of Cooperation.* New York: Basic Books.

Baron, J. (1997). The illusion of morality as self-interest: A reason to cooperate in social dilemmas. *Psychological Science, 8*, 330–335.

Baron, J. (2001). Confusion of group-interest and self-interest in parochial cooperation on behalf of the group. *Journal of Conflict Resolution, 45*, 283–296.

Berg, J., Dickhaut, J., McCabe, K. (1995). Trust, reciprocity, and social history. *Games and Economic Behavior, 10*, 21–142.

Blinder, A. S., Morgan, J. (2005). Are two heads better than one? An experimental analysis of group vs. individual decision making, *Journal of Money, Credit and Banking, 37*, 789–811.

Bornstein, G. (1992). The free rider problem in intergroup conflicts over step-level and continuous public goods. *Journal of Personality and Social Psychology, 62*, 597–606.

Bornstein, G. (2003). Intergroup conflict: Individual, group, and collective interests. *Personality and Social Psychology Review, 7*, 129–145.

Bornstein, G., Ben-Yossef, M. (1994). Cooperation in intergroup and single-group social dilemmas. *Journal of Experimental Social Psychology, 30*, 52–67.

---

[11] A recent study of the beauty contest game by Sutter (2005) showed that unitary groups of four members do not perform any better than two-member groups (although, as in Kocher & Sutter, 2005, both two-person and four-person groups outperformed individuals). Similar findings were reported by Pallais (2005) with regard to the Ultimatum game.

Bornstein, G., Erev, I. (1994). The enhancing effect of intergroup competition on group perform-ance. *International Journal of Conflict Management, 5,* 271–284.

Bornstein, G., Yaniv, I. (1998). Individual and group behavior in the ultimatum game: Are groups more "rational" players? *Experimental Economics, 1,* 101–108.

Bornstein, G., Budescu, D., Zamir, S. (1997). Cooperation in intergroup, two-person, and *n*-person games of Chicken. *Journal of Conflict Resolution, 41,* 384–406.

Bornstein, G., Budescu, D., Kugler, T., Selten, R. (in press). Repeated price competition between individuals and between teams. *Journal of Economic Behavior and Organization.*

Bornstein, G., Gneezy, U., Nagel, R. (2002). The effect of intergroup competition on intragroup coordination: An experimental study. *Games and Economic Behavior.*

Bornstein, G., Rapoport, A., Kerpel, L., Katz, T. (1989). Within and between group communication in intergroup competition for public goods. *Journal of Experimental Social Psychology, 25,* 422–436.

Bornstein, G., Schram, A., Sonnemans, J. (2004). Do democracies breed chickens? Forthcoming in R. Suleiman, D. V. Budescu, I. Fischer & D. Messick (eds.), *Contemporary Psychological Research on Social Dilemmas.* Cambridge: Cambridge University Press.

Brams, S. (1975). *Game Theory and Politics: International Relations Games.* New York: The Free Press.

Brewer, M. B., Kramer, R. M. (1986). Choice behavior in social dilemmas: Effects of social identity, group size, and decision framing. *Journal of Personality and Social Psychology, 50,* 543–549.

Budescu, D. V, Rapoport, A., Suleiman, R. (1990). Resource dilemmas with environmental uncer-tainty and asymmetric players. *European Journal of Social Psychology, 20,* 475–478.

Camerer, C. (1995). Individual decision making. In A. Roth & J. Kagel (eds.), *Handbook of Experimental Economics.* Princeton, NJ: Princeton University Press.

Campbell, D. T. (1965). Ethnocentric and other altruistic motives. In D. Levine (ed.), *Nebraska Symposium on Motivation.* Lincoln: University of Nebraska Press.

Campbell, D. T. (1972). On the genetics of altruism and the counter-hedonic components in human culture. *Journal of Social Issues, 28,* 21–37.

Cason, T. N., Mui, V. (1997). A laboratory study of group polarization in the team dictator game. *Economic Journal, 107,* 1465–1483.

Chamberlin, E. (1929). Duopoly: Values where sellers are few. *Quarterly Journal of Economics, 43,* 63–100.

Coleman, J. (1990). *Foundations of Social Theory.* Cambridge, MA: Harvard University Press.

Colman, A. M. (1995). *Game Theory and Its Applications.* Oxford: Butterworth-Heinemann.

Conradt, L., Roper, T. J. (2003). Group decision-making in animals. *Nature, 42,* 155–158.

Cooper, D. J., Kagel, J. H. (2005). Are two heads better than one? Team versus individual play in signaling games. *American Economic Review, 95,* 477–509.

Cooper, R. (1999). *Coordination Games: Complementarities and Macroeconomics.* Cambridge: Cambridge University Press.

Coser, L. A. (1956). *The Function of Social Conflict.* Glencoe, IL: Free Press.

Cox, J. C. (2002). Trust, reciprocity, and other-regarding preferences: Groups vs. individuals and males vs. females. In R. Zwick & A. Rapoport (eds.), *Advances in Experimental Business Research.* New York: Kluwer Academic Publishers.

Davis, J. H. (1992). Some compelling intuitions about group consensus decisions: Theoretical and empirical research, and interpersonal aggregation phenomena: Selected examples, 1950–1990, *Organizational Behavior and Human Decision Processes, 52,* 3–38.

Dawes, R. M. (1980). Social dilemmas. *Annual Review of Psychology, 31,* 169–193.

Dawes, R. M., Messick, D. M. (2000). Social dilemmas. *International Journal of Psychology, 35,* 111–116.

Deutsch, M. (1973). *The Resolution of Conflict.* New Haven, CT: Yale University Press.

Elbittar, A., Gomberg, A., Sour, L. (2004). Group decision-making in ultimatum bargaining: An experimental study. Unpublished manuscript.

Erev, I., Bornstein, G., Galili, R. (1993). Constructive intergroup competition as a solution to the free rider problem: A field experiment. *Journal of Experimental Social Psychology, 29,* 463–478.

Gunnthorsdottir, A., Rapoport, A. (2006). Egalitarian vs. proportional profit-sharing rules in multi-level collective action problems. *Organizational Behavior and Human Decision Processes, 101*, 184–199.

Hardin, R. (1982). *Collective Action*. Baltimore, MD: The Johns Hopkins University Press.

Hardin, R. (1995). *One for All: The Logic of Intergroup Conflict*. Princeton, NJ: Princeton University Press.

Hastie, R., Kameda, T. (2005). The robust beauty of majority rules in group decisions. *Psychological Review, 112*, 494–508.

Heinsohn, R. (1997). Group territoriality in two populations of African lions. *Animal Behavior, 53*, 1143–1147.

Hill, G. W. (1982). Group versus individual performance: Are $n + 1$ heads better than one? *Psychological Bulletin, 91*, 517–539.

Insko, C. A., Schopler, J. (1987). Categorization, competition, and collectivity, in C. Hendrick, (ed.), *Group Processes* (Vol. 8, pp. 213–251). New York: Sage.

Isaac, R. M., Walker, J. M. (1994). Group size and the voluntary provision of public goods: Experimental evidence utilizing large groups. *Journal of Public Economics, 54*, 1–36.

Jervis, R. (1978). Cooperation under the security dilemma. *World Politics, 30*, 167–186.

Kahneman, D., Knetsch, J., Thaler, R. (1986). Fairness as a constraint on profit seeking: Entitlements in the market. *American Economic Review, 76*, 728–741.

Kahneman, D., Slovic, P., Tversky, A. (eds.) (1982). *Judgment Under Uncertainty: Heuristics and Biases*. Cambridge: Cambridge University Press.

Kelley, H. H., Thibaut, J. W. (1978). *Interpersonal Relations: A Theory of Interdependence*. New York: Wiley.

Kerr, L. N., MacCoun, R. J., Kramer, G. P. (1996). Bias in judgment: Comparing individuals and groups. *Psychological Review, 103*, 687–719.

Kocher, M. G., Sutter, M. (2005). The decision maker matters: Individual versus group behavior in experimental beauty-contest games. *The Economic Journal, 115*, 200–223.

Kocher, M. G., Sutter, M. (in press). Individual versus group behavior and the role of the decision making procedure in gift-exchange experiments. *Empirica*.

Kollock, P. (1998). Social dilemmas: The anatomy of cooperation. *Annual Review of Sociology, 24*, 183–214.

Komorita, S., Parks, C. (1995). Interpersonal relations: Mixed-motive interaction. *Annual Review of Psychology, 46*, 183–207.

Kramer, R. M., Brewer, M. B. (1984). Effects of group identity on resource use in simulated social dilemmas. *Journal of Personality and Social Psychology, 46*, 1044–1057.

Kugler, T., Bornstein, G. (2005). Individual and groups as players in bilateral conflicts. Unpublished manuscript.

Kugler, T., Bornstein, G., Kocher, M. G., Sutter, M. (in press). A trust game between individuals and groups: Groups are less trusting than individuals but just as trustworthy. *Journal of Economic Psychology*.

Ledyard, J. O. (1995). Public goods: A survey of experimental research. In A. Roth & J. Kagel (eds.), *Handbook of Experimental Economics*. Princeton, NJ: Princeton University Press.

Levine, R., Campbell, D. (1972). *Ethnocentrism: Theories of Conflict, Ethnic Attitudes and Group Behavior*. New York: John Wiley.

McKelvey, R., Palfrey, T. (1992). An experimental study of the centipede game. *Econometrica, 60*, 803–836.

Messick, D. M., Allison, S. T., Samuelson, C. D. (1988). Framing and communication effects on group members' responses to environmental and social uncertainty. In S. Maital (ed.), *Applied Behavioral Economics* (Vol. 2, pp. 677–700). New York: New York University Press.

Nalbantian, H., Schotter, A. (1997). Productivity under group incentives: An experimental study. *American Economic Review, 87*, 314–341.

Palfrey, T., Rosenthal, H. (1983). A strategic calculus of voting. *Public Choice, 41*, 7–53.

Pallais, A. (2005). The effect of group size on ultimatum bargaining. Unpublished manuscript.

Probst, T., Carnevale, P., Triandis, H. (1999). Cultural values in intergroup and single-group social dilemmas. *Organizational Behavior and Human Decision Processes, 77*, 171–191.

Putnam, R. D. (1988). Diplomacy and domestic politics: The logic of two-level games. *International Organization, 42*, 427–460.

Rabbie, J. M. (1982). The effects of intergroup competition on intragroup and intergroup relationships. In V. J. Derlega & J. Grzelak (eds.), *Cooperation and Helping Behavior: Theories and Research*. New York: Academic Press.

Rapoport, A., Amaldoss, W. (1999). Social dilemmas embedded in between-group competitions: Effects of contest and distribution rules. In M. Foddy, M. Smithson, S. Schneider, & M. Hogg (eds.), *Resolving Social Dilemmas: Dynamic, Structural, and Intergroup Aspects*. Philadelphia: Psychology Press, Taylor & Francis.

Rapoport, A., Bornstein, G. (1987). Intergroup competition for the provision of binary public goods. *Psychological Review, 94*, 291–299.

Rapoport, A., Bornstein, G. (1989). Solving public goods problems in competition between equal and unequal size groups. *Journal of Conflict Resolution, 33*, 460–479.

Rapoport, A., Bornstein, G., Erev, I. (1989). Intergroup competition for public goods: Effects of unequal resources and relative group size. *Journal of Personality and Social Psychology, 56*, 748–756.

Robert, C., Carnevale, P. J. (1997). Group choice in ultimatum bargaining. *Organizational Behavior and Human Decision Processes, 72*, 256–279.

Schopler, J., Insko, C. A. (1992). The discontinuity effect in interpersonal and intergroup relations: Generality and mediation. In W. Strobe & M. Hewstone (eds.), *European Review of Social Psychology*. Chichester, UK: John Wiley.

Sherif, M. (1966). *In Common Predicament: Social Psychology of Intergroup Conflict and Cooperation*. Boston: Houghton Mifflin.

Snidal, D. (1986). The game theory of international politics. In K. Oye (ed.), *Cooperation Under Anarchy*. Princeton, NJ: Princeton University Press.

Stein, A. A. (1976). Conflict and cohesion: A review of the literature. *Journal of Conflict Resolution, 20*, 143–172.

Suleiman, R. (1997). Provision of step-level public goods under uncertainty: A theoretical analysis. *Rationality and Society, 9*, 163–187.

Sutter, M. (2005). Are four heads better than two? An experimental beauty-contest game with teams of different size. *Economics Letters, 88*, 41–46.

Tajfel, H. (1982). Social psychology of intergroup relations. *Annual Review of Psychology, 33*, 1–39.

Tajfel, H., Turner, J. C. (1979). An integrative theory of intergroup conflict. In W. G. Austin & S. Worchel (eds.), *The Social Psychology of Intergroup Relations*. Monterey, CA: Brooks/Cole.

Takacs, K. (2001). Structural embeddedness and intergroup conflict. *Journal of Conflict Resolution, 45*, 743–769.

Tirole, J. (1988). *The Theory of Industrial Organization*. Cambridge, MA: MIT Press.

Turner, J. C. (1975). Social comparison and social identity: Some prospects for intergroup behavior. *European Journal of Social Psychology, 5*, 5–34.

Turner, J. C., Brown, R. J., Tajfel, H. (1979). Social comparison and group interest in intergroup favoritism. *European Journal of Social Psychology, 9*, 187–204.

Van Huyck, J., Battalio, R., Beil, R. (1990). Tacit coordination games, strategic uncertainty, and coordination failure. *American Economic Review, 80*, 234–248.

Velicer, G. (2003). Social strife in the microbial world. *Trends in Microbiology, 11*, 330–337.

Wildschut, T., Pinter, B., Vevea, J. L., Insko, C. A., Schopler, J. (2003). Beyond the group mind: A quantitative review of the interindividual–intergroup discontinuity effect. *Psychological Bulletin, 129*, 698–722.

Wilson, M. L., Hauser, M. D., Wrangham, R. W. (2001). Does participation in intergroup conflict depend on numerical assessment, range location, or rank for wild chimpanzees? *Animal Behavior, 61*, 1203–1216.

Chapter 4
How Do We React to Feedback in Social Dilemmas?

Eric van Dijk, David De Cremer, Laetitia B. Mulder, and Jeroen Stouten

How Do We React to Feedback in Social Dilemmas?

Social dilemmas depict mixed-motive situations in which personal interests and collective interests are at odds (e.g., Dawes, 1980; Komorita & Parks, 1995). In answering the question of how people deal with such conflicting motives, experimental research has used a variety of experimental games that are modeled after real-life situations. Two of the main types are the "public-good dilemma" and the "resource dilemma." Research on social dilemmas has primarily concentrated on the provision of public goods (i.e., the public-good dilemma) and the maintenance of scarce resources (i.e., the resource dilemma). In both situations, individual and collective interests may be in conflict. In the case of public goods, people may reason that it is in the interest of the collective to provide public goods and services (e.g., Medicare or public television) but that they are personally better off if they do not contribute. The maintenance of scarce resources refers to issues like the energy problem: It is in the collective's interest to restrict consumption, but individuals may want to consume excessively.

In the typical experimental study on social dilemmas, group members make their decisions privately and anonymously (for overviews, see, e.g., Dawes, 1980; Messick & Brewer, 1983; Komorita & Parks, 1995; Weber et al., 2004). Often these decisions are single decisions such that group members take their decisions in a kind of social vacuum in which they do not have prior information about how their group fared or what their fellow group members decided. Whereas these characteristics may be witnessed in real-life situations, it may be argued that many decisions are not taken in a social vacuum. In this chapter, we draw attention to the fact that many decisions are taken in situations where people do have some social information available. So how do people decide when they can rely on such social information? And does it matter what such feedback looks like?

Situations in which group members make their decisions in ignorance of the decisions made by the other group members have been referred to as *situations of social uncertainty* (Messick et al., 1988). A *situation of social certainty* would thus be a situation in which one has to decide while knowing what the other group

43

A. Biel et al. (eds.), *New Issues and Paradigms in Research on Social Dilemmas.*

members have decided in the dilemma you currently face. It may be appropriate to note here that when in this chapter we refer to a situation in which people receive feedback about what others did, we do not interpret this as a situation of social certainty. That is, we concentrate on situations in which group members do not know what their fellow group members *currently* decide. The issue that we would like to address is how, in such a situation of social uncertainty, people base their decisions on the feedback information they receive about their fellow group members.

When trying to make their decision in situations of social uncertainty, people may be highly motivated to rely on any feedback they may have available regarding their group and their fellow group members. In the current chapter, we distinguish between *explicit feedback* and *implicit feedback*. Explicit feedback refers to the situation where group members are explicitly informed about how their group has done in the past (e.g., was the group successful in securing collective interest?) or what each individual group member decided in the past (e.g., did some of the current group members free-ride in the past? Who are they?). Implicit feedback refers to situations where group members are informed about some characteristics of the dilemma that allow them to form expectations regarding their fellow group members. An example of this form would be a situation where group members learn that a sanctioning situation is introduced. By itself, this aspect does not provide explicit information about the group. Implicitly, however, it may signal that group members are not to be trusted and that group members are motivated to put their own interests first (Mulder et al., 2006).

In addition, we distinguish between various reactions to feedback. Social dilemma research is characterized by a strong focus on choice behavior, and in particular on whether or not people cooperate to further the collective interest. But the behavioral repertoire is not restricted to the decision to cooperate or not. In addition to this behavioral reaction of "elementary" cooperation (cf. Yamagishi, 1988), people may want to change the structural aspects of the dilemma that they face, for instance, by installing a sanctioning system, or by installing leadership. In addition, more recent approaches have focused on the willingness to ostracize defectors and the tendency that people may have to leave their group. Finally, we will also discuss a neglected aspect in social dilemmas: the relation among feedback, emotions, and emotion-based behaviors.

Explicit Feedback

Effects on Cooperation

In one of the first systematic studies to investigate the effects of feedback regarding others' behavior, Schroeder et al. (1983) manipulated in a resource dilemma context the feedback that participants received about their fellow group members' prior behavior. For example, in their Experiment 2, they put their participants in what they termed a "consuming-feedback" condition and a "conserving-feedback" condition, in which the fellow group members either did or did not consume excessively from a common resource. The results indicated that participants conformed to the decisions of their fellow group members. Thus, feedback indicating high consumption by others led to higher consumption by the participant, and feedback indicating restraint led to restraint. These findings were then primarily interpreted as being indicative of a motivation of group members to adopt the "correct" strategy. The observed tendency to do what others do was viewed as a display of a motivation to determine what would be an appropriate response (see also Smith & Bell, 1994; Parks et al., 2001; Pillutla & Chen, 1999).

Conformity, and relying on feedback about others' prior behavior to determine what would be the correct strategy, is not the only effect that feedback may have, however. As Messick and Brewer (1983) already noted, seeing others defect may also induce oneself to defect because it may reduce the felt responsibility to honor the collective interests. Thus, people may reason that if others apparently put their own interests first, they might as well do that too. The motivation to avoid being the sucker (Kerr, 1983) may add to this "defection breeds defection" explanation (see also Fleishman, 1988). In agreement with this, Messick et al. (1983) found that when participants facing a resource dilemma were provided with feedback that others overused the common resource, they subsequently tended to increase their own harvests. Participants receiving feedback indicating that others did not overuse the pool remained cooperative.

Interestingly, Messick et al. (1983) did not only study whether the group members' harvesting behavior was affected by collective feedback (i.e., did they respond to collective defection with defection and collective cooperation with cooperation?). In addition, these researchers provided their participants with (bogus) feedback about the variance of the individual harvests of the other group members. This variance was either low or high. In the low-variance conditions, the harvests of the fellow group members did not vary much. The results indicated that high variance had a detrimental effect on cooperation, suggesting that the presence of some non-cooperative group members may be enough for people to put their own interests first.

Chen and Bachrach (2003) investigated reactions to defection by manipulating the feedback on the number of defectors. In 5-person groups, participants played 16 consecutive trials of a linear public-good dilemma in which group members had to decide whether or not to contribute their endowments (10 per trial) to provide a public good. After every four trials, they received (bogus) feedback on investment decisions. They received feedback either that one of their fellow group members defected or that two members defected. Chen and Bachrach also manipulated whether the alleged defectors were always the same group members (the "fixed-pattern conditions") or whether defection was spread randomly among the group members. The results indicated not only that participants were less likely to contribute after learning that two other members defected than when learning that one member defected. The results also indicated that participants were especially likely to defect in the fixed-pattern conditions. It thus seems that people are less tolerant of free riding if it is the same free rider again and again. Chen and Bachrach explained this phenomenon by suggesting that the attribution for defection is likely to be different for people who free-ride all the time than for people who do not. In the former case, an internal attribution is likely to be made. A second, but related explanation is that in the case of a consistent free rider, people may feel that apparently they cannot influence this person. Thus, reactions to free riders may be related to feelings of self-efficacy and perceived criticality (cf. Chen et al., 1996; De Cremer & Van Dijk, 2002a; Kerr, 1989).

The presence of consistent free riders, or "bad apples" (Ouwerkerk et al., 2005), may be highly disturbing for the collective interests. As Stouten et al. (2007) showed, people especially seek (and ask for) explanations for the behavior of non-cooperative members. Moreover, Kurzban et al. (2001) argued that people may especially care about the least cooperative member of a group. In a public-good setting, they demonstrated that people tend to adjust their own contributions to those of the lowest contributor. These findings seem in agreement with Kerr's (1995) remarks, who noted that such turning to defection can be interpreted as a tailored response to observed inequity, aimed to restore equity.

Collective Failure Does Not Always Lead to Defection

As we already briefly noted, reactions to feedback may be partly affected by the attribution that people make for the failure. In agreement with this notion, Rutte et al. (1987) investigated whether people reacted differently to scarcity in a resource dilemma when it could be attributed to the other members in the group than when it could be attributed to the environment. They found that people did not react as negatively to scarcity if it was due to the environment. De Cremer and Van Dijk (2002b) showed that collective failure does not inevitably induce group members to respond with defection, even if it does not seem to be caused by environmental factors. Investigating responses to collective failure and success in a resource dilemma, they demonstrated that people who strongly identify with their group may even respond to collective failure with increased cooperation. The main reasoning was that for strong identifiers, collective-failure feedback may act as a signal that the group needs better coordination and performance. As a consequence, people who identify strongly with their group may decide to increase their contributions to the group. When people identify less strongly with their group, failure may lead to defection.

It thus seems that after failure feedback, individual differences in group identification strongly affect choice behavior and that high identification with the group may then result in highly cooperative behavior. Similar positive effects of failure feedback have recently been documented regarding another individual difference measure: social value orientations. Social value orientations are considered to be individual differences in how people evaluate outcomes for themselves and others in interdependent situations (Kuhlman & Marshello, 1975; Messick & McClintock, 1968). Most people can be classified as a prosocial, a competitor, or an individualist (Van Lange, 1999). Prosocials strive for maximizing joint outcomes and equality in outcomes (see also Eek & Gärling, this volume). Individualists want to maximize their own outcome, regardless of the other's outcome. Competitors aim to maximize the difference between outcomes for self and other. These latter two—individualists and competitors—are often taken together and defined as proselfs (Van Lange & Kuhlman, 1994), as they both assign more weight to their own outcomes than to the other's outcomes.

Van Dijk et al. (2005) presented participants a 4-person resource dilemma in which the group would obtain a bonus if they succeeded in restricting their harvests by not harvesting more than 220 chips from a collective resource of 400 chips. In addition, they assessed the group members' social value orientations. Participants first played a trial in which they did not receive feedback. The results showed that group members predominantly adhered to the equal division rule on the first trial. Moreover, social value orientations did not affect choice behavior. This finding is in agreement with the previous research showing a strong preference for the equal division rule in resource dilemmas (e.g., Allison & Messick, 1990). In order to investigate the effects of feedback, Van Dijk et al. (2005) then informed the participants either that the collective harvests were too high (i.e., collective-failure feedback) or that the group had succeeded in restricting their harvests (i.e., collective-success feedback). Subsequently, participants played a second trial. After having received success feedback, most participants did on the second trial what they had done on the first trial: They again adhered to the equal division rule. After feedback indicating collective failure, however, things were different. In that case, the harvests on trial 2 were moderated by social value orientations in the sense that proselfs increased their harvests whereas prosocials again restricted their harvests.

Although the finding that prosocials remained cooperative after collective failure can be seen as being in line with the observation that high identifiers behave cooperatively after collective failure, it should be noted that the interpretation that Van Dijk et al. (2005) offered was different from the reasoning provided by De Cremer and Van Dijk (2002b). Van Dijk et al. (2005) related their findings to the general notion that Snyder and Ickes (1985) put forward regarding the importance of individual differences. Snyder and Ickes (1985) reasoned that situations may differ with regard to the extent that they provide salient cues for behavior. In this respect, they distinguished between "strong" and "weak" situations and stated that (p. 904) "'strong' situations tend to be those that provide salient cues to guide behavior … 'weak' situations tend to be those that do not offer salient cues to guide behavior." Moreover, they then also reasoned that individual differences will play a more important role in weak situations than in strong situations. Based on this general insight, Van Dijk et al. (2005) reasoned that failure feedback may signal to group members that they are facing a weak situation, in which apparently the dilemma at hand does not provide salient cues for successful coordination.

It is tempting to also interpret the findings on the effects of individual differences in group identification on cooperation after failure feedback as indirect evidence for Snyder and Ickes' (1985) framework. Whether this is appropriate would be an interesting issue for future research. Nevertheless, regardless of the underlying psychological process, these findings on the effects of individual differences do show that collective failure (i.e., defection) does not inevitably breed defection.

Feedback, Ostracism, and Exit

In most dilemmas, group members are stuck with their fellow group members. They cannot leave their group, and they have no power to expel others from the group. In the absence of feedback, these additional features may not yield additional insights. But when it comes to how people deal with negative feedback (either collective failure or high variance), the issue becomes more prominent.

Preferences to exit after collective-failure feedback were recently studied by Van Vugt and Hart (2004). They investigated how people react to collective failure in a public-good dilemma by giving their participants a possibility to leave the group. Their findings revealed that exit reactions to collective failure were moderated by group identification. People who identified strongly with their group were more likely to be loyal and remain with their failing group than were group members who only showed weak identification with their group. We do not know of research on the relation between preferences to exit (or its counterpart, loyalty) and variance feedback. It may be reasoned, however, that in that case identification will play a moderating role, too.

Research on ostracism does not study whether people want to exit themselves, but whether people want to show others the exit. In a recently published overview, Ouwerkerk et al. (2005) report on some early findings of their research project on the relation between ostracism and cooperation in social dilemmas. In this context, they also investigated how people reacted to an uncooperative member (i.e., the "bad apple"). The findings not only revealed that the presence of a bad apple may increase defection but also indicated that when group members were given the opportunity to vote in order to ban one member from the group (and thus exclude this group member from future outcomes of the group), an overwhelming majority of their participants voted to exclude the bad apple. Moreover, referring to other studies with a similar paradigm, Ouwerkerk et al. (2005) noted that people experienced more pleasure when a bad apple was excluded from the group than when it happened to "a good guy."

Emotional Reactions to Feedback

Social dilemma research has primarily focused on behavior. As the preliminary findings on ostracism we discussed above show, reactions to feedback (e.g., failure feedback, variance) may not be limited to overt behavior, however. In particular, reactions may extend to emotions, which in turn may affect future behavior and decision making (see e.g., Lerner et al., 2004; Loewenstein & Lerner, 2002; Schroeder et al., 2003). In seems plausible that collective-failure feedback and feedback indicating high variance among the group members' decisions may evoke negative emotions. We only know of one previous study, however, that explicitly investigated this effect. Stouten et al. (2005) investigated how prosocials and proselfs reacted to variance feedback in a public-good dilemma. In this case, the variance was made very explicit in the sense that after making their decisions in a step-level, public-good dilemma, participants were informed that one of the group members had contributed considerably less than an equal share of the threshold. Thus, one member appeared to violate the equality rule. In terms of the bad apple research (Ouwerkerk et al., 2005), one could say that participants learned that there was one bad apple in their group. Note that if in a threshold dilemma one member contributed less than an equal share, this would normally imply that contributions had been made in vain and that the public good would not be provided. This would, of course, be disturbing to both proselfs and prosocials. In their study, however, Stouten et al. (2005) added a manipulation that allowed them to distinguish between reactions to collective failure and the feedback indicating the presence of a member violating the equality rule. After informing the participants that the total contribution fell below the threshold needed for provision because one member had violated the equality rule by contributing less than an equal share, participants were exposed to a manipulation of outcome feedback. Half of the participants learned that, even though the contributions fell short, the public good would be provided after all. Thus, for these participants what seemed like failure turned out to be a success after all. For the other half of the participants, the negative outcome was not altered.

Stouten et al. (2005) assessed positive emotions (e.g., happy, elated) as well as negative emotions (e.g., angry, disappointed). The findings indicated that the emotional reactions of proselfs to the feedback indicating the presence of a violator of the equality rule were less negative and more positive if they learned that the public good was provided after all than if they learned that the outcome remained unchanged. In contrast, prosocials were not affected by the manipulation of outcome feedback. Regardless of whether or not the public good was provided after all, they were angry and unhappy. Stouten et al. (2005) regarded these findings as indicative of their proposition that adherence to the equal division rule may be primarily instrumental for proselfs, whereas for prosocials adherence and violation of equal division are more regarded in moral terms (see also Van Lange, 1999). It is clear that more research on emotional reactions is needed, especially since it has been acknowledged that emotional reactions may be seen as instigators for behavioral reactions such as revenge, retaliation, and exclusion (cf. Darley & Pittman, 2003; Schroeder et al., 2003; Stouten et al., 2007).

Feedback and Structural Solutions

The research on the effects of feedback on choice behavior suggests that collective failure and high variance may induce people to defect. In part, this may be due to people's tendencies to reciprocate others' behavior and to focus on the least cooperative member. That feedback induces more than conformity is apparent from the research on emotional reactions. A similar conclusion can be reached on the basis of the research on preferences for structural solutions, that is, solutions that change the outcome structure of the dilemma. The study of Messick et al. (1983) that we cited earlier, for example, did not only assess how variance and collective feedback affect the individual's decision to cooperate or defect. They also addressed the participants' preference to change the structure by installing an autocratic leader who would decide for all group members what to do. Both high-variance and collective-failure feedback induced a stronger preference for such a leader (see also Samuelson et al., 1984; Samuelson & Messick, 1986).

It is interesting to see that social value orientations also play a moderating role in the case of preferences for structural solutions. In a resource dilemma setting, Samuelson (1993) manipulated collective-failure feedback by confronting participants with either moderate overuse or extreme overuse. They then assessed whether this had a different effect on the subsequent preferences of prosocials versus proselfs to opt for autocratic leadership. As it turned out, proselfs predominantly opposed the leadership solution, regardless of the extent of the overuse. Prosocials, however, were responsive to the feedback manipulation and were more in favor of installing a leader after extreme overuse (see also De Cremer, 2000).

Why would people object to installing an autocratic leader even after being confronted with collective failure? As Van Dijk et al. (2003) argued, an important reason may be that people view autocratic leadership as a threat to their individual freedom (cf. Brehm, 1966, 1972). It may be that especially proselfs respond to this possibility, which would indeed explain the low preference of proselfs for the leadership solution in the Samuelson (1993) study. As may be noted from our selective overview, most studies on preferences for leadership option have used the resource dilemma. Only a few studies (e.g., De Cremer, 2000; Van Vugt & De Cremer, 1999) investigated leadership in public-good settings. Van Dijk et al. (2003), however, compared preferences for the leadership solution in step-level, public-good dilemmas and resource dilemmas. Their study suggested that collective failure in a public-good dilemma may be conceived as more negative than collective failure in a resource dilemma. The basic argument was that collective failure in the public-good dilemma generally implies that people end up with lower outcomes than they started out with (i.e., when the public good is not provided, group members end up with the endowments they started with, minus the contributions they made in vain). In the resource dilemma, collective failure not necessarily implies that group members are eventually worse off compared to how they started. After all, the typical case in the resource dilemma is that people start out with nothing, apart from the collective resource, and end up with the endowments they harvested from the collective resource. This brighter perspective in the resource dilemma was mimicked in the preferences for the leadership solution. Especially in the public-good dilemma, collective-failure feedback evoked a preference for leadership. Apparently, the sense of personal loss in the public-good dilemma "helped" to overcome the reluctance to give up the decisional freedom.

Implicit Feedback

The Case of Sanctioning Systems

As our selective review on the effects of explicit feedback shows, especially high-variance feedback and collective-failure feedback have been found to lead to a preference for structural solutions such as the installment of leadership and sanctioning systems. The fact, however, that people may view such structural solutions as remedies for defection and inequality opens an interesting possibility that essentially reverses the causal chain. If people are confronted with the presence of structural solutions such as leadership and sanctioning systems, they may infer that these solutions are needed because apparently (some) people cannot be trusted to put the collective interests first. In a way, it resembles the connection between rain and an umbrella. If it rains when you want to go out, you may want to carry an umbrella. And if you see somebody carry an umbrella, you may infer that it probably rains. In a similar vein, the mere presence of a sanctioning system may induce a belief that the sanctioning system is there for a reason and that people would not cooperate if it were not for the sanctioning system. As a consequence, it may decrease people's belief that the others are *internally* motivated to cooperate.

The first evidence for this possibility was presented in Mulder et al. (2005), who showed that the mere presence of a sanctioning system made people more *pessimistic* about the chances to realize the collective goal in a subsequent social dilemma situation. In a subsequent study, Mulder et al. (2006) tested this possible negative effect of sanctioning systems on trust in greater detail by introducing the "removing the sanction" paradigm (RTS). In this paradigm, participants first experience a dilemma situation with a sanctioning system that is subsequently removed. Decisions that people make in this latter situation are then compared with the decisions people make who never experienced a sanctioning system (for more specific details, see Mulder et al., 2006). In all three experiments that we conducted using the RTS paradigm, trust in fellow group members was lower for participants who had previously experienced a sanctioning system than for those who had not. These findings suggest that the sanctioning system undermined trust in fellow group members. Additionally, in two of the three experiments, the initial level of trust (i.e., before introduction of the sanctioning system) was either measured or manipulated. These studies showed that when there was a high level of initial trust, the sanctioning system undermined trust and resulted in a low cooperation level (lower than the cooperation level of those who had not experienced a sanctioning system). Thus, experiencing a sanctioning system in one situation decreased cooperation in a subsequent situation.

The mere presence of a sanctioning system may also affect how people deal with feedback regarding group success or failure. As Mulder et al. (2005) showed, collective failure and success are attributed differently depending on whether the failure and success were obtained in the presence or absence of a sanctioning system. The presence of a sanctioning system appears to imply its own necessity when it comes down to the question of whether one needs the system to ensure collective success. When observing collective success in the presence of a sanctioning system, people may attribute the success to the sanctioning system, and thus support the sanctioning system. When observing collective failure in the presence of a sanctioning system, people may reason that there is definitely a great need for a sanctioning system (and maybe even that the sanctions should be increased).

The insights we developed above pertained to reactions to collective failure and success. A similar line of reasoning could be developed, however, for reactions to variance feedback. Thus, in the presence of a sanctioning system, feedback indicating low variance may be taken as evidence that apparently the sanctioning system is successful and may induce people to cooperate. Feedback indicating high variance may convince people of the necessity to have a sanctioning system to reduce variance. Another issue to acknowledge is that the reasoning need not be restricted to sanctioning systems. In principle, each structural solution could induce similar inferences. Earlier, we noted that collective failure and high variance may call for leadership. Therefore, it may also be expected that people may regard the presence of leadership as implicit feedback signaling that apparently things would go wrong in the absence of leadership.

Implicit Feedback: The Case of Emotions

We already discussed that feedback may elicit emotional reactions, which may consequently instigate positive or negative behavioral reactions in social dilemmas. In addition, emotions may also serve as feedback in themselves and thus classify as a form of implicit feedback. According to appraisal theory (Roseman, 1984; Scherer, 1988; Smith & Ellsworth, 1985), the experience of emotions is strongly dependent on the cognitive appraisals (judgments) of the social situation at hand (Ellsworth & Scherer, 2003). In more general terms, this literature draws attention to the strong connection between experienced emotions and the appraisals people make. Smith and Ellsworth (1985), for example, argued that the emotion of anger is accompanied by perceptions of certainty and control, whereas the emotion of fear is related to uncertainty and low perceptions of control. For social dilemma research, these insights are especially relevant because uncertainty is generally conceived as one of the main causes of defection (for an overview of the effects of uncertainty in social dilemmas, see, e.g., Van Dijk et al., 2004). Future research is urged to examine the role that appraisal processes play as an instance of implicit feedback in social dilemmas.

In this respect, it is also relevant to acknowledge that emotions exert influence not only at the intrapersonal level but also at the interpersonal level. First of all, emotions may evoke reciprocal emotions in others (e.g., people get angry if they are confronted with others who express anger; see Keltner & Haidt, 1999; Hatfield et al., 1994). In addition, the emotions others express may provide us with important information about their main motives and about how they evaluate their social situation (e.g., Barrett & Campos, 1987; Keltner & Gross, 1999). Put differently, the emotions of others may serve as a signal of implicit feedback in social interactions. The benefits of such an interpersonal approach have already been demonstrated in the context of negotiations (see, e.g., Van Kleef et al., 2004a, b). But it may also be highly relevant to social dilemma settings. Let us take the example of anger again. If people express anger toward their fellow group members, one might infer that the group has experienced collective failure and/or that the anger results from violation of a social standard or norm (e.g., the equal division rule). If so, this emotion-based inference might induce people to cooperate less or even leave the group (e.g., Wubben et al., 2005).

Taken together, from our review it becomes clear that emotions can also be looked upon as important feedback signals in social dilemmas (albeit at the implicit level). It is our belief that research examining emotions at both the intrapersonal and interpersonal levels is also needed to deepen our understanding of how people coordinate their decisions in social dilemmas and how these processes are related to what psychologists refer to as signals of feedback.

Conclusion

To understand how people make their decisions in social dilemma situations, we need to take into account how people deal with social information. Feedback plays an important role in the decision-making process. Previous research has traditionally concentrated on explicit feedback. In doing so, it has primarily focused on collective feedback (failure vs. success) and individual feedback (variance, the presence of free riders), and their effect on cooperation and preference for structural change. More recently, the scope of the research has expanded. Research has started to incorporate additional behavioral reactions such as social exclusion (in terms of banning people from the group), exit (leaving the group), and retribution and punishment. By also including emotional reactions in the analysis, research is bound to provide a more complete picture of the effects of feedback in social dilemmas. As our distinction between implicit and explicit feedback illustrates, the process underlying decision making in social dilemmas is complex, and even partly bidirectional. Conditions like collective failure and high variance may contribute to negative emotional reactions and induce people to opt for structural solutions like sanctioning systems and leadership. The process of sense-making and social inferences may in turn be considered as valuable feedback and, as such, as new input in the decision process.

References

Allison, S. T., Messick, D. M. (1990). Social decision heuristics in the use of shared resources. *Journal of Behavioral Decision Making*, *3*, 195–204.

Barrett, K. C., Campos, J. J. (1987). Perspective on emotional development II: A functionalist approach to emotions. In J. D. Osofsky (ed.), *Handbook of Infant Development* (2nd ed., pp. 555–578). New York: Wiley.

Brehm, J. W. (1966). *A Theory of Psychological Reactance.* New York: Academic Press.

Brehm, J. W. (1972). *Responses to Loss of Freedom: A Theory of Psychological Reactance.* Morristown, NY: General Learning Press.

Chen, X.-P., Au, W. T., Komorita, S. S. (1996). Sequential choice in a step-level public goods dilemma: The effects of criticality and uncertainty. *Organizational Behavior and Human Decision Processes, 65,* 37–47.

Chen, X.-P., Bachrach, D. G. (2003). Tolerance of free-riding: The effects of defection size, defection pattern, and social orientation in a repeated public goods dilemma. *Organizational Behavior and Human Decision Processes, 90,* 139–147.

Darley, J. M., Pittman, T. S. (2003). The psychology of compensatory and retributive justice. *Personality and Social Psychology Review, 7,* 324–336.

Dawes, R. M. (1980). Social dilemmas. *Annual Review of Psychology, 31,* 169–193.

De Cremer, D. (2000). Leadership in social dilemmas—not all prefer it: The moderating effect of social value orientation. *Group Dynamics: Theory, Research and Practice, 4,* 330–337.

De Cremer, D., Van Dijk, E. (2002a). Perceived criticality and contributions in public good dilemmas: A matter of feeling responsible to all? *Group Processes & Intergroup Relations, 5,* 319–332.

De Cremer, D., Van Dijk, E. (2002b). Reactions to group success and failure as a function of group identification: A test of the goal-transformation hypothesis in social dilemmas. *Journal of Experimental Social Psychology, 38,* 435–442.

Ellsworth, P. C., Scherer, K. R. (2003). Appraisal processes in emotion. In R. J. Davidson, K. R. Scherer & H. H. Goldsmith (eds.), *Handbook of Affective Sciences* (pp. 572–595). New York: Oxford University Press.

Fleishman, J. A. (1988). The effects of decision framing and others' behavior on cooperation in a social dilemma. *Journal of Conflict Resolution, 32,* 162–180.

Hatfield, E., Cacioppo, J. T., Rapson, R. L. (1994). *Emotional Contagion.* New York: Cambridge University Press.

Keltner, D., Gross, J. J. (1999). Functional accounts of emotions. *Cognition and Emotion, 13,* 467–480.

Keltner, D., Haidt, J. (1999). Social functions of emotions at four levels of analysis. *Cognition and Emotion, 13,* 505–521.

Kerr, N. L. (1983). Motivation losses in small groups: A social dilemma analysis. *Journal of Personality and Social Psychology, 45,* 819–828.

Kerr, N. L. (1989). Illusions of efficacy: The effects of group size on perceived efficacy in social dilemmas. *Journal of Experimental Social Psychology, 25,* 287–313.

Kerr, N. L. (1995). Norms in social dilemmas. In D. Schroeder (ed.), *Social Dilemmas: Social Psychological Perspectives* (pp. 31–47). New York: Pergamon Press.

Komorita, S. S., Parks, C. D. (1995). Interpersonal relations: Mixed-motive interaction. *Annual Review of Psychology, 46,* 183–207.

Kuhlman, D. M., Marshello, A. (1975). Individual differences in game motivation as moderators of preprogrammed strategic effects in prisoner's dilemma. *Journal of Personality and Social Psychology, 32,* 922–931.

Kurzban, R., McCabe, K., Smith, V. L., Wilson, B. J. (2001). Incremental commitment and reciprocity in a real-time public goods game. *Personality and Social Psychology Bulletin, 27,* 1162–1673.

Lerner, J. S., Small, D. A., Loewenstein, G. F. (2004). Heart strings and purse string: Carryover effects of emotions on economic decisions. *Psychological Science, 15,* 337–341.

Loewenstein, G. F., Lerner, J. S. (2002). The role of affect in decision making. In R. J. Davidson, K. R. Scherer & H. H. Goldsmith (eds.), *The Handbook of Affective Sciences* (pp. 619–642). Oxford: Oxford University Press.

Messick, D. M., Allison, S. T., Samuelson, C. D. (1988). Framing and communication effects on group members' responses to environmental and social uncertainty. In S. Maital (ed.), *Applied Behavioural Economics* (Vol. 2, pp. 677–700). Brighton, UK: Wheatsheaf.

Messick, D. M., Brewer, M. B. (1983). Solving social dilemmas: A review. In L. Wheeler & P. Shaver (eds.), *Review of Personality and Social Psychology* (Vol. 4, pp. 11–44). Beverly Hills, CA: Sage.

Messick, D. M., McClintock, C. G. (1968). Motivational basis of choice in experimental games. *Journal of Experimental Social Psychology, 4,* 1–25.

Messick, D. M., Wilke, H., Brewer, M. B., Kramer, R. M., Zemke, P. E., Lui, L. (1983). Individual adaptions and structural change as solutions to social dilemmas. *Journal of Personality and Social Psychology, 44,* 294–309.

Mulder, L. B., Van Dijk, E., De Cremer, D., Wilke, H. A. M. (2006). Undermining trust and cooperation: The paradox of sanctioning systems in social dilemmas. *Journal of Experimental Social Psychology, 42,* 147–162.

Mulder, L. B., Van Dijk, E., Wilke, H. A. M., De Cremer, D. (2005). The effect of feedback on support for a sanctioning system in a social dilemma: The difference between installing and maintaining the sanction. *Journal of Economic Psychology, 26,* 443–458.

Ouwerkerk, J. W., Kerr, N. L., Gallucci, M., Van Lange, P. A. M. (2005). Avoiding the social death penalty: Ostracism, and cooperation in social dilemmas. In K. D. Williams, J. P. Forgas & W. von Hippel (eds.), *The Social Outcast: Ostracism, Social Exclusion, Rejection, and Bullying.* (pp. 321–332). New York: Plenum Press.

Parks, C. D., Sanna, L. J., Berel, S. R. (2001). Actions of similar others as inducements to cooperate in social dilemmas. *Personality and Social Psychology Bulletin, 27,* 345–354.

Pillutla, M. M., Chen, X. P. (1996). Social norms and cooperation in social dilemmas: The effects of context and feedback. *Organizational Behavior and Human Decision Processes, 78,* 81–103.

Roseman, I. J. (1984). Cognitive determinants of emotions: A structural theory. In P. Shaver (ed.), *Review of Personality and Social Psychology* (Vol. 5, pp. 11–36). Beverly Hills, CA: Sage Publications.

Rutte, C. G., Wilke, H. A. M., Messick, D. M. (1987). Scarcity or abundance caused by people or the environment as determinants of behavior in the resource dilemma. *Journal of Experimental Social Psychology, 23,* 208–216.

Samuelson, C. D. (1993). A multiattribute evaluation approach to structural change in resource dilemmas. *Organizational Behavior and Human Decision Processes, 55,* 298–324.

Samuelson, C. D., Messick, D. M. (1986). Alternative structural solutions to resource dilemmas. *Organizational Behavior and Human Decision Processes, 37,* 139–155.

Samuelson, C. D., Messick, D. M., Rutte, C. R., Wilke, H. (1984). Individual and structural solutions to resource dilemmas in two cultures. *Journal of Personality and Social Psychology, 47,* 94–104.

Schroeder, D. A., Jensen, T. D., Reed, A. J., Sullivan, D. K., Schwab, M. (1983). The actions of others as determinants of behavior in social dilemmas. *Journal of Experimental Social Psychology, 19,* 522–539.

Schroeder, D. A., Steel, J. E., Woodell, A. J., Bembeneck, A. F. (2003). Justice within social dilemmas. *Personality and Social Psychology Review, 7,* 374–387.

Scherer, K. R. (1988). *Facets of Emotion: Recent Research.* Hillsdale, NJ: Erlbaum.

Smith, C. A., Ellsworth, P. C. (1985). Patterns of cognitive appraisal in emotion. *Journal of Personality and Social Psychology, 48,* 813–838.

Smith, J. M., Bell, P. A. (1994). Conformity as a determinant of behavior in a resource dilemma. *Journal of Social Psychology, 134,* 191–200.

Snyder, M., Ickes, W. (1985). Personality and social behavior. In G. Lindzey & E. Aronson (eds.), *Handbook of Social Psychology* (Vol. 2, pp. 883–947). New York: Lawrence Erlbaum.

Stouten, J., De Cremer, D., Van Dijk, E. (2007). Managing equality in social dilemmas: Emotional and retributive implications. *Social Justice Research, 20,* 53–67.

Stouten, J., De Cremer, D., Van Dijk, E. (2005). All is well that ends well, at least for proselfs: Emotional reactions to equality violation as a function of social value orientation. *European Journal and Social Psychology, 35,* 767–783.

Van Dijk, E., De Cremer, D., De Kwaadsteniet, E. W. (2005). Tacit coordination and social value orientations in resource dilemmas: When feedback gets in the way of coordination. Unpublished manuscript.

Van Dijk, E., Wilke, H., Wit, A. (2003). Preferences for leadership in social dilemmas: Public good dilemmas versus resource dilemmas. *Journal of Experimental Social Psychology, 39,* 170–176.

Van Dijk, E., Wit, A., Wilke, H., Budescu, D. V. (2004). What we know (and do not know) about the effects of uncertainty on behavior in social dilemmas. In R. Suleiman, D. V. Budescu, I. Fischer & D. M. Messick (eds.), *Contemporary Psychological Research on Social Dilemmas* (pp. 315–331). New York: Cambridge University Press.

Van Kleef, G. A., De Dreu, C. K. W., Manstead, A. S. R. (2004a). The interpersonal effects of anger and happiness in negotiations. *Journal of Personality and Social Psychology, 86,* 57–76.

Van Kleef, G. A., De Dreu, C. K. W., Manstead, A. S. R. (2004b). The interpersonal effects of emotions in negotiations: A motivated information processing approach. *Journal of Personality and Social Psychology, 87,* 510–528.

Van Lange, P. A. M. (1999). The pursuit of joint outcomes and equality in outcomes: An integrative model of social value orientations. *Journal of Personality and Social Psychology, 77,* 337–349.

Van Lange, P. A. M., Kuhlman, D. M. (1994). Social value orientations and impressions of partner's honesty and intelligence: A test of the morality effect. *Journal of Personality and Social Psychology, 67,* 126–141.

Van Vugt, M., De Cremer, D. (1999). Leadership in social dilemmas: The effects of group identification on collective actions to provide public goods. *Journal of Personality and Social Psychology, 76,* 587–599.

Van Vugt, M., Hart, C. M. (2004). Social identity as social glue: The origins of group loyalty. *Journal of Personality and Social Psychology, 86,* 585–598.

Weber, J. M., Kopelman, S., Messick, D. M. (2004). A conceptual review of decision making in social dilemmas: Applying a logic of appropriateness. *Personality and Social Psychology Review, 8,* 281–307.

Wubben, M., De Cremer, D., Van Dijk, E. (2005). The informative nature of emotions in social dilemmas. Unpublished manuscript.

Yamagishi, T. (1988). The provision of a sanctioning system in the United States and Japan. *Social Psychology Quarterly, 51,* 265–271.

Chapter 5
Group-Based Trust in Social Dilemmas

Margaret Foddy and Robyn Dawes

Introduction

In a world of strangers, whom should we trust? In the last two decades, there has been increased attention to trust between individuals, trust in organizations, and trust in groups (e.g. Cook, Hardin & Levi, 2005; Gambetta & Hamill, 2005; Kramer, 1999; Molm, 2006; Yamagishi & Yamagishi, 2004). In this chapter we address the question of trust that arises from shared membership in groups in settings which do not provide the opportunity for development of a personal history of obligation between two or more parties, nor information about the reputation of a particular person, nor an organization. Further, the situations we investigate do not involve "assurance", or encapsulated interest (Hardin, 2001; Yamagishi & Yamagishi, 1994). Rather, we examine those situations where individuals have little information about others, and no guarantees of favorable treatment. In these contexts, we argue that people employ a range of heuristics which are not necessarily less reliable than calculations based on strict individual self interest. We will refer to this as "social assurance", to distinguish it from institutional assurance and formal sanctions.

Why is social assurance important? Trust is essential to decisions people make to enter into exchange and other relationships with others (Foddy, Yamagishi & Platow 2006; Yamagishi & Kiyonari, 2000). In the modern world, it has become increasingly rare to know these others personally, or to have intact networks of obligation. Still, if people were to choose the option of trusting only those who could suffer sanctions for not being trustworthy, many forms of commerce and joint action would be impossible. It does not take a catalogue of instances to show that people "take chances" with strangers, and civil society relies on the fact that such trust is normally rewarded with behavior that takes into account the effects of the trusted person's behavior on the person who invested trust.

Trust is particularly important in situations described as "social dilemmas" (Dawes, 1980; Dawes & Messick, 2000; Foddy, Smithson, Schneider & Hogg, 1999; Kollock; 1998). Dilemmas are characterized by a reward structure that presents individuals with a choice between an alternative that may possibly lead to a good personal outcome, with the risk of a reduced joint outcome, and an alternative

A. Biel et al. (eds.), *New Issues and Paradigms in Research on Social Dilemmas.*
© Springer 2008

that puts the chooser at risk of exploitation, but produces a jointly optimal outcome, should all people decide to cooperate (Dawes, 1980; Komorita & Parks, 1996). The important feature of dilemmas is that if all people refuse to cooperate, they do worse, collectively, and individually, than if all had cooperated (Dawes, 1980; Kollock, 1998).

Key issues in the analysis of behavior in dilemmas are expectations about others' behavior, and the focal actor's orientation toward group and individual gain (Kramer & Goldman, 1995; Van Lange & Kuhlman, 1994). Taken from a strictly economic point of view, a person should "defect" in risky situations, to avoid exploitation, and also take the chance of gaining at the expense of others in the group. In a dilemma structure, trust in others should be low, because it is rational for all actors to defect, but in so doing, they undermine the collective good, and by definition, their own gain. The strict view of economically rational behavior seems to be waning, with economists building in social dimensions to their models (Camerer, 2003a, b; Cox, 2004). However, it still provides a useful baseline model against which to assess behavior in social dilemmas. Research shows that not every one chooses the self-interested option, and indeed, cooperation is often the modal choice (Caporael, Dawes, Orbell & Van de Kragt, 1989; Ostrom, 1998; Yamagishi, et al., 2005).

The question is, how to build a model of human decisions in dilemma settings that combines social and economic heuristics, and does not relegate social determinants of trust to the "irrational"? In this paper, we explore how shared group membership, a social psychological concept, may inform theories of choice in social dilemmas.

There are many variables that can influence social values and expectations of cooperation in social dilemmas. We will treat "trust" as relating to expectations, that is, an expectation of benevolent treatment from another, or at least, not harmful treatment (Dasgupta, 1988; Foddy, Yamagishi, & Platow, 2006). Yamagishi, et al. (2005) extend the definition of trust to "trustful behaviour", as acts by which an individual voluntarily exposes himself to greater positive and negative externalities produced by the actions of others. Thus, trusting behavior is a risky act that may produce more positive outcomes than failure to trust, but there is a co-existing chance that the outcomes will be negative (Kramer, 1999; Molm, 2006; Lawler, 2003).

The important contribution of this chapter is to show that abstract group membership may modify expectations of benevolent treatment from others, and that this sets in train expectations for reciprocity, trust, and altruism (Cox, 2004). For this, we draw on the theory of social identity (Brown, 2000; Tajfel & Turner, 1986; Turner & Reynolds, 2001), and a theory of generalized exchange, proposed by Yamagishi and others (Buchan, Croson & Dawes, 2002; Yamagishi & Kiyonari, 2001).

Social identity theory claims that when individuals identify with a particular group, they do so in part to maximize self esteem, through positive evaluations of the group, and self as part of that group (Brown, 2000). Brewer (2000) found that individuals rated positive traits such as "trustworthy" and "cooperative" as significantly more common in their own group than in other groups, and suggested that ingroup favouritism and cooperation arise in part from positive self-identification a group. Turner and Reynolds (2000) and Hogg and Abrams (1990; Abrams & Hogg, 2001) argue that a process of "depersonalization" occurs when a person identifies with a group, making self and other members of the group "interchangeable". In this sense, cooperation with others in the group benefits self at the same time it benefits the group, and theoretically, should induce higher level of trust in positively valued others, who will be expected to value one's interests, just as self values theirs.

Alternatively, it has been suggested that a group heuristic, incorporating an expectation of generalized reciprocity from ingroup members, produces both trust and cooperation among people with common group membership, but not necessarily a history of interaction. When people find themselves in an interdependent relationship with a fellow group member, the exchange "heuristic" is activated, resulting in an expectation that others in their group will treat them well. Yamagishi and Kiyonai (2000) reported that simple identification with a group was not necessary or sufficient to produce ingroup favouritism; they argued, rather, that cooperation grew out of an expectation of generalized reciprocity, which was accompanied by positive affect towards the group, but that the expectations were the most important causal factor. Their evidence included studies showing that when generalized trust was blocked, no ingroup favoritism was shown. Placed in the context of Dawes' key paper on social dilemmas (1980), it seems that trust and a desire for the collective good may both be necessary for cooperation (see also Foddy & Veronese, 1996).

Previous Research on Group-Based Trust

Whatever the mechanism for group-based trust, and there may be more than one working conjointly, there is surprisingly little research which explores the conditions under which group-based trust in strangers may occur. Recent studies have shown the importance of category membership to trust in strangers (Foddy, et al., 2006; Yuki & Brewer, 2005). These authors have asserted that it is often necessary to invest trust in others about whom we have little information and no assurance mechanisms in place (Cook, et al., 2005). As in the "minimal group" situation (Tajfel, Billig, Bundy & Flament, 1971), there are few cues on which to base impressions of others, and the important decision: "Shall I trust person x?" There are several varieties of "groups" that may evoke group-based trust: face to face groups, with a long or short history; organizations of individuals who are interdependent and pursuing a common goal; minimal groups, in which people do not interact directly, and the basis of group formation is arbitrary and often trivial (Tajfel, et al, 1971); and categorical groups of strangers who share one or more similarity but do not usually know many members of the category (such as fans of sports teams, members of the same university, citizens of a country). This chapter is concerned with the last meaning of "group", and the way in which mutual group membership can provide an initial basis for trust in an interdependent setting.

A brief summary is provided here of studies showing a strong tendency to trust others who are from the same group or category as the focal person. This first body of studies did not, however, involve a social dilemma, but rather, tested the limits of group-based trust in a context in which the focal person was entirely dependent on another for rewards. The rest of the chapter describes a study which expands the study of group based trust to reciprocal relationships in a trust dilemma (Berg et al. 1995).

Unilateral Trust in an Ingroup Member

The allocator studies

A simple paradigm was used for a series of studies of whether people would place trust in another person, who had complete control over the allocation of an endowment (Foddy et al., 2006). In these studies, the recipient had simply to choose between the share of the endowment already allocated by someone from an "ingroup", or an "outgroup" allocator, who had dictatorial rights to keep all the endowment ($20), or give some to the recipient.

The main finding of these studies was that participants strongly preferred the allocation of an ingroup member. The specific nature of the social category used to operationalise shared group membership made little difference to the preference for an ingroup allocator. A range of ingroups and outgroups were used across studies: university or college attended; faculty of enrolment; major at university; all of these produced similar effects. Given a choice of an allocation from an ingroup or an outgroup stranger, people preferred the allocation of a fellow group member. This held true even when the ingroup was fellow economics students, a group for whom the stereotype includes strong individual self interest. While levels of trust and expectations of fair treatment were high for the ingroup, they were also relatively high for all groups. These results suggest that people have a learned and generalized belief that strangers will be trustworthy, and that ingroup strangers may be trusted the most.

This ingroup preference was *not* evident if information was provided that the allocator did not know the group membership of the recipient. In other words, mutual knowledge of shared group membership was important (Foddy, et al., 2006). We hypothesized that recipients' trust of ingroup members arises from taking the perspective of the allocator, who, like any other group member, feels obliged to treat fellow group members well. This obligation cannot arise without mutual knowledge: the allocator cannot be expected to act benignly if the identity of the recipient is not known, and the recipient has no reason to trust someone on the basis of group membership, unless she knows the allocator recognizes the common link. Trust may be facilitated by a positive stereotype of the ingroup, but requires mutual identification of common group membership.

A further study using the allocator paradigm introduced real allocators who divided their endowment between self, and a recipient who was from the same, or a different group (Hoffarth & Foddy, 2006). Allocators knew that they would play the roles of both allocators and recipient, but with different partners, who varied in group membership (same or different from the participant). This study showed that group-based trust is well founded: allocators gave away just under half of their endowments. In this case, the effects of mutual group membership were weaker than in the allocators choice studies described above. However, it was clear that people did expect, and received a considerable share of funds from someone who was under no obligation to give anything.

Limits on the allocator choice studies

The allocator paradigm is useful to study *relative* trust in ingroup members, compared with others from an outgroup. However, recipients have no choice to leave the situation; they are forced to express a preference between one allocator or another. Such a preference might be weak, but still lead a majority of people to choose an ingroup allocator. Indeed, while the proportion of people choosing an ingroup allocator was generally high (around 70–85%), participants' expectations of the amounts of money the allocators would share were significantly, but not greatly, different.

Follow up studies were conducted using the allocator choice paradigm, but included a third choice, to opt for a sure thing, rather than have to choose one of two allocators. For psychology students, less than a third (28%) preferred the sure thing option; among those rejecting the sure thing option, many more recipients chose the ingroup (other Psychology students), compared to the outgroup (Economics students), allocator—56% and 16% respectively of the total sample of 50 students. These experiments indicated that many participants regarded having to choose between two allocators as a risky option. While they could gain more by opting for the choice of allocators than choosing the sure thing, their fate would be in the hands of an unknown stranger, and they might get nothing. Choice of the sure thing was not associated with low group identification Results from similar allocators studies offering a sure thing (Hoffarth & Foddy, 2006) have shown that between 25% and 50% of recipients in this paradigm prefer the sure thing. In a sense, choosing the sure thing is equivalent to choosing not to play at all (van Lange & Visser, 1999), and such a choice may indicate lower baseline levels of trust in both ingroup and outgroup strangers than is indicated when a person has to place trust in one person or the other.

Trust when the Situation is Interdependent

The allocator studies produced important evidence for shared group membership as a basis for relative trust. However, the substantial proportion of people opting for a sure thing makes us cautious about whether group-based trust will operate in settings of mutual dependence, rather than the unilateral setting used in the allocator paradigm.

The Prisoner's Dilemma has been the source of many insights into the factors which determine cooperation in dilemmas. In particular, expectations of cooperation from another has been shown to be an important factor for one's own willingness to cooperate (Caporael et al., 1989); Komorita & Parks, 1996; Rapoport, 1966), although this has not usually been referred to as "trust". However, as many authors have pointed out, trust and cooperation are confounded in the simultaneous Prisoner's Dilemma (Ostrom, 1998 Yamagishi, 2002). A player who chooses to cooperate in a PD may expect (trust) the other to do the same, or may be expressing a preference to cooperate. Yamagishi and Kiyonari (2000) showed that cooperation was higher for dyads composed of members of the same (minimal) group, but again, it is not possible to separate cooperation motivated by ingroup liking, and cooperation based on a stronger expectation of higher cooperation from an ingroup member.

To study group-based trust in an interdependent setting, we adapted the "trust game" (Berg et al., 1995), which has been used extensively to separate an initial act of entrustment, and the subsequent trustworthiness, or lack thereof, shown in an interdependent interaction (Camerer, 2003b; Wilson & Eckel, 2006). This is a simple sequential game in which the experimenter provides an endowment to Player A, who decides how much, if any, of the endowment to give to, or invest in, Player B. Whatever is sent by Player A (the sender) is then tripled in value by the experimenter, and Player B (the receiver)[1], decides how much, if anything, to send back to the sender, A. Player B is entirely free to keep all of the funds, and indeed, will maximize his or her gains by so doing. Player A's decision to send any funds is a risky, *trusting* act; the receiver's decision to return any is interpreted as an act demonstrating trustworthiness, and cooperation. The total return to the group, that is sender plus receiver outcomes, is higher if the sender decides to trust, than if she decides to keep the endowment. However, since the funds returned by the receiver to the sender do not increase in value, there is no change to the possible *joint gain* to the group, whether the receiver chooses to cooperate or not. Research has shown that people do in fact trust strangers in this game, with senders parting with substantial parts of their endowment, and receivers return the trust at high levels (Ostrom, 1998 Camerer, 2003a, b). The appeal of the Trust Game is that it separates, to some extent, trust and cooperation, through the roles of sender and receiver, and the rules of the game. The rules define the game as one in which entrustment can produce more group gain than staying with a sure thing. The roles are important, because the sender has to entrust money to make any further transaction, and any further gain, possible. The sender takes all the risk by entrusting funds. She may also be signaling a willingness to cooperate, or at least, to share profits, but since this is a one-shot, anonymous game, there is no future for the particular dyad. The receiver has no risks to face; she may decide to take all of the profit, or share some. Again, this dyad has no immediate future, and so "cooperation" is not really required. Thus, the separation of the roles makes the Trust Game particularly useful for an examination of the effects of shared group membership. A person may feel safer in trusting a fellow

---

[1] Researchers using the Trust Game often refer to Person A as the "trustor", and Person B as the "trustee". For clarity in describing the experiment, we adopt the terms "sender" and "recipient".

group member, and a receiver may prefer to reciprocate such trust with a higher return. Since the structure of the game is identical for both ingroup and outgroup dyads, any differences in their behavior must be due to group factors. The studies reported in this chapter do not allow a detailed analysis of particular reasons for reciprocation by the receiver; the aim is to establish whether mutual group membership affects entrustment, reciprocation, or both.

Some researchers have used the Trust Game to vary characteristics of the players (e.g. gender, Croson & Buchan, 1999), and also cues to the identity of the partner (e.g. attractiveness, Wilson & Eckel, 2006) that might affect expectations about trustworthiness. In the study reported below, we provided information to participants about a fairly trivial category membership (faculty of enrolment), that was shared, or not shared, by the two participants. The research question was: does shared group membership activate a group heuristic such that senders are more willing to entrust their endowment to an ingroup member, and will receivers be more willing to reciprocate that trust, if it occurs, by returning higher amounts to the sender?

Overview of the Design

Participants in the study were volunteers from first year classes in the Faculty of Arts and Social Sciences (Arts) and Faculty of Science/Engineering (Science) at a Canadian University. For most first year students, faculty of enrolment is not a highly salient identity category, but on the basis of arguments made earlier, shared category membership should activate both positive evaluations of fellow group members, and an anticipation of better treatment of ingroup members. Participants were 51 students from Arts and 33 from Science, who were randomly assigned to the role of sender or receiver, in either an ingroup (Arts-Arts, 16 pairs, Science-Science, 7 pairs) or an outgroup (Arts sender-Science receiver, 11 pairs), or (Science sender, Arts receiver, 8 pairs). In all, 84 students participated in the study (33 males; 51 females). No gender differences were found on any of the relevant dependent variables. For purposes of this paper, dyads were collapsed into "same/ingroup", or "different/outgroup", because Faculty of enrolment was not of theoretical interest, and there were no differences on the relevant dependent variables resulting from the Faculty designation of the individuals. The design was thus a 2 × 2 factorial: type of dyad (ingroup - both sender and receiver from same Faculty, or outgroup - sender and receiver from different Faculties), and role (sender or receiver). The first factor was a between groups variable; although sender and receiver were separate individuals, we treated their data as correlated, and therefore dealt with role as a repeated measures factor.

Procedure

When participants arrived for the study, they were seated at a desk where there were signs that identified their Faculty of enrolment, and the role to which they had been assigned (sender or receiver). To prime group identity, we asked students what faculty they were from, made a point of telling them which faculty the student they were paired with was from, and then asked them to complete a 15-item group identification questionnaire (Foddy & Hogg, 1999), with items varied to be relevant to their particular faculty (e.g., "I feel similar to other Arts students", or "I feel similar to other Science students"). Items were rated on a 9-point scale. This also gave a measure of degree of identification with their faculty.

To preserve anonymity, participants did not see one another at any time during the study. In cases where more than one dyad was being tested, Senders were seated in one room and Receivers in another, and instructed not to speak to one another. The only information they had about the person they were paired with was that person's Faculty of enrolment. There was no deception involved.

Participants were then given a one-page sheet of written instructions (specific to sender or receiver) as well as a flow chart of the decision-making task. Senders were told that they were being given a "cheque" for $5 and that they had to decide whether or not they would like to send a portion of their $5, or even all of it, to the receiver. The instructions made it clear that any portion of the money they decided to send would be tripled in value by the experimenter when it was sent to the receiver; examples of this tripling were provided. They were informed that the receiver also had been given a $5 "cheque", which the receiver could keep; both endowments were good for exchange for dollars.

Both players were told that once receivers had received the (tripled) funds from the sender, they had the option of sending a portion of the money back or keeping all of it; examples of this were also provided. All participants were told that the complete exchange would take place once only, that is, from sender, to receiver, and back to sender. Finally, senders were told that if they decided not to send any money to the receiver, they could keep the initial $5 that they had been given, and the session was over. In such a case, both the sender and receiver would leave with their initial endowments of $5 in cash.

The first "move" was made by the senders, who wrote a cheque for the amount of their endowment they wished to send; they then answered questions about what the receiver would get from the amount sent, and what they estimated the receiver would return. The receivers also completed a questionnaire which asked what they anticipated the sender would send, and comprehension questions about what such an amount would provide to the receiver, and leave the sender. Once the sender's (tripled) amount was delivered, receivers wrote a cheque for the amount they wished to return, and completed a questionnaire which asked for the reasons for their choices; they also rated the fairness of the sender's choice of amount to send. Both participants were given a six-item trust questionnaire (Yamagishi & Yamagishi, 1994) while the experimenter prepared the payoff to each person. Participants were debriefed separately, paid the money that resulted from the exchange, and dismissed separately.

As in previous studies using the Berg et al. trust game, we interpreted the choice of the sender to give part or all of his endowment to the receiver, as trusting behaviour, or "entrustment". The person undertook a risky behavior, presumably expecting to get back a share of funds sent; senders' expectations about returns were assessed by questions. If the receiver did return funds to the sender, this was interpreted as demonstrating trustworthy behaviour in response to entrustment; we also refer to this as making a cooperative choice, because it increases the benefits of the sender, at a cost to the receiver, who could have returned nothing at all. Because the game was not repeated, and players were anonymous, there are no negative consequences possible to the receiver who defects.

Results

The unique feature of our adaptation of the Trust Game is the introduction of shared or unshared category membership. The key questions are addressed by comparison of senders and receivers in the conditions of shared category membership with participants in the mixed dyads, those where group membership was not shared:

1. Are ingroup senders more likely to send all or part of their funds to ingroup receivers?
2. Do ingroup senders expect higher return from ingroup receivers?
3. Do ingroup receivers return a higher amount to ingroup senders?
4. Does reciprocation of the senders' trust occur at a higher level for ingroup dyads?
5. Do higher levels of entrustment of funds by the senders produce higher benefits to the sender, regardless of group identity of the receiver?
6. Is joint gain higher in groups where there is shared group identity?

Only 2 senders, both in outgroup dyads, chose not to send any part of their endowments. Five receivers failed to return any funds, all in outgroup (mixed faculty) dyads. Amounts sent and returned were continuous; this was not a send nothing-send all version of the Trust Game. It is nevertheless noteworthy that very few senders chose the sure thing option.

The effect of dyad type on amount sent: Entrustment

Of their $5 endowment, senders from ingroup dyads (sender and receiver from same faculty), sent higher amounts than did senders in mixed dyads, M_{same} = 3.43 (sd =1.13) and $M_{different}$ = 2.71 (sd = 1.50) respectively, but these means did not differ significantly from one another, $F(1, 41) = 3.17$, $p = .082$.

Senders' expectations of return

The sender's expected return from the receivers was converted to an index of "expected benefit", which was expressed as the difference score (amount expected back - amount sent). The means for this index did not differ as a function of dyad similarity (Means 1.22 and 1.21, for same and mixed dyads, respectively).

Effect of dyad type on amount returned by receiver

Receivers' expectations of the amount of money they would be sent did not differ significantly (M = 3.98 for ingroup receivers; M = 3.47 for mixed dyads, sd's 2.9 and 1.6 respectively). The expectations of receivers suggested that they anticipated the senders would place a reasonably high level of trust in the receiver, well above the "rational" expectation of zero, and more than half of the senders' endowments. The amounts sent were below the amounts expected, as noted above. Examination of the receivers' ratings of the fairness of the amounts sent showed no difference for ingroup vs. outgroup dyads; this result is not surprising, given that amounts sent did not differ by dyad type. The amount of money available to the receiver to divide between herself and the sender was the receiver's initial endowment of $5, plus the tripled amount of money sent by the sender. The mean proportion of available funds returned to the senders for the ingroup (same faculty) receivers was M = .38 (sd .11), and M = .25 for mixed dyads (sd .18). Five receivers, all in outgroup dyads, returned nothing.

Because the amounts sent to the receiver varied widely, so did the funds available to return. For clarity, we calculated an index of "benefit to the sender", (mean amount returned - mean amount sent), which controls for the variation, and indicates how much better off the sender was after obtaining the amount allotted to them by the receiver; it is possible for this index to be negative, if the receiver returned less than the amount the sender had entrusted. The benefit to the sender was significantly greater for the ingroup dyads, M = $2.66, (sd 1.81), vs. M = $0.84, (sd 2.69) for outgroup dyads, F (1, 41) = 6.82, p = .013.

Do higher levels of entrustment produce higher levels of return?

Although the initial levels of entrustment were not significantly higher for ingroup senders compared with outgroup senders, they were higher. We investigated whether initial amount sent to the receiver was correlated with benefit to the sender, and found a significant correlation (r = .355, p = .021). Comparing ingroup and outgroup dyads, the correlation was high and significant for ingroup dyads (r = .731, p < .001), and for outgroup dyads, there was no significant relationship between amount sent, and the benefit to the sender (r = .005, p =.98). This difference can be seen more clearly in Figure 5.1, where we first divided the entire sample into "high entrusters", those above the median of $3.00, and "low entrusters", those equal to or below the median amount sent by senders. A 2 × 2 ANOVA (dyad type by entrustment), showed that higher entrustment led to higher benefits to senders, but only for those in the ingroup dyads. There was a significant effect for dyad

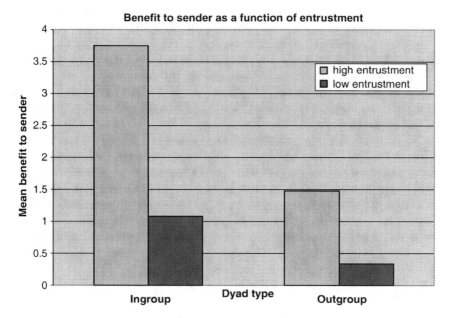

Figure 5.1 Benefit to sender as a function of entrustment

similarity, F (1, 41) = 7.76, p = .008, and a significant interaction of dyad similarity with level of entrustment, F (1, 41) = 4.83, p = .034). The benefits of placing high trust in a receiver from one's own group were high, but even low entrusters in the ingroup condition did better than those in the outgroup, mixed dyad condition, where a high initial entrustment produced less benefit. The relationship between entrustment and reciprocation did not seem to depend on expected amounts from the sender, and did not depend on level of ingroup identification, or general trust levels.

Joint gain to dyads

The receiver in the Trust Game is in an advantaged position, and the results of final outcomes to sender and receiver reflect this difference. A repeated measures ANOVA (with dyad type as a between groups factor, and "role" of sender/receiver), revealed a significant main effect for role, F (1, 40) = 14.145, p < .01. Receivers did better than senders, with net gain (endowment plus amount taken from the tripled amount sent by the sender) higher for receivers than senders (Means 9.37, sd 2.9, versus 6.84, sd 2.4) respectively. However, the difference between sender and receiver was lower for ingroup dyads (significant interaction of role and dyad similarity). Because the Trust Game has a maximum joint gain of $20, it is of interest to compare the joint gain to the dyads in the two dyad types. An ANOVA of the total to the dyad, which is simply a function of net gain to senders and receivers, showed no significant difference due to dyad type, F (1,40) = 3.17, p = .082. While being in an ingroup dyad reduced the gap between sender and receiver outcomes, it did not make the ingroup dyads significantly more successful. Both dyad types did well, with total amounts to the dyad of $16.89 for ingroup dyads, and $15.42 for outgroup dyads. Contrasted with the non-cooperative joint gain of $10, it is clear that participants realized the advantages of the exchange relationship. In the Trust Game, it is equally efficient from a dyad point of view for the receiver to keep all of the tripled funds from the sender, and maximally efficient for the sender to entrust all $5 in the receiver.

Overall, the results from the Trust Game were consistent with those from the Allocator Choice studies. Shared group membership produces a weak tendency to trust others from the same group, and "primes the pump" or reciprocity, in that fellow group members in the role of recipient and allocators, were more inclined to return a profit to the senders in response to their entrustment. Again, the differences were not large between ingroup and outgroup dyads, and trust without assurance was cautious, but high enough to allow participants to risk some of their funds.

Discussion

Interdependence creates opportunities for gain, but it also creates risks of loss, uncertainty, and the desire to reduce uncertainty. Social dilemmas are a special and ubiquitous form of interdependence, because actors are tempted, and know their partners are tempted, to impose costs on others in order to improve their own gain. This realization is the beginning for both trust and distrust (Kramer, 1999). At the initiation of a relationship with a stranger, there is often a scarcity of information that could reduce or increase the risk of a negative outcome. We have suggested one factor, shared group membership, that may increase expectations of benevolent treatment, and our results are consistent with the claim that this shared membership activates a heuristic, or short-cut, that may draw on past experiences of successful transactions with group members. However, this trust occurs without negotiation (Molm, 2006; Molm, Takahashi, & Peterson, 2000), and is not surrounded by institutional guarantees and sanctions. It is in this sense that socially based trust is "irrational", it is not assurance (Yamagishi & Yamagishi, 1994). It may nevertheless be as reliable as institutional trust and sanctions. Our studies show that group-based trust is easily evoked; it might just as easily be destroyed if a group member does not act in a group favoring manner. The resilience of trust is an important topic for future research, but the ease of activation of "fast trust" in group members suggests it will not be easily destroyed as a heuristic. There are many other cues or signs of trustworthiness of others that do not required shared group identity (Gambetta & Hamill, 2005; Wilson & Eckel, 2006).

With the recognition of the social assurance of group membership, people are also likely to be aware of its fragility (Kramer, 1999). We agree with Cook, Hardin & Levi (2005) that trust should be seen as a relational concept, and that it occurs when one party to a relationship believes that the other person has an incentive to take the interests of the first party into account. The main point of difference in our account is the nature of those perceived incentives. Further, we agree with Hardin et al. that when wide-scale cooperation is needed, trust may not be an adequate mechanism to ensure successful transactions. Indeed, trust may not be necessary when other mechanisms are in place: reputational systems, laws of contract, surveillance systems, and so on. Still, processes at the micro level provide a foundation for people to recognize the benefits of trust, and the circumstances under which it may need to be transformed into assurance.

The studies reported in this paper open up a range of research questions at the micro level. These include the conditions under which defecting ingroup members may be ejected or excluded from a group, or from group benefits (Williams, Forgas & von Hippel, 2005). A further important direction is to make links with the literature on negotiated, compared with reciprocal and generalized exchange (Molm, 2006; Lawler, 2003). Group-based trust should also be studied in repeated interaction, where the history of exchanges in particular relationships may have different effects for ingroup and outgroup members.

References

Abrams, D. & Hogg, M. (1990). *Social identity theory: Constructive and critical advances.* London: Harvester Wheatsheaf.

Berg, J., Dickhaut, J., & McCabe, K. (1995). Trust, reciprocity, and social history. *Games and Economic Behavior, 10,* 122–142.

Brann P., & Foddy, M. (1987). Trust and the consumption of a deteriorating common resource. *Journal of Conflict Resolution, 31,* 615–630.

Brewer, M. B. (2000). Social identity theory and change in intergroup relations. In D. Capozza & R. Brown (Eds.), *Social identity processes* (pp. 117–131). London: Sage Publications.

Brown, R. (2000). Social identity theory: Past achievements, current problems and future challenges. *European Journal of Social Psychology, 30,* 745–778.

Buchan, N. R., Croson, R. T. A. & Dawes, R. M. (2002). Swift neighbors and persistent strangers: A cross-cultural investigation of trust and reciprocation in social exchange. *American Journal of Sociology, 108,* 168–206.

Camerer, C.F. (1997). Progress in behavioral game theory. *Journal of Economic Perspectives, 11,* 167–188.

Camerer, C.F. (2003a). Behavioral game theory: Experiments in strategic interaction. In: C. F. Camerer & E. Fehr (Eds.), *Roundtable series in behavioral economics* (pp. 121–135). New York, Sage & Princeton University Press.

Camerer, C.F. (2003b). Behavioural game theory: Plausible formal models that predict accurately. *Behavioral and Brain Sciences, 26,* 157–158.

Caporael, L., Dawes, R.M., Orbell, J.M. & van de Kragt, A. (1989). Selfishness examined: Cooperation in the absence of egoistic incentives. *Behavioral and Brain Science, 12,* 227–248.

Cook, K.S., Hardin, R. & Levi, M. (2005). *Cooperation without trust?* New York: Russell Sage Foundation.

Cook, K. S., Yamagishi, T., Cheshire, C., Cooper, R., Matsuda, M., & Mashima, R. (2005). Trust building via risk taking: A cross-societal experiment. *Social Psychology Quarterly, 68,* 121–142.

Cox, C.C. (2003). How to identify trust and reciprocity. *Games and Economic Behavior, 46*, 260–281.

Croson, R. & Buchan, N. (1999). Gender and culture: International experimental evidence from Trust Games. *American Economic Review, 89*, 386–91.

Dasgupta, P. S. (1988). Trust as commodity. In D. Gambetta (Ed.), *Trust: Making and breaking cooperative relations* (pp. 49–72). New York: Basil Blackwell.

Dawes, R.M. 1980. Social dilemmas. *Annual Review of Psychology, 31*, 161–93.

Dawes, R.M. & Messick, D.M. (2000). Social dilemmas. In: *International Journal of Psychology: Special Issue on Diplomacy and Psychology, 35*, 111–116.

Eckel, C.C, & Wilson, R.K. (2004). Is trust a risky decision? *Journal of Economic Behavior & Organization, 55*, 447–56.

Foddy, M., & Hogg, M. (1999). Impact of leaders on resource consumption in social dilemmas: The intergroup context. In M. Foddy, M. Smithson, S. Schneider, & M. Hogg (Eds.), *Resolving social dilemmas: Dynamic, structural, and intergroup aspects* (pp. 309–330). Philadelphia, PA: Psychology Press.

Foddy, M., Smithson, M., Schneider, S. & Hogg, M. (Eds.). (1999). *Resolvings social dilemmas: Dynamic, structural, and intergroup aspects*. Philadelphia, PA: Psychology Press.

Foddy, M., Yamagishi, T., & Platow, M. (2006). *Stereotypes and Expectations in group-based trust*. Unpublished manuscript.

Foddy, M., & Veronese, D. (1996). Does knowing the jointly rational solution make you want to pursue it? Motivational orientation, information, and behavior in two social dilemmas. In W.B.G. Liebrand and D.M. Messick (Eds.), *Frontiers in social dilemma research* (pp. 135–155). Berlin: Springer-Verlag.

Gambetta, D. & Hamill, H. (2005). *Streetwise*. New York: Russell Sage Foundation.

Hardin, R. (1991). Trusting persons, trusting institutions. In: R.J. Zeckhauser, *The Strategy of choice*, pp. 185–209. Cambridge, Mass: MIJ Press.

Haslam, S. A. (2000). *Psychology in organizations: The social identity approach*. London: Sage Publications.

Hoffarth, M. & Foddy, M. (2006). *Do economists trust economists?* Unpublished manuscript.

Hogg, M. A., & Abrams, D. (1988). *Social identifications: A social psychology of intergroup relations and group processes*. London: Routledge.

Hogg, M.A., & Mullin, B.A., (1999). Joining groups to reduce uncertainty: Subjective uncertainty reduction and group identification. In D. Abrams, D. & M. A. Hogg (Eds.), *Social identity and social cognition* (pp. 249–279). Oxford: Blackwell.

Kollock, P. (1997). Transforming social dilemmas: Group identity and cooperation. In: P. Danielson (Ed.), *Modeling rational and moral agents* (pp. 186–210). Oxford: Oxford University Press.

Kollock, P. 1998. Social dilemmas: The anatomoy of coopration. *Annual Review of Sociology, 24*, 183–214.

Komorita, S.S., & Parks, C.D. (1996). S*ocial dilemmas*. Boulder, CO: Westview Press.

Kramer, R. M. (1999). Trust and distrust in organizations. *Annual Review of Psychology, 50*, 569–98.

Kramer, R. M., & Tyler, T. R. (Eds.). (1996). *Trust in organisations: Frontiers of theory and research*. Thousand Oaks, CA: Sage.

Kramer, R., & Brewer, M. (1984). Effects of group identity on resource use in a simulated commons dilemma. *Journal of Personality and Social Psychology, 46*, 1044–1057.

Kramer, R. & Goldman, L. (1995). Helping the group or helping yourself? Social motives and group identification in resource dilemmas. In D.S. Schroeder (Ed.), *Social dilemmas: Perspectives on individuals and groups* (pp. 49–67). Westport, CT: Praeger.

Kramer, R., & Wei, J. (1999). Social uncertainty and the problem of trust in social groups: The social self in doubt. In T. Tyler, R. Kramer, & O. John (Eds.), *The psychology of the social self* (pp.145–167). Mahwah, NJ: Lawrence Erlbaum Associates.

Lawler, E. (2003). Interaction, emotion, and collective identities. In: P.J. Burke, T.J. Owens, R. Serpe & P.A. Thoits (Eds.), *Advances in identity theory and research*. pp 231–247. New York: Kluwer Academic/Plenum.

Mansbridge, J. (1995). Rational Choice Gains by Losing. *Political Psychology, 16* (1), 137–155.

Messick, D.M. (1999). Alternative logics for decision making in social settings. *Journal of Economic Behavior and Organization, 39,* 11–28.

Molm, L. (2006). The social exchange framework. In P.J. Burke (Ed.), *Contemporary social psychological theories* (pp. 24–45). Stanford, CA: Stanford University Press.

Molm, L.D, Takahashi, N. & Peterson, G. (2000). Risk and trust in social exchange: An experimental test of a classical proposition. *American Journal of Sociology, 105,* 1396–1427l.

Rapoport, A. (1966). *N-person game theory: Concepts and applications.* Ann Arbor: University of Michigan Press.

Ostrom, E. (1998). A behavioral approach to the rational choice theory of collective action. *American Political Science Review 92,* 1–22.

Smithson, M., & Foddy, M. (1999). Theories and strategies for the study of social dilemmas. In M. Foddy, M. Smithson, S. Schneider, & M. Hogg (Eds.), *Resolving social dilemmas: Dynamic, structural and intergroup perspective* (pp. 1–14). Philadelphia, PA: Psychology Press.

Tajfel, H., Billig, M., Bundy, R., & Flament, C. (1971). Social categorization in intergroup behaviour. *European Journal of Social Psychology, 1,* 149–178.

Tajfel, H. & Turner, J.C. (1986). The social identity theory of intergroup behavior. I: S. Worchel & W.G. Austin (Eds.), *The psychology of intergroup relations* (pp. 7–24). Chicago: Nelson Hall.

Turner, J. C., & Reynolds, K.J. (2001). The social identity perspective in intergroup relations: Theories, themes, and controversies. In R. Brown, & S. L. Gaertner (Eds.), *Blackwell handbook of social psychology: Intergroup processes* (pp. 133–152). Malden, MA: Blackwell Publishers.

Van Lange, P.A.M. & Kuhlman, D.M. (1994). Social value orientations and impressions of partner's honesty and intelligence: A test of the might versus morality effect. *Journal of Personality and Social Psychology, 67,* 126–141.

Van Lange P.A.M. & Visser, K. (1999). Locomotion in social dilemmas: How people adapt to cooperative, Tit-for-tat, and non-cooperative partners. *Journal of Personality and Social Psychology, 77,* 762–773.

Williams, K., Forgas, J. & von Hippel, W. (2005). *The social outcast.* Philadelphia, PA: Psychology Press.

Wilson, R.K, & Eckel, C.C. (2006). Judging a book by its cover: Beauty and expectations in the trust game. *Political Research Quarterly, 59,* 189–202.

Yamagishi, T. (2000). *Risk Taking and Trust Building.* Unpublished manuscript. Russell Sage Foundation.

Yamagishi, T., Makimura, Y., Foddy, M., Matsuda, M., Kiyonari, T., & Platow, M.J. (2005). Comparisons of Australians and Japanese on group-based cooperation. *Asian Journal of Social Psychology, 8,* 173–190.

Yamagishi, T., Kanazawa, S., Mashima, R. & Terai, S. (2005). Separating trust from cooperation in a dynamic relationship. *Rationality and Society, 17,* 275–308.

Yamagishi, T., & Kiyonari, T. (2000). The group as the container of generalized reciprocity. *Social Psychology Quarterly, 63,* 116–132.

Yamagishi, T., & Yamagishi, M. (1994). Trust and commitment in the United States and Japan. *Motivation and Emotion, 18,* 129–166.

Yuki, M., Maddux, W.W., Brewer, M.B.B. & Takemura, K. (2005). Cross-cultural differences in relationship- and group-based trust. *Personality and Social Psychology Bulletin, 31,* 48–62.

Chapter 6
Promoting Cooperation in Social Dilemmas via Fairness Norms and Group Goals

Ali Kazemi[1,2] and Daniel Eek[1,2]

Introduction

In everyday life, people often encounter situations where their personal interests are at odds with the welfare of a larger collective to which they belong. What seems to be an individually rational choice may later have detrimental effects on the well-being of the group. Such conflicts of interest are referred to as social dilemmas (Dawes, 1980). Social dilemmas are formally defined as situations in which (1) individual outcomes for non-cooperative behavior or defection are larger than outcomes for cooperative behavior (favoring the collective interest), regardless of how other members in a collective behave; but (2) if all members adhere to this individually rational behavior, all members will acquire a lower payoff in the end as compared to if all had chosen to cooperate in the first place.

The theoretical framework in research on decision making in social dilemmas was for a long time expected utility or rational choice theory (e.g., Camerer, 1990). According to this theory, people should choose the option with the largest expected utility. Thus, the rational (dominant) decision in a social dilemma is always to defect (e.g., Dawes, 1980), that is, to benefit the own interest. However, that greed and economic incentives are the primary drivers of choice has been shown to be too limited of a perspective (e.g., Dawes & Thaler, 1988). Instead, in order to understand decision making in social dilemmas, modern theorizing in psychology has adopted a multiple-motives approach according to which both economic and non-economic motives are argued to influence choice behavior (e.g., De Cremer, 2002; Kerr, 1995; Tyler & Degoey, 1995). The present chapter adopts the latter approach and investigates the interplay between self-interest, fairness, and group goal in determining public-good allocation decisions.

Whereas previous social dilemma research has investigated the antecedents of cooperation in terms of public-good provision (e.g., Eek & Biel, 2003), the present chapter focuses on antecedents of cooperation in terms of public-good allocation

[1]Göteborg University, Sweden, [2]University of Skövde, Sweden

Corresponding author: Ali Kazemi, School of Technology and Society, University of Skövde, P.O. Box 408, SE-541 28, Skövde, Sweden, Email: ali.kazemi@his.se

A. Biel et al. (eds.), *New Issues and Paradigms in Research on Social Dilemmas.*
© Springer 2008

(Kazemi & Eek, in press; Kazemi et al., 2005a, b, 2006). Thus, in effect, this research conceptualizes cooperation more broadly than traditionally. Markóczy (2004) defined cooperation as joint behavior directed toward a goal in which members of a collective have a common interest. Similarly, Batson (1994) discussed cooperation in terms of "acting for the public good." Kazemi et al. (2005a, b, 2006) posited that people realize different group goals by following appropriate norms of fairness (i.e., equity, equality, need)[1] for resource allocation. Viewed in this way, an allocation satisfying a certain group goal can be regarded as a cooperative behavior in the sense that the individual disregards individual interests by helping the group to fulfill a certain social goal.

The chapter is organized as follows. We begin with providing a selective brief overview of previous research concerning the role of distributive fairness for decision making in social dilemmas. The subsequent section reviews research focusing on the effects of fairness and group goal on public-good allocations (Kazemi & Eek, in press; Kazemi et al., 2005a, b, 2006). This research is based on two related assumptions. The first is that the problems of public-good dilemmas are twofold. Specifically, people must first be motivated to contribute to provide or maintain public goods. Then, once provided, the way the benefits should be distributed must be determined. While the first has gained considerable attention (e.g., Dawes, 1980; Dawes et al., 1977; Eek et al., 1998; Van Lange et al., 1992; Wilke, 1991), the second has been largely neglected. In this research, both aspects of public-good dilemmas are considered. The second assumption is that different collective goals are operative in social dilemmas and that they may explain why people allocate public goods according to different allocation principles without being influenced by the provision aspect of the public good (i.e., self-interest). The chapter ends with some attempts to advance theoretical and practical implications of this line of research.

Distributive Fairness and Cooperation in Social Dilemmas

Social dilemma research has during the last four decades highlighted the role of cooperation for a functional society (e.g., Messick & Brewer, 1983). As a consequence, this research has been predominantly concerned with identifying factors that promote cooperation and thereby increase the welfare of the group or society at large (for an overview, see Komorita & Parks, 1994). Notions about the role of fairness as a crucial factor for cooperation in social dilemmas emerged early (Marwell & Ames, 1979). Although this still is a relatively unexplored area, some significant work has been done during the last two decades. Combining the two

---

[1] Theory and empirical research have focused on three principal allocation principles: equality, equity, and need (e.g., Deutsch, 1975, 1985). *Equality* prescribes that individuals receive the same rewards regardless of possible individual differences. *Equity*, also referred to as the merit or proportionality rule, implies that the outcome received by the individual is proportional to his or her contribution, ability, or performance (e.g., Adams, 1965). The principle of *need* prescribes that the outcome is proportional to need.

fields of social justice and social dilemmas has proven to be fruitful, as both are concerned with two important issues of interdependency and self-interest (cf. Tyler & Dawes, 1993; Tyler & Degoey, 1995). More recently, De Cremer and Van Dijk (2003) and Schroeder et al. (2003; see also Schroeder et al., this volume) emphasized the value of integrating research on justice, ethics, and decision making in research on social dilemmas. De Cremer and Van Dijk (2003) noted that research on decision making has increasingly taken into account how contextual factors, such as fairness, affect individual decision making. Similarly, Schroeder et al. (2003) argued that free riding in social dilemmas awakes notions of fairness as it results in beneficial resource asymmetry for the free riders and in sucker payoffs for the cooperators.

Two major paradigms have been employed in social dilemma research: resource dilemmas, which refer to situations in which each group member decides how much to harvest from a common resource that he or she has free access to, and public-good dilemmas, which refer to situations in which group members, through individual contributions, provide a common resource from which all can benefit. We begin by discussing the role of fairness in resource dilemmas and continue with the role of fairness in public-good dilemmas, ending this section with considering research that compares the two dilemma types with regard to fairness conceptions.

Resource Dilemmas and Fairness

Wilke et al. (1986) reported that a majority of participants considered it fair that a person who had participated longer in an experiment should take more from the resource than those who had participated shorter (i.e., equity). When no information was given about the time invested by participants, no such effect was observed.

In the GEF hypothesis, Wilke (1991) proposed that people facing resource dilemmas are by nature greedy in the sense that they prioritize their personal gains before the welfare of others. Wilke argued further that although people are greedy, their greed is restrained by a motive to utilize the resource efficiently and a call for being fair in terms of ensuring that others harvest an equal amount (i.e., equality). Thus, a resource dilemma might be viewed as a coordination task in which individuals pursue outcome maximization within the constraints of not taking more than their fair share and that the common resource does not deplete.

Wade-Benzoni et al. (1996) compared symmetric (where people have equal access to the resource) and asymmetric resource dilemmas (unequal access) with regard to interpretations of fairness and harvesting behavior. They argued and found that the equality rule was conceived as fair in symmetric settings, whereas it was more difficult to decide what a fair allocation would be in asymmetric settings. Overharvesting (i.e., non-cooperation) was more frequently found in asymmetric than in symmetric resource dilemmas, suggesting that asymmetric resource dilemmas are more complex and thus lead to ambiguity in deciding what is fair.

Public-Good Dilemmas and Fairness

Marwell and Ames (1979) showed that high-endowment participants, who were able to provide the public good themselves, contributed significantly more than did low-endowment participants (i.e., equity). Marwell and Ames interpreted this to mean that participants behaved in a way they conceived as fair. Furthermore, a majority of participants considered investing half or more of their tokens as fair. Wit et al. (1992) found that contributing in proportion to one's assets or interest (profit) position was conceived as fair in public-good dilemmas. The more assets participants possessed, the more they felt obliged to contribute. Accordingly, the higher the individual's profit position, the more he or she felt obliged to contribute (i.e., equity). Wit et al. (1992) suggested that the relative cost of contributing one or more resource units is reduced the more assets one possesses and that this was the basis of fairness concerns. Van Dijk and Wilke (1993) extended these results by studying interest asymmetry and concluded that high-interest people do not contribute more to public goods than low-interest people unless the asymmetry of interest is considered to be unjustified.

Biel et al. (1997) and Eek et al. (1998, 2001) examined the relevance of distributive fairness in real-life public-good dilemmas by focusing on how perceived fairness of different public-good distributions affected willingness to pay (i.e., cooperation). Biel et al. (1997) surveyed parents' willingness to pay for municipal child care and related willingness to pay to how fair the distribution of quality of child care was perceived. The results indicated that equality was perceived as the fairest principle for distribution and that parents were willing to pay the most when equality was prevalent. Eek et al. (1998) replicated and extended these results in experiments where participants rated how fair they considered distributions of a public good (i.e., child care) according to the principles of equity, equality, and need. They found that perceived fairness of the public good's distribution mediated the effect of allocation principle on contributions to the public good. Thus, fairness perceptions accounted for positive effects of endorsed allocation strategies on cooperation.

Comparing Fairness Conceptions in Resource and Public-Good Dilemmas

Van Dijk and Wilke (1995) regarded fairness norms as coordination rules. They found that participants in the public-good dilemma based their choices on the equity rule and that participants in the resource dilemma based their choices on the equal final outcomes rule even though the objective payoff structure in both types of dilemma was identical (see also Van Dijk & Grodzka, 1992; Van Dijk et al., 1999). Van Dijk and Wilke (2000) extended these results and demonstrated that it is the behavior that is focused (e.g., giving or keeping some of the endowments in a public-good dilemma) and not the social dilemma type per se that affects people's fairness judgments and preferences. Thus, the give-some and leave-some dilemmas (i.e., low-outcome focus) both invoked a preference for the equity rule, whereas the keep-some and the take-some dilemmas (i.e., high-outcome focus) invoked a stronger preference for the equal final outcomes rule.

Explaining the Importance of Fairness in Social Dilemmas

Two lines of research integrating social justice and social dilemma research may be discerned.[2] One line (e.g., Van Dijk et al., 1999; Wit et al., 1992) initiated the idea of fairness as an important motive in social dilemmas, manifested through coordination rules such as equity and equality. In general, the effects of fairness on cooperation in this line of research were examined by first asking participants what they perceive as fair to take from or contribute to a collective resource and then measuring their actual harvests or contributions. Another line of research (e.g., Eek & Biel, 2003; Eek et al., 1998, 2001) investigated the validity of the GEF hypothesis to account for cooperation in public-good dilemmas and examined, in particular, how fair people perceived different distributions of the public good to be and how much they correspondingly were willing to contribute.

This research suggests that fairness guides cooperation and downplays the role of self-interest in social dilemmas where individuals find themselves trapped between cooperative choices benefiting collective interests on the one hand and competitive choices benefiting individual interests on the other. An intriguing question is why fairness plays such a paramount role for how people behave in social dilemmas. A number of accounts are outlined in the following. One explanation is that fairness is a strong societal norm. Norms are often defined as socially anchored expectations about proper conduct "enforced by the threat of sanctions or the promise of reward" (Kerr, 1995, p. 33). Norms are widely shared and internalized through the process of socialization (Scott, 1971; Sherif, 1966).

Fairness may also be important for self-presentational concerns. Distribution of desirable and limited resources confronts involved parties with a motivational dilemma. On the one hand, they want to maximize their own gains. On the other hand, they strive to be perceived as fair because fairness is seen as a moral virtue (cf. Folger, 1998) and a desirable personal characteristic. It has, for instance, been found that fair people are perceived as more trustworthy and reliable (cf. Tyler, 1994; Tyler & Lind, 1992).

---

[2] A third line of research (e.g., De Cremer, 2002, 2003; Tyler & Degoey, 1995) that investigates the effects of procedural fairness on cooperation in social dilemmas has been omitted in this chapter due to the present focus on distributive fairness. Thus, instead of targeting the perceived fairness of final outcome distributions, this line of research examines the quality of the formal and informal aspects of the procedures enacted by authorities in making outcome decisions.

Another answer to the role of fairness in decision making and social encounters is to be found in Tyler (2005), who advanced the social value activation model positing that self-interest and outcome favorability have less impact on people's behavioral decisions when actions are viewed in terms of social values (e.g., justice, morality). An implication is that if a justice frame is activated, people will exhibit fairness considerations. When this happens, people display high levels of decision acceptance and satisfaction without too much attention to gains and losses. If a justice frame is not triggered, decisions will primarily be based on self-interest concerns, that is, in terms of gains and losses.

Moreover, to follow norms promotes collective action (e.g., Kerr, 1995), in particular, when communication is not possible, as often is the case in social dilemma research. Hence, actions of interdependent individuals can tacitly be coordinated in an efficient way (e.g., Van Dijk & Wilke, 1995) when others realize each other's motives; that is, by being fair, they signal to others that they do not intend to take advantage of them.

Finally, fairness has also been proposed by recent theorizing in procedural justice to be instrumental in managing uncertainty in social encounters. Uncertainty management theory (Lind & Van den Bos, 2002) posits that activation of fairness processes is an indication of fairness judgments' being utilized to settle some important social or psychological issue. Lind and Van den Bos suggest that fairness serves people in managing uncertain situations by giving them "confidence that they will ultimately receive good outcomes and because it makes the possibility of loss less anxiety-provoking" (2002, p. 195).

Fairness Norms and Group Goals in Social Decision Making

Recently, we initiated a new line of research that extends the notion of collective interest in previous social dilemma research. Specifically, the notion of collective interest is elaborated and thus considered to be composed of performance or economic goals on the one hand and relational or socio-emotional goals on the other (Kazemi & Eek, in press; Kazemi et al., 2005a, b, 2006). Drawing on this extended notion of collective interest, we also extended research on fairness in social dilemmas by showing that endorsement of distributive fairness norms in social dilemmas is related to the nature of the collective goal that a group pursues. Furthermore, in contrast to previous research positing the maximization of economic benefits to oneself as the ultimate goal (e.g., Kreps, 1990), it was argued that striving toward group goals (e.g., performance, harmony, a sense of responsibility, or social concern) would minimize the pursuit of self-interest in social dilemmas.

A fundamental proposition in this research is that how public goods are distributed is important for the extent to which different group goals are achieved. This proposition is derived from Deutsch (1975, 1985), who suggested that norms of allocation are not adopted because of an intrinsic justice value but because of the goals they realize. Deutsch (1975, 1985) argued that adopting equity promotes effectiveness and productivity. The rationale is that individuals performing better, contributing more, or possessing higher abilities will be entitled and legitimized to gain more of the collective's resources. For instance, it may be argued that the capability of high-skilled individuals will eventually lead to an enlargement of the common wealth, which justifies that high-skilled individuals receive a larger share of the common resource. In contrast, whenever enjoyable social relations and harmony are salient in a social relationship, the equality rule is most likely to be employed because it does not differentiate between the members of the collective and, therefore, reduces outbreaks of possible conflicts resulting from differential treatments. Equity is believed to impair enjoyable social relations, since it may signal unequal status or unequal worth of the group members. The need principle is endorsed in situations in which individuals' welfare and a sense of social concern and responsibility for others are in focus. Since needs differ and needy individuals may have limited capabilities or opportunities to make contributions, allocations in accordance equity would prove to be detrimental to the personal welfare and development of those in need. Mannix et al. (1995) asked participants to role-play as vice presidents of a private company and to distribute a number of instructional videos among three different company divisions that differed in terms of past performance. They systematically varied what they called culture (economically oriented, relationship-oriented, and personal development-oriented) by means of an extract from a speech by the company founder. The results partially supported Deutsch's theory in showing an effect of culture. However, the role of fairness for outcome allocation was not considered.

We argue that group goals define desired future states that frame the allocation decision or provide a reason as to why a public good should be distributed according to one principle rather than another (cf. Weber et al., 2004). Pillutla and Chen (1999) showed that people cooperate more in social dilemmas involving non-economic decisions (i.e., contributing to a social event) than in those involving economic decisions (i.e., investing in a joint investment fund). Similarly, Tenbrunsel and Messick (1999) argued that the effect of sanctions on cooperation depends on the decision frame (i. e., business vs. ethical) invoked since it induces different processing. They found that a business frame triggers a calculative decision process whereby the strength of the sanction affects the extent to which people choose to cooperate, whereas an ethical frame triggers a non-calculative process leading to a cooperation heuristic that is unaffected by the strength of the sanction. Although these studies are relevant in that they are all concerned with decision frames and context-dependent decision making, they do not specifically address the issue that we raise in our research.

To reiterate, our research extends previous research on fairness in social dilemmas in that we examine the hypothesis that people prefer to allocate public goods according to different principles. These principles differ in terms of perceived fairness. We propose that the fairness perceptions and allocations depend on the induced group goal. More specifically, in contrast to previous research (e.g., Van Dijk & Wilke, 1995, 2000) showing that a proportionality principle (i.e., equity) is perceived as fair in public-good dilemmas, we will demonstrate in several studies that other principles (i.e., equal share, equal final outcomes, and need) are also perceived as fair in public-good dilemmas to the extent that they are conducive to achieving a certain group goal.

Preferences for Public-Good Allocations

Kazemi et al. (2005a) investigated preferences (according to equity, equality, or equal final outcomes) for allocating a public good among group members who had contributed unequally in providing the good. In five-person groups, all participants made an initial contribution to a successful provision of the public good and were subsequently told that they randomly had been selected as the leader of their group. Their task as the leader was to allocate the public good among the other four group members. The question posed in Study 1 was whether the preferred allocation of the good was determined by what is considered to be a fair distribution. Previous research shows that the equality principle is chosen because it is considered to be fair if social comparison information (i.e., others' cooperative intentions and behavior) is lacking or uncertain (cf. Allison et al., 1992). However, if such information is available, the equity or need is perceived as fairest (Lamm & Schwinger, 1983; Schwinger & Lamm, 1981; Van Dijk & Wilke, 1995). In this study we provided participants with false feedback indicating that the other group members had contributed unequally. Thus, compared to other principles, equality was expected to be perceived as unfair. Therefore, we predicted that participants would prefer to use other principles than equality in their allocations.

Twenty undergraduates participated. A within-group design was employed with allocation principle as a factor with three levels (i.e., equity, equality, and equal final outcomes). Participants' allocations constituted the main dependent variable referred to as allocation preference. Following the allocation task, participants' perceived fairness of the different principles was measured.

The results showed that participants took individual contributions to the public good into account and expressed a stronger preference for equity and equal final outcomes than equality in their allocation decisions. The predictions that equality would be perceived as less fair and that it would be endorsed less than equity and equal final outcomes were supported. As hypothesized, perceived fairness was a significant predictor of preference for the equity and equal final outcomes principles.

Study 1 thus provides evidence for the dominant preference of two contribution-based allocation principles (i.e., equity and equal final outcomes) over equality. When the group goal was unspecified, fairness perceptions determined the preferred distribution of the public good. Participants did not differentiate between the equity and equal final outcomes principles. In Study 2, we investigated how the group goal affects public-good allocation. More specifically, by introducing the group goal, we expected that participants would differentiate among all principles. We also expected participants to adopt the equality principle when it was instrumental in achieving certain goals (i.e., harmony and enjoyable social relations). This implies that equality may be adopted in public-good allocations even when individual contributions are unequal.

Sixty undergraduates were randomly assigned to three groups in which the group goal was varied (economic productivity vs. harmony vs. social concern) as a between-groups factor. Apart from this, Study 2 was identical to Study 1. The manipulation of the group goal was introduced after contributions had been made. In the *economic productivity* condition, the instructions read (translated from Swedish), "Your group has a long-term goal of economic productivity. Hence, economic profit is the primary driving force. The emphasis is on measuring achievements with precision." In the *harmony* condition, the instructions read, "Your group has a long-term goal of harmony. Hence, maintenance of enjoyable relations is the primary driving force. The emphasis is on enhancing the group spirit and fellowship." In the *social concern* condition, the instructions read, "Your group has a long-term goal of social concern. Hence, giving help and support to fellow group members is the primary driving force. The emphasis is on being considerate and taking responsibility for other members."

The results showed that fairness and the group goal had independent effects on allocation preferences. As predicted, the group goal proved to be effective in differentiating between the preference for equity and equal final outcomes. Thus, equity was preferred when people were motivated to realize economic productivity in a group, and inducing the group goal of harmony made participants allocate according to equal final outcomes. Equality was found to be preferred when it was conducive to realizing the group goal of social concern. Thus, as hypothesized, when contributions are unequal, endorsement of equality may still occur if it is directed toward a given group goal. Moreover, the finding that equity and equal final outcomes were perceived as fairer than equality as well as the finding that their endorsement in allocations correlated with the perceived fairness of allocation principle were replicated.

Promoting Unselfish Public-Good Allocations via Group Goals and Distributive Fairness

In Kazemi et al. (2005a), participants allocated the public good between others, which did not make possible an assessment of the role of self-interest. Self-interest concerns were addressed in Kazemi et al. (2005b).

Major and Deaux (1982) distinguished between four different allocation paradigms: allocations to others only, allocations to self only, individual allocations to self and others, and group allocations to self and others. In Study 1 in Kazemi et al. (2005b), we employed a paradigm where participants evaluated allocations made by a group leader. The main dependent variable was allocation instrumentality. Allocation instrumentality was defined as the perception of the different distributive principles with regard to their potential in fulfilling certain group goals.

Data were collected for 180 participants in 5-person groups. The group goal (economic productivity vs. harmony vs. social concern) was manipulated between groups, and the allocation principle (equity vs. equality vs. equal final outcomes) measured within groups. In contrast to our previous studies, one of the other group members was appointed as the leader. Subsequently, the group goal was induced in the same way as in Kazemi et al. (2005a). Thereafter, the public-good dilemma was presented. Contribution decisions were followed by an announcement of a decision from the group leader regarding the allocation of the public good. Subsequently, participants assessed perceived fairness and instrumentality (e.g., "To what extent do you perceive that employing allocation principle X will lead to a realization of goal X?") of this first allocation decision and were informed that the experiment was over. Shortly after this, they learned that the leader had decided to change the first allocation decision and presented two alternative allocations. Participants were then asked to evaluate these alternative allocations in terms of fairness and instrumentality.

Results revealed no significant effects of group goals on the perceived instrumentality of allocations. Instead, the data clearly indicated that fairness predicted the instrumentality of allocations. These results may suggest that participants in the role of recipients were less concerned with whether or not group goals were realized than participants in the role of leaders in the previous studies. Furthermore, a tentative but tenable explanation is that as recipients, participants may not have seen it as their responsibility to realize the group goal (cf. Folger et al., 1995).

In Study 2 in Kazemi et al. (2005b), we used the allocation-to-self-and-others paradigm (Major & Deaux, 1982) in which participants were both recipients and allocators of the public good. The issue of responsibility was thus taken into account, and it became possible to examine the role of self-interest for allocations more directly. It was conjectured that the salience of fairness and group goals would promote unselfish allocations. It was hypothesized that the fairness of public-good allocations would be affected by the group goal. In contrast to this hypothesis, a self-interest hypothesis predicted that the fairness of public-good allocations depends on the individual's outcome following the public-good allocation (cf. De Dreu, 1996; Messick & Sentis, 1979). Thus, participants making no contribution (0) or an equal-share (30) contribution = equality as fair those contributing more (40 or 60) = equity as fair, while those contributing more (40 or 60) would benefit from and therefore consider equity as fair (i.e., an egocentric bias in fairness perceptions).

Seventy-two participants were randomly assigned to one of four contribution conditions (i.e., contribution: 0 vs. 30 vs. 40 vs. 60). All participants were told that they belonged to a four-person group. The procedure was the same as in the previous studies except that participants were instructed to make seven instead of one contribution choice. First, they chose the amount that they preferred most to contribute, the second time they chose the second most preferred contribution, and so forth. The seventh contribution was thus their least preferred contribution. They were told that one of the seven contribution choices would then be randomly selected as their valid one. In this way, the amount of contribution to the public good was manipulated between participants. Thereafter, participants were given a table with entries showing group members' initial endowments and their possessions after contributions as well as how much of the outcome each member would receive according to the three proposed allocation principles. The induced group goal was a within-groups factor. Following the inducement of each goal, participants allocated SEK 240 between themselves and the other members. Subsequent to each allocation, participants also rated the fairness of the allocation principles.

One's own contribution to the public good (i.e., self-interest) had no significant effects on the perceived fairness or allocation preferences. In support of the predictions, the group goal of economic productivity increased fairness of allocations according to equity, and the group goals of harmony and social concern increased fairness of allocations according to equality. These findings suggest that allocations in public-good dilemmas may not primarily depend on self-interest but on group goals justifying a specific allocation.

Fairness Mediates the Effects of Group Goal on Public-Good Allocations

Some questions remain to be answered concerning the main hypothesis that the group goal affects public-good allocations. One concerns whether the relationship between group goal and allocation preference holds in asymmetric public-good dilemmas. Since previous research (Kazemi et al., 2005a, b; Mannix et al., 1995) shows that different goals lead to different allocation decisions, we argued in Kazemi et al. (2006) that differences in initial endowments should not be crucial for dividing the public good if a group goal is made salient. Thus, it was hypothesized that the relationship of group goals to allocation preferences generalizes to asymmetric public-good dilemmas.

Another issue that was raised in Kazemi et al. (2006) concerned identification of an alternative allocation principle to equal final outcomes that was not based on initial contributions. In this way, we could use an allocation principle that was more differentiated from the equity and equality principles. Specifically, in Kazemi et al. (2005a, b), the equal final outcomes principle was defined on the basis of participants' post-contribution possessions. In this way, the equal final outcomes principle was like a hybrid of the equity principle (in the sense that participants received more the more they contributed) and the equality principle (in the sense that participants ended up with the same amount of resources). By asking participants to indicate their need for money to purchase course readings, the allocation principle of need was identified in Kazemi et al. (2006) and was operationalized independently of participants' contributions to the public good, making this principle distinct from the equity and equality principles.

Furthermore, to investigate to what extent participants were driven by self-interest, allocation information was manipulated. Half of the participants learned that their allocations were public (i.e., revealed to others in their group), while the other half learned that their allocations would remain private. In contrast to the fairness-group goal hypothesis (e.g., Deutsch, 1975), a self-interest hypothesis (cf. De Dreu, 1996; Messick & Sentis, 1979) stressed that people are primarily motivated by maximizing their own economic benefits. Thus, on the one hand, if the self-interest notion is valid, private allocations should result in higher allocations to self as compared to public allocations. On the other hand, if the fairness-group goal hypothesis is valid, participants should make allocations that are instrumental in achieving a certain group goal irrespective of whether the allocations are private or public.

The fairness-group goal hypothesis also implies a relationship between perceived fairness of allocations and group goal. Previous research (Kazemi et al., 2005a, b; Mannix et al., 1995) has not provided any explanation for the observed relationship between group goal and public-good allocation. Thus, the third purpose was to extend the above line of reasoning by examining why people striving for a certain group goal prefer a specific way of public-good allocation. We believe that people have subjective theories about appropriate means for the realization of different group goals. These theories emanate from different norms of fairness. Specifically, different group goals activate different fairness norms, which in turn guide public-good allocations. Thus, it was hypothesized that the effect of group goal on public-good allocation was mediated by perceived fairness.

In 4-person groups, 72 participants were randomly assigned to one of four experimental conditions according to a 2 [endowment position: SEK 60 (low) vs. SEK 120 (high)] × 2 (allocation: public vs. private) factorial design. Participants were first asked to indicate their personal need the current semester for money to purchase course literature. They were further informed that this estimation would be used as a basis for working on the upcoming group tasks. Participants were bogusly told that those assigned to a high-endowment position had indicated a greater need than those assigned to a low-endowment position. Thus, half of them received SEK 60, while the other half received SEK 120. Participants were further informed that another group member had received the same amount of endowments as they themselves, whereas the other two members had received either a lower (i.e., SEK 60) or a higher (i.e., SEK 120) amount.

The public-good dilemma was then presented. After their contribution decisions, participants were informed that the public good had been provided. A table with handwritten entries was then given to the participants showing group members' initial endowments, their contribution decisions, their post-contribution possessions, and how much each member would receive from the public good according to the equity, equality, and need principles. Subsequently, group goal was induced in the same way as in the previous studies. For each goal, participants divided the public good and rated the fairness of each of the three principles.

The results clearly indicated that the relationship of group goal and preferred allocations previously observed also holds in asymmetric public-good dilemmas. Thus, as expected, when the group goal was economic productivity, allocations corresponded more to equity; when the group goal was harmony, allocations corresponded to equality; and when the group goal was social concern, allocations corresponded more to need. The hypothesis that fairness mediates the effects of group goal on allocation preferences was also supported, suggesting that perceived fairness explains why people pursuing a certain goal tend to prefer a specific allocation. Furthermore, the results did not reveal any significant effects of allocation information on public-good allocations. That is, being informed that allocations would remain private did not incur higher self-allocations than being informed that allocations would be public. These results conceptually replicate the findings reported by Kazemi et al. (2005b).

Generalizing Effects of the Group Goal on Profit Allocations to Cost Allocations

The question of how to divide losses or negative outcomes has not received much attention in social dilemma research. Furthermore, previous research on distributive justice has not been conclusive concerning the effects of resource valence on fairness perceptions and allocation preferences. Some previous studies show that people prefer equity for allocation of positive outcomes and equality for allocation of negative outcomes (e.g., Meeker & Elliot, 1987; Törnblom & Jonsson, 1985, 1987), while others show the reverse pattern (e.g., Lamm & Kayser, 1978; Mannix et al., 1995; Törnblom & Ahlin, 1998; Sondak et al., 1995). In Kazemi and Eek (in press), we addressed the issue of positive and negative outcome allocations by adopting the group goal approach. Thus, allocation preference variations within each level of resource valence were expected to be explained by the extent to which people think that their allocations help accomplish a certain group goal. Expressed differently, the allocation principle that is preferred in the context of positive and negative outcome allocations is related to the group goal that the allocation promotes.

The assumption is that people bring implicit goals to interdependent group situations. These goals differ in nature. Some are performance- and productivity-oriented, others are oriented toward harmony and solidarity, while yet others are focused on social responsibility and commitment to the group (cf. Deutsch, 1975). The ways people allocate outcomes, positive as well as negative, are implicitly affected by the goals that they embrace. An aim was therefore to investigate whether our previous results generalize to allocation of negative outcomes.

In contrast to the previous studies, we did not manipulate the group goal. Instead, we measured the group goal. Specifically, we measured to what extent participants believed that their allocations promoted realization of several different group goals. Thus, by measuring several different group goals, we could use factor analysis to examine the dimensionality of the group goal construct, hence testing the validity of the assumed three-dimensionality (Kazemi et al., 2005a, b, 2006).

One hundred participants were randomly assigned to one of two groups where resource valence was either positive or negative. As in Kazemi et al. (2006), participants were instructed to indicate their personal need for money to purchase course literature the current semester and were bogusly told that those assigned to a high-endowment position had indicated a greater need than those assigned to a low-endowment position. In reality, all participants were assigned to the low-endowment position. After participants made their contribution decisions, the resource valence was manipulated. Half were told that the provision threshold had not been reached (i.e., the deficit condition), whereas the other half were told that the provision threshold had been outreached (i.e., the surplus condition). In both groups, the distance to the provision threshold was said to be SEK 600. Subsequently, all participants were asked to divide the deficit (or surplus) among themselves and fellow group members. In the surplus condition, participants were told that in spite of the initial information that contributions beyond the threshold would not be given back to group members, the experimenter had now decided to do so. In the deficit condition, participants were told the experimenter had decided to give the group another chance to provide the public good.

Subsequent to the allocation task, participants assessed the perceived fairness of the allocation principles of equity, equality, and need. Following this, the extent to which participants believed that their allocations promoted realization of different group goals was measured.

The results showed that a two-factor solution of the group goal construct provided the most parsimonious description of the data. Furthermore, as predicted for the allocation of positive outcomes (i.e., surplus), it was found that relationship-oriented goals predicted preferences for the allocation principle of equality, whereas performance-oriented goals predicted preferences for the allocation principle of equity. The same held true for the allocation of negative outcomes. This suggests that people implicitly have different orientations or goals in mind in group situations that influence the way they prefer to allocate positive as well as negative outcomes.

Discussion and Conclusions

The research on fairness in social dilemmas that was reviewed indicates that people are prone to contribute to the establishment of common resources (i.e., public-good dilemma) or to utilize existing resources (i.e., common resource dilemma) more restrictedly as fairness norms tacitly coordinate actions (e.g., Van Dijk et al., 1999).

As group goals and resource allocation are integral parts of all social groups, knowledge in advance of how to distribute collective resources in order to realize these goals is essential to group functioning and effectiveness. Our results show that public-good allocation according to different norms of fairness depends on group goal. This finding is also consistent with previous research showing that decision frames influence the way people behave in social dilemmas (e.g., Pillutla & Chen, 1999; Tenbrunsel & Messick, 1999).

An integrative theory for how decisions are made in social dilemmas is the appropriateness framework recently developed by Weber et al. (2004). The definition of the situation is the core element. Drawing on March (1994), the appropriateness framework states that people making decisions in social dilemmas ask themselves, "What does a person like me do in a situation like this?" (p. 281). Weber et al. (2004) argue that this question highlights the interaction among the three elements of recognition, identity, and rules. Recognition refers to categorization based on event prototypes. The more novel the situation encountered is, the more difficult and resource-consuming the categorization process will be. Integral to the categorization process is also a consideration of how others perceive the same situation and what others would expect the individual to do given the situation. Identity pertains to "all the idiosyncratic factors that individuals bring with them into a social situation" (p. 283). Personal history, personality, social motives, and gender are all subsumed under identity. In contrast to the rational choice theories, the appropriateness framework assumes decision making to be rule-based rather than outcome-based. Rules are assumed to facilitate choice behavior by limiting the options. This framework is relevant to our research in the sense that it supports the contention that people try to employ rules when making decisions about how to realize different group goals, which indicates, as previously shown, that their decisions are less outcome-based. Thus, when goals are defined as desired future states, they help to frame the allocation decision or provide a cause for why a public good should be distributed in accordance with one rule rather than another. This line of reasoning is supported by the appropriateness framework in that features or details of a social situation (in this case, group goal) may have a large impact on decision making if those features or details alter people's conceptions of appropriateness (in this case, norms of fairness).

Extensions and Implications

In order to survive and prosper, every organized group must first adapt to the external environment surrounding it and, second, maintain cohesion and prevent the group from disintegration. Preventing disintegration is largely dependent on the extent to which the group manages to attain various collective goals. Allocation of resources takes place in all social settings. In an allocation task, the individual sometimes is the allocator. At other times, he or she is the recipient. In either case, a number of psychological and contextual factors influence the individual's behavior. In this chapter, the emphasis has been on investigating the role of group goal for allocators' and recipients' fairness perceptions in social dilemmas. Some goals are certainly more salient than others in various contexts. Austin (1980) reported that whereas college roommates dividing a group resource overlooked individual differences in performance and thus divided according to the equality principle, strangers dividing a group resource took individual differences in performance into account and thus divided according to the equity principle. In a related vein, Eek et al. (2001) found that the equity principle was perceived as fairer than equality in privately provided child care, whereas equality was perceived as fairer in child care provided by the municipality. As collectives such as municipalities and a group of roommates probably are more concerned with relational goals (i.e., harmony and social concern) than performance-related goals (i.e., economic productivity), these findings are consistent with the present results concerning the relationship between the group goal and public-good allocation. This implies that the application of a certain principle can be justified in one context or organizational culture but not in another (cf. Mannix et al., 1995).

Various goals may also vary in importance depending on a group's development phase or the social occasion it is facing. For instance, sororities or fraternities, which in Deutsch's (1975) terms are "solidarity-oriented groups," do not in all of their activities employ the equality principle or consider it as fair or appropriate. Goode (1978) challenged Deutsch's view that social groups, depending on their goal orientation, are governed by a single dominant justice principle. Instead, Goode suggested that different principles apply to different phases or occasions in a group's life rather than one principle always being dominant for a group. From another point of view, Törnblom (1992) objected to Deutsch's unconditional propositions by noting that "it seems gratuitous to claim that the shouldering of responsibility for a recipient's welfare would elicit need-oriented allocations. Of course this may depend on whose needs are recognized (e.g., those of a child or prisoner) and on the nature of the allocator's responsibilities (e.g., those of a parent or a prison guard)" (p. 214). This objection highlights the importance of taking the type of social relationship into account. Thus, in real-life settings, there is usually a mixture of different goals at some point in time, which makes it difficult, if not impossible, to adhere to one principle only.

A Note on the Public-Good Dilemma Paradigm

The present volume focuses on new issues and paradigms in social dilemma research. Thus, in the following, some attention is devoted to aspects of the public-good paradigm used in our research. First, in contrast to the traditional public-good paradigm (e.g., Van Dijk & Wilke, 1995), a degree of uncertainty about how the public good would be distributed was introduced. Thus, when deciding how much to contribute, participants were not certain about how much they would benefit from the public good should it be provided. In real-life public-good dilemmas, people are probably seldom certain about how public goods will be distributed. To exemplify, when citizens pay taxes, they are uncertain about how the accumulated tax pool will be allocated. Thus, each citizen knows that he or she will receive something but not how much. Second, the public-good dilemma paradigm was extended to allow other principles than equality to be applied in the allocation of public goods. To measure allocation preferences and investigate the effects of fairness and group goal on allocation preferences, participants in Kazemi et al. (2005a) were told that they as leaders would not receive anything from the public good. Consequently, non-excluda-bility did not apply in the allocation of the public good. However, it is argued that this public-good simulation comes closer to real life than those utilized in previous research. For example, contributing to charities is often given as an example of a public-good dilemma (e.g., Cornes & Sandler, 1996). Yet, it is clear that non-excludability does not apply in this case and that there is usually a person or a group who determines how the charitable resources are allocated to others.

Another aspect of non-excludability is whether public goods in real life are public in the sense that they are accessible to all people. As Foddy (2005) argues, excluding or restricting people's access to scarce public goods is a common structural solution that governmental agencies apply. Immigration policy, health care, voting, and driver's license are examples of this type of solution that show that public goods are provided only for some "publics" or "groups" that some-how qualify for benefiting from the public good. Foddy concluded that the pub-lics who contribute to the provision and the publics who benefit from its provision vary. Given that real-life public goods are amenable to allocations based on other principles than equality, such as equity, need, and equal final outcomes, we believe that the present research addresses an important issue that has been overlooked in previous social dilemma research. Furthermore, as noted by Messick (1995), even though there may be consensus about implementing equality in the allocation of a public good, problems can arise. Specifically, the type of resource to be allocated is important. Messick discusses the problem of identifying ways to allocate an expensive carpet between two persons who have equal claims to the carpet. Clearly, it is easier to divide a continuous resource like money equally. Thus, real-life public goods cannot always be allocated equally, because "public" does not mean "accessible to all people" (Foddy, 2005) and because public goods differ with regard to the properties of the resource that constitutes them (Messick, 1995). In conclusion, we believe that our research contributes to experimental public-good dilemma research in that we used a paradigm that mimics real-life public goods in a way that has not been recognized in prior research.

Acknowledgments This research was made possible by financial support from the Swedish Research Council (Grant 421-2001-4697) to Daniel Eek. We thank Tommy Gärling and Anders Biel for valuable comments on a previous version of this chapter. We also would like to thank Eric Van Dijk for valuable discussions.

References

Adams, J. S. (1965). Inequity in social exchange. In L. Berkowitz (ed.), *Advances in Experimental Social Psychology* (pp. 267–299). New York: Academic Press.

Allison, S. T., McQueen, L. R., Schaerfl, L. M. (1992). Social decision making processes and the equal partitionment of shared resources. *Journal of Experimental Social Psychology, 28*, 23–42.

Austin, W. (1980). Friendship and fairness: Effects of type of relationship and task performance on choice of distributive rules. *Personality and Social Psychology Bulletin, 6*, 402–408.

Batson, D. C. (1994). Why act for the public good? Four answers. *Personality and Social Psychology Bulletin, 20*, 603–610.

Biel, A., Eek, D., Gärling, T. (1997). Distributive justice and willingness to pay for municipality child care. *Social Justice Research, 10*, 63–80.

Camerer, C.F. (1990). Behavioral game theory. In R.M. Hogarth (ed.), *Insights in Decision Making* (pp. 311–336). Chicago: University of Chicago Press.

Cornes, R., Sandler, T. (1996). *The Theory of Externalities, Public Goods, and Club Goods.* Cambridge: Cambridge University Press.

Dawes, R. M. (1980). Social dilemmas. *Annual Review of Psychology, 31*, 169–193.

Dawes, R. M., McTavish, J., Shaklee, H. (1977). Behavior, communication, and assumptions about other people's behavior in a common dilemma situation. *Journal of Personality and Social Psychology, 35*, 1–11.

Dawes, R. M., Thaler, R. H. (1988). Anomalies: Cooperation. *Journal of Economic Perspectives, 2*, 187–197.

De Cremer, D. (2002). Respect and cooperation in social dilemmas: The importance of feeling included. *Personality and Social Psychology Bulletin, 28*, 1335–1341.

De Cremer, D. (2003). Non-economic motives predicting cooperation in public good dilemmas: The effect of received respect on contributions. *Social Justice Research, 16*, 367–377.

De Cremer, D., Van Dijk, E. (2003). Fairness and ethics in social decision making. *Social Justice Research, 16*, 191–194.

De Dreu, C. K. W. (1996). Gain-loss frame in outcome-interdependence: Does it influence equality or equity considerations? *European Journal of Social Psychology, 26*, 315–324.

Deutsch, M. (1975). Equity, equality, and need: What determines which value will be used as the basis for distributive justice? *Journal of Social Issues, 31*, 137–149.

Deutsch, M. (1985). *Distributive Justice: A Social Psychological Perspective.* New Haven, CT: Yale University Press.

Eek, D., Biel, A. (2003). The interplay between greed, efficiency, and fairness in public-goods dilemmas. *Social Justice Research, 16*, 195–215.

Eek, D., Biel, A., Gärling, T. (1998). The effect of distributive justice on willingness to pay for municipality child care: An extension of the GEF hypothesis. *Social Justice Research, 11*, 121–142.

Eek, D., Biel, A., Gärling, T. (2001). Cooperation in asymmetric social dilemmas when equality is perceived as unfair. *Journal of Applied Social Psychology, 31*, 649–666.

Foddy, M (2005). Exclusion and inclusion in social dilemmas: Who do you toss out of the lifeboat? Paper presented at the XIth International Conference on Social Dilemmas, Krakow, Poland.

Folger, R. (1998). Fairness as a moral virtue. In M. Schminke (ed.), *Managerial Ethics: Moral Management of People and Processes* (pp. 13–34). Mahwah, NJ: Erlbaum.

Folger, R., Sheppard, B. H., Buttram, R. T. (1995). Equity, equality, and need: Three faces of social justice. In B. Benedict & J. Z. Rubin (eds.), *Conflict, Cooperation, and Justice: Essays Inspired by the Work of Morton Deutsch* (pp. 261–289). San Francisco: Jossey-Bass.

Goode, W. J. (1978). *The Celebration of Heroes: Prestige as a Control System.* Berkeley: University of California Press.

Kazemi, A., Eek, D. (in press). Effects of group goal and resource valence on allocation preferences in public good dilemmas. *Social Behavior and Personality*.

Kazemi, A., Eek, D., Gärling, T. (2005a). *Effects of Fairness and Distributive Goal on Preferred Allocations in Public Good Dilemmas* (Göteborg Psychological Reports, 35, No. 4). Sweden: Göteborg University, Department of Psychology.

Kazemi, A., Eek, D., Gärling, T. (2005b). *Effects of Fairness, Group Goal, and Self-Interest on Allocation Preferences in Step-Level Public Good Dilemmas* (Göteborg Psychological Reports, 35, No. 5). Sweden: Göteborg University, Department of Psychology.

Kazemi, A., Eek, D., Gärling, T. (2006). *The Interplay Between Greed, Fairness, and Group Goal in Allocation of Public Goods* (Göteborg Psychological Reports, 36, No. 2). Sweden: Göteborg University, Department of Psychology.

Kerr, N. L. (1995). Norms in social dilemmas. In D. Schroeder (ed.), *Social Dilemmas: Perspectives on Individuals and Groups* (pp. 31–47). Westport, CT: Praeger.

Komorita, S. S., Parks, C. D. (1994). *Social Dilemmas*. Madison, WI: Brown & Benchmark.

Kreps, D. M. (1990). *Game Theory and Economic Modelling*. Oxford: Clarendon.

Lamm, H., Kayser, E. (1978). The allocation of monetary gain and loss following dyadic performance: The weight given to effort and ability under conditions of low and high intra-dyadic attraction. *European Journal of Social Psychology, 8*, 275–278.

Lamm, H., Schwinger, T. (1983). Need consideration in allocation decisions: Is it just? *Journal of Social Psychology, 119*, 205–209.

Lind, E. A., Van den Bos, K. (2002). When fairness works: Toward a general theory of uncertainty management. In B. M. Staw & R. M. Kramer (eds.), *Research in Organizational Behavior* (Vol. 24, pp. 181–224). Greenwich, CT: JAI Press.

Major, B., Deaux, K. (1982). Individual differences in justice behavior. In J. Greenberg & R. L. Cohen (eds.), *Equity and Justice in Social Behavior* (pp. 43–76). New York: Academic Press.

Mannix, E. A., Neale, M. A., Northcraft, G. B. (1995). Equity, equality, or need? The effects of organizational culture on the allocation of benefits and burdens. *Organizational Behavior and Human Decision Processes, 63*, 276–286.

March, J. (1994). *A Primer on Decision-Making: How Decisions Happen*. New York: Free Press.

Markóczy, L. (2004). Multiple motives behind single acts of co-operation. *International Journal of Human Resource Management, 15*, 1018–1039.

Marwell, G., Ames, R. E. (1979). Experiments on the provision of public goods. I: Resources, interest, group size, and the free-rider problem. *American Journal of Sociology, 84*, 1335–1360.

Meeker, B. F., Elliott, G. C. (1987). Counting the costs: Equity and the allocation of negative group products. *Social Psychology Quarterly, 50*, 7–15.

Messick, D. M. (1995). Equality, fairness, and social conflict. *Social Justice Research, 8*, 153–173.

Messick, D. M., Brewer, M. B. (1983). Solving social dilemmas: A review. In L. Wheeler & P. Shaver (eds.), *Review of Personality and Social Psychology* (pp. 11–44). Beverly Hills, CA: Sage Publications.

Messick, D. M., Sentis, K. P. (1979). Fairness and preference. *Journal of Experimental Social Psychology, 15*, 418–434.

Pillutla, M. M., Chen, X. -P. (1999). Social norms and cooperation in social dilemmas: The effects of context and feedback. *Organizational Behavior and Human Decision Processes, 78*, 81–103.

Schroeder, D. A., Steel, J. E., Woodell, A. J., Bembenek, A. F. (2003). Justice within social dilemmas. *Personality and Social Psychology Review, 7*, 374–387.

Schwinger, T., Lamm, H. (1981). Justice norms in allocation decisions: Need consideration as a function of resource adequacy for complete need satisfaction, recipients' contributions, and recipients' interpersonal attraction. *Social Behavior and Personality, 9*, 235–241.

Scott, J. F. (1971). *Internalization of Norms*. Englewood Cliffs, NJ: Prentice-Hall.

Sherif, M. (1966). *The Psychology of Social Norms*. New York: Harper Torchbooks.

Sondak, H., Neale, M. A., Pinkley, R. L. (1995). The negotiated allocation of benefits and burdens: The impact of outcome valence, contribution, and relationship. *Organizational Behavior and Human Decision Processes, 64*, 249–260.

Tenbrunsel, A. E., Messick, D. M. (1999). Sanctioning systems, decision frames, and cooperation. *Administrative Science Quarterly, 44*, 684–707.

Törnblom, K. Y. (1992). The social psychology of distributive justice. In K. R. Scherer (ed.), *Distributive Justice from an Interdisciplinary Perspective* (pp. 177–284). Cambridge: Cambridge University Press.

Törnblom, K. Y., Ahlin, E. (1998). Mode of accomplishing positive and negative outcomes: Its effects on fairness evaluations. *Social Justice Research, 11*, 423–442.

Törnblom, K. Y., Jonsson, D. R. (1985). Subrules of the equality and contribution principles: Their perceived fairness in distribution and retribution. *Social Psychology Quarterly, 48*, 249–261.

Törnblom, K. Y., Jonsson, D. R. (1987). Distribution vs. retribution: The perceived justice of the contribution and equality principles for cooperative and competitive relationships. *Acta Sociologica, 30*, 25–52.

Tyler, T. R. (1994). Psychological models of the justice motive. *Journal of Personality and Social Psychology, 67*, 850–863.

Tyler, T. R. (2005). Managing conflicts of interest within organizations: Does activating social values change the impact of self-interest on behavior? In D. A. Moore, D. M. Cain, G. Loewenstein, & M. H. Bazerman (eds.), *Conflicts of Interest: Challenges and Solutions in Business, Law, Medicine, and Public Policy* (pp. 13–35). New York: Cambridge University Press.

Tyler, T. R., Dawes, R. M. (1993). Fairness in groups: Comparing the self-interest and social identity perspectives. In B. A. Mellers & J. Baron (eds.), *Psychological Perspectives on Justice: Theory and Applications* (pp. 87–108). New York: Cambridge University Press.

Tyler, T. R., Degoey, P. (1995). Collective restraint in social dilemmas: Procedural justice and social identification effects on support for authorities. *Journal of Personality and Social Psychology, 69*, 482–497.

Tyler, T. R., Lind, E. A. (1992). A relational model of authority in groups. In M. Zanna (ed.), *Advances in Experimental Social Psychology* (Vol. 25, pp. 115–191). San Diego: Academic Press.

Van Dijk, E., Grodzka, M. (1992). The influence of endowments asymmetry and information level on the contribution to a public step good. *Journal of Economic Psychology, 13*, 329–342.

Van Dijk, E., Wilke, H. A. M. (1993). Differential interests, equity, and public good provision. *Journal of Experimental Social Psychology, 29*, 1–16.

Van Dijk, E., Wilke, H. A. M. (1995). Coordination rules in asymmetric social dilemmas: A comparison between public good dilemmas and resource dilemmas. *Journal of Experimental Social Psychology, 31*, 1–27.

Van Dijk, E., Wilke, H. (2000). Decision-induced focusing in social dilemmas: Give-some, keep-some, take-some, and leave-some dilemmas. *Journal of Personality and Social Psychology, 78*, 92–104.

Van Dijk, E., Wilke, H., Wilke, M., Metman, L. (1999). What information do we use in social dilemmas? Environmental uncertainty and the employment of coordination rules. *Journal of Experimental Social Psychology, 35*, 109–135.

Van Lange, P. A. M., Liebrand, W. B. G., Messick, D. M., Wilke, H. A. M. (1992). Introduction and literature review. In W. Liebrand, D. M. Messick, & H. Wilke (eds.), *Social Dilemmas: Theoretical Issues and Research Findings* (pp. 3–28). Oxford: Pergamon.

Wade-Benzoni, K. A., Tenbrunsel, A. E., Bazerman, M. H. (1996). Egocentric interpretations of fairness in asymmetric, environmental social dilemmas: Explaining harvesting behavior and the role of communication. *Organizational Behavior and Human Decision Processes, 67*, 111–126.

Weber, J. M., Kopelman, S., Messick, D. M. (2004). A conceptual review of decision making in social dilemmas: Applying a logic of appropriateness. *Personality and Social Psychology Review, 8*, 281–307.

Wilke, H. A. M. (1991). Greed, efficiency and fairness in resource management situations. In
    W. Stroebe & M. Hewstone (eds.), *European Review of Social Psychology* (Vol. 2, pp. 165–187).
    New York: Wiley & Sons.
Wilke, H. A. M., De Boer, K. L., Liebrand, W. B. G. (1986). Standards of justice and quality of
    power in a social dilemma situation. *British Journal of Social Psychology, 25,* 57–65.
Wit, A., Wilke, H., Oppewal, H. (1992). Fairness in asymmetric social dilemmas. In W. Liebrand,
    D. Messick, & H. Wilke (eds.), *Social Dilemmas: Theoretical Issues and Research Findings*
    (pp. 183–197). Oxford: Pergamon.

Chapter 7
Bringing Back Leviathan into Social Dilemmas

Mizuho Shinada and Toshio Yamagishi

Introduction

More than three and a half centuries ago, the great ancestor of the contemporary social dilemma researchers, Thomas Hobbes, published the most influential book on social dilemmas ever (Hobbes, 1651) and argued that social order cannot be maintained without authority that controls individuals' unrestricted pursuit of self-interest. According to Hobbes, people who prefer peace (mutual cooperation) to a war of all against all (mutual defection) should agree to give birth to *Leviathan*, or a government or authority that enforces social order.

In "the tragedy of commons," Garrett Hardin (1968) talks about the modern version of the Hobbesian problem of social order. In this influential article, Hardin uses a parable of English commons to illustrate how and why communities fail to maintain their resources. Consider the pasture that is open to all herdsmen in a village. Suppose there is no rule for regulating the use of the pasture or social institutions that enforce such rules. Each herdsman can freely add his sheep on the common pasture. The increase in the demand for wool in fact induced English villagers to add more sheep than the pasture could sustain. This "rational" behavior of each herdsman produced depletion of grasses on the commons. This familiar parable drew the attention of the general public in the 1970s when people became aware of resource problems on a global scale. Hardin's (1968) recommendation for the prevention of the "tragedy" echoes that of Hobbes'; he recommended that coercion—"coercion, mutually agreed upon by the majority of the people affected" (Hardin, 1968, p. 1247)—not conscience, provides a solution to the tragedy. He even stated that "a call for voluntary compliance would be counterproductive" (Hardin, 1977, p. 129).

Hardin's recommendation for coercion as the solution to the social dilemma problem created much controversy in various fields, inviting criticism because of its brutal Hobbesian appearance (Crowe, 1969; Fox, 1985; Lynn & Oldenquist, 1986; Stillman, 1975; Taylor, 1976, 1982). Subsequent studies of social dilemmas in psychology mostly ignored the recommendation—mutual coercion mutually agreed upon—by the two giants of social dilemma research, and mostly focused on how and among whom "voluntary compliance" emerges (for reviews of psychological studies of social dilemmas, see Dawes, 1980; Kollock, 1998; Messick & Brewer, 1983; Stroebe &

A. Biel et al. (eds.), *New Issues and Paradigms in Research on Social Dilemmas.*
© Springer 2008

Frey, 1982), except for limited and sporadic attempts to pursue psychological implications of their recommendations (e.g., Yamagishi, 1988a, b). Meanwhile, the two giants' recommendations have met much warmer greetings in economics. Another earlier giant in social dilemma research, Mancur Olson (1965), emphasized selective incentives as a solution to the public-good problem even before Hardin's (1968) influential article, though not as early as Hobbes'. Especially during the last decade, experimental economists have revitalized social dilemma researchers' interest in "coercion" as a solution to the social dilemma problem. The purpose of this chapter is to provide a review of the studies and findings on the use and effectiveness of sanctions conducted in recent years mostly by experimental economists, and add a few suggestions for future studies from social psychological perspectives.

Experimental research on social dilemmas in economics has grown rapidly for the past couple of decades. Economics was once regarded as a non-experimental science like astronomy (Samuelson & Nordhaus, 1985) when Hardin's article and Olson's book were published; it was taken for granted that economic activities were so complicated that manipulating theoretically relevant factors while controlling for relevant other factors was impossible. However, this view has changed drastically between 1948, when the first experiment in economics was conducted to test the neoclassical theory of perfect competition (Chamberlin, 1948), and 2002, when Vernon Smith, who participated in Chamberlin's experiment as a graduate student, received a Nobel Prize in economics. In the interim, experimental economists have produced experimental evidence against the assumption of *homo economicus,* who cares only for his or her own self-interest. For example, the contribution rate for public good is persistently higher than the zero predicted by such a self-interested model of humans (Isaac et al., 1984; see Ledyard, 1995; Rabin, 1998 for reviews).

The discrepancy between the traditional theory and experimental results has driven several economists to develop a theory of "social preferences" that incorporates preferences for other-regarding behavior as well as self-interested behavior (Camerer, 2003; Fehr & Schmidt, 1999; Levine, 1998; Rabin, 1993). Similar to their counterpart in social psychology—researchers of social value orientation—they explain individual differences in social behavior in terms of differences in social preferences. Faced with experimental evidence indicating other-regarding social preferences including preferences for fairness and reciprocity, the main concern of rationally minded economists has increasingly focused on the development of theories to explain why humans have such other-regarding social preferences. For them (as well as for the authors of this chapter), explaining social preferences means finding adaptive advantages for acquiring such preferences. The question is, under what socio-institutional arrangement does the behavior guided by such preferences bring in self-interest (or interest to one's kin who shares one's gene)? One promising theoretical direction in this endeavor of explaining other-regarding preference or behavioral pattern has been provided by studies of indirect reciprocity (Brandt & Sigmund, 2005; Nowak & Sigmund, 1998; Takahashi & Mashima, 2003). In a generalized exchange system, being conditionally altruistic toward other conditional altruists makes the conditional altruist more successful than egoists in procuring resources. Another promising theoretical development is in the direction of "strong reciprocity" (Fehr & Fischbacher, 2003;

Gintis, 2000), which includes sanctioning behavior. The adaptive advantage of having a preference for strong reciprocity and sanctioning against free riders (often called the altruistic punishment or third-party punishment; Fehr & Fischbacher, 2004; Fehr & Gächter, 2002) has been proposed based on some evolutionary mechanisms such as cultural transmission and cultural group selection (Fehr & Fischbacher, 2003; Fehr et al., 2002). Our goal in this chapter is to give a sample of research on sanctioning behavior mostly conducted during the last decade by experimental economists. The rest of this chapter is organized into three sections. The first section provides a brief review of research findings about solving social dilemmas in psychology, especially focusing on "structural solutions" (Messick & Brewer, 1983). In the second section, we will look at some of the recent studies of sanctions, most of which are conducted by experimental economists. In the third section, we will propose possible contributions that psychologists can provide to the study of sanctions in social dilemmas.

The Structural Approach to Solving Social Dilemmas

According to Messick and Brewer (1983), solutions to the social dilemma problem are more or less classified as either individual solutions or structural solutions. Individual solutions are the ones that alter individual cognition and motivation to make them more willing to engage in cooperative behavior. Researchers who are interested in individual solutions study factors that affect individuals' behavior in social dilemmas such as communication (Bixenstine & Douglas, 1967; Bixenstine et al., 1966; Rapoport et al., 1962), information about others' choices (Dawes et al., 1977), trust in other group members (Messick et al., 1983), social values and responsibility (McClintock & Liebrand, 1988; Sweeney, 1973; Van Lange et al., 1997; Van Lange & Kuhlman, 1994), ingroup identity (Kramer & Brewer, 1984, 1986), self-monitoring (Boone et al., 1999; Danheiser & Granziano, 1982; De Cremer et al., 2001; Kurzban & Houser, 2001), and personal history and experience (Bettenhausen & Murnighan, 1985, 1991).

While advancing research on individual solutions, psychologists also pursued possibilities of structural solutions. Structural solutions alter the incentive structure of a social dilemma in such a way as to eliminate inconsistency between individuals' incentives and collective consequences. To change the payoff structure directly is the most straightforward implementation of a structural solution. A large number of studies were conducted to investigate how changes in the payoff structure affect participants' cooperative behavior. Results of these studies generally support the view that participants' cooperation behavior is negatively related to the cost of cooperation and positively tied to the benefit of cooperation (Bonacich et al., 1976; Goehring & Kahan, 1976; Kelley & Grzelak, 1972; Komorita et al., 1980; Marwell & Ames, 1979, 1980; Stern, 1976; Yamagishi, 1988a). Changes in the payoff structure may also involve the form of the production function rather than the magnitude of the cost and benefit of cooperation. The form of the production function that translates contributions made by the group members to the level of the public good produced include linear, disjunctive, conjunctive, step-level, and other forms (Dawes et al., 1986; Sato & Yamagishi, 1986; Van de Kragt et al., 1983; Yamagishi & Sato, 1986). Van de Kragt et al. (1983) reported that introducing the minimal contributing sets (MCS) enhances cooperation. Participants in their study were told that the public good would be supplied only if a specified number of contributors (or more) were reached. The provision rates were higher in the MCS condition than in a linear condition in which the level of public good was linearly related to the number of contributors. Dawes et al. (1986) found similar results. Yamagishi and Sato (1986) found that fear and greed play different roles with different forms of the production function. Other structural changes that were found to enhance cooperative behavior is small group size (Bonacich et al., 1976; Fox & Guyer, 1977; Marwell & Schmidt, 1972), territorialization of the commons (Cass & Edney, 1978; Messick & McClelland, 1983), and leadership (Messick et al., 1983).

Changes to the payoff structure can be introduced through administration of sanctions or selective incentives in the form of punishments of non-cooperators and rewards for cooperators. Caldwell (1976) was the first to examine the effect of mutual sanctioning in an n-person prisoner's dilemma game. In this study, participants played several trials of a five-person prisoner's dilemma game. They were randomly assigned to one of three conditions: the information-only condition, the talk-only condition, and the sanction condition. In the information-only condition, participants played a repeated n-person prisoner's dilemma game with feedback information about other players' decisions. Participants in the talk-only condition were allowed to talk with other members. Participants in the sanction condition were given opportunities to vote to impose penalties on each member, though the penalty did not cost any to the voters, in addition to talk with other members. The results clearly showed the effect of punishments; the opportunity for sanctions raised the level of cooperation from 46% to 65%, while communication per se did not significantly yield higher cooperation. Subsequent studies of punishment (Sato, 1987; Yamagishi, 1986a, 1988a, b, 1992) provided further evidence of the effectiveness of sanctions for enhancing cooperation in social dilemmas.

Demonstration of the power of punishment as a means to improve cooperation in social dilemmas failed to instigate much interest among social dilemma researchers; rather, it was met with serious criticisms. Most criticisms against the use of sanctions concerned either psychological or structural "side effects" of the use of sanctions. First, the negative psychological consequences of administrating sanctions have been pointed out. The negative psychological implications are summarized in Taylor's view that sanctions are like drugs; the more we use it, the more we need it (Taylor, 1976). Sanctions may work as a source of overjustification (Lepper et al., 1973) of intrinsic motivation for cooperation and thus destroy intrinsic motivation for cooperation (Yamagishi, 1990a). Enforcement of sanctions also destroys sense of community (Fox, 1985; Taylor, 1976, 1982) and sometimes makes people strive for uncontrolled means to free-ride (Bell et al., 1989; Mulder et al., 2003). The negative effects of sanctions to reduce intrinsic motivation for cooperation pointed out by these people have long escaped empirical investigation, but Mulder et al. (2006) recently demonstrated this effect in their study in which the experience of playing a public-good game under the threat of sanctions reduces participants' level of cooperation once the threat is removed, even below the level that prevailed before experiencing sanctions.

The structural implications of sanctions concern several issues. The first issue is how to reach an agreement about the sanctioning rules. Hobbes' Leviathan is created by the consent of the people who prefer peace to war. Similarly, Hardin (1968) emphasized that mutual coercion as a solution to the social dilemma problem has to be mutually agreed upon. Given the diversity in interests and values among major players in the real-life social dilemma makes it extremely hard for them to agree on a particular rule for sanctions (Crowe, 1969). The second issue concerns the cost for enforcing sanctions. In the extreme example of a totalitarian regime, damages to psychological welfare and quality of life may be imposed by strict enforcement of sanctions (Lynn & Oldenquist, 1986). Even in a more liberal regime, the administrative cost of enforcing sanctions may exceed the benefits produced by the enhanced level of cooperation (Edney & Harper, 1978; Tullock, 1977). How to share and provide the cost for enforcing sanctions is the central issue in the structural implications of sanctions. This is often called the *second-order social dilemma problem* (Oliver, 1980; Yamagishi, 1986a, b). Once sufficient sanctions are provided and make all people cooperate for the provision of a public good, everyone benefits from the public good regardless of whether or not one participated in the sanctioning activities. In this regard, sanctions are a public good and face the same problem that the original public good faces. It is not individually rational—against one's own short-term self-interest— to engage in sanctioning activities, in the same way contributions to a public good are not rational. If this is, in fact, the case, sanctions create a new dilemma in the way of solving the original dilemma problem (Yamagishi, 1986a, b).

Partly because of these difficulties that sanctions as a solution to the social dilemma problem face, and partly because of psychologists' intrinsic interest in psychological issues rather than social structural issues, structural solutions in general, and sanctions as a means for structural changes in particular, have never received a wide array of attention among psychologists working on the problem of social dilemmas, except in applied studies of real-life problems such as traffic congestion (Van Vugt et al., 1996a, b) and surveillance and monitoring in companies (Tenbrunsel & Messick, 1999). During the last couple of decades, in which psychologists have been more or less silent on structural solutions, economists have picked up the topic and have developed an impressive array of research. In the following section, we will review the recent studies on sanctions conducted mostly by experimental economists.

Research on Sanctions and Sanctioning Behavior

As we mentioned above, most of the research on sanctions is conducted by experimental economists. We refer you to Camerer (2003), Kagel and Roth (1995), and Rabin (1998) for an overview of the research by experimental economists on social dilemmas in general and, instead, focus our discussion on their studies of sanctions. Let us start with a brief discussion of a particular feature of the sanctioning studies conducted by experimental economists; most of their studies deal with sanctions as individual behavior to another individual rather than a behavior taken by an institution that imposes a penalty on free riders. This feature of sanctions that experimental economists study is appropriate when the goal of the researchers is in individuals' motivations or preferences that make them sanction other people, rather than the effectiveness of various enforcing schemes. In other words, their orientation in their sanctioning studies is very much psychological rather than structural. This orientation creates a fertile ground for exchanges of ideas and research activities between psychologists and economists, as we will discuss in the next section of this chapter.

Their rather psychological orientation goes back to the "surprising" finding that people actually expend their own resources (viz. money) to retaliate unfair treatments by others (Guth et al., 1982; Fehr & Fischbacher, 2003). This finding is no surprise to psychologists who have been studying such behavior with such descriptive theories as equity theory (Adams, 1963) and frustration-aggression hypothesis (Dollard et al., 1939). However, such findings were, in fact, surprising for economists who had been operating under the assumption that people maximize their own payoffs. Rejection of unfair offers in ultimatum game experiments with monetary costs to the participant that sometimes are worth a few months' earnings (Cameron, 1999; Fehr et al., 2002) surprised some economists and prompted them to pursue a new model of humans that is capable of explaining such behavior. The result of this endeavor came out as new theories of social preference that explain irrational, fairness-based behavior observed in ultimatum and related games (Bolton, 1998; Falk & Fischbacher, 2006; Sobel, 2005).

One way of explaining social preference that produces behavior reducing payoff to the individual such as cooperation, retaliation, and pursuit of fairness is to regard it as a means to enhance the long-term benefit to the individual or to those genetically related to him. For example, cooperation between genetically related individuals, or altruistic behavior toward kin members, can be a means to enhance inclusive fitness, as presented in the theory of kin selection (Hamilton, 1964). Cooperation in a long-lasting relationship can be explained in terms of reciprocal altruism (Axelrod & Hamilton, 1981; Trivers, 1971) that is equivalent to the tit-for-tat strategy in repeated PD games (Axelrod & Hamilton, 1981). The theories of indirect reciprocity (Milinski et al., 2001; Nowak & Sigmund, 1998) and costly signaling (Zahavi, 1977) suggest that cooperation can evolve even in large groups when cooperators build up reputations through cooperative, altruistic, and/or fairness-enhancing behavior. While admitting that the ultimate causes of social preferences are founded on fitness-enhancing mechanisms such as those mentioned above and others including cultural transmission and cultural group selection (Boyd et al., 2003), experimental economists who take the social preference approach aspire to demonstrate the existence of social preferences that make people engage in behavior that reduces their own immediate payoff. In order to demonstrate the existence of such social preferences, their experiments are designed to eliminate the possibility of explaining their target behavior in terms of long-term, indirect benefits to the actor herself *within the experimental setting*. That is, their experiments are typically designed to allow them to draw a conclusion that the participant's social preferences can be the sole explanation of the target behavior; no long-term, indirect implications of the behavior to her self-interest that explain the behavior exist in the experimental settings.

Research on sanctioning behavior by experimental economists more or less share this design feature with their studies of social preferences in general. Fehr and Gächter (2002), for example, showed in their influential article experimental findings from a study using such a design feature that people engage in altruistic punishment that brings no benefit to the participants themselves while being costly to them. This study stimulated other researchers' interests in sanctioning behavior and prompted subsequent studies, some of which we show next.

Altruistic Punishment

Cooperation in public-good games has been widely studied in psychology and economics in both repeated and one-shot experiments. Yamagishi (1986a, 1988a, b, 1992) studied sanctions in repeated public-good games. And yet, Fehr and Gächter (2002) were the first to study a public-good game with sanctions in a repeated one-shot setting. They examined the effect of the opportunity of mutual sanctions among group members in a public-good game. Each round of their game consisted of two stages. In the first stage, participants decided on the level of their contribution for a four-person public good as described below. In each trial they received an endowment of 20 money units (MUs), and each contributed any units of it (between 0 and 20 MUs) to a group project. They kept the money that they did not contribute. For every MU invested in the project, each of the four group members earned 0.4 MUs, whereas 1 MU that participants kept was exactly 1 MU. If all group members kept all MUs, each participant earned only 20 MUs, while if all of them invested their 20 MUs, each of them would earn $0.4 \times 80 = 32$ MUs. After the decision, they were informed about the investments by each of the other participants. In the second stage, participants assigned in the punishment condition decided how many MU points (between 0 and 10) they would use to reduce earnings of each of the other group members. For each point a participant used, three points were subtracted from the target member's earnings. This game was repeated for six trials, while group membership changed from trial to trial such that no participant ever met another participant more than once. In this repeated one-shot design, there was no opportunity for reputation building and direct reciprocity since participants never met anyone who knew what they had done in the previous games; thus, punishers were not able to expect any indirect benefit (through enhanced reputation) from engaging in costly punishment. Their punishment might enhance the target member's cooperation in future trials, but when it happened, they would not be in the same group and thus would not enjoy the benefit of enhanced cooperation from the target member. This feature of the game makes it impossible to explain the participant's punishment behavior in terms of his long-term benefit. Punishment behavior in this game is thus purely altruistic, since the benefit produced by the costly punishment goes only to others. Fehr and Gächter (2002) call such punishment in the repeated one-shot game "altruistic punishment." They found that 84% of the participants in the punishment condition punished at least once, and 34% punished more than five times during the six trials. The effect of punishment was very clear. The average contribution in the punishment condition was higher than that in the no-punishment condition in any of the periods. In the final period, 59% of the participants in the no-punishment condition contributed nothing, while 39% in the punishment condition contributed their entire endowment. Fehr and Gächter (2000) also included another condition in which participants kept interacting with the same set of members (partner condition) and compared the effect of punishment in the repeated one-shot game (stranger condition). They found that the contribution rate was much higher in the punishment/partner condition (close to 100% toward the end of repeated trials) than in the punishment/stranger condition (of which the overall cooperation rate was 58%), whereas contributions in the no-punishment/stranger condition approached zero toward the end of repeated trials. They found not much difference in the use of sanctions between the partner and the stranger conditions. In either condition, those whose contribution levels were above average were hardly punished at all, whereas among the below-average contributors, the degree to which their contributions fell short of the average was strongly related to the amount of punishment they received. Furthermore, the size of punishment given to free riders at each level of free riding (i.e., the size of deviation from the average) was not much different between the two conditions either. These results suggest that punishment behavior is mostly based on a social preference rather than considerations of long-term self-interest.

Carpenter and Matthews (2002) reported that participants pay costs for punishing free riders in another group as well as in their own group. Their participants were assigned to a 4-person group whose members stayed through all 10 periods (i.e., equivalent to the partner condition in Fehr & Gächter, 2000). The experimental session consisted of two separate four-person groups playing the same public-good game simultaneously and independently of each other. Participants benefited only from their group's contribution to a public good. However, they were provided with opportunities to punish any one of the other seven players regardless of which group they belonged to. Since the group membership stayed the same during the 10 trials, punishing members of their own group may serve the punisher's own interest through enhancing other members' cooperation level. However, punishing members of the other group was useless as a means to improve their self-interest; it only helped the cooperation level in the other group. They found that opportunities to punish only members of their own group raised contributions as in the partner treatment in Fehr and Gächter (2000). They also found that when participants were provided with opportunities to punish outgroup members as well as ingroup members, cooperation rates increased even more, higher than in the condition in which only ingroup punishment was allowed. About 50% of participants punished outgroup members at least once, whereas they punished ingroup members much more heavily than outgroup members.

These experimental results suggest that people punish non-cooperators even when there is no possibility that their punishment behavior improves their self-interest. These findings made the researchers conclude that at least some of the punishment behavior observed in their studies is based on the participants' social preference that internally instigates them to engage in punishment behavior. The social preference for punishing non-cooperators, however, may not be strong enough to overcome fear of retaliation. Most experimental studies of sanction behavior share a design feature of anonymity of punishers. That is, participants are informed of who contributed how much, but are not typically informed who punished whom. This feature provides the punisher immunity from retaliation from the punished. When this immunity from retaliation was not provided in an experiment in which the punisher's identity was revealed, Nikiforakis (2004) found that opportunities of punishment did not have a positive effect on cooperation.

While the above studies suggest that punishment behavior is not a strategy to ensure long-term self-interest, it has been shown not to be free of cost-benefit considerations. Anderson and Putterman (2006), using a repeated one-shot game, showed punishment behavior to increase as the cost for the punishment was reduced. Their participants repeated a voluntary contribution game in a three-person group with a different set of players for each trial. They manipulated the costs of punishment as a within-subject factor over five trials; 0 to 120 experimental cents were required to subtract one experimental dollar from the earnings of the target of punishment. Their results indicate that the size of punishment administered by the participants was negatively related to its cost for the punisher, and positively related to the target member's degree of free riding. The negative relationship between the size of punishment and the cost of punishment was robustly observed at each level of the target's free riding. Carpenter (forthcoming-a) conducted an experiment similar to Anderson and Putterman's (2006) and reported that a 1% increase in the cost of punishment reduces the quantity of punishment delivered by 1.22%. There results, taken together with the result that people punish free riders even when they earn nothing from such behavior, suggest that people derive psychological satisfaction from punishing free riders, but they pay to "purchase" the satisfaction.

Motivations Behind Sanctions

Based on the evidence provided by several studies that people pay substitute costs to deliver punishment while expecting no return for it, some researchers think that they are ready to pose a new question: "It is no longer the question whether there is informal sanctioning. The problem, which is not yet understood, however, is why people sanction and, in particular, why they sanction others' cooperative or defective behavior" (Falk et al., 2005, p. 2017). As shown below, the answer to this question requires information about who punishes whom. In earlier studies that used punishment schemes that were prepared by the researcher (McCusker &

Carnevale, 1995; Yamagishi, 1986a, b, 1992), the target of punishment—the least cooperative member—was fixed and thus was not the topic of the study. The earlier researchers overlooked this issue simply because they assumed that punishments would be directed to free riders. This assumption is mostly true. Most punishments are imposed by cooperative members on less cooperative members. In Fehr and Gächter (2002), 74.2% of all punishments were delivered by above-average contributors and directed to below-average contributors. Also, as mentioned earlier, Fehr and Gächter (2000) and Carpenter and Matthews (2002) found that most punishments were directed toward below-average contributors. How shall we explain this pattern? Price et al. (2002) proposed an evolutionary explanation, *fitness differential theory*, of why cooperators punish defectors. According to this explanation, cooperative behavior cannot evolve in a population of "egoists" unless cooperators eliminate the benefits free riders earn. They further argued that punishment eliminates free riders' fitness advantage by reducing free riders' earnings. Since the "goal" of punishment in evolutionary terms is in the reduction or reversal of free riders' fitness advantage, the proximate or psychological mechanism to execute this "goal" should be found in a punitive sentiment or a desire to harm free riders. This evolutionary "goal" is achieved by harming free riders more than the cost they bear to impose such harm to free riders. In other words, people should have a competitive social value orientation—maximization of relative gain—toward free riders. This kind of social value or social preference, they argue, is likely to be "hardwired" into our motivational circuitry, and that is why game players punish free riders even when it is costly to do so.

According to the fitness differential theory briefly summarized above, cooperators should punish free riders because a penalty reduces free riders' payoffs more than it reduces the punisher's payoffs. However, Falk et al. (2005) found that cooperators punish defectors even when the punishment does not reduce the payoff difference between the punisher and the punished. Participants in their study played a one-shot, three-person prisoner's dilemma game. They first decided whether or not to cooperate and then were provided with an opportunity to subtract money from each of the other group members. However, delivering punishment in one condition of this study was very costly; the cost for delivering punishment is as expensive as the harm delivered to the target. That is, they were required to pay one token to subtract one token from the target. They compared this condition with another condition in which punishment was less costly—1 token afforded 2.5 to 3.3 tokens of punishment. They were informed of all members' choices in the public-good game and decided how much they should pay to subtract money from each of the other three. In the less costly punishment (1 token affording 2.5 to 3.3 tokens of penalty) condition, 69% of cooperators paid costs to reduce defectors' earnings, and only 7% of them paid costs to reduce cooperators' earnings. In the high-cost condition in which one token afforded one token of penalty, the pattern was almost exactly the same; 60% of cooperators punished defectors and none of them punished cooperators. Furthermore, a similar but less pronounced pattern of punishing defectors regardless of the fine-to-fee ratio was observed among defectors. When punishment was effective (1:2.5–3.3), 40% of defectors punished other defectors, and 34% of them punished cooperators. When punishment was costly (1:1), only 2% of defectors punished other defectors, and none of them punished cooperators. These findings are inconsistent with the fitness differential theory proposed by Price and his associates, since, first of all, defectors punish other defectors, and, second, cooperators (and defectors) deliver punishment in the same way when such behavior does not eliminate or reduce free riders' advantages as when it eliminates or reduces the difference. That is, cooperators' punitive behavior was not driven by competitive social preference as assumed in the fitness advantage theory. Falk et al. (2005) suggested that retaliation (i.e., the desire to harm those who committed unfair acts, rather than to reduce the fitness advantage of free riders) seems to be the most likely motive for punishment by cooperators, not spiteful or competitive motivation (i.e., the desire to maximize the payoff difference between self and other).

Falk and his associates also compared the results from the "strategy method" with those from the "specific response method" and found some significant differences between the two. This advises us to use some caution in interpreting the finding of punishment by defectors. With the use of strategy method, participants are provided with a number of scenarios in which other participants' choices are systematically varied and are asked to make their own decision. They are instructed that they will be rewarded for their own and other participants' choices in a randomly chosen scenario. With the use of the specific response method, participants actually face a decision environment and make decisions in a particular environment. The strategy method is similar to the "role-playing experiment" advocated in social psychology in the 1960s and 1970s as a means to avoid using deception (Kelman, 1967). The only difference from the role-playing experiment in social psychology is that participants in the strategy method are actually paid according to their choices in one scenario. While social psychologists have never resolved the problem of internal validity associated with role-playing experiments, economists are more convinced of the validity of the strategy method (Hertwig & Ortmann, 2001). The strategy method has been used frequently in experimental economics because researchers can elicit a large number of responses without actually letting their participants face real decision tasks repeatedly. It also has the advantage of studying the effect of stimuli combinations that rarely occur in natural settings; it is a convenient means to study such effects without artificially creating the stimuli combination by deceiving participants. While some studies report no difference in the results produced by the two methods (e.g., Cason & Mui, 1998; Brandts & Charness, 2000) on some behavior, Falk et al. (2005) reported that 34% of the defectors punished cooperators with the strategy method while only 17% of them did so with the specific response method. Interpretation of such a difference is difficult at this stage. On the one hand, defectors may simply be thinking that they *would* behave in a socially desirable manner when they respond to the strategy method, whereas concerns for self-interest become more salient to them in the specific response method.

Group Size

Group size has been known to be negatively related to the level of cooperation in social dilemmas (e.g., Kerr & Bruun, 1983; Marwell & Schmitt, 1972). The negative effect of group size on cooperation has mostly been attributed to correspondent changes in the incentive structure; for example, benefit from one's own contribution is reduced in larger groups. However, the negative effect of group on cooperation is also observed even when the incentive parameters are kept constant over different group sizes (Bonacich et al., 1976; Sato, 1988; Yamagishi, 1990b), while the negative effect disappears in others studies with the constant parameters (Isaac & Walker, 1988; Isaac et al., 1994). The "residual" negative size effect has been explained in terms of a decline in the influence a change in one's behavior has on other participants (Bonacich et al., 1976; Dawes, 1980; Kerr, 1989) or reduced expectation for other members' cooperation (Yamagishi, 1990b). Compared to the abundance of studies of group size on cooperation, experimental studies of the effect of group size on sanctions is limited. Yamagishi (1992) partially confirmed his prediction, in a comparison of four-person and eight-person groups, that people would be more willing to contribute to the provision of a punishment system in larger groups than in smaller groups. His results showed that high-trusters increased their contribution to the punishment system in larger groups, whereas the effect of group size on punishment was in the opposite direction among low-trusters. Bowles et al. (2001) compared 5-person groups with 10-person groups in a repeated one-shot public-good game with punishment. They also compared MPCR (marginal per capita return; the ratio of benefit from public good allocated to each player to the cost for its provision) in two conditions; it was set at 0.3 in one condition, and 0.5 in the other. After participants were informed of the other members' contribution level, they were provided with an opportunity to reduce other participants' earnings. Each point they paid reduced the punished member's payoff in the same trial by 10%. The results of their study revealed a positive effect of group size on both cooperation and punishment; participants paid more money for delivering punishment and cooperated more in 10-person groups than in 5-person groups. They also showed that MPCR was positively related to both cooperation and punishment. Carpenter (forthcoming-b) also manipulated both group size and MPCR and partially replicated Bowles et al.'s (2001) findings. As in Bowles et al. (2001), Carpenter found a positive relationship between MPCR and both cooperation and punishment. Furthermore, he found more cooperation in larger groups than in smaller groups. However, the effect of group size was in the opposite direction to the one found by Bowles and his associates. Carpenter found that participants delivered less punishment in larger groups than in smaller groups.

Why does group size have a positive effect on cooperation and punishment (though not observed in Carpenter, forthcoming-a) with sanction opportunities present, while it has a negative effect on cooperation in the absence of sanction opportunities? Yamagishi (1992) predicted the positive effect of group size on punishment based on his structural goal/expectation approach. According to the goal/expectation approach proposed by Pruitt and Kimmel (1977), people are motivated to cooperate when they realize the need for mutual cooperation. However, motivation to cooperate is not sufficient for them to actually cooperate. The motivated people need to feel that their goodwill will not be exploited by others. Based on this goal/explanation approach, Yamagishi (1986a, b) proposed that people realize the need for establishing a sanctioning system when the need for mutual cooperation is strongly felt and, at the same time, when they realize voluntarily based mutual cooperation is hard to achieve. Yamagishi (1988a) conducted an experiment to test this idea and found that the seriousness of a social dilemma (greater benefit from cooperation and greater cost of cooperation) induced his participants to contribute more to the establishment of a sanctioning system. Group size is a factor that makes voluntarily based cooperation harder to achieve, and thus, Yamagishi (1992) argued, people are more strongly motivated to contribute to establish a sanctioning system.

In contrast to Yamagishi's (1992) psychological explanation, Casari (2005) proposed a structural explanation of the positive effect of group size on punishment. Casari (2005) argued that how the cost of punishment each player bears is translated to the penalty delivered to a particular player affects the level of punishment provided in general, and how group size is related to the level of punishment, in particular. According to Casari (2005), punishment technologies commonly used in experiments are classified into two categories depending on the fine-to-fee ratio: the "neutral" and the "non-neutral" punishment technologies. A neutral technology lets a player punish another with a constant fine-to-fee ratio in all circumstances. Studies that used this technology include Fehr and Gächter (2002), Sefton et al. (2002), Page et al. (2005), Carpenter (forthcoming-a), Andreoni et al. (2003), and Anderson and Putterman (2006). In contrast, a non-neutral technology allows the fine-to-fee ratio to vary with members' behavior in the first stage. The most extreme case of this technology is when only defectors can be punished, like in a legal system. Fehr and Gächter (2000), Bowles et al. (2001), Carpenter (forthcoming-b), Masclet et al. (2003), and Nikisforakis (2004) adopted this type of technology. For example, in Bowles et al. (2001), the earnings of the punished member in a public-good game were reduced by 10% for each punishment point received. This makes the size of the fine vary according to the earnings of the punished in the public-good game. With the use of this technology, it costs less to deliver the same fine to a cooperator than to a defector who earned more than a cooperator in the public-good game. This should produce the finding that participants spend more of their money to punish defectors than to punish cooperators, even when their goal is to deliver the same level of punishment to defectors and cooperators. If this is, in fact, the case, the generally observed pattern that participants spend more of their own money to punish defectors than cooperators can be artificially inflated than the actual pattern produced by social preference for retaliation, fairness, or spite. Casari (2005) further argued that the positive effect of group size on punishment may be mediated by an increase in the fine-to-fee ratio when a non-neutral technology is used. This is because the total benefit each player receives from a public good increases in larger groups, as in the case of a public good characterized by non-excludability from consumption. The increase in the benefit to each member from the public good also increases the fine-to-fee ratio. The positive effect of group size on cooperation and punishment observed in experiments using a non-neutral technology can be a result of the increase in the fine-to-fee ratio rather than a product of some social preferences. Casari (2005) advised using a neutral punishment technology in the study of social preferences as a motivator of punishment behavior in social dilemmas. Providing a definite answer to the question of whether group size increases sanctioning behavior and cooperation needs to wait for further studies; it is an important topic for future research since it has serious implications for possible solutions in the large-scale social dilemmas we face in real life. Experimental research on social dilemmas has been criticized for a lack of generalizability of its findings, such that what works well in small groups may not work well in larger groups. The positive effect of group size seems to imply that what works fine in small groups will work better in larger groups.

Punishments and Rewards

Comparisons of rewards and punishments as reinforcers are one of the most traditional topics in psychology (Skinner, 1938). In the behaviorist tradition, positive reinforcers (i.e., rewards) are usually more effective than negative ones (i.e., punishments) except in certain conditions (Bandula, 1969; Millenson, 1967). Platt (1973), who analyzed the commons dilemma from the behaviorist perspective, proposed a solution in terms of administration of immediate negative consequences, such as punishment of inappropriate behavior. While the distinction between positive and negative frames drew the attention of social dilemma researchers (social dilemmas versus social fences—see Messick & Brewer, 1983; give-some versus take-some type of social dilemmas—see Hamburger, 1974; Hamburger et al., 1975), and a general conclusion that a positive frame is more conducive to cooperation than a negative frame even when the payoff structures are held constant (Komorita & Barth, 1985), studies that compared positive sanctions (i.e., rewards) and negative sanctions (punishments) are relatively few.

Rapoport and Au's (2001) experiment is an example of such a study; they compared the reward condition with the penalty condition using a repeated one-shot game with no feedback about outcomes in each trial. In each trial, participants played a common pool resource dilemma (Gardner et al., 1990), taking a private share of the resource from a common resource pool. The private share of the common resource pool became theirs insofar as the total amount requested by all the members of a five-person group was kept below a threshold; once the total amount was exceeded, they lost their share. In the reward condition, the member who requested the least amount was given a bonus by the experimenter. In the penalty condition, the experimenter imposed a penalty on the member who requested the largest amount. The size of the bonus and the penalty were the same. Both rewards (bonus) and punishments (penalty) had a positive effect on cooperation, but the effect of punishments was stronger than that of rewards.

However, McCusker and Carnevale (1995) reported a finding from their experiment that is opposite to the finding by Rapoport and Au (2001). Their participants played a repeated dilemma game in a seven-person group consisting of the same set of participants across trials. Information about other players' decisions—actually pre-programmed by the experimenter—was given to the participant. In each trial, participants decided how much to contribute in a public-good game, and then they were given an opportunity to contribute to a "reward fund" (reward condition) or a "penalty fund" (penalty condition). In the reward condition, the sum of money contributed to the reward fund was given to the most cooperative member. In the penalty condition, the sum of money contributed to the penalty fund was deducted from the least cooperative member's earnings. Participants contributed more to the reward fund than to the penalty fund, and their cooperation level was higher in the reward condition than in the penalty condition.

Sefton et al. (2002) compared the effects of rewards, punishments, and the combination of both using a repeated public-good game in a four-person group in which they played with the same set of members while their ID was varied in each trial. After receiving feedback about the members' contributions in the public-good game, their participants were given an opportunity to assign between zero and six tokens to each of the other three members for either punishing or rewarding him. Each token cost 10 cents to the rewarder/punisher and delivered the same 10 cents of reward or fine to the target member. Participants in the reward and punishment condition were given a choice of using the tokens for either rewarding or punishing each of the other members. At the end of each trial, participants were informed of their earnings in that trial, including rewards and/or fines they received. The cooperation level in any one of these three conditions was higher than that in the baseline condition (i.e., no-punishment, no-reward condition). The cooperation level in the public-good game was the highest when participants were able to provide both punishments and rewards (i.e., reward and punishment condition), while no difference was found between the punishments-alone condition and the rewards-alone condition. While the cooperation level was not statistically different between the punishment condition and the reward condition, the use of rewards in the reward condition was less frequent than the use of punishments in the sanction condition. At the same time, the use of rewards was more frequent than the use of punishments in the reward and punishment condition.

Walker and Halloran (2004) found no effect of either punishments or rewards despite the fact that they used a similar design to the one used by Sefton et al. (2002) with the following changes. First, Walker and Halloran (2004) used a repeated one-shot game instead of the repeated game with no history used by Sefton and his associates. Second, no feedback of the other members' rewarding and/or punishing behavior was provided. Finally, the value of each token for punishment or rewarding was much smaller than in the Sefton et al. study; one token for punishments or rewards was worth one-fifth of one token used in the public-good game, while the ratio was one to one in Sefton et al. (2002). The lack of effect of sanctions (either punishments or rewards) and cooperation in this study may be attributed to any one of the three changes in Walker and Halloran's (2004) study. First, the effects on punishments and rewards may require that a game be repeated among the same set of people. Second, the lack of the effect may be due to the unavailability of information about other members' sanctioning behavior rather than to the repeated nature of the game. Finally, the size of punishments and rewards may have been too small to have an impact on participants. To identify the roles that these factors play in sanctioning behavior is an important topic for future study.

An interesting twist to the reward versus punishment controversy concerns the second-order sanctions (Cinyabuguma et al., 2006; Kiyonari et al., 2005, 2007). Second-order sanctions are sanctions on sanctions (punishment of non-punishers, rewarding of rewarders, etc.). One of the criticisms of sanctions as a solution to the social dilemma problem is that sanctions themselves are a public good and thus create a "second-order social dilemma" (Oliver, 1980; Yamagishi, 1986a, b). Axelrod (1986) provided an answer to this criticism in the form of "meta-norms." According to him, meta-norms involve sanctions of non-enforcers of norms (e.g., those who do not punish defectors). If those who enforce norms (those who punish defectors) also enforce meta-norms (punish those who do not punish defectors), and those who do not enforce norms do not enforce meta-norms, the second-order social dilemma problem disappears within a certain range of parameters. Yamagishi and Takahashi (1994) reanalyzed this issue with a computer simulation and concluded that meta-norms are not really needed insofar as the "linkage" or behavioral consistency between two levels of dilemmas exists between the cooperation and punishment, instead of punishment and meta-punishment as argued by Axelrod (1986). In order to test Yamagishi and Takahashi's (1994) claim, Kiyonari et al. (2005, 2007) examined three kinds of behavior—cooperation, punishment, and meta-punishment—in a four-person group. Results of their study show a fair amount of consistency between cooperation and punishment as observed in other studies in which those who punish defectors are mostly cooperators. However, they did not find consistency between punishment and meta-punishment; actually, meta-punishment occurred only very rarely. Kiyonari et al. (2005, 2007) replicated this finding and, in addition, found that the meta-sanctions in the positive direction—i.e., rewards to those who reward cooperators—occur frequently and are consistent with the first-order rewarding (rewards to cooperators). The positive chain of reward giving is likely to survive and prosper as suggested by the indirect reciprocity literature (Brandt & Sigmund, 2005; Milinski et al., 2001; Nowak & Sigmund, 1998; Takahashi & Mashima, 2003), but the negative chain of punishment giving seems to stop at the second step.

Social Sanctions

The studies we presented above all used monetary sanctions in the form of a fine or rewards. This fixation with money is a matter of convenience in conducting research; it is not based on a conviction that only monetary sanctions are important. Social approval and disapproval are important means to control our behavior in social life. Earlier exchange theorists in sociology (Homans, 1961; Emerson, 1972) emphasized the importance of non-monetary rewards and sanctions. Blau (1964) argued that informal sanctions such as peer pressure, gossip, and social ostracism are effective deterrents against defection in social exchange. Some economists who recognize the effects of social sanctions have constructed theoretical models to include peer pressure (Kandel & Lazear, 1992; Barron & Gjerde, 1997) and avoidance of social disapproval (Akerlof, 1980; Hollander, 1990). Bowles and Gintis (2003) proposed an evolutionary model of social emotions according to which some social emotions such as shame coevolve with other emotions motivating punishment of antisocial actions.

Masclet et al. (2003) argued that a sanctioning behavior using monetary fines in Fehr and Gächter (2000) was a vehicle to express disapproval of others' free-riding behavior. They argue that facing expression of disapproval from other members in itself, even without being monetarily penalized, would increase players' level of contribution. They conducted an experiment in which they compared monetary sanctions with non-monetary sanctions. Their participants played a repeated public-good game in a four-person group. They decided on the level of contribution for a public good between 0 to 20 experimental currency units (ECUs). In addition, participants in the non-monetary punishment condition had an opportunity to inform the target member of their level of disapproval. They did not pay for their ECUs for this action. For participants in the monetary punishment condition, the ECUs they spent on punishment were used to reduce the target member's earnings. In this experiment, the non-monetary sanctions—expressions of disapproval—raised the average contribution from 6.6 ECUs in the no-punishment treatment to 8.97 ECUs, while monetary punishment had about twice as strong an effect and raised it from 6.0 ECUs to 11.1 ECUs. The effect of the non-monetary punishment did not emerge in a repeated one-shot game.

Noussair and Tucker (2005) compared three conditions: monetary punishment, non-monetary punishment, and bother punishment—both monetary and non-monetary punishments. The average contribution to the public-good game was higher in the monetary punishment condition than in the non-monetary punishment condition. Furthermore, the average contribution level was not higher in the bother punishment condition than in the monetary punishment condition, indicating that adding non-monetary punishment to monetary punishment did not make people cooperate more. On the other hand, participants' earnings after deducting costs for monetary punishment and fine were larger in the bother punishment condition than in the monetary punishment condition. That is, about the same effect was achieved in the bother punishment condition despite the fact that participants spent less money for punishment when they could express their disapproval. Non-monetary punishment replaced some of the effects of monetary punishment.

The relatively weak power of non-monetary punishment observed in these studies may be due to the fact that disapproval was communicated without face-to-face interactions. The cooperation-enhancing effect of face-to-face communication has been extensively studied since the early days of social dilemma research (e.g., Bixenstine et al., 1966; Brechner, 1977; Dawes et al., 1977; Edney & Harper, 1978; Jerdee & Rosen, 1974; Rapoport et al., 1962), and the well-established effect is, at least partly, due to social approval and disapproval exchanged in face-to-face communication (Ostrom et al., 1992).

The effect of a non-monetary sanction in a face-to-face situation has also been examined outside the laboratory. Barr (2001) reports results of a public-good game with punishment conducted in rural communities in Zimbabwe. Interestingly, participants in this study who had witnessed the disapproval of those who contributed only a small amount increased their contribution by even more than those directly criticized. This result suggests the indirect effect of social disapproval as a warning to the third party, in addition to its direct effect as a punishment to a transgressor. Single-mindedly focusing on the direct effect of non-monetary punishment and concluding that it has only weak power on enhancing cooperation is thus premature; more research is needed on the indirect effect on non-monetary sanctions.

One issue surrounding non-monetary sanctions concerns its costless nature; does the power of non-monetary sanctions depend on its cost-free nature? A study by Carpenter et al. (2004) showing that their participants were willing to pay money to signal their disapproval of free riding suggests that this is not the case. In their study, Thai and Vietnamese participants in urban slums in their respective countries who played a repeated voluntary contribution game with social sanctions paid monetary costs to display a picture of an unhappy face (34% of Thai participants and 25% of Vietnamese participants disapproved at least once).

Net Benefits of Sanctions

Early critics of sanctions as a means to solve social dilemma problems raised the issue that the costs of sanctions may exceed their benefits (Crowe, 1969; Fox, 1985; Lynn & Oldenquist, 1986; Stillman, 1975; Taylor, 1976, 1982). The costs of sanctions include long-term as well as short-term costs. Short-term costs are monetary costs for monitoring free riders and delivering sanctions upon them. Long-term costs include reduction in intrinsic motivation for cooperation (Taylor, 1976; Yamagishi, 1990a) and the sense of community (Fox, 1985; Taylor, 1976, 1982). We will later discuss recent studies on the negative psychological effect of sanctions; we focus on the short-term, monetary costs in this section. As presented earlier in this chapter, most studies of sanctions report the cooperation-enhancing effect of punishment (e.g., Bowles et al., 2001; Carpenter, forthcoming-b; Carpenter & Matthews, 2002; Masclet et al., 2004; Fehr & Gächter, 2002; Yamagishi, 1986, 1988a, b, 1992). However, the short-term monetary costs including both the cost for the punisher as well as the penalty paid by the punished often exceeded the extra benefits derived from the enhanced level of cooperation (Bochet et al., 2006; Carpenter & Matthews, 2002; Ostrom et al., 2002). It seems to be obvious that the net benefit of sanctions depends on several structural factors such as the MPCR of contribution in the public-good game and the fine-to-fee ratio in the sanctioning game. When the MPCR is high, only a small improvement in the cooperation level produces a large benefit, and thus the net benefit of punishment is more likely to be in the black. Also, an improvement in cooperation and the benefit from a public good can be achieved by a small fee when the fine-to-fee ratio is large. In lieu of this interpretation, Yamagishi (1986) found that the net benefit of punishment was positive with a high fine-to-fee ratio, whereas it was negative with a low fine-to-fee ratio. Given the fact that the net effect of sanctions is positive or negative depends on the nature of some parameters characterizing the game, it is impossible to draw a *general* conclusion on the overall benefit of sanctions. Instead of drawing a general conclusion, we need to pay attention to the specifics of the social dilemma problem to see if sanctions are useful and desirable as its solution.

Future Directions

As presented above, most of the recent research on sanctions in social dilemmas has been conducted by experimental economists. This is not surprising given the fact that psychologists are not as interested in social structural factors as social scientists. An interesting irony, however, is that the interest of experimental economists who work on sanctions is mostly focused on the psychology of sanctioning behavior, as briefly discussed earlier. Their primary research goal is to demonstrate the operation of social preferences that make people sanction free riders. It seems to the authors of this chapter that there is a lot for psychologists to contribute to this endeavor. We will present below some recent developments by social psychologists which we think enrich studies of sanctions in social dilemmas. Strong methodological positions taken by experimental economists (cf., Hetwig & Ortmann, 2001)—such as the use of monetary incentives and rules against the use of deception—may keep the fruit of some psychological research from having an impact on economists, but we believe that it will not take too long for an eventual collaboration between the two to emerge since sanctions are the place where psychology meets structure. We will present a few research topics that may turn out to be fertile grounds for psychologists' contributions to the sanctioning research in social dilemmas.

The Dark Side of Sanctions

As mentioned earlier, the use of sanctions advocated by the precursors of social dilemma researchers was heavily criticized because of its potential negative consequences. Social psychologists had been concerned with the negative consequences of extrinsic incentives that occur in the form of depletion of intrinsic motivation (Deci & Ryan, 1985; Lepper et al., 1973). It was thus natural for those who had been trained in social psychology to think about the dark side of sanctions in the context of social dilemmas. The anticipated negative consequences included loss of intrinsic motivation to cooperate and of sense of community (Fox, 1985; Taylor, 1976, 1982; Yamagishi, 1990a) in addition to excessive cost for administrating sanctions (Edney & Harper, 1978; Tullock, 1977). Economists' focus on the motivational foundations of sanctioning behavior, on the other hand, made them less concerned with such negative consequences of sanctions. It is of some interest to note that it is psychologists working in business schools who conducted experimental research on negative psychological consequences of sanctions. Tenbrunsel and Messick (1999) conducted the first experiment focused on the negative psychological consequences of sanctions. In their studies, Tenbrunsel and Messick (1999) compared the strong sanction condition and the weak sanction condition with the no-sanction condition. They found that the cooperation level in the weak sanction condition was lower than that in the no-sanction condition, whereas the cooperation level in the strong sanction condition was higher than that in the no-sanction condition. They explained these findings in terms of the framing effect. Threats of sanctions make participants think of the game situation as one in which people are driven by extrinsic incentives. That is, participants see the game situation in a "business frame" when the threat of sanctions exists. In the absence of such salient extrinsic incentives, participants tend to see the game situation as one in which people seek to cooperate. They see the game in a moral frame (cf. the might-over-morality literature on this issue; Kelley & Stahelski, 1970; Liebrand et al., 1986). In the weak sanction condition, participants see the game in a business frame, and yet the sanctions are not strong enough to make them cooperate as rational actors. When the sanction is strong enough, even those who have adopted a business frame do cooperate since cooperation is a rational strategy under strong sanctions.

Another, more recent study by Mulder et al. (2006) demonstrates that a sanctioning system in social dilemmas undermines trust—the belief that other members are motivated to cooperate. They developed a "removing the sanction" paradigm in which participants play a social dilemma twice. In the first phase, they play a public-good game in which a sanctioning system is either present (sanction condition) or not (no-sanction condition). In the second phase, they play the same game without a sanctioning system in both conditions. The goal of their experiments was to demonstrate that the cooperation level in the second phase is lower in the sanction condition than in the no-sanction condition. This would indicate that the experience of playing a public-good game under a sanctioning system makes them less cooperative once the sanctioning system is taken away. In one of their experiments, participants played a 4-person public-good game in which each decided how many of 100 chips (each worth EUR 0.05) to contribute for the provision of a public good. In addition, the participant who contributed the smallest number of coins faced a fine of EUR 5.00. Their trust—expected contribution by other members—was measured at each phase. The average level of trust in other members in the second phase was found to be lower in the sanction condition than in the no-sanction condition, as expected. Further, participants' level of cooperation in the second phase was found to be lower in the sanction condition, though the difference was not statistically significant. Their second experiment found a significant difference in cooperation between sanction and no-sanction conditions among high-trusters [whose levels of trust were measured through Yamagishi's (1986a) trust scale administered in a pre-experimental questionnaire], though not among low-trusters. Sanctions in this study undermined participants' willingness to trust others and cooperate, when and only when the level of their trust in the absence of sanctions is already high.

Social Value Orientations

Social value orientations in psychology are equivalents of social preferences in economics. One of the social preferences economists consider relevant to sanction behavior is *inequity aversion* (Fehr & Schmidt, 1999; Bolton & Ockenfels, 2000). Its equivalent—equality orientation—has been discussed in the social value orientation (SVO) literature to explain reciprocal or conditional cooperation behavior (Van Lange, 1999; Van Lange et al., 1997). Although the social value orientation literature has focused on behavior in social dilemmas (i.e., cooperation and defection), implications of SVO for sanctioning behavior will be a challenging topic for future research. Since sanctions (either rewards for cooperators or punishments of defectors) reduce the difference in payoffs to cooperators and defections, equality-seekers are the ones who should deliver sanctions. No one has directly examined if this prediction is supported. Pinpointing a particular social value orientation that is directly tied to sanctioning behavior may provide an interesting and challenging avenue for SVO researchers.

In extending the SVO research to include sanctions, one challenge is how to explain sanctions against unintended defection. The concept of SVO has been used in two contexts—consequence-based and rule-based contexts. In the consequence-based model of SVO, inequity-averters are motivated to reduce the payoff difference between cooperators and defectors by rewarding the former and punishing the latter. Intentions of cooperation and defection should not matter in this model. As experiments using truncated ultimatum games have shown, punishment of unintended unfair behavior is rather rare (Falk et al., 2003; Ohmura & Yamagishi, 2005). According to the rule-based model (Messick, 1999; Weber et al., 2004), SVO involves more than differential assignments of weights to various components of utilities. It is also related to the way a game player defines the game situation

("What kind of situation is this?") and the appropriate behavior in that situation ("What would a person like me do in a situation like this?) (Messick, 1999; Weber et al., 2004). In this approach, players make decisions not by comparing utilities of outcomes, but by following rules or heuristics that are appropriate for the situation. SVO is important as an indicator of how a game player defines the game situation and what kind of decision rules or heuristics she applies to it. According to the rule-based view of SVO, the intentions of cooperators and defectors should matter. This is because some of the rules or heuristics are directly tied to the perceived intentions of others. Psychological contributions are of critical importance on this issue.

Ingroup, Outgroup, and Sanctions

Are sanctions directed more toward members of one's own group, or toward members of another group? Does it matter if the sanctions are in the form of rewards or sanctions in determining which group they are directed to? Are rewards directed toward members of one's own group, and punishments more toward members of another group? These are questions of both theoretical and practical importance. There are several competing theoretical grounds to answer these questions. Social identity theory would predict that rewards are directed toward ingroup members (i.e., members of one's own group) and punishments toward outgroup members. This is because providing extra rewards to ingroup members and punishments to outgroup members increases the advantage of ingroup over outgroup, enhancing the positive distinction between the two groups. This prediction competes with another prediction based on the view of sanctions as a means of improving cooperation within one's own group. According to this perspective, paying costs to reward cooperators and punish defectors outside one's own group is a waste, and thus both rewards and punishments should be directed toward ingroup members. And yet, another prediction is possible by adding a "group-selection" aspect to the second perspective. This perspective provides a similar prediction as that from the social identity perspective; rewards toward ingroup members and punishments toward outgroup members provide a fitness advantage to one's own group vis-à-vis other groups. This perspective, however, provides a prediction concerning who in the other group is different from the social identity perspective; *punishing cooperators*, not defectors, in other groups provides a fitness advantage to one's own group. As discussed in the previous section, Carpenter and Mathews' (2002) participants punished ingroup members more than outgroup members in a repeated game, supporting the second approach. Shinada et al. (2004) conducted an experiment in which participants were provided with opportunities to punish members of their own group and those of another group. When they had such opportunities, they had been informed that there would be no future trials, eliminating considerations for future self-interest. Two three-person groups played a public-good game within each group. When the subject was chosen as a "monitor," he was given an opportunity to spend money to reduce the earnings of each of the other two members of his own group and of the three members of the other group. The results of this experiment were rather mixed. Cooperators punished mostly ingroup defectors, whereas defectors punished mostly outgroup defectors. Furthermore, in a partial replication of this in which the fine-to-fee ratio was reduced from 3:1 in the above study to 1:1, defectors stopped punishing outgroup defectors (Shinada et al., 2005). None of the above three approaches can explain these findings. These studies provide more puzzles than answers and invite further theoretical and empirical research efforts.

Goren et al.'s (2005) study addresses another issue of the effect of intergroup conflicts on sanctions. Intergroup conflicts have been known to make people cooperate more within each group (Bornstein & Ben-Yossef, 1994). Goren et al. (2005) hypothesized in this study that intergroup conflicts also promote sanctioning behavior within each group as a means to enhance cooperation there. Although their findings were not strong enough to draw a conclusion on this hypothesis either way, this study points to an important issue to be pursued. Furthermore, recent studies in experimental economics report the "parochial" nature of punishment in real social groups where the members have strong mutual rapport (Bernhard et al., 2006; Goette et al., 2006). Parochial nature of punishment means that third parties are more lenient if the norm violator belongs to their group, whereas they punish outgroup members who harm an ingroup victim. These results are intriguing, but we need to conduct further carefully designed studies before we draw firm conclusions based on the data obtained from real social groups.

Direct and Indirect Effects of Sanctions

We started this chapter with Hobbes. While studies of sanctions seem to represent our renewed interest in Hobbes, the most important insight in his discussion of Leviathan is missing from the contemporary studies of sanctions in social dilemmas. What is missing in the contemporary research on sanctions is Hobbes' insight that Leviathan's role is not in the direct control of its subjects but in the protection of peace. Hobbes starts his argument with the assumption that people come to prefer peace to war of all against all. Using terminology of the contemporary social dilemma research, Hobbes assumed that people are conditional cooperators instead of rational defectors who care only about their own short-term self-interests. People are willing to cooperate if they are assured that their cooperation will not be exploited by others. Leviathan's role is in providing this assurance rather than forcing everyone to cooperate against their will.

Yamagishi's (1986a, b, 1988, 1992) earlier work on the provision of a sanctioning system was based on this idea of Hobbes. In these studies, Yamagishi emphasized the indirect effect of sanctions as a protector of peace rather than the direct effect as a coercer of peace. The costs, psychological as well as monetary, of providing sanctions, he argued, are much lower if the aim of sanctions is to convince conditional cooperators that it is safe to cooperate than if it is to force everyone to cooperate against his or her will. In his earlier studies, however, Yamagishi did not directly investigate the importance of the indirect effect of sanctions vis-à-vis the direct effect of sanctions. Almost two decades after Yamagishi pointed out the importance of the indirect effect of sanctions (and close to four centuries after Hobbes pointed out the same idea), Eek et al. (2002), Loukopoulos et al. (2006), and Shinada & Yamagishi (in press) conducted experiments to demonstrate the importance of the indirect effect of sanctions. Eek et al. (2002) called the indirect effect a "spill-over effect" and studied the relative size of the two types of effects by varying the target of punishment. In one condition, the participant alone was subject to punishment; since other members were not subject to punishment, only the direct effect was expected in this condition. In another condition, all members excluding the participant were subject to punishment; only the indirect effect was expected in this condition. They found a substantial indirect effect among prosocials and no indirect effect among proselfs. In a replication of this experiment, Loukopoulos and his associates (2006) found a significant indirect effect in both prosocials and proselfs, although the size of the indirect effect was only a fraction of the direct effect.

Shinada & Yamagishi (in press) noticed a potential problem in the above experiments that might have artificially reduced the size of indirect effect; the indirect effect was not completely excluded from the direct effect in those experiments. Participants in these studies knew that the other members knew they were subject to punishment; thus, they would be less afraid of their defection. The direct effect manipulation thus could have produced the indirect effect as well. Shinada & Yamagishi (in press) used a different technique and demonstrated that the indirect effect substantially explains the effect of sanctions. Their participants played a three-person, one-shot public-good game, under two punishment conditions. In the global punishment condition, all three members faced punishment. When punished, the amount of money the participant kept was reduced by half. In the direct effect condition, only the participant was told that only he or she had a chance of being punished and that the other two members would not be informed of anything about punishment. Therefore, the participant in the direct effect condition couldn't expect the other members to cooperate under the sanction system since they knew nothing about sanctions. The average cooperation level of participants in the direct punishment condition who faced the possibility of punishment alone (0.43) was greater than that observed in the no-punishment condition (0.30), indicating that the direct effect of punishment can boost cooperation. Players in the global punishment condition who faced punishment together with their group members contributed significantly more money (0.54) compared to those in the direct effect condition. Thus, the size of the indirect effect is almost as big as that of the direct effect.

This result—increased cooperation over and above what was possible by the direct effect alone—provides evidence for the strong indirect effect of punishment. Furthermore, regression analysis indicated that the effect of punishment was mediated by the expectation in the net effect condition; a sanction system has indirectly increased contribution by changing beliefs about others. While not ruling out the importance of the direct effect of punishment, these results demonstrate that "ruling by the sword" alone is insufficient to convince people to behave in a mutually beneficial manner. As Hardin (1968) and Ostrom (1990) argued, the key to a successful sanctioning system is consent by the people involved; voluntary acceptance enhances the efficacy of punishment with the indirect effect. While the direct effect depends more on the actual controlling power of a social institution, the indirect effect depends more on the conviction that other members believe in its power. A sanctioning system supported by a shared belief system would be more effective than sanction by "sword" alone.

Let us conclude this chapter with the following final remark. Sanctions are where psychology meets structure. Studies of sanctioning systems and sanctioning behavior, we believe, will be a fertile ground for a truly interdisciplinary research endeavor to study human cooperation.

References

Adams, J. S. (1963). Toward an understanding of inequity. *Journal of Abnormal and Social Psychology, 67*, 422–436.

Akerlof, G. (1980). A theory of social custom, of which unemployment may be one consequence. *Quarterly Journal of Economics, 94*, 749–775.

Anderson, C. M., Putterman, L. (2006). Do non-strategic sanctions obey the law of demand? The demand for punishment in the voluntary contribution mechanism. *Games and Economic Behavior, 54*, 1–24.

Andreoni, J., Harbaugh, W., Vesterlund, L. (2003). The carrot or the stick: Rewards, punishments, and cooperation. *American Economic Review, 93*, 893–902.

Axelrod, R., Hamilton, W. D. (1981). The evolution of cooperation. *Science, 211*, 1390–1396.

Axelrod, R. (1986). An evolutionary approach to norms. *American Political Science Review, 80*, 1095–1111.

Bandula, A. (1969). *Principles of Behavior Modification*. New York: Holt, Rinehart and Winston.

Barr, A. (June 2001). Social dilemmas and shame-based sanctions: Experimental results from rural Zimbabwe (The Centre for the Study of African Economies Working Paper Series, #149).

Barron, J. M., Gjerde, K. P. (1997). Peer pressure in an agency relationship. *Journal of Labor Economics, 15*, 234–254.

Bell, P. A., Petersen, T. R., Hautaluoma, J. E. (1989). The effect of punishment probability on overconsumption and stealing in a simulated commons. *Journal of Applied Social Psychology, 19*, 1483–1495.

Bernhard, H., Fischbacher, U., Ernst, F. (2006). Parochial altruism in humans. *Nature, 442*, 912–915.

Bettenhausen, K. L., Murnighan, J. K. (1985). The emergence of norms in competitive decision-making groups. *Administrative Science Quarterly, 30*, 350–372.

Bettenhausen, K. L., Murnighan, J. K. (1991). The development of an intragroup norm and the effects of interpersonal and structural challenges. *Administrative Science Quarterly, 36*, 20–35.

Bixenstine, V. E., Douglas, J. (1967). Effect of psychopathology on group consensus and cooperative choice in a six-person game. *Journal of Personality and Social Psychology, 5*, 32–37.

Bixenstine, V. E., Levitt, C. A., Wilson, K. R. (1966). Collaboration among six persons in a prisoner's dilemma game. *Conflict Resolution, 10*, 488–496.

Blau, P. M. (1964). *Exchange and Power in Social Life*. New York: John Wiley and Sons, Inc.

Bochet, O., Page, T., Putterman, L. (2006). Communication and punishment in voluntary contribution experiments. *Journal of Economic Behavior and Organization, 60*, 11–26.

Bolton, G. E. (1998). Bargaining and dilemma games: From experimental data towards theoretical synthesis. *Experimental Economics, 1*, 257–281.

Bonacich, P., Shure, G. H., Kahan, J. P., Meeker, R. J. (1976). Cooperation and group size in the N-person prisoner's dilemma. *Journal of Conflict Resolution, 20*, 687–705.

Boone, C., De Brabander, B., Van Witteloostuijn, A. (1999). The impact of personality on behavior in five prisoner's dilemma games. *Journal of Economic Psychology, 20*, 343–377.

Bornstein, G., Ben-Yossef, M. (1994). Cooperation in intergroup and single-group social dilemmas. *Journal of Experimental Social Psychology, 30*, 52–57.

Bowles, S., Carpenter, J., Gintis, H. (2001). Mutual monitoring in teams: The effects of residual claimancy and reciprocity (Santa Fe Institute working paper #98-08-074E).

Bowles, S., Gintis, H. (2003). Prosocial emotions (Santa Fe Institute working paper #02-07-028).

Boyd, R., Gintis, H., Bowles, S., Richerson, P. J. (2003). The evolution of altruistic punishment. *Proceedings of the National Academy of Sciences of the United States of America, 100*, 3531–3535.

Brandt, H., Sigmund, K. (2005). Indirect reciprocity, image scoring, and moral hazard. *Proceedings of the National Academy of Sciences of the United States of America, 102*, 2666–2670.

Brandts, J., Charness, G. (2000). Hot vs. cold: Sequential responses and preference stability in experimental games. *Experimental Economics, 2*, 227–238.

Brechner, K. C. (1977). An experimental analysis of social traps. *Journal of Experimental Social Psychology, 14*, 552–564.

Brewer, M. B., Kramer, R. M. (1986). Choice behavior in social dilemmas: Effects of social identity, group size, and decision framing. *Journal of Personality and Social Psychology, 50*, 543–549.

Caldwell, M. D. (1976). Communication and sex effects in a five-person prisoner's dilemma game. *Journal of Personality and Social Psychology, 33*, 273–280.

Camerer, C. (2003). *Behavioral Game Theory: Experiments in Strategic Interaction*. Princeton, NJ: Princeton University Press.

Cameron, L. (1999). Raising the stakes in the ultimatum game: Experimental evidence from Indonesia. *Economic Inquiry, 37*, 47–59.

Carpenter, J., Matthews, P. (2002). Social reciprocity (Middlebury College Department of Economics working paper).

Carpenter, J. (forthcoming-a). The demand for punishment. *Journal of Economic Behavior and Organization*.

Carpenter, J. (forthcoming-b). Punishing free-riders: How group size affects mutual monitoring and the provision of public goods. *Games and Economic Behavior*.

Carpenter, J., Matthews, P., Ong'Ong'a, O. (2004). Why punish? Social reciprocity and the enforcement of prosocial norms. *Journal of Evolutionary Economics, 14*, 407–429.

Casari, M. (2005). On the design of peer punishment experiments. *Experimental Economics, 8*, 107–115.

Cason, T., Mui, V. (1998). Social influence in the sequential dictator game. *Journal of Mathematical Psychology, 42*, 248–265.

Cass, R., Edney, I. I. (1978). The commons dilemma: A simulation testing the effects of resource visibility and territorial division. *Human Ecology, 6*, 371–386.

Chamberlin, E. H. (1948). An experimental imperfect market. *Journal of Political Economy, 56*, 95–108.

Cinyabuguma, M., Page, T., Putterman, L. (2006). Can second-order punishment deter perverse punishment? *Experimental Economics, 9*, 265–279.

Crowe, B. L. (1969). The tragedy of the commons revisited. *Science, 166*, 1103–1107.

Danheiser, P. R., Graziano, W. G. (1982). Self-monitoring and cooperation as a self-presentational strategy. *Journal of Personality and Social Psychology, 42*, 497–505.

Dawes, R. M. (1980). Social dilemmas. *Annual Review of Psychology, 31*, 169–193.

Dawes, R. M., McTavish, J., Shaklee, H. (1977). Behavior, communication and assumptions about other people's behavior in a commons dilemma situation. *Journal of Personality and Social Psychology, 35*, 1–11.

Dawes, R. M., Orbell, J. M., Van de Kragt, A. (1986). Organizing groups for collective action. *American Political Science Review, 80*, 1171–1185.

De Cremer, D., Snyder, M., Dewitte, S. (2001). "The less I trust, the less I contribute (or not)?" The effects of trust, accountability and self-monitoring in social dilemmas. *European Journal of Social Psychology, 31*, 93–107.

Deci, E. L., Ryan, R. M. (1985). *Intrinsic Motivation and Self-Determination in Human Behavior.* New York: Plenum Press.

Dollard, J., Doob, L., Miller, N. E., Mowrer, H. O., Sears, R. R. (1939). *Frustration and Aggression.* New York: Yale University Press.

Edney J. J., Harper, C. S. (1978). The commons dilemma: A review of contributions from psychology. *Environmental Management, 2*, 491–507.

Eek, D., Loukopoulos, P., Fujii, S., Gärling, T. (2002). Spill-over effects of intermittent costs for defection in social dilemmas. *European Journal of Social Psychology, 32*, 801–813.

Emerson, R. (1972). Exchange theory, Part I: A psychological basis for social exchange. Part II: Exchange relations and networks. In J. Berger, M. Zelditch Jr. & Anderson, B. (eds.), *Sociological Theories in Progress* (pp. 38–83). Boston: Houghton-Mifflin.

Falk, A., Fehr, E., Fischbacher, U. (2005). Driving forces of informal sanctions. *Econometrica, 73*, 2017–2030.

Falk, A., Fischbacher, U. (2006). A theory of reciprocity. *Games and Economic Behavior, 54*, 293–315.

Fehr, E., Fischbacher, U. (2003). The nature of human altruism: Proximate patterns and evolutionary origins. *Nature, 425*, 785–791.

Fehr, E., Fischbacher, U. (2004). Third-party punishment and social norms. *Evolution and Human Behavior, 25*, 63–87.

Fehr, E., Fischbacher, U., Gächter, S. (2002). Strong reciprocity, human cooperation and the enforcement of social norms. *Human Nature, 13*, 1–25.

Fehr, E., Gächter, S. (2000). Cooperation and punishment in public goods experiments. *American Economic Review 90*, 980–994.

Fehr, E., Gächter, S. (2002). Altruistic punishment in humans. *Nature, 415*, 137–140.

Fehr, E., Schmidt, K. M. (1999). A theory of fairness, competition and cooperation, *Quarterly Journal of Economics, 114*, 817–868.

Fehr, E., Tougareva, E., Fischbacher, U. (2002). Do high stakes and competition undermine fairness? Evidence from Russia (Working paper No. 120, University of Zurich).

Fox, D. R. (1985). Psychology, ideology, utopia, and the commons. *American Psychologist, 40*, 48–58.

Fox, J., Guyer, M. (1977). Group size and others' strategy in an N-person game. *Journal of Conflict Resolution, 21*, 323–338.

Gardner, R, Ostrom, E., Walker, J. (1990). The nature of common-pool resource problems. *Rationality and Society, 2*, 335–358.

Gintis, H. (2000). Strong reciprocity and human society. *Journal of Theoretical Biology, 206*, 169–179.

Goehring, D. J., Kahan, J. P. (1976). The uniform n-person prisoner's dilemma game. *Journal of Conflict Resolution, 20*, 111–128.

Goette, L., Huffman, D., Meier, S. (2006). The impact of group membership on cooperation and norm enforcement: Evidence using random assignment to real social groups. *American Economic Review, 96*, 212–216.

Goren, H., Bornstein, T., Kugler, T. (July 2005). The effect of punishment on cooperation in single-group and inter-group social dilemmas. Paper presented at the 11th International Conference of Social Dilemma, Krakow, Poland.

Guth, W., Schmittberger, R., Schwarze, B. (1982). An experimental analysis of ultimatum bargaining. *Journal of Economic Behavior and Organization, 3,* 37–88.

Hamburger, H. (1974). Take-some: A format and family of games. *Behavioral Science, 19,* 28–34.

Hamburger, H., Guyer, M., Fox, J. (1975). Group size and cooperation. *Journal of Conflict Resolution, 19,* 503–531.

Hamilton, W. D. (1964). The genetical evolution of social behaviour. I and II. *Journal of Theoretical Biology, 7,* 1–16; 17–32.

Hardin, G. (1968). The tragedy of the commons. *Science, 162,* 1243–1248.

Hardin, G. (1977). Rewards of pejoristic thinking. In G. Hardin & J. Baden (eds.), *Managing the Commons* (pp. 126–134). San Francisco: W. H. Freeman.

Hertwig, R., Ortmann, A. (2001). Experimental practices in economics: A methodological challenge for psychologists? *Behavioral and Brain Science, 24,* 383–451.

Hobbes, T. (1651). *Leviathan.* Cambridge: Cambridge University Press.

Hollander, H. (1990). Social exchange approach to voluntary cooperation. *American Economic Review, 80,* 1157–1167.

Homans, G. C. (1961). *Social Behavior: Its Elementary Forms.* New York: Harcourt Brace.

Isaac, M., Walker, J. (1988). Group size effects in public goods provision: The voluntary contribution mechanism. *Quarterly Journal of Economics, 103,* 179–199.

Isaac, M., Walker, J., Williams, A. (1994). Group size and the voluntary provision of public goods. *Journal of Public Economics, 54,* 1–36.

Isaac, R. M., Walker, J., Thomas, S. (1984). Divergent evidence on free-riding: An experimental examination of possible explanations. *Public Choice, 43,* 113–150.

Jerdee, T. H., Rosen, B. (1974). Effects of opportunity to communicate and visibility of individual decisions on behavior in the common interest. *Journal of Applied Social Psychology, 21,* 190–197.

Kagel, J. H., Roth, A. E. (eds.) (1995). *Handbook of Experimental Economics.* Princeton, NJ: Princeton University Press.

Kandel, E., Lazear, E. (1992). Peer pressure and partnerships. *Journal of Political Economy, 100,* 801–817.

Kelley, H. H., Grzelak, J. (1972). Conflict between individual and common interest in an N-person relationship. *Journal of Personality and Social Psychology, 21,* 190–197.

Kelley, H. H., Stahelski, A. J. (1970). Social interaction basis of cooperators' and competitors' beliefs about others. *Journal of Personality and Social Psychology, 16,* 66–91.

Kelman, H. C. (1967). Human use of human subjects: The problem of deception in social psychological experiments. *Psychological Bulletin, 67,* 1–11.

Kerr, N. L., Brunn, S. E. (1983). Dispensability of member effort and group motivation losses: Free-rider effects. *Journal of Personality and Social Psychology, 44,* 78–94.

Kerr, N. L. (1989). Illusions of efficacy: The effects of group size on perceived efficacy in social dilemmas. *Journal of Experimental Social Psychology, 25,* 287–313.

Kiyonari, T., Barclay, P., Wilson, M., Daly, M. (2005). Do second-order sanctions solve the second-order free rider problem? Manuscript in preparation.

Kiyonari, T., van Veelen, M., Yamagishi, T. (2007). Can second-order punishment solve the puzzle of human cooperation in one-shot games? Paper submitted for publication.

Kollock, P. (1998). Social dilemmas: The anatomy of cooperation. *Annual Review of Sociology, 24,* 183–214.

Komorita, S., Barth, J. M. (1985). Components of reward in social dilemmas. *Journal of Personality and Social Psychology, 48,* 364–373.

Komorita, S. S., Sweeney, J., Kravitz, D. A. (1980). Cooperative choice in the n-person dilemma situation. *Journal of Personality and Social Psychology, 38,* 504–516.

Kramer, R. M., Brewer, M. B. (1984). Effects of group identity on resource use in a simulated commons dilemma. *Journal of Personality and Social Psychology, 46,* 1044–1057.

Kurzban, R., Houser, D. (2001). Individual differences in cooperation in a circular public goods game. *European Journal of Personality, 15*, S37–S52.

Ledyard, J. (1995). Public goods: A survey of experimental research. In J. Kagel & A. Roth (eds.), *The Handbook of Experimental Economics* (pp. 111–194). Princeton, NJ: Princeton University Press.

Lepper, M. R., Greene, D., Nisbett, R. E. (1973). Undermining children's intrinsic interest with extrinsic reward: A test of the overjustification hypothesis. *Journal of Personality and Social Psychology, 29*, 129–137.

Levine, D. K. (1998). Modeling altruism and spitefulness in experiments. *Review of Economic Dynamics, 1*, 593–622.

Liebrand, W. B., Jansen, R. W., Rijken, V. M., Shure, C. J. (1986). Might over morality: Social values and the perception of other players in experimental games. *Journal of Experimental Social Psychology, 22*, 203–215.

Loukopoulos, P., Eek, D., Gärling, T., Fujii, S. (2006). Palatable punishment in real-world social dilemmas? Punishing others increase cooperation among the unpunished. *Journal of Applied Psychology, 36*, 1274–1279.

Lynn, M., Oldenquist, A. (1986). Egoistic and nonegoistic motives in social dilemmas. *American Psychologist, 41*, 529–534.

Marwell, G., Ames, R. (1979). Experiments in the provision of public goods, I: Resources, interest, group size and the free rider problem. *American Journal of Sociology, 84*, 1335–1360.

Marwell, G., Ames, R. (1980). Experiments on the provision of public goods, II: Provision points, stakes, experience and the free rider problem. *American Journal of Sociology, 85*, 926–937.

Marwell, G., Schmitt, D. R. (1972). Cooperation in a three-person prisoner's dilemma. *Journal of Personality and Social Psychology, 21*, 376–383.

Masclet, D., Noussair, C., Tucker, S., Villeval, M. (2003). Monetary and nonmonetary punishment in the voluntary contributions mechanism. *American Economic Review, 93*, 366–380.

McClintock, C. G., Liebrand, W. B. G. (1988). Role of interdependence structure, individual value orientation, and another's strategy in social decision making: A transformal analysis. *Journal of Personality and Social Psychology, 55*, 396–409.

McCusker, C., Carnevale, P. J. (1995). Framing in resource dilemmas: Loss aversion and the moderating effects of sanctions. *Organizational Behavior and Human Decision Processes, 61*, 190–201.

Messick, D. M. (1999). Alternative logics for decision making in social settings. *Journal of Economic Behavior & Organization, 39*, 11–28.

Messick, D. M., Brewer, M. B. (1983). Solving social dilemmas. *Review of Personality and Social Psychology, 4*, 11–44.

Messick, D. M., McClelland, C. L. (1983). Social traps and temporal traps. *Personality and Social Psychology Bulletin, 9*, 105–110.

Messick, D. M., Wilke, H., Brewer, M. B., Kramer, R. M. (1983). Interpersonal relations and group processes. *Journal of Personality and Social Psychology, 44*, 294–309.

Milinski, M., Semmann, D., Bakker, T. C. M., Krambeck, H. (2001). Cooperation through indirect reciprocity: Image scoring or standing strategy? *Proceedings of the Royal Society of London Series B: Biological Sciences, 268*, 2495–2501.

Millenson, J. R. (1967). *Principles of Behavioral Analysis*. New York: Macmillan.

Mulder, L. B., van Dijk, E., De Cremer, D., Wilke, H. (2003). Sanctioning systems in social trilemmas. Paper presented at the 10th International Conference on Social Dilemmas.

Mulder, L. B., Van Dijk, E., De Cremer, D., Wilke, H. (2006). Undermining trust and cooperation: The paradox of sanctioning systems in social dilemmas. *Journal of Experimental Social Psychology, 42*, 147–162.

Nikiforakis, N. S. (March 2004). Punishment and counter-punishment in public goods games: Can we still govern ourselves? (University of London, Department of Economics, Royal Holloway Discussion Paper Series No. dpe04/5).

Noussair, C., Tucker, S. (2005). Combining monetary and social sanctions to promote cooperation. *Economic Inquiry, 43*, 649–660.

Nowak, M. A., Sigmund, K. (1998). Evolution of indirect reciprocity by image scoring. *Nature, 393*, 573–577.

Ohmura, Y., Yamagishi, T. (2005). Why do people reject unintended inequity? Responders' rejection in a truncated ultimatum game. *Psychological Reports, 96*, 533–541.

Oliver, P. (1980). Rewards and punishments as selective incentives for collective action: Theoretical investigations. *American Journal of Sociology, 85*, 1356–1375.

Olson, M. (1965). *The Logic of Collective Action: Public Goods and the Theory of Groups.* Cambridge, MA: Harvard University Press.

Ostrom, E. (1990). *Governing the Commons: The Evolution of Institutions for Collective Action.* New York: Cambridge University Press.

Ostrom, E., Walker, J., Gardner, R. (1992). Covenants with and without a sword: Self-governance is possible. *American Political Science Review, 86*, 404–417.

Page, T., Putterman, L., Unel, B. (2005). Voluntary association in public goods experiments: Reciprocity, mimicry and efficiency. *The Economic Journal, 115*, 1032–1053.

Platt, J. (1973). Social traps. *American Psychologist, 28*, 641–651.

Price, M. E., Cosmides, L., Tooby, J. (2002). Punitive sentiment as an anti-free rider psychological device. *Evolution and Human Behavior, 23*, 203–231.

Pruitt, D. G., Kimmel, M. J. (1977). Twenty years of experimental gaming: Critique, synthesis, and suggestions for the future. *Annual Review of Psychology, 28*, 363–392.

Rabin, M. (1993). Incorporating fairness into game theory and economics. *American Economic Review, 83*, 1281–1302.

Rabin, M. (1998). Psychology and economics. *Journal of Economic Literature, 35*, 11–46.

Rapoport, A., Au, W. T. (2001). Bonus and penalty in common pool resource dilemmas under uncertainty. *Organizational Behavior and Human Decision Processes, 85*, 135–165.

Rapoport, A., Chammah, A., Dwyer, C. A., Gyr, J. (1962). Three-person non-zero-sum nonnegotiable games. *Behavioral Science, 7*, 38–58.

Samuelson, P., Nordhaus, W. (1985). *Economics.* New York: McGraw-Hill.

Sato, K., Yamagishi, T. (1986). Two psychological factors in the problem of public goods. *Japanese Journal of Experimental Social Psychology, 26*, 89–95 (in Japanese).

Sato, K. (1987). Distribution of the cost of maintaining common resources. *Journal of Experimental Social Psychology, 23*, 19–31.

Sato, K. (1988). Trust and group size in a social dilemma. *Japanese Psychological Research, 30*, 88–93 (in Japanese).

Sefton, M., Shupp, R., Walker, J. (2002). The effect of rewards and sanctions in provision of public goods (The Centre for Decision Research and Experimental Economics working paper no. 2002-2).

Shinada, M., Yamagishi, T. (In Press), Punishing free-riders: Direct and indirect promotion of cooperation. *Evolution and Human Behavior.*

Shinada, M., Yamagishi, T., Ohmura, Y. (2004). False friends are worse than bitter enemies: "Altruistic" punishment of in-group members. *Evolution and Human Behavior, 25*, 379–393.

Shinada, M., Yamagishi, T., Yamamoto, Y. (July 2005). Third-party punishment of in-group and out-group members. Paper presented at the 11th International Conference of Social Dilemma, Krakow, Poland.

Skinner, B. F. (1938). *The Behavior of Organisms.* New York: Appleton-Century-Crofts.

Sobel, J. (2005). Interdependent preferences and reciprocity. *Journal of Economic Literature, 43*, 392–436.

Stern, P. C. (1976). Effect of incentives and education on resource conservation decisions in a simulated commons dilemma. *Journal of Personality and Social Psychology, 34*, 1285–1292.

Stillman, P. G. (1975). The tragedy of the commons: A re-analysis. *Alternatives, 4*, 12–15.

Stroebe, W., Frey, B. S. (1982). Self-interest and collective action: The economics and psychology of public goods. *British Journal of Social Psychology, 21*, 121–137.

Sweeney, J. W. (1973). An experimental investigation of the free-rider problem. *Social Science Research, 2*, 227–292.

Takahashi, N., Mashima, R. (2003). The emergence of indirect reciprocity: Is the standing strategy the answer? (21st Century "Center for the Study of Cultural and Ecological Foundations of the Mind" Working Paper Series No. 29).

Taylor, M. (1976). *Anarchy and Cooperation*. New York: Wiley.

Taylor, M. (1982). *Community, Anarchy and Liberty*. New York: Cambridge University Press.

Tenbrunsel, A. E., Messick, D. M. (1999). Sanctioning systems, decision frames, and cooperation. *Administrative Science Quarterly, 44*, 684–707.

Trivers, R. (1971). The evolution of reciprocal altruism. *Quarterly Review of Biology, 46*, 35–57.

Tullock, G. (1977). The social costs of reducing social cost. In G. Hardin & J. Baden (eds.), *Managing the Commons* (pp. 147–156). San Francisco: Freeman.

Van de Kragt, A., Orbell, J., Dawes, R. M. (1983). The minimal contribution set as a solution to public goods problems. *American Political Science Review, 77*, 112–122.

Van Lange, P. A. M. (1999). The pursuit of joint outcomes and equality in outcomes: An integrative model of social value orientation. *Journal of Personality and Social Psychology, 77*, 337–349.

Van Lange, P. A. M., Kuhlman, D. M. (1994). Social value orientations and impressions of partner's honesty and intelligence: A test of the might versus morality effect. *Journal of Personality and Social Psychology, 67*, 126–141.

Van Lange, P. A. M., Agnew, C. R., Harinck, F., Steemers, G. E. M. (1997a). From game theory to real life: How social value orientation affects willingness to sacrifice in ongoing close relationships. *Journal of Personality and Social Psychology, 73*, 1330–1344.

Van Lange, P. A. M., Otten, W., De Bruin, E. M. N., Joireman, J. A. (1997b). Development of prosocial, individualistic, and competitive orientations: Theory and preliminary evidence. *Journal of Personality and Social Psychology, 73*, 733–746.

Van Vugt, M., Van Lange, P. A. M., Meertens, R. M. (1996a). Commuting by car or public transportation? Social dilemma analysis of travel mode judgements. *European Journal of Social Psychology, 26*, 373–395.

Van Vugt, M., Van Lange, P. A. M., Meertens, R. M., Joireman, J. A. (1996b). How a structural solution to a real-world social dilemma failed: A field experiment on the first carpool lane in Europe. *Social Psychology Quarterly, 59*, 364–374.

Walker, J., Halloran, M. A. (2004). Rewards and sanctions and the provision of public goods in one-shot settings. *Experimental Economics, 7*, 235–247.

Weber, J. M., Kopelman, S., Messick, D. M. (2004). A conceptual review of decision making in social dilemmas: Applying a logic of appropriateness. *Personality and Social Psychology Review, 8*, 281–307.

Yamagishi, T., Sato, K. (1986). Motivational bases of the public goods problem. *Journal of Personality and Social Psychology, 50*, 67–73.

Yamagishi, T. (1986a). The provision of a sanctioning system as a public good. *Journal of Personality and Social Psychology, 51*, 110–116.

Yamagishi, T. (1986b). The structural goal/expectation theory of cooperation in social dilemmas. *Advances in Group Processes, 3*, 51–87.

Yamagishi, T. (1988a). Seriousness of social dilemmas and the provision of a sanctioning system. *Social Psychology Quarterly, 51*, 32–42.

Yamagishi, T. (1988b). The provision of a sanctioning system in the United States and Japan. *Social Psychology Quarterly, 51*, 265–271.

Yamagishi, T. (1990a). *Social Dilemmas*. Tokyo: Science Press (in Japanese).

Yamagishi, T. (1990b). Factors mediating residual effects of group size in social dilemmas. *The Japanese Journal of Psychology, 61*, 162–169 (in Japanese).

Yamagishi, T. (1992). Group size and the provision of a sanctioning system in a social dilemma. In W. B. G. Liebrand, D. M. Messick & H. A. M. Wilke (eds.), *Social Dilemma: Theoretical Issues and Research Findings* (pp. 267–287). Oxford: Pergamon Press.

Yamagishi, T., Takahashi, N. (1994). Evolution of norms without metanorms. In U. Schulz, W. Albers & U. Mueller (eds.), *Social Dilemmas and Cooperation* (pp. 311–326). Berlin: Springer-Verlag.

Zahavi, A. (1977). The cost of honesty (Further remarks on the handicap principle). *Journal of Theoretical Biology, 67*, 603–605.

Chapter 8
Effectiveness of Coercive and Voluntary Institutional Solutions to Social Dilemmas

Yuval Samid and Ramzi Suleiman

Introduction

In his seminal paper on "The Tragedy of the Commons," Hardin (1968) analyzes the danger of excessive use of common resources. His discussion deals with common pastures, freedom of the seas, overcrowded national parks, pollution, and excessive population growth. Hardin rules out the appeal to conscience because it is self-eliminating in some cases and pathogenic in most cases. He claims that if the inherent logic of the commons dilemma generates tragedy, then the structure of the dilemma should be changed, and the structural change should introduce some form of coercive measure. For instance, the use of parking meters and traffic fines is required to keep downtown shoppers temperate in their use of parking spaces: "We need not actually forbid a citizen to park as long as he wants to; we need merely make it increasingly expensive for him to do so. Not prohibition, but carefully biased options are what we offer him" (Hardin, 1968, p. 1247). Hardin states that although we may not enjoy coercion, we must recognize that voluntary temperance would favor the conscienceless. The only kind of coercion Hardin recommends is "mutual coercion, mutually agreed upon by the majority of the people affected" (1968, p. 1247).

Yamagishi (1986, 1988a, b, 1992) tested the efficiency of a coercive mechanism in the form of sanctions. In a public-good dilemma or game, players could contribute a portion of their endowments for the provision of a sanctioning system. The sum of the money contributed to the sanctioning system was multiplied by a fixed factor and reduced from the least cooperative player. Yamagishi found that the use of a sanctioning system increased contributions, but when the sanctioning factor equaled 1 (i.e., the sum contributed to the sanctions equaled the reduction), the profit increase was offset by the cost of the sanctioning system. With a higher sanctioning factor, both cooperation and profits increased (Yamagishi, 1986). Yamagishi also found that contributions to sanctions increased when players were low in giving trust (Yamagishi, 1986) and when they exhibited or expected lower levels of cooperation, as in large groups (Yamagishi, 1992), with less cooperative subjects (Japanese vs. Americans; Yamagishi, 1988b) and with more extreme public-good dilemmas (Yamagishi, 1988a).

A. Biel et al. (eds.), *New Issues and Paradigms in Research on Social Dilemmas.*
© Springer 2008

Dawes's (1980) rejects using coercion as a general solution to commons dilemmas, or social dilemmas, which is the term Dawes uses. His first objection concerns the danger in the control given to the coercive institution. The coercive "solutions are essentially the same as Hobbes's (1651) Leviathan. ... There is empirical evidence that those societies where people are best off ... are those whose governments correspond least to Hobbes's authoritarian Leviathan" (Orbell & Rutherford, 1973, cited by Dawes, 1980, p. 174). His second objection relates to the fact that in many dilemmas, when all are coerced to cooperate, the cost of the coercive system could exceed its benefits. His third objection concerns peoples' response to coercive systems, which "apparently create, or at least exacerbate, a motivation to get around the rules" (Dawes, 1980, p.175).

The negative motivational effects of sanctions were tested in a recent series of experiments (Mulder et al., 2005, 2006a–c). The experiments showed that the mere presentation of a sanctioning system reduces the trust that others will cooperate without sanctions (Mulder et al., 2005). Moreover, they found that the removal of an effective sanctioning system reduces cooperation below the levels achieved without sanctions (Mulder et al., 2006b, Experiments 2 and 3). The results lend support to Dawes' (1980) third reservation by showing that when people have the opportunity to get around the rules, the sanctioning system becomes ineffective (Mulder et al., 2006c). A good example is the problem of garbage reduction. If a local government chooses to encourage people to reduce or recycle garbage by charging a fee (sanction) for every kilogram of unrecycled garbage that an individual puts on his or her doorstep, people may burn their garbage, or throw it in the bushes or in an illegal dumpsite (Van Meegeren, 1997).

Another way to increase people's cooperative actions is by organizing their contributions. Dawes et al. (1986) introduced two mechanisms for organizing cooperation in a step-level public-good dilemma. One is the *money-back guarantee*, in which contributions are returned if the public goods are not supplied. The second is the *fair share*, which enforces all non-contributors to contribute their endowments when the public goods are supplied. While the first mechanism reduces the *fear* of being "suckered," or "gypped," the second reduces the *greed* to free-ride on others' contributions. The *money-back guarantee* is a form of voluntary organization; the *fair share* is, in fact, a sanction through which contributions are enforced when a sufficient number of others cooperate.

In an experiment to be reported below, players in an iterated *n*-person prisoner's dilemma (NPD) game could choose an institutional solution, which combines a sanctioning system with an organized voluntary contribution, similar to the *money-back guarantee mechanism*. In the modified game, players could either play the standard NPD game by choosing between "defection" and "cooperation" or join an institutional solution presented to the subjects as a *collective decision*. The collective decision prescribed collective cooperation, but only when the players who joined this institution profited from cooperation; otherwise, it defected. The choice to join the collective decision offered participants an opportunity to cooperate in an organized manner, while avoiding being suckered or gypped. As such, the collective decision mechanism ensured profitable cooperation, or a money-back guarantee. Under the coercive conditions of the experiment, joining the collective decision imposed a "fine" on non-participants, and for its coercive service, the collective decision charged a "fee" from participants. To operational-ize Hardin's (1968) recommendation for "mutual coercion, mutually agreed upon by the majority of the people affected," the fine was increased, progressively, as a function of the number of players who joined the collective decision. With the organized cooperation and the sanctioning system, the collective decision operates as a "central authority." The more support it receives, the more powerful it becomes in forcing others to support it.

The experimental conditions included four types of "authority games" in which levels of fees and fines were manipulated. Different levels of fees and fines resulted in different equilibria. Motivated by Dawes' (1980) reservations regard-ing the cost-effectiveness of coercive mechanisms, the present experiment was designed to answer two questions: (1) What is the minimal effective coercion necessary for eliciting institutional cooperation, and (2) to what extent will indi-viduals lend support to a cost-deficient, exploitative institution that employs excessive coercion? The minimal coercion necessary to elicit cooperation was tested using *non-coercive* and *moderately coercive* institutions. The support received by an exploitative authority was tested using *exploitative* and *dominating* institutions.

The payoff matrices corresponding to the four types of the modified "authority prisoner's dilemma" (APD) games are presented in Table 8.1.[1] The top two rows of payoffs in each matrix represent a standard, six-player NPD game. This game was played in the control condition, and in other conditions when nobody chose to join the authority. The third row from top represents the payoffs for a given player who chooses authority, and the two rows below show the payoffs for other players, when the focal player joins the authority. Moving down, each grouping of three rows represents payoffs for the case where another player joins the authority. The bottom, shaded rows show the payoffs when the authority cooper-ates collectively.

In the non-coercive APD game (Table 8.1a), the standard "all-defect" equilib-rium (denoted by α) is weakened by the authority choice, which yields the same payoff for one or two players who join the authority, and higher payoffs when three or more players join the authority. The non-coercive APD game results in a new equilibrium (denoted by β) in which three players join the authority and three others defect. This equilibrium is the most profitable one and therefore is the game-theoretical prediction for the non-coercive APD game. The reader should notice that this equilibrium is an asymmetric one, in the sense that it results in a significant inequality in payoffs. Thus, defectors in this equilibrium receive a payoff of 51 NIS, which amounts to more than twice the payoff (of 24 NIS) received by author-ity supporters. As could be expected, for players who compare their own payoffs to

[1] In all matrices, the number of players was n = 6 and the endowments were e = 15 New Israeli Shekels (NIS). At the time of the experiment 5 NIS equaled about 1 Euro. A player's contribution was multiplied by 4 and divided equally between the other 5 players.

Table 8.1 Payoff matrix (in NIS[2]) for four types of an Authority Prisoners Dilemma (APD) game

A: Non-Coercive Authority (fee=fine=0)

Number of other players choosing A:	Focal player's choice	Number of other players choosing C:					
		0	1	2	3	4	5
0	$C_{0,c+1}$:	0	12	24	36	48	60
	$D_{0,c}$:	15^α	27	39	51	63	75
	$A_{1,c}$:	15	27	39	51	63	75
1	$C_{1,c+1}$:	0	12	24	36	48	
	$D_{1,c}$:	15	27	39	51	63	
	$A_{2,c}$:	15	27	39	51	63	
2	$C_{2,c+1}$:	0	12	24	36		
	$D_{2,c}$:	15	27	39	51		
	$A_{3,c}$:	24^β	36	48	60		
3	$C_{3,c+1}$:	36	48	60			
	$D_{3,c}$:	51^β	63	75			
	$A_{4,c}$:	36	48	60			
4	$C_{4,c+1}$:	48	60				
	$D_{4,c}$:	63	75				
	$A_{5,c}$:	48	60				
5	$C_{5,c+1}$:	60					
	$D_{5,c}$:	75					
	$A_{6,c}$:	60					

B: Moderately Coercive Authority (16% fee & 10% progressive fine)

Number of other players choosing A:	Focal player's choice	Fine & Fee deduction	Number of other players choosing C:					
			0	1	2	3	4	5
0	$C_{0,c+1}$:	0%	0	12	24	36	48	60
	$D_{0,c}$:	0%	15^α	27	39	51	63	75
	$A_{1,c}$:	16%	12.6	22.7	32.8	42.8	52.9	63
1	$C_{1,c+1}$:	10%	0	10.8	21.6	32.4	43.2	
	$D_{1,c}$:	10%	13.5	24.3	35.1	45.9	56.7	
	$A_{2,c}$:	16%	12.6	22.7	32.8	42.8	52.9	
2	$C_{2,c+1}$:	20%	0	9.6	19.2	28.8		
	$D_{2,c}$:	20%	12	21.6	31.2	40.8		
	$A_{3,c}$:	16%	20.2^β	30.2	40.3	50.4		
3	$C_{3,c+1}$	30%	25.2	33.6	42			
	$D_{3,c}$:	30%	35.7^β	44.1	52.5			
	$A_{4,c}$:	16%	30.2	40.3	50.4			
4	$C_{4,c+1}$:	40%	28.8	36				
	$D_{4,c}$:	40%	37.8	45				
	$A_{5,c}$:	16%	40.3	50.4				
5	$C_{5,c+1}$:	50%	30					
	$D_{5,c}$:	50%	37.5					
	$A_{6,c}$:	16%	50.4^γ					

(continued)

[2] 5 NIS (New Israeli Shekels) = 1 Euro, at the time of the experiment.

Table 8.1 (continued)

C: Exploitative Authority (80% fee & 30% progressive fine)

Number of other players choosing A:	Focal player's choice	Fine & Fee deduction	Number of other players choosing C:					
			0	1	2	3	4	5
0	$C_{0,c+1:}$	0%	0	12	24	36	48	60
	$D_{0,c:}$	0%	15^α	27	39	51	63	75
	$A_{1,c:}$	80%	3	5.4	7.8	10.2	12.6	15
1	$C_{1,c+1:}$	30%	0	8.4	16.8	25.2	33.6	
	$D_{1,c:}$	30%	10.5	18.9	27.3	35.7	44.1	
	$A_{2,c:}$	80%	3	5.4	7.8	10.2	12.6	
2	$C_{2,c+1:}$	60%	0	4.8	9.6	14.4		
	$D_{2,c:}$	60%	6	10.8	15.6	20.4		
	$A_{3,c:}$	80%	4.8	7.2	9.6	12		
3	$C_{3,c+1}$	90%	3.6	4.8	6			
	$D_{3,c:}$	90%	5.1	6.3	7.5			
	$A_{4,c:}$	80%	7.2	9.6	12			
4	$C_{4,c+1:}$	120%	−9.6	−12				
	$D_{4,c:}$	120%	−12.6	−15				
	$A_{5,c:}$	80%	9.6	12				
5	$C_{5,c+1:}$	150%	−30					
	$D_{5,c:}$	150%	−37.5					
	$A_{6,c:}$	80%	12^γ					

D: Dominating Authority (16% progressive fee & 30% progressive fine)

Number of other players choosing A:	Focal player's choice	Fine & Fee deduction	Number of other players choosing C:					
			0	1	2	3	4	5
0	$C_{0,c+1:}$	0%	0	12	24	36	48	60
	$D_{0,c:}$	0%	15^α	27	39	51	63	75
	$A_{1,c:}$	0%	15	27	39	51	63	75
1	$C_{1,c+1:}$	30%	0	8.4	16.8	25.2	33.6	
	$D_{1,c:}$	30%	10.5	18.9	27.3	35.7	44.1	
	$A_{2,c:}$	16%	12.6	22.7	32.8	42.8	52.9	
2	$C_{2,c+1:}$	60%	0	4.8	9.6	14.4		
	$D_{2,c:}$	60%	6	10.8	15.6	20.4		
	$A_{3,c:}$	32%	16.3	24.5	32.6	40.8		
3	$C_{3,c+1:}$	90%	3.6	4.8	6			
	$D_{3,c:}$	90%	5.1	6.3	7.5			
	$A_{4,c:}$	48%	18.7	25	31.2			
4	$C_{4,c+1:}$	120%	−9.6	−12				
	$D_{4,c:}$	120%	−12.6	−15				
	$A_{5,c:}$	64%	17.3	21.6				
5	$C_{5,c+1:}$	150%	−30					
	$D_{5,c:}$	150%	−37.5					
	$A_{6,c:}$	80%	12^γ					

Choices: C - Cooperation; D - Defection; A - Authority; Gray: when Authority cooperates
Equilibria: α - All Defect equilibrium (6D); β - Intermediate equilibrium (3A,3D); γ - All support Authority equilibrium (6A)

those of others, this inequality would arouse feelings of unfairness. To estimate the effect of this type of social comparison, the non-coercive APD game was played under two feedback conditions: (1) full feedback, under which players received information about their own payoffs and about the payoffs of others, and (2) partial feedback, under which players received information about their payoffs but not about others' payoffs. Both types of feedback included information about the number of players who made each choice, so players could, in fact, inform themselves about others' payoffs in the charts handed to them. Social comparison was thus not eliminated under the partial feedback condition but reduced by presenting less informative feedback.

As can be seen in Table 8.1b, in the moderately coercive APD game, a 16% fee is charged from authority participants and a progressive fine is imposed on non-participants. The fine is increased by 10% for each player who joins the authority. This game has three equilibria. In addition to the α and β equilibria described above, the 50% fine imposed on the non-supporter of authority when all others support it creates a new, "all-support-authority" equilibrium (denoted by γ). Note that in comparison to the non-coercive APD game, the 30% fine, imposed on defectors, when three players support the authority, reduces the inequality in payoffs at the β equilibrium.

The γ equilibrium is the most profitable one; therefore, it is the game-theoretical prediction for the moderately coercive APD game. The fine rate for this condition was chosen in order to meet the minimal coercion necessary for achieving a large-scale cooperation. For this level of fines, only when five players support authority does the defector earns less than authority supporters do. Therefore, it seems like the minimal level of effective coercion.

Table 8.1c presents the payoffs for the exploitative APD game. The authority charges an exploitative fee of 80% from participants and imposes a progressive fine that increases by 30% for each player who joins the authority. The game has two equilibria, the standard α (all-defect) equilibrium, and the γ (all-support-authority) equilibrium. An inspection of the payoff matrix reveals that when fewer than three others support the authority, the authority choice is dominated by defection. Therefore, when groups begin the game with low authority support, there is no incentive for any player to switch from defection to authority support. In this game, the α equilibrium dominates the γ equilibrium and the authority dose not provide a profitable solution for the dilemma. Although the exploitative APD game employs excessive coercive power, it nevertheless accords with Hardin's (1968) "mutual coercion, mutually agreed upon by the majority of the people affected," since only when the majority of players (4 or 5 out of 6) support authority do defectors earn less than authority-supporters.

The dominating APD game (Table 8.1d) imposes a 30% progressive fine like the exploitative APD game, but the fee in this condition is progressive, increasing by 16% for every other player who joins the authority. When all six players support the authority, the deductions in the two conditions are equal. Like the exploitative APD game, the game has the two equilibria (α and γ). The α (all-defect) equilibrium dominates the γ (all-support-authority) equilibrium. Nonetheless, its dominance is somewhat weak, because when all others defect, a player who joins the authority will be indifferent between authority support and defection. The dominating APD game differs from the exploitative APD game in the employment of a progressive fee, which, except for the all-defect equilibrium, renders the authority choice dominant over defection. The game theory prediction is the dominating all-defect equilibrium, but if one player switches to authority, then the rational players should also do the same, and the result would be convergence to the dominated, "all-support-authority" equilibrium. This game does not conform to Hardin's (1968) "mutual coercion, mutually agreed upon." The authority's coercive power is enforced by a single player, and the game has the form of a *social trap* (Platt, 1973). The dominating APD game resembles a tyrant who enforces stricter rules as he gets more power and support. An institution that puts its own good before the good of its members and has the power to change and enforce the rules might act in this manner. It would start by offering non-costly participation, but once it receives support, it would use its coercive power to exploit supporters.

To illustrate the various types of authority, consider as an example the maintenance of a stairway by a group of tenants who share an apartment house. The tenants can wash the stairs at their own floors (cooperate), hoping that others will do the same and that the whole stairway will be kept clean. Alternatively, tenants can jointly pay someone to wash the stairway. If the number of tenants who pay is not sufficient to wash the stairway, the tenants who paid will reclaim their money. In this example, the tenants' association organizes cooperation, while securing a money-back guarantee as in the non-coercive APD game. Alternatively, the tenants' association can pay a maintenance company, which will take the effort of collecting payment from all tenants. If enough money is collected, the maintenance job will be accomplished; otherwise, payments will be returned after the deduction of collecting costs (fee). If the majority of tenants participate, the maintenance company can legally enforce payment on the few who did not pay (fine). In this example, the maintenance company functions like in the moderately coercive APD game. It charges a fixed fee for its profits and collecting efforts and imposes a progressive fine on non-participants, the size of which depends on the relative number of participating tenants.

In the exploitative APD game, the cost of coercion becomes higher than the outcomes when all the individuals are coerced to cooperate. For instance, the enforcing of fishing quotas in the oceans could be as costly as fishing itself. Maritime nations could issue restrictions on fishing volumes, but ocean patrols would have to patrol the oceans to prevent illegal fishing. When fish become abundant, fishing vessels can cover less mileage to catch the same quota, but the patrols must cover more mileage to restrict illegal fishing. As fish become abundant and fishing becomes more profitable, the enforcement of fishing quotas becomes more costly. In this way, there is no profit from a coercive solution to the dilemma.

The dominating APD game is not necessarily similar to a tyrant-governed institution. In the fishing example, suppose that when fish become scarce, the government subsidizes a coercive ocean patrol. In this case, all fishermen will be better off if they restrict themselves to the quotas. However, when fish become abundant and fishermen earn high profits, the government would stop the subsidy and fishermen would pay high license fees to cover the costs of increased ocean patrols. With this kind of subsidy, a well-meaning government turns an exploitative APD game into a dominating APD game. At first, fishermen will support the coercive solution, only to learn later that they are better off with freedom of the seas and fewer fish, than with abundant fish and inflated license fees.

The examples described above illustrate some aspects of the dynamics emerging in situations, which could be modeled by each of the four APD games. To explore these dynamics empirically, each game was played for 280 trials. The game-theoretical predictions for the different games are the β equilibrium, prescribing an intermediate (50%) support for the non-coercive authority, full support of the moderately coercive authority (the γ equilibrium), and no support (α equilibrium) for the exploitative and dominating authorities.

Method

Participants

Two hundred and fifty two subjects (169 females and 83 males, 18 to 41 years old with a median age of 24) participated in 42 groups of 6 players each. Participants were recruited via billboard ads at the University of Haifa campus. The ads stated that they could earn up to 75 NIS (about 15 Euro) contingent on their gains in a decision-making experiment.

Experimental Conditions

In the full feedback condition, five groups played the standard NPD game as control condition. Six groups played the non-coercive APD game, another 6 groups played the moderately coercive APD game, 10 groups played the exploitative APD game, and 3 groups played the dominating APD game. In the partial feedback condition, six groups played the non-coercive APD game and six groups played the dominating APD game.

Procedure

The experiment was computer-controlled. Upon arrival, each participant was escorted to a private booth. Instructions were provided on the computer screen, and all participants' replies and decisions were registered via the mouse. At the beginning of each session, subjects had to mark their gender and age. All further instructions addressed subjects according to their gender (in Hebrew, verbs and pronouns are gender-specific). The instructions for the experiment stated:

> In this experiment you will participate in a game with five other players. The game will be played for many rounds. In each round, you will receive an allocation of 15 NIS, which you can contribute or keep to yourself. When a player contributes, the contribution will be multiplied by 4 and distributed evenly among all the other players. A contributing player receives only the benefits of others' contributions. A non-contributing player receives the benefits of others' contributions in addition to his allocation.

Further instructions presented the payoffs received if all players contributed and if all players kept their allocations. Under the authority conditions, players were given the choice to join a "collective decision" as a third alternative to the "contribute" or "keep" choices. The instructions regarding the collective decision stated that "Allocations will be contributed only when contribution is profitable for those players who chose to join the collective decision" (i.e., when three or more players choose the collective decision). In the coercive authority conditions, the system of fees and fines was presented. Further instructions presented the outcomes when all players chose the collective decision. Players were advised to study the payoff matrix on the complementary paper. They were told, "Although the collective decision is managed by the computer, one can think of it as a representative body which charges a fee from its members and enforces a fine on non-members." At any time during the experiment, players could review the instructions or ask for the experimenter's assistance by pressing at the appropriate on-screen button.

Before the experimental phase, participants played two phases of practice trials. The first phase consisted of 21 trials in which participants replied to a computer-generated random series, which included all possible combinations of other players' choices. The second phase consisted of 50 practice games. The outcomes obtained in the two practice phases were not included in the participants' monetary payments.

In the full information condition, following each trial participants received feedback about the number of other participants who made each choice (i.e., how many others chose to contribute, not contribute, or join the collective decision). In addition, they were informed about their own payoffs, about the payoffs resulting from each choice, and about whether or not a collective contribution was implemented. Similar feedback was given in the partial feedback condition, except that no information was given to participants about the earnings of others who made a different choice than theirs. Throughout the experiment, the percentage of fees and fines appeared on the participants' screens.

The experiment ended after 280 trials or after an hour and a half, whichever came first. Upon termination of the experiment, participants received feedback about their average earnings. They were then invited, one at a time, to the experimenter room, paid their earnings, and released separately from the laboratory.

Results

Non-Coercive Authority

In the non-coercive APD game with full feedback, none of the groups converged to the dominant β equilibrium. All six groups showed similar dynamics, with authority support alternating between 0% and 50%. In fact, the equilibrium was rarely reached and never sustained. The average support[3] for authority was 27.5% (SD = 4.61%). To estimate efficiency, we calculated the total number of contributions made by authority supporters (collective cooperation) and by players who chose to contribute individually (direct cooperation). The aggregate number of contributions accounted for only 12.0% (SD = 4.28%) of the total number of players' choices and did not differ significantly from the contribution rate (15.7%, SD = 7.82%) obtained under the control condition, $t(9) = 1.01$, $p = 0.34$. These results indicate that the non-coercive authority is an inefficient mechanism for enhancing contributions.

As previously mentioned, we speculated that the inequality embedded in the asymmetric β equilibrium could arouse feelings of unfairness among authority supporters who compared their payoffs to the higher payoffs received by defectors. The partial feedback condition was designed to attenuate the effects of social comparisons. In this condition, the rate of support for the non-coercive authority was 43.8% (SD = 7.36%), which is significantly higher than the support rate of 27.5% in the *full feedback* condition, $t(10) = 4.61$, $p < 0.001$. The results for the six groups in this condition were relatively stable. Three groups oscillated below the β equilibrium, reaching equilibrium only for short intervals (of about 10 trials each). Two other groups oscillated around the β equilibrium, and a sixth group maintained authority support of above 50% (the β equilibrium), alongside a 20% rate of voluntary cooperation. In this group, authority support and voluntary cooperation declined slowly, and the group converged to the β equilibrium toward the last trials of the game. The aggregate rate of contributions in the partial feedback condition reached 37.2% (SD = 15.38%), which is significantly higher than the 12% contribution rate obtained under full feedback and the 15.7% contribution rate obtained in the control (standard NPD) condition, $F(2,14) = 10.03$, $p < 0.01$[4]

For the 50 practice trials and the 280 experimental trials, Figure 8.1 presents the aggregate contribution rates obtained under the control, NPD game and under the APD game with full and with partial feedbacks. The figure shows that the contribution rate under the APD game with partial feedback is substantially higher than the rates obtained under the two other conditions and that this difference was sustained throughout all the experimental trials. This result, coupled with the significantly higher rate of support for authority in the partial (vs. full) feedback, lends support to the negative effect of explicit information about others' profits. As hypothesized,

---

[3] Calculated for 6 groups of 6 players each over 280 experimental trials.
[4] A Post-Hoc Tukey-Kramer (Kramer, 1956) test showed that both differences are significant ($\alpha = 0.05$).

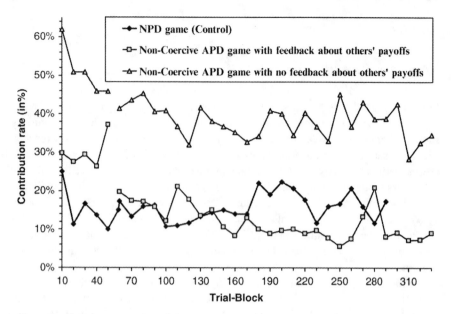

Figure 8.1 The contribution rate obtained for a standard NPD game and two conditions of a non-coercive APD game

this information might have hindered convergence to the β equilibrium, due to the social comparison, facilitated by feedback about others' payoffs.

Moderately Coercive Authority

The results for the six groups in the moderately coercive APD game reveal three patterns. As can be seen in Figure 8.2, these patterns fit the three equilibria. One group (Figure 8.2a) converged to the "all-defect" (α) equilibrium. Two groups (Figures 8.2b and c) oscillated around the β equilibrium, with group C shifting twice from the more profitable "all-support-authority" (γ) equilibrium to the β equilibrium at the beginning of the experimental trials. Three other groups converged to the γ equilibrium in the first 120 trials and sustained this state for the rest of the game. The rate of support for authority under this condition was 64.0% (SD = 29.65%). The fact that different groups converged to different equilibria suggests that the values of fines and fees in this game have created an "intermediate" situation and that an incremental change in fines could increase authority support.

Exploitative Authority

The exploitative APD game tested whether the authority will receive support even when it depletes the players' profits. The results for this condition were highly

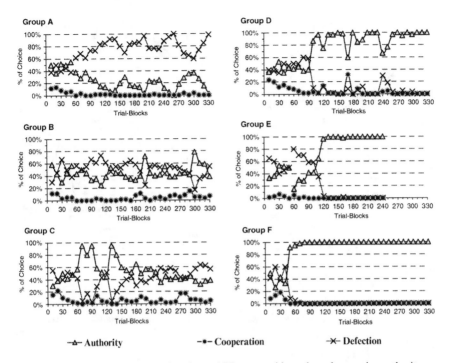

Figure 8.2 Rates of A, C & D choices in an APD game with moderately coercive authority

diverse; thus, more groups were run in order to allow a better examination of the game's dynamics. The results of 10 groups revealed that the rate of support for this type of authority was relatively low (18.9%, SD = 18.2%). Figure 8.3 shows that only one group (group A) out of ten, converged to the inefficient γ equilibrium. In five other groups (groups B to F), participants supported the authority for some consecutive trials. In the remaining four groups (groups G to J), the authority hardly received any support.

Dominating Authority

All three groups that played the dominating APD game with full feedback showed similar patterns of convergence toward the inefficient "all-support-authority" (γ) equilibrium. Overall, the mean rate of authority support was 88.3% (SD = 3.9%). Due to the homogeneity of the results, three groups seemed sufficient for estimating the population mean. Results from another six groups, which played the same game with partial feedback, showed a similar convergence toward the γ equilibrium. The results across trials for all nine groups are shown in Figure 8.4. In the partial feedback condition, the mean rate for authority support was 83.1% (SD = 12.3%), not significantly different from the mean rate reported for the full feedback condition, $t(7) = 0.70$, $p = 0.51$. When the two feedback conditions were analyzed together, a mean support rate of 84.8% (SD = 10.2%) was obtained.

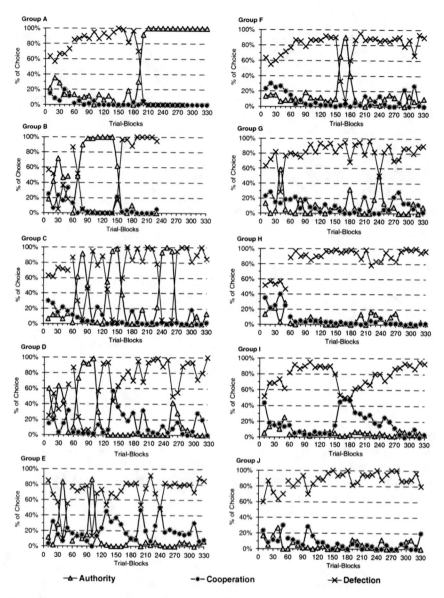

Figure 8.3 Rates of A, C & D choices in an APD game with exploitative authority

Summary

Means and SDs for the four APD games are given in Table 8.2. A one-way ANOVA revealed significant differences between the rates of authority support under the five conditions, $F(4,32) = 23.05$, $p < 0.0001$. As can be seen, the SDs obtained under the various conditions are highly diverse. Because of this, post-hoc tests

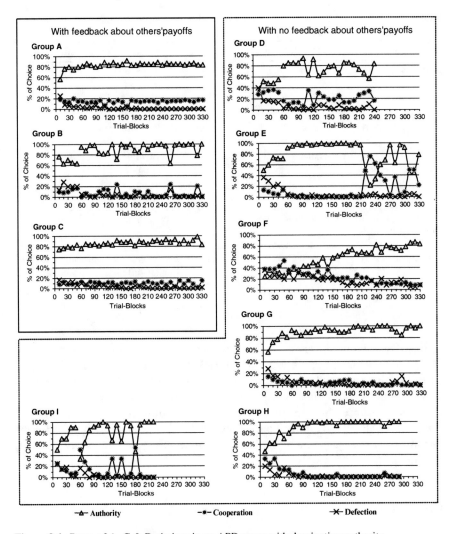

Figure 8.4 Rates of A, C & D choices in an APD game with dominating authority

(Sidak, 1967) were conducted by approximate t-tests based on the assumption that the variances are unequal (Satterthwaite, 1946). The results revealed three significantly distinct clusters of means. Based on the corresponding rate of authority support, each cluster could be associated with one of the game's three equilibria. Cluster a, which yields the lowest authority support, could be associated with convergence to the "all-defect," α equilibrium. Cluster b, with almost 50% authority support, could be associated with convergence to the β equilibrium, and cluster c, with the highest authority support, could be associated with convergence to the "all-support-authority," γ equilibrium.

Table 8.2 Means (and Standard Deviations) of Authority Support for the Five Experimental Conditions of the APD Game

Type of Authority	Type of feedback	No. of groups	Proportion of Authority support
Non-coercive	Regular	6	**27.49%**[a]
			(4.61%)
	Partial	6	**43.82%**[b]
			(7.36%)
Moderately coercive	Regular	6	**63.95%**[a,b,c,d]
			(29.65%)
Exploitative	Regular	10	**18.94%**[a]
			(18.23%)
Dominating	Regular and Partial	9	**84.82%**[c]
			(10.25%)

[a/b/c] Means with the same letter are not significantly different [Sidaks' (1967) post-hoc for independent t-tests].

[d] Due to independency between t-tests, each comparison yielded different confidence intervals. This explains why support of the *moderately coercive authority* was not significantly different from other conditions, although other comparisons, with smaller differences between means, reached significance.

Based on this classification, we may summarize the results by saying that for the non-coercive APD game, if given full feedback the groups converged to the α (all-defect) equilibrium, and under partial feedback to the β (50% authority support–50% defection) equilibrium. For the moderately coercive APD game, results are inconclusive, since different groups converged to different equilibria. For the exploitative APD game, most groups converged to the α equilibrium, and for the dominating APD game all groups converged to the γ (all authority support) equilibrium.

Discussion

Motivated by Hardin's (1968) "mutual coercion, mutually agreed upon" principle, we tested a novel institutional solution to public-good dilemmas. We constructed four variants of a modified NPD game with authority (APD). In all APD games, the "authority" makes the contribution decisions on behalf of its participants and contributes only when contribution is profitable for participants; otherwise, it withholds its contribution. Except for the non-coercive APD game, in all investigated games the authority charged a fee from participants and imposed a fine on non-participants. In addition to the "all-defect" equilibrium for the standard game, this structural change created one or two additional equilibria, depending on the rates of fees and fines. In the non-coercive APD game, another dominant equilibrium (which we call the β equilibrium) is when 50% of the players join the authority and the remaining 50% defect. In the moderately coercive APD game, the additional equilibria are the

β equilibrium and an "all-support-authority" dominant equilibrium (which we call the γ equilibrium). The exploitative and the dominating APD games have an all-support-authority (γ) equilibrium that is dominated by the "all-defect" equilibrium.

The results lend partial support to the equilibrium predictions. They were strongly supported for the non-coercive APD game with partial feedback and for the exploitative APD game, but were refuted for the non-coercive APD game with full feedback and for the dominating APD game. For the moderately coercive APD game, the predicted all-support-authority (γ) equilibrium received fair support, with a 64.0% rate of support for the authority, and with 3 out of 6 groups converging to the predicted equilibrium after 120 trials.

Despite this support, we think that the observed changes across trials in these games, even when it eventually resulted in convergence to a predicted equilibrium, may be better explained by a reinforcement-based principle. As, for instance, the exploitative APD game's payoff matrix clearly shows, the payoffs for players' decisions reinforce convergence to the game-theoretical prediction. In this game, groups that do not start with substantial support for authority have no individual or collective incentive to switch to the "all-support-authority" equilibrium. A similar reasoning applies to the dominating APD game. Although the game-theoretical prediction for this game prescribes convergence to the dominant "all-defect" solution, the uniform convergence of all groups to the dominated "all-support-authority" equilibrium could be explained by the obvious pattern of reinforcement, which, unless all group members avoid the authority choice, is bound to drive the group to the "all-support-authority" solution.

A reinforcement-based principle could also explain why, when feedback is partial, the groups in the non-coercive APD game converged to the predicted β equilibrium and why, for full feedback, the groups were driven away from the same equilibrium. In the first condition, if fewer than 50% of the group members support the authority, others will be indifferent between supporting the authority and defecting, but if 50% or more of the group members support the authority, then everyone else is better off. Taken together, under this condition, a reinforcement-based learning process will eventually push the group toward the predicted equilibrium. Under the second condition, providing feedback reveals the high asymmetry at the β equilibrium and the clear advantage of being a defector rather than an authority supporter. Here again, a reinforcement-based principle with a social reference point could explain the high defection rate (see Figure 8.1) and the failure to converge to the predicted equilibrium.

Like the money-back-guarantee mechanism studied by Dawes et al. (1986), in the non-coercive APD game it is ensured that authority supporters do not waste their money if contribution is not profitable. Notwithstanding, the high level of cooperation achieved under partial feedback stands in contrast to results obtained by Dawes et al. (1986), showing that, compared to the effective fair-share mechanism, the money-back-guarantee mechanism is ineffective for enhancing cooperation (Dawes et al., 1986). This apparent discrepancy may mainly be attributed to two differences between the non-coercive mechanism and the money-back-guarantee mechanism in step-level PG games. First, in our experiment we used a repeated game, whereas

Dawes et al. (1986) employed a one-shot game. Second, the step-level PG dilemma is a game of coordination (Rapoport & Eshed-Levy, 1989) in which excessive contributions are wasted. In such a game, the money-back guarantee does not provide remedy to the redundancy problem. In contrast, the step-level contribution arising from the money-back guarantee of the APD game ensures that one's contribution is never redundant, since any additional contribution (beyond the "threshold" that renders contributions profitable) will increase the collective earnings.

Further research is needed to understand the effects of different structural and psychological variables on the contributions in repeated APD games. Nonetheless, our preliminary investigation highlights two possible solutions for the notorious failure in achieving and sustaining cooperation in situations, which could be modeled by NPD games. First, as long as information about others' payoffs is concealed, cooperation could be significantly enhanced if group members are encouraged to self-organize and manage their contributions collectively. The high rate of cooperation observed in the non-coercive APD game with partial feedback points to the possible effectiveness of this simple, and relatively costless, arrangement. Second, cooperation could be significantly enhanced by a coercive "fees-fines" device, as the one investigated here. The drawback with this device is that ensuring collective cooperation might entail using a fees-fines system, which consumes all participants' benefits, rendering cooperation unworthy for all participants. Note that an organization of this type, like the dominating APD game investigated here, continues to gain its participants' support, albeit the exploitation of all their benefits. Avoiding a "Leviathan," which puts its interest in "eminence" and "power to rule" (Hobbes, 1651) above the interest of its participants, requires that the cost-benefit ratio be kept fixed. It is not the coercive power per se, as Dawes (1980) suggests, that must be restricted, but rather the costs (fees) an organization charges for its services. In the fishing-quota example, described in the introduction, a successful and lasting cooperation creates abundance, which increases the temptation to defect and, subsequently, inflates the cost of coercive measures needed to prohibit defection. In a social dilemma as such, an increase in the cost-benefit ratio seems to be the only way for maintaining resource abundance. Even in such situations, further increase in the cost-benefit ratio should be prohibited. This could be achieved if the organizing institution forecasts the cost-benefit ratio for expected future abundance and applies the expected ratio when offering its coercive services.

The fact that in some trials the exploitative authority was supported by "the majority of the people affected" (Hardin, 1968, p. 1247) could be interpreted in two opposed directions. The pessimist would argue that the majority rule does not make the authority immune from exploitation. The optimist would argue that exploitation could not flourish through democratic means.

References

Dawes, R. M. (1980). Social dilemmas. *Annual Review of Psychology, 31,* 169–195.

Dawes, R. M., Orbell, J. M., Simmons, R. T., Van de Kragt, A. J. C. (1986) Organizing groups for collective action. *American Political Science Review, 80,* 1171–1185.

Hardin, G. (1968). The tragedy of the commons. *Science, 162,* 1243–1248.

Hobbes, T. (1651). *Leviathan, or The Matter, Forme, & Power of a Common-Wealth Ecclesiasticall and Civill.* London: Green Dragon in St. Pauls Church-yard.

Kramer, C. Y. (1956). Extension of multiple range tests to group means with unequal numbers of replications. *Biometrics, 12,* 307–310.

Mulder, L. B., Van Dijk, E., De Cremer, D., Wilke, H. A. M. (2005). The effect of feedback on support for a sanctioning system in a social dilemma: a question of installing or maintaining the sanction. *Journal of Economic Psychology, 26,* 443–458.

Mulder, L. B., Van Dijk, E., De Cremer, D. (2006a). Fighting noncooperative behavior in organizations: The dark side of sanctions. In E. A. Mannix & M. A. Neale (eds.), *Ethics in Groups, Vol. 8, (research on managing groups and teams)* (pp. 59–82). Stamford, CT: JAI Press.

Mulder, L. B., Van Dijk, E., De Cremer, D., Wilke, H. A. M. (2006b). Undermining trust and cooperation: The paradox of sanctioning systems in social dilemmas. *Journal of Experimental Social Psychology, 42,* 147–162.

Mulder, L. B., Van Dijk, E., De Cremer, D., Wilke, H. A. M. (2006c). When sanctions fail to increase cooperation in social dilemmas: Considering the presence of a defective alternative defective option. *Personality and Social Psychology Bulletin, 32,* 1312–1324.

Orbell, J. M., Rutherford, B. (1973). Can Leviathan make the life of man less solitary, poor, nasty, brutish, and short? *British Journal of Political Science, 3,* 383–407.

Platt, G. (1973). Social traps. *American Psychologist, 28,* 641–651.

Rapoport, A., Eshed-Levy, D. (1989) Provision of step-level public goods: Effects of greed and fear of being gypped. *Organizational Behavior and Human Decision Processes, 44,* 325–344.

Satterthwaite, F. W. (1946). An approximate distribution of estimates of variance components. *Biometrics Bulletin, 2,* 110–114.

Sidak, Z. (1967). Rectangular confidence regions for the means of multivariate normal distributions. *Journal of the American Statistical Association, 62,* 626–633.

Van Meegeren, R. C. F. (1997). *Communicatie en maatschappelijke acceptatie. Een onderzoek naar de houding ten aanzien van de "dure afvalzak" in Barendrecht. [Communication and social acceptance. A study of the attitude to the "expensive garbage bag" in Barendrecht].* Wageningen Universiteit, Wageningen.

Yamagishi, T. (1986). The provision of a sanctioning system as a public good. *Journal of Personality and Social Psychology, 51,* 110–116.

Yamagishi, T. (1988a). Seriousness of social dilemmas and the provision of a sanctioning system. *Social Psychology Quarterly, 51,* 32–42.

Yamagishi, T. (1988b). The provision of a sanctioning system in the United States and Japan. *Social Psychology Quarterly, 51,* 264–270.

Yamagishi, T. (1992). Group size and the provision of a sanctioning system in a social dilemma. In W. B. G. Liebrand, D. M. Messick. & H. A. M. Wilke (eds.), *Social Dilemmas* (pp. 267–287). Oxford: Pergamon Press.

Chapter 9
A Recursive Model for Changing Justice Concerns in Social Dilemmas

David A. Schroeder, Alicia F. Bembenek, Kimberly M. Kinsey, Julie E. Steel, and Andria J. Woodell

In 2003, we (Schroeder et al., 2003) presented an analysis of justice concerns and considerations of fairness within social dilemma situations. At that time, we perceived the various types of justice criteria (i.e., distributive, procedural, restorative, retributive) as evolving in a more or less sequential manner as the status of a common resource pool or the threat to a public good changed for the worse over time. Social dilemmas are intriguing mixed-motive situations in which those involved must make choices between acting in their own best interests versus acting for the well-being of a group, and the decisions made can lead to unequal outcomes among the group members. These asymmetries make social dilemma situations particularly well suited for the study of how members of these groups strive to find fair and just accommodations to the self-interest vs. communal interest conflicts operating upon them.

Because many social dilemmas are iterative and dynamic, they also provide an excellent context within which to explore how these accommodations might shift over time as the parameters of the situation change as a consequence of the choices made by the group (see Ostrom, 1990, for examples). For instance, in the case of common pool dilemmas, as people repeatedly harvest from some resource pool and thereby alter the status of the resource, the consideration that needs to be given to the protection of the pool (and especially to the protection of one's *own* outcomes) will be modified as well. We think individuals caught in social dilemmas look for solutions and social arrangements that will provide a measure of stability to answer the longitudinal concerns of how they are going to protect this common pool or how they are going to provide for the public good.

In addition to concerns for the stability and continued viability of some common good, we believe potential or actual differences among the payoffs received by group members may challenge the cooperator's sense of fairness and justice; individuals disadvantaged by the competitive actions of others may begin to question their role as "suckers" in their group settings. If, as former baseball manager Leo Durocher once said, "Nice guys finish last," what are the "losers" to do? Overharvesters in common pools dilemmas and free riders in public-good dilemmas are always going to be at a competitive advantage relative to the cooperators, and we think that those who have been disadvantaged (as well as some who recognize the folly of defecting but have nonetheless continued to overharvest or free-ride to protect themselves from

A. Biel et al. (eds.), *New Issues and Paradigms in Research on Social Dilemmas.*

being suckers) will want to consider options other than a *laissez-faire*, free choice for all situation. They will recognize the necessity of imposing some restraint on the actions of others to avoid further exploitation; they may also realize that if restraints are not imposed on the group, then every member of the group will fall prey to the dire predictions of Garrett Hardin (1968) that "ruin is the destination toward which all men rush, each pursuing his own best interests, ... freedom in the common brings ruin to all" (p. 1244).

By recognizing the injustices that may arise in social dilemma situations and that some limits must be placed on the behavioral options available, groups will want to try to find some fair and just resolution to the individualistic versus group tensions (Barnett, 2000). This tension represents the very essence of social dilemmas. While those calling for the development of means to protect the common goods might want to retain their own freedoms to act as they wish, these same individuals would be reluctant to grant similar freedom to others. That is, while they believe they can trust themselves to act in a fair and socially responsible manner, they are less certain that they can trust others to work for the common good. We see the introduction of explicit justice concerns as a novel and potentially important addition to our understandings of decision making in social dilemmas. In essence, we are suggesting a need to take into account individuals' appraisals of the fairness of outcomes among group members caught in social dilemmas and their steps that they then take to ensure fair and just outcomes for all group members.

Justice Concerns in Social Dilemmas

In our 2003 paper, we tried to explore distributive, procedural, restorative, and retributive justice concerns within social dilemmas. In this chapter, we will build on our initial work in this area and now present a more comprehensive, "recursive" model (see Figure 9.1). This model not only recognizes the emergence of different justice concerns as the group uses the common resource pool but also helps to differentiate between the actions that might be taken following violations of the rules and regulations that have been established to protect the common resource. To understand the processes underlying the emergence of the different justice concerns, we will also discuss possible "triggers" that lead groups and their members to shift from one justice concern to another.

Briefly, we believe that within particular social dilemma situations (e.g., settings in which resources are abundant and therefore no regulation is imposed), *distributive justice* concerns prevail so long as equity exists among group members. However, when some threshold of inequity is reached in the distribution of the group members' individual outcomes, justice motivations shift to *procedural concerns* as the group begins the process of establishing standardized rules and regulations to guarantee equitable allocations of resources among group members in the future and perhaps some measure of long-term protection of the common resource.

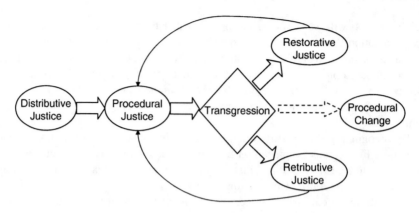

Figure 9.1 The recursive model of justice concerns within social dilemmas

If violations of the agreed-upon procedural system subsequently occur (i.e., over-harvesting, defections, free riding, represented by the "Transgression" component in Figure 9.1), the group must shift its central justice concerns once again. Depending on the nature of the violations (e.g., frequency, magnitude, perceived motivations of the transgressors), group members may (1) seek *restorative justice* to make the situation fair once again, (2) seek *retributive justice* not only to restore fairness but also to punish the defector, or (3) enact procedural change as a means to make the justice system more effective and responsive to the needs of the group.

Distributive Justice Concerns

We start our consideration by taking a look at distributive justice issues: What fairness criterion is used to judge whether or not fair allocations have been made among the parties in the social dilemma? The primary standard for judgments of fairness has been whether there has been an *equitable* distribution of resources among group members; that is, whether there is proportionality between the inputs and the outcomes of each member of the group (e.g., Walster et al., 1976). For those individuals who have offered the most to the group product or group effort, it is generally considered fair and equitable for those contributors to realize a greater proportion of the outcome. Conversely, the equity norm prescribes that individuals who have contributed less should realize less in the final allocation.

Note that equity does not necessarily imply equality. Equal distributions can be recognized as a special case of equity theory—circumstances in which each individual's input is perceived as being equal (e.g., all members of the same ingroup), resulting in the perception that the outcome for each individual should be equal as well. There may be some unique situations in which the group judges a fair distribution by acknowledging more than the ratio of input and outcomes alone; for example, if a certain amount of some resource is necessary for individual survival, groups may try to ensure that all members receive that subsistence level, regardless of their personal means. Frohlich and Oppenheimer (1992) made this sort of suggestion, arguing that in the allocation of certain public services and protections, people endorse plans that guarantee an equality-based subsistence floor representing a safety net for everyone (something akin to the intent of the Social Security system in the United States). However, after the safety net has been provided, groups see that the standards for what passes as the fair allocations of resources can then shift to an equity criterion based on an individual's merits and personal contributions to the system. This blending of equality and equity rules ensures a more responsive form of fairness to all.

"Triggers" for Change

In common pool dilemmas, the shared resource pool may initially be of sufficient capacity that there is no immediate problem with allowing all members of the group to have free access. Those involved may not be concerned about differential outcomes; as long as each individual perceives that he or she is satisfying his or her personal needs, the situation is fair and just. At some point, however, as use of the pool approaches the carrying capacity, as depletion of the pool appears imminent, or as one's outcomes no longer satisfy needs (or wants) or remain comparable to those of others, we believe that people will start to become concerned about the common good of the group, concerned for the resource viability for the future, and especially concerned about their own prospects. They may not have recognized a need for resource conservation at the outset, but as the "shadow of the future" becomes darker and darker and the personal implications of the deteriorating situation become more unfavorable, individuals may recognize that free access may not be an effective or efficient way for a group to operate within most social dilemmas. As the threat of losing the resource becomes clearer, there is a greater tension between the value people place on their own liberties and the constraints they feel may need to be placed on the group as a whole (Barnett, 2000). John Baden (1998) suggested that there will be the recognition of necessity for some constraint on the individual freedom in order to preclude greater loss in the future, and we believe this recognition of necessity will trigger problem-solving efforts that will result in the development of new procedures that will help ensure the group's well-being.

Procedural Justice Concerns

As we have noted, social dilemmas are usually iterative; there are constantly evolving changes in the status of the resource pool or need for some public good and continuing relationships among group members. Throughout this ongoing process, the individuals involved—singly and collectively—continue to evaluate their satisfaction with their own outcomes (Schroeder et al., 1995). When individual group members become dissatisfied with their own outcomes or concerned about the future of the resource for all, the group may turn to procedural justice considerations in its attempt to ensure overall joint satisfaction in the long run. Fair procedures produce beneficial results that are not only limited to the increased satisfaction of the individuals involved but also continued or improved resource viability and stability (e.g., Brockner & Wiesenfeld, 1996; De Cremer & Tyler, 2005). The favorable effects of fair procedures can be attributed to their ability to directly or indirectly impact prosocial behaviors in dilemmas. In particular, fair procedures decrease defection and increase cooperation by (1) increasing distributive satisfaction (Brockner et al., 1994; Brockner & Wiesenfeld, 1996), (2) soliciting group members' input, reducing future uncertainty in allocation decisions and outcomes (Thibaut & Walker, 1975; Van den Bos & Lind, 2002), (3) engaging the group members, leading to increased future cooperation (De Cremer & Tyler, 2005), and (4) introducing specific allocation solutions and possible sanctions for future defectors (e.g., Platt, 1973; Messick & Brewer, 1983; Dolsak & Ostrom, 2003).

Increasing Distributive Satisfaction

Individuals who have had a "voice" or a measure of input in the development of resource allocation procedures are typically committed to the use of those procedures and are therefore likely to perceive the results of the application of those rules as being fair. As a consequence, those who have contributed to the formulation of the allocation guidelines are less likely to defect themselves as a means of "leveling the playing field" when differences in the distributions are observed; they will trust that everything will "even out" in the long run. In addition, Brockner and his colleagues (Brockner et al., 1994; Brockner & Wiesenfeld, 1996) suggested that a group member's determination of whether he or she has been treated fairly is based more on whether agreed-upon procedures have been followed than on the magnitude or objective nature of the resource allocation received.

Reducing the Uncertainty

Based on the work of Thibaut and Walker (1975), individuals prefer a voice concerning the decisions and outcomes that affect them. That is, they want to have input about what the goals of the group should be and how the group should go about achieving those goals. By allowing group members voice and gaining input from those directly involved, there is a belief that there will be a fair method determined for the distribution goals of the group as a whole. Allocation procedures may often be established in response to perceptions that a current allocation scheme (e.g., "freedom in the commons") will lead to unfair distributions; however, a recent study in our lab found that individuals prefer to enact explicit procedures to determine subsequent resource allocations, regardless of whether the group member had been overbenefited, underbenefited, or treated equitably in previous interactions. That is, even if individuals have received a fair distribution of some resource, they prefer to have established procedures in place to guide future interactions and guarantee that these interactions will result in fair outcomes.

More recently, Van den Bos and Lind (2002) have suggested that one implicit objective underlying an individual's need for control (as suggested in Thibaut & Walker, 1975) is the desire to reduce uncertainty in one's life. Van den Bos and Lind have proposed an uncertainty management model suggesting that in ambiguous situations (i.e., where one does not have sufficient information) individuals will search for pertinent information (e.g., the fairness of the procedures used) in order to better understand their circumstances. Furthermore, individuals assume that if the currently utilized procedures are fair, then the situation in which they are involved is secure.

Although not the primary focus of their theory, we believe that the implications for prosocial behaviors are considerable. In fact, Van den Bos and Lind (2002) briefly stated that the reduction of uncertainty is important in social dilemma situations and that uncertainty reduction is central in establishing trust (Holmes & Rempel, 1989). In addition, research by De Cremer and Stouten (2003) has suggested that cooperative efforts between individuals are the result of increased trust.

Engaging the Group Members

Fair procedures not only increase the control and reduce the uncertainty (bolstering trust among individuals) but also, according to Tyler and Blader's (2000, 2003) group engagement model, satisfy social needs for validation and respect and promote a sense of belonging among those in the group. In addition, De Cremer and Tyler (2005) have argued that increasing the perceptions of respect among group members by the adoption of fair procedures will result in increased prosocial decisions within the group (see also Dovidio et al., 2006). De Cremer and Tyler stated that procedural fairness "activates people's intrinsic motivation to promote the interests and viability of the group" (p. 154), enhancing trust within the group and thereby increasing cooperation.

Introducing Specific Allocation Solutions and Possible Sanctions

A fourth feature of procedural justice, and perhaps the one having the greatest impact on the actual behavior of group members, involves the use of structural solutions for social dilemmas (e.g., Schroeder et al., 1995). These solutions (often the product of the information exchange when group members have been given voice) define (either formally or informally) the rules and procedures for the allocation process (e.g., Platt, 1973; Messick & Brewer, 1983; Dolsak & Ostrom, 2003; Ostrom, 1990) and, in some cases, the procedures may also specify the actions the group may take against defectors and free riders who fail to abide by the rules (e.g., Yamagishi, 1986). With the implementation of structural solutions, the group is trying to implement procedures that will ensure fair distribution of resources for all members and prevent (or at the least delay) the depletion of a common resource pool that would be lost if some intervention were not taken.

Informal Procedures

Because we have all been socialized within ongoing social systems, we cannot examine behavior in social dilemmas without recognizing that we all have had common normative "training" histories of how to deal with problems akin to these distribution problems. As a result, informal procedures may emerge more or less spontaneously when the need for action has been recognized. Kerr (1995) has described the nature of "general interaction norms" that individuals have acquired through the socialization process, and van Dijk and Wilke (1995; van Dijk et al., 1999) have more recently discussed what they call "tacit coordination rules" by which simply being a member of a group elicits a basic goal of ensuring fairness among the group members. In addition, Russell Hardin (1982) explored norms and conventions as representing general guidelines for appropriate behaviors, and he also argued that these conventions may include how to seek redress for transgressions. These analyses would serve to corroborate Posner's (2000) claims that, "In a world with no law and rudimentary government, order of some sort would exist. The order would appear as routine compliance to social norms and the corrective infliction of sanctions on those who violate them, including stigmatization of the deviant and ostracism of the incorrigible" (p. 3).

In his book *Order Without Law* (1991), Ellickson provided an exemplary case history of the social transition of Shasta County, California, from a largely agricultural area to a mixed-use county of "ranchette" owners living among life-long cattlemen who grazed their stock on open range. According to Ellickson, as the transition was taking place in response to the changing demographics of the region, reactions to transgressions (particularly trespassing cattle) were often handled informally according to a norm-based series of implicit, escalating steps. When a violation of the norms was first recognized, the wronged party would simply begin to spread "truthful negative gossip" about the transgressor's failing to do the right thing; because of the citizens' general obsession with neighborliness, corrective action was typically taken promptly in order for the transgressor to avoid having the reputation of his family name in some way soiled. Only rarely did disputants actually seek remedies within the legal system. According to Ellickson, reactions to trespass conflicts were "generally resolved *not* in 'the shadow of the law' but, rather, *beyond* that shadow. Most rural residents are consciously committed to an overarching norm of cooperation among neighbors... . Allegiance to this norm seems wholly independent of legal entitlements" (1991, pp. 52–53, emphases in the original). It is interesting to note that the citizens also lived by a norm that minor transgressions should simply be tolerated or "lumped," recognizing the advantages of "reciprocal lumping" compared to the costs in time and money of having to deal with incidents of little consequence (p. 54).

Formal Procedures

Such informal, norm-based justice procedures may not always be sufficient to restrain selfish interests that affect resource allocations, and in some cases, the attempts of individuals to deal personally with transgressors may actually exacerbate the problems if everyone is left to his own retaliatory devices. To avoid these situations, more formal procedures may be needed, and Tyler (Tyler & Blader, 2000) and Posner (2000) have suggested that formal social arrangements will emerge to control and restrain the most competitive and destructive urges of group members.

Recall that Garrett Hardin's prescription for dealing with the adverse outcomes that he believed to be the inevitable consequence of unrestrained consumption in common pool dilemmas (and, by extension, rampant free riding in public-good dilemmas) was "mutual coercion, mutually agreed upon" (1968, p. 1247). Hardin argued that socio-political action was the only solution for social dilemmas and that individuals must come together to have the group decide how it would manage its resources (another example of the importance of voice for determining fair procedures). Furthermore, because of the personal benefits that individuals would realize by overharvesting the commons if left to their own devices, he saw the coercion that would be inherent in social contracts as being necessary to promote cooperation and to discourage defection and free riding.

Hardin's prescription is very similar to that offered by Rawls (1971, 1999, 2001) in his notion of "justice as fairness." Rawls argued that the fair terms of social cooperation are given by agreements or social contracts freely entered into by those involved. Rawls, like Hardin, is granting to the group the responsibility of finding its own solution, but that solution is again one to which everyone must agree (i.e., mutually agreed upon) and one with which everyone must abide by (i.e., mutual coercion). These agreements are entered into by "free and equal individuals," and the most powerful are not allowed to dictate what the rules of allocation are going to be.

There are costs involved with the implementation of formal procedures (R. Hardin, 1982), however, as compared to the informal arrangements that Ellickson (1991) described. For example, there can be significant coordination costs for formalizing the procedures and costs associated with learning the applicable laws and regulations. Systems must be put in place for the administration of these new rules and for the imposition of sanctions for those who violate these rules; of course, these systems often require some investment of the group's resources (e.g., taxes paid to support the judicial system) and can become a "second-order" social dilemma (Ostrom, 2001). On the other hand, significant benefits can be realized by having such procedures in place. Of perhaps greatest importance is that formal procedures may increase trust and reduce the fear of those individuals in the social dilemma (De Cremer & Tyler, 2005). If individuals can trust that others will not take advantage because of the rules and regulations that are in place, they will be more likely to cooperate, limit harvests, and contribute to the public good. Individuals may not really trust others, but they do trust the situation with its formal rules in place enough to be cooperative and abide by the prescriptions themselves. Explicit procedural justice systems may be a form of a social glue that can hold the group together through that promotion of trust, reduction of fear, suppression of greed, and even suggestion of mutual respect among the individuals who are involved (e.g., De Cremer & Tyler, 2005).

If formal procedures are in place, who is to pay the cost of enforcement and impose the sanctions? Ernst Fehr and his colleagues (e.g., Fehr & Gächter, 2002) introduced the concept of "altruistic punishment" and the notion that each member of the group should be willing to bear some costs to punish transgressors, even if all members have not been directly harmed by the transgressor's actions. They suggested that groups are not only interested in punishing those who have transgressed but are also interested in punishing those who do not contribute to the punishment of the transgressor. These "second-order" free riders are willing to benefit from the sanctions imposed and paid for by other group members, but they are unwilling to make their fair contribution to the support of the sanctioning system (Ostrom, 2001). Fehr and Gächter (2002) approached the sanctioning issue from an evolutionary-based view of self-sacrificial altruism, but recent work by Carlsmith and Wilson (2005) has shown that strong egoistic motivations may also be operating within punishment systems. They suggested that individuals feel good and derive satisfaction from the awareness that the defector is being punished in some way, either by the victim or by other agents. They have labeled this "hedonistic punishment."

Reactions to Violations: Restorative and Retributive Justice

Procedural justice systems, whether formal or informal, are means of social control that move individuals away from individual rationality and toward a group rationality criterion that is intended to ensure a fair and just distribution of resources that promotes the common good. Despite a group's best efforts to institute fair and just procedural justice systems and to make explicit the consequences that would be suffered for defections, each individual's decision-making process is ultimately reduced to a personal cost-benefit analysis that will continue to factor in selfish, individual rationality considerations. Walster et al. (1976, p. 5) made this egoistic point most succinctly: "So long as individuals perceive that they can maximize their outcomes by behaving equitably, they will do so. Should they perceive that they can maximize their outcomes by behaving inequitably, they will do so." Defection has been recognized as an inevitable occurrence; however, the group members' reactions toward those who transgress are not as easily described, predicted, or explained, and trying to understand possible reactions of victims toward transgressors has been the crux of our own conceptual and empirical research efforts over the past several years.

We believe that one of two types of justice concerns will emerge in response to violations of agreed-upon procedures and defections from the common good. One is *restorative* or compensatory justice; restorative reactions are primarily self-focused and intended to make restitution to victims (i.e., the cooperators in the social dilemma) for past transgressions and/or to restore social order (Darley, 2002). The notion of restoration is to make the victims whole again by compensating them for costs they have been forced to bear by the defector's actions (e.g., Tyler et al., 1997; Darley & Pittman, 2003). The second type of justice concern that may be activated is *retributive* or punitive justice; retributive reactions are driven by the joint goals of compensation to the victim and punishment of the offender (Darley & Pittman, 2003). Retribution has also been discussed as a means of restoring social order (Rawls, 1971, 1999; Bradley, 2003), but retribution primarily serves a punitive function, although the motive for punishment may differ. As outlined in Table 9.1, punishment of the offender may serve the purpose of deterrence (e.g., Nagin, 1998; Bradley, 2003; Crombag et al., 2003), re-education of the perpetrator (e.g., Miller, 2001), just deserts (e.g., Darley, 2002; Carlsmith et al., 2002), increasing positive affect (e.g., hedonic punishment; Carlsmith & Wilson, 2005), reasserting the integrity of the group and its values (Tyler et al., 1997), and/or lowering the status of the offender (Vidmar, 2001). Although making clear distinctions between restorative and retributive justice is not always easy (because many writers

Table 9.1 Factors Impacting Restorative or Retributive Reactions to Defections

	Restorative	Retributive
Type of defection (e.g., Tyler et al., 1997)	Material	Symbolic
Magnitude of defection (e.g., Steel, 2004)	Lesser	Greater
Attributions of cause (e.g., Steel, 2004; Bembenek et al., 2005)	Accidental	Intentional
Frequency of defection (e.g., Bembenek et al., 2005)	Fewer	Greater
Group membership of defector (e.g., Woodell et al., 2002)	Ingroup	Outgroup
Underlying Motives		
Restore victim (e.g., Tyler et al., 1997; Darley & Pittman, 2003)	Present	Present
Restore social order (e.g., Darley, 2002; Bradley, 2003)	Present	Present
Punishment of the transgressor	Absent	Present
Deterrence (e.g., Bradley, 2003; Crombag et al., 2003)	Absent	Present
Re-educate/reduce future defections (e.g., Miller, 2001)	Absent	Present
Just deserts (e.g., Darley, 2002; Carlsmith et al., 2002)	Present	Present
Hedonic punishment (e.g., Carlsmith & Wilson, 2005)	Absent	Present
Reassert group values (e.g., Vidmar, 2001)	Absent	Present
Lower status of offender (e.g., Vidmar, 2001)	Absent	Present
Affective Factors		
Negative affect (e.g., Steel, 2004)	Present	Present
Moral outrage (e.g., Wright, 2000; Darley & Pittman, 2003)	Absent/Low	Present/High

have used the terms synonymously), we believe there are multiple factors that determine whether the reaction to defection will, in fact, be restorative or retributive in nature, and these factors and motives can be used to differentiate the two types of responses (see Table 9.1).

Restorative Justice

When restorative justice concerns are paramount, group members react against a transgressor with the underlying motives of restoring the status quo for victims, requiring the transgressor to make amends, and compensating those who have been harmed by the transgressor's actions (e.g., Darley, 2002; Darley & Pittman, 2003). Restorative efforts are primarily victim-focused in nature, and the primary action taken toward transgressors is that they must relinquish their ill-gotten advantage. The defector who overharvests in a common pool dilemma or free-rides for some public good may be asked to make restitution.

The objective nature of the offense is one of the critical factors in determining if restorative concerns will be foremost in the minds of those who have been disadvantaged. For example, Tyler and his colleagues (Tyler et al., 1997; Tyler & Blader, 2000) have suggested that restorative justice may be most easily employed when there has been some form of material loss. In such cases, it is relatively straightforward to assign value to the loss that has been experienced, and therefore it is easy to require that the wrongdoer make proportionate amends. When the loss suffered is of relatively low magnitude, simply asking for compensation equal to the loss to be made will likely be sufficient to "balance the books" for the victim and allow the ongoing relationship to continue (Steel, 2004). While this solution to the infraction can be easily accomplished when the cost to the victim is material or monetary, minor violations of interactional justice (e.g., insults, displays of disrespect) can often be resolved by the transgressor acknowledging the *faux pas* and offering an apology (e.g., Goffman, 1959; Miller, 2001).

Causal attributions made by victims to explain transgressions are often the primary predictor for either restorative or retributive efforts, with accidental defections resulting in restorative attempts and intentional defections leading to retributive efforts. For example, the frequency of transgressions may play an important role in determining whether restitution for the harm will be sufficient. Committing a single infraction (e.g., exceeding an agreed-upon harvesting quota from some jointly held resource pool) may require some repayment to compensate other shareholders, and some warning about future incidents may be issued. A single transgression by an individual who has otherwise abided by the procedural justice rules and regulations is likely to be attributed to some set of external circumstances that led to what would be judged an accident (e.g., Kelley, 1973). One minor mistake by the transgressor would not necessarily lead to an attribution of intentional harm, and restitution to make those who have been harmed whole again would be a satisfactory response for the transgressor (Steel, 2004). In fact, mistakes do happen, and those who have inadvertently caused harm by their actions may be willing to compensate those who have suffered.

In an attempt to find empirical evidence for these claims (using scenarios of defections in a public-good dilemma—contributions to a class project), we (Bembenek et al., in preparation) manipulated the frequency of the transgressions and found that after a single transgression, individuals more strongly believed that the defector's behavior was due to situational factors as compared to cases in which two or more defections had occurred. Conversely, individuals endorsed internal attributions for the defection to a greater extent after two or more defections as compared to one. We also measured endorsements of particular behavioral responses toward the defector and found that individuals reported a greater preference to "do nothing in response to [the defector's] actions" after only one transgression (see also Bies & Tripp, 1996) as compared to two or more incidents; however, relatively extreme retributive responses (i.e., removing the defector from the group) were more strongly endorsed after two or more defections.

Finally, the group membership of the defector may affect attributions for the defection as well as victims' justice-seeking efforts. Based on recent evidence (Bembenek et al., in preparation), it appears that after one defection, victims tended to believe that an ingroup defector's behavior was more likely to have been caused by external circumstances than was an outgroup defector's behavior. Consistent with this view, victims are less likely to recommend penalizing an ingroup defector as compared to an outgroup defector. We suggest that the attributions of intentionality and subsequent reactions to defections may be influenced by the defector's group membership; although ingroup transgressors are not well liked because of their actions, group membership appears to confer on the defector some measure of "benefit of the doubt" about the intent of their action and may protect them from punishment (Woodell et al., 2002).

The idea of granting the benefit of the doubt may also come into play in those social dilemma situations in which the defector has played an ambiguous role in the situation (Steel, 2004). Instances in which it is unclear to other group members why an individual acted in a particular way will result in vague and indeterminate attributions of intentionality for the transgressor's actions, even if everyone knows that something contrary to the outcome expected by the procedural justice rules occurred. Transgressors may understand the role these factors play and may intentionally try to obscure their intent and to hide behind the inability of those making judgments to unequivocally label the transgressor as having intentionally caused harm. If defectors are able to avoid attributions of intentionality for their wrongdoing and hide behind a shield of "plausible deniability," restitution may be all that is asked to restore a sense of justice among those who have been harmed.

Retributive Justice

But when defectors consistently take advantage of their fellow group members, when the stakes for the defections become high, or when only insincere apologies are offered (that is, when defectors are seen as having intentionally exploited the group), those who have followed the rules may feel that the matter cannot be satisfactorily resolved simply by having the transgressor make restitution for the wrong that was done (e.g., Agrawal, 1994; Steel, 2004; Darley & Pittman, 2003). Exploited members of the group who have had their trust violated may feel that justice has truly been reestablished only when some retribution and punishment have been meted out for the violation. While restorative justice concerns seem to focus primarily on the victim and asks the defector to set things right, a group's retributive justice concerns are primarily other-focused and driven by the desire to punish the transgressor. A review of the literature suggests that retribution serves many purposes and the underlying motives of punishment vary. Most individuals endorse honorable motives of deterrence (Bradley, 2003; Crombag et al., 2003) and re-education with the intent of reductions in future offences (Miller, 2001); however, Darley and his colleagues have found stronger evidence of a "just deserts" motive (Darley, 2002; Darley et al., 2000; Carlsmith et al., 2002) in which "the perpetrator deserves to be punished for the past harm he or she committed [and] the punishment is a valuable end in itself and needs no further justification" (Darley et al., 2000, p. 660).

As mentioned above, in addition to deterrence, re-education, and just-deserts motives, some recent evidence suggests that punishing a defector may also serve a satisfying hedonic function for those who have been harmed by transgressors' actions (Carlsmith & Wilson, 2005). Group members who have been harmed by the selfish actions of others seem to use retribution to assuage their moral indignation; retributive justice requires the defector not only to make compensation but to be punished as well. (In fact, we think of retribution as to "restore, and a little more.") As Carlsmith and Wilson pointed out in their work on hedonic punishment, retribution feels good, so there may be a reward for those imposing the punishment on the transgressor.

Other motives for seeking retributive justice may include the notion of asserting the group values and increasing the cohesiveness of the group as the defectors are punished and the cooperators are rewarded for their loyalty to the group (Tyler et al., 1997; Vidmar, 2001; De Cremer & Tyler, 2005). In line with the group engagement model, taking retributive action against a transgressor reasserts the integrity and value of the group. It may be seen as validating and bolstering the group's identity and demonstrating that the group does have the authority to expect and even require honest relationships among the members of the group that conform to the agreed-upon procedures for resource allocations.

Retribution also tends to lower the status of the defector in the eyes of the other group members (e.g., Vidmar, 2001) and, in line with the interactional justice criterion, concomitantly raises the self-esteem of the cooperating group members who did keep the faith, who did abide by the rules, and who did follow the dictates of the formal system in place. It raises self-esteem as they assert power over the offender—no one is above the law and the rules were established to serve the goals of fairness and justice in the group.

Finally, a central role of affective reactions in retribution for defections and transgressions has been suggested by some writers, but it has not yet received much attention by researchers. Although the conditions that we have described as precursors to restorative justice would seem to lead to rather "cool" decision making, intentional attempts to take advantage of fellow group members that we have suggested to be a precursor to retributive actions may be expected to arouse strong emotional reactions and "hot" cognitions. Wright (2000) said that in cases of retribution, "we are driven by something deeper and hotter than sheer reason, by a feeling of moral indignation, of just grievance" (p. 24), and he suggests moral indignation is the trigger for retribution. Recent theory (Darley & Pittman, 2003) has also suggested that the degree of moral outrage contributes to the type of justice-seeking response that will be displayed; according to these researchers, "low moral outrage" results in restorative justice efforts, but "high moral outrage" results in a desire to seek retribution. Work in our lab has consistently found the expected arousal of negative affect in victims of defections (Steel, 2004; Woodell, 2005; Bembenek, 2006), but we have not yet demonstrated the mediational role of emotions in the display of retribution, retaliation, and revenge.

When Restoration and Retribution "Miss the Mark"

In addition to restorative and retributive actions, our recursive model suggests a third option that may come into play if the members of the group begin to realize the need to impose restorative or retributive actions upon transgressors with great frequency or to note that the transgressions are of great magnitude. This realization may lead group members to consider whether specific procedural justice rules are meeting the intended purposes and needs of the group and perhaps to assess the overall fairness of the rules that are in place. For example, repeated violations of the 18th Amendment to the U.S. Constitution prohibiting the manufacture and sale of alcoholic beverages in the 1920s and 1930s and more recent examples in which drivers consistently exceeded the 55-mile per hour speed limit on interstate highways led to the repeal of these laws to bring them in line with conventional behaviors. Dissatisfaction with the outcomes resulting from the application of the established procedural justice rules pushed the group beyond some justice "tipping point" (Gladwell, 2000), at which point the group entertained the need for new forms of procedural justice (i.e., new structural solutions) to evolve (e.g., Ostrom, 1990).

We would return to our roots in the social dilemma literature that dealing with the resource management problems is an iterative process. As members of a group receive feedback about how well their procedures are doing and monitor the success (and failure) of the procedures that are in place to ensure justice and fairness, the members may recognize the need to make adjustments to their system. In some cases, the adjustments may be relatively minor, but in other cases, the overall situation may have changed to such an extent (e.g., the once-abundant supplies of fossil fuels begin to approach "the end of oil"; Roberts, 2004) that something akin to a justice paradigm shift (Kuhn, 1970) may be required.

Implications of the Recursive Model for Understanding Decisions in Social Dilemmas

As we step back a bit and take a look at our proposed recursive justice model, it is important to make explicit that we believe that the desired equilibrium state for the members of a group is, in fact, the preservation of the procedural policies that are serving the ultimate goal of distributive justice and fairness. The group members will consistently return to procedural justice concerns after dealing with instances of defection and taking the steps necessary to restore justice to ensure fair outcomes and the fair application of the procedural justice rules. Within that context, we see restorative and retributive justice actions as being instrumental means to the end of maintaining procedural justice, rather than being ends in and of themselves. The end stasis of the group's actions will be at the procedural justice level to realize the distributional, instrumental, and interactional benefits that established procedures provide and, perhaps more importantly, to avoid that ruin in the commons toward which Garrett Hardin (1968) claimed we are all rushing.

Acknowledgments   The authors gratefully acknowledge the support for this work provided by the Marie Wilson Howells Fund, Department of Psychology, University of Arkansas. Portions of this chapter have been presented at the 10th International Conference on Social Dilemmas, Marstrand, Sweden, August 2003, and the conventions of the Society of Experimental Social Psychology, Ft. Worth, Texas, October 2004, and the Society for Personality and Social Psychology, New Orleans, January 2005.

References

Agrawal, A. (1994). Rules, rule making, and rule breaking: Examining the fit between rule systems and resource use. In E. Ostrom, R. Gardner & J. Walker (eds.), *Rules, Games, and Common-Pool Resources*. Ann Arbor: University of Michigan Press.

Baden, J. A. (1998). A new primer for the management of common-pool resources and public goods. In J. A. Baden & D. S. Noonan (eds.), *Managing the Common* (2nd ed., pp. 51–62). Bloomington: Indiana University Press.

Barnett, R. (2000). *The Structure of Liberty: Justice and the Rule of Law*. Oxford: Oxford University Press.

Bembenek, A. F. (2006). Retaliation as a function of justice violations: The possible mediational role of negative affect. *Unpublished doctoral dissertation*, University of Arkansas.

Bembenek, A. F., Woodell, A. J., Kinsey, K., Schroeder, D. A. (in preparation). The effects of group membership and repeated transgressions on retributive responses.

Bies, R. J., Tripp, T. M. (1996). Beyond distrust: "Getting even" and the need for revenge. In R. M. Kramer & T. R. Tyler (eds.), *Trust in Organizations: Frontiers of Theory and Research* (pp. 246–260). Thousand Oaks, CA: Sage.

Bradley, G. (2003). Retribution: The central aim of punishment. *Harvard Journal of Law and Public Policy, 27*, 19–31.

Brockner, J., Konovsky, M., Cooper-Schneider, R., Folger, R., Martin, C. L., Bies, R. J. (1994). The interactive effects of procedural justice and outcome negativity on the victims and survivors of job loss. *Academy of Management Journal, 37*, 397–409.

Brockner, J., Wiesenfeld, B. M. (1996). An integrative framework for explaining reactions to decisions: Interactive effects of outcomes and procedures. *Psychological Bulletin, 120*, 189–208.

Carlsmith, K. M., Darley, J. M., Robinson, P. H. (2002). Why do we punish? Deterrence and just deserts as motives for punishment. *Journal of Personality and Social Psychology, 83*, 284–299.

Carlsmith, K. M., Wilson, T. D. (2005). Hedonic punishment. Unpublished manuscript.

Crombag, H., Rassin, E., Horselenberg, R. (2003). On vengeance. *Psychology, Crime, & Law, 9*, 333–344.

Darley, J. M. (2002). Just punishments: Research on retributional justice. In M. Ross & D. T. Miller (eds.), *The Justice Motive in Everyday Life* (pp. 314–333). New York: Cambridge University Press.

Darley, J. M., Carlsmith, K. M., Robinson, P. H. (2000). Incapacitation and just deserts as motives for punishment. *Law and Human Behavior, 24*, 659–683.

Darley, J. M., Pittman, T. S. (2003). The psychology of compensation and retributive justice. *Personality and Social Psychology Review, 7*, 324–336.

De Cremer, D., Stouten, J. (2003). When do people find cooperation must justified? The effect of trust and self-other merging in social dilemmas. *Social Justice Research, 16*, 41–52.

De Cremer, D., Tyler, T. R. (2005). Managing group behavior: The interplay between procedural justice, sense of self, and cooperation. In M. P. Zanna (ed.), *Advances in Experimental Social Psychology* (Vol. 37, pp. 151–218). San Diego: Elsevier Academic Press.

Dolsak, N., Ostrom, E. (2003). The challenges of the commons. In N. Dolsak & E. Ostrom (eds.), *The Commons in the New Millennium* (pp. 3–34). Cambridge, MA: MIT Press.

Dovidio, J. F., Piliavin, J. A., Schroeder, D. A., Penner, L. A. (in press, 2006). *The Social Psychology of Prosocial Behavior*. Mahwah, NJ: Lawrence Erlbaum Associates.

Ellickson, R. C. (1991). *Order Without Law: How Neighbors Settle Disputes*. Cambridge, MA: Harvard University Press.

Fehr, E., Gächter, S. (2002). Altruistic punishment in humans. *Nature, 415*, 137–140.

Frohlich, N., Oppenheimer, J. A. (1992). *Choosing Justice: An Experimental Approach to Ethical Theory*. Berkeley: University of California Press.

Gladwell, M. (2000). *The Tipping Point: How Little Things Can Make a Big Difference*. Boston: Little Brown.

Goffman, E. (1959). *The Presentation of Self in Everyday Life*. Garden City, NY: Doubleday Anchor.

Hardin, G. (1968). The tragedy of the commons. *Science, 162*, 1243–1248.

Hardin, R. (1982). *Collective Action*. Baltimore, MD: The Johns Hopkins University Press.

Holmes, J. G., Rempel, J. K. (1989). Trust in close relationships. In C. Hendrick (ed.), *Close Relationships: Review of Personality and Social Psychology* (Vol. 10, pp. 187–220). London: Sage.

Kelley, H. H. (1973). The processes of causal attribution. *American Psychologist, 28*, 107–128.

Kerr, N. L. (1995). Norms in social dilemmas. In D.A. Schroeder (ed.), *Social Dilemmas: Perspectives on Individuals and Groups* (pp. 31–47). Westport, CT: Praeger.

Kuhn, T. S. (1970). *The Structure of Scientific Revolutions* (2nd ed.). Chicago: University of Chicago Press.

Messick, D. M., Brewer, M. B. (1983). Solving social dilemmas. In L. Wheeler & P. R. Shaver (eds.), *Review of Personality and Social Psychology* (Vol. 4, pp. 11–44). Beverly Hills, CA: Sage Publications.

Miller, D. T. (2001). Disrespect and the experience of injustice. *Annual Review of Psychology, 52*, 527–553.

Nagin, D. (1998). Deterrence and incapacitation. In M. Tonry (ed.), *The Handbook of Crime and Punishment* (pp. 345–368). New York: Oxford University Press.

Ostrom, E. (1990). *Governing the Commons: The Evolution of Institutions for Collective Action*. Cambridge: Cambridge University Press.

Ostrom, E. (2001). Reformulating the commons. In J. Burger, E. Ostrom, R. B. Norgaard, D. Policansky & B. D. Goldstein (eds.), *Protecting the Commons: A Framework for Resource Management in the Americas* (pp. 17–41). Washington, DC: Island Press.

Posner, E. A. (2000). *Law and Social Norms*. Cambridge, MA: Harvard University Press.

Platt, J. R. (1973). Social traps. *American Psychologist, 28*, 641–651.

Rawls, J. (1971, 1999). *A Theory of Justice*. Cambridge, MA: Harvard University Press.

Rawls, J. (2001). *Justice as Fairness: A Restatement*. (E. Kelly, ed.). Cambridge, MA: Belknap Press.

Roberts, P. (2004). *The End of Oil: On the Edge of a Perilous New World*. New York: Houghton-Mifflin.

Schroeder, D. A., Sibicky, M. E., Irwin, M. E. (1995). A framework for understanding decisions in social dilemmas. In D. A. Schroeder (ed.), *Social Dilemmas: Perspectives on Individuals and Groups* (pp. 183–199). Westport, CT: Praeger.

Schroeder, D. A., Steel, J. E., Woodell, A. J., Bembenek, A. F. (2003). Justice within social dilemmas. *Personality and Social Psychology Review, 7*, 374–387.

Steel, J. E. (2004). When procedural change isn't enough: Restorative and retributive justice-seeking and the "recognition of necessity." Unpublished doctoral dissertation, University of Arkansas.

Thibaut, J., Walker, L. (1975). *Procedural Justice: A Psychological Analysis*. Hillsdale, NJ: Lawrence Erlbaum.

Tyler, T. R., Blader, S. L. (2000). *Cooperation in Groups: Procedural Justice, Social Identity, and Behavioral Engagement*. Philadelphia: Psychology Press.

Tyler, T. R., Blader, S. L. (2003). The group engagement model: Procedural justice, social identity, and cooperative behavior. *Personality and Social Psychology Review, 7*, 349–361.

Tyler, T. R., Boeckmann, R. J., Smith, H. J., Huo, Y. J. (1997). *Social Justice in a Diverse Society*. Boulder, CO: Westview Press.

Van den Bos, K., Lind, E. A. (2002). Uncertainty management by means of fairness judgments. In M. P. Zanna (ed.), *Advances in Experimental Social Psychology* (Vol. 34, pp. 1–60). San Diego: Academic Press.

van Dijk, E., Wilke, H. A. M. (1995). Coordination rules in asymmetric social dilemmas: A comparison of public goods dilemmas and resource dilemmas. *Journal of Experimental Social Psychology, 31*, 1–27.

van Dijk, E., Wilke, H. A. M., Wilke, M., Metman, L. (1999). What information do we use in social dilemmas? Environmental uncertainty and the employment of coordination rules. *Journal of Experimental Social Psychology, 35*, 109–135.

Vidmar, N. (2001). Retribution and revenge. In J. Sanders & V. L. Hamilton (eds.), *Handbook of Justice Research in Law* (pp. 31–63). New York: Kluwer Academic/Plenum.

Walster, E., Berscheid, E., Walster, G. W. (1976). New directions in equity research. In L. Berkowitz & E. Walster (eds.), *Advances in Experimental Social Psychology* (Vol. 9, pp. 1–42). New York: Academic Press

Woodell, A. J. (2005). The cognitive and affective precursors to retributive justice. Unpublished doctoral dissertation, University of Arkansas.

Woodell, A. J., Schroeder, D. A., Steel, J. E., Bembenek, A. F. (May 2002). Are all transgressors created (and treated) equal?: The influence of group membership on retribution. Poster presented at the Midwestern Psychological Association, Chicago.

Wright, R. (2000). *Nonzero: The Logic of Human Destiny*. New York: Pantheon Books.

Yamagishi, T. (1986). The provision of a sanctioning system as a public good. *Journal of Personality and Social Psychology, 51*, 110–116.

Chapter 10
The Emergence of Generalized Exchange by Indirect Reciprocity

Rie Mashima and Nobuyuki Takahashi

One of the characteristics that differentiate human beings from other species is their tendency to help non-kin even when there is no expectation of future interactions. Most religions consider such altruistic behavior a virtue at the highest level. In a society, such behavior constitutes generalized exchange. However, from the perspectives of social exchange theory, rational choice theory, and evolutionary theory, the existence of generalized exchange is a theoretical puzzle. How can generalized exchange exist? How does generalized exchange emerge, and how is it maintained? Recently, research in evolutionary biology has demonstrated that indirect reciprocity is the principle that makes generalized exchange possible. The first part of this chapter reviews recent theoretical studies on generalized exchange and concludes with the current debate on whether or not "to regard the enemy's friend as an enemy" is necessary in order to maintain generalized exchange. The remainder will introduce our first attempt to empirically examine whether people actually have such a tendency to evaluate others.

Previous Solutions to Generalized Exchange

Until the 1990s, a vast majority of research on cooperation focused on restricted (direct) exchange in which two actors exchange resources with each other. A typical example of restricted exchange is the prisoner's dilemma game. The principle that makes people give resources to others in restricted exchange settings is direct reciprocity. Direct reciprocity dictates as follows: If A helps B now, then B will help A in the future, whereas if A does not help B now, then B will not help A in the future. Research on reciprocal altruism in biology (e.g., Trivers, 1971), that is, the tit-for-tat (TFT) strategy[1] in both biology and the social sciences is quite well-known (e.g., Axelrod, 1984; Oskamp, 1971; Wilson, 1971; Yamagishi, 1995).

---

[1] In an iterated PD, an actor adopting TFT starts with cooperation. In subsequent rounds, he cooperates if and only if the partner cooperated on the previous round. Otherwise, he defects.

A. Biel et al. (eds.), *New Issues and Paradigms in Research on Social Dilemmas.*
© Springer 2008

However, TFT can be applied only in the situation of restricted exchange with repeated interaction between pairs of actors. In contrast to restricted exchange, generalized exchange inherently involves more than two actors. There is no one-to-one correspondence between what two actors directly give to and receive from each other. In order for generalized exchange to occur, A's giving to B should not be reciprocated by B's giving to A, but by C's giving to A, where C is a third party. This is the principle called indirect reciprocity. Therefore, we know that generalized exchange exists if indirect reciprocity is present. However, what makes indirect reciprocity work? How can giving behavior be rational or adaptive in such generalized exchange settings where there is no guarantee of return by a third party and individuals can free-ride?

A breakthrough was made by Nowak and Sigmund (1998a, b).[2] They assumed that if actors adopt certain kinds of conditional strategies that help "good" recipients but not "bad" recipients, giving resources to others will eventually pay off. The theoretical framework proposed and subsequent research conducted by Nowak and Sigmund (1998a, b) have attracted much attention. Several additional studies have been performed, and researchers are currently debating how a recipient's reputation is determined. Before reviewing some of the details of these studies, we will first summarize the theoretical framework and its common assumptions.

Theoretical Framework

Most of the theoretical work in this area has been conducted using either mathematical analysis or computer simulation. In the following discussion, we will use terminology consistent with an evolutionary approach, based on the principle that what works well for an actor is more likely to be used again while what turns out poorly is more likely to be discarded. Axelrod (1986) argued that there could be several different interpretations of this principle. One is a purely biological mechanism in which more effective individuals are more likely to survive and reproduce. The second concerns the role of reinforcement in learning theory in which actors learn by trial and error, retaining effective strategies and refining those that turn out poorly.[3] In this chapter, we adopt technical terms associated with the first interpretation (i.e., gene, natural selection, generation, and mutation) because it is the easiest way to illustrate the content.

The existence of a population of individuals is assumed. On each round, a pair of individuals is chosen randomly. One individual is in the role of a donor, and the other individual is in the role of a recipient. The donor may give to the recipient at a cost of value c to herself. Consequently, the recipient receives a benefit of value

---

[2] Also see Takagi (1996), Takahashi and Yamagishi (1996), and Takahashi (2000) for an earlier attempt.

[3] A third one is observational learning in that the actors observe each other, and those with poor performance tend to imitate the strategies of those they observe doing better.

b ($> c$). If the donor decides not to give to the recipient, both individuals receive zero. In this sense, this is a one-shot, one-sided prisoner's dilemma game. In addition, each individual assigns a reputation score, s, to every other individual participating reflecting the individual's past behavior. Typically, an individual who plays the role of donor decides whether to give based on the recipient's reputation score. If the score is "good" (i.e., if the donor believes that the recipient is a good person), the donor will give to the recipient. If the score is "bad" (i.e., if the donor believes that the recipient is a bad person), the donor will not give to the recipient. The subjective definition of "good" and "bad" is determined by each individual's strategy. Some individuals may consider an individual "good" while some other individuals may consider the *same* individual "bad."

Several "rounds" make up one generation. Since a new pair of individuals is chosen randomly in each round, the possibility of direct reciprocity is negligible. At the end of each generation, "natural selection" occurs. The individuals whose cumulative earnings are low reproduce less offspring, whereas the individuals whose cumulative earnings are high reproduce more offspring. Then, "mutation" occurs. Mutation changes the value of each individual's gene(s) by a small probability.

Representation of Strategies

A donor assigns a score to a recipient by using two types of information based on the recipient's previous behavior as a donor. The two types are first-order information (the recipient's previous behavior) and second-order information: the reputation score of the recipient's previous recipient. Thus, we have four genes that assign the score to others (see Table 10.1).[4] Strategies are represented by the sets of these four genes.

Each gene determines whether a particular type of other should be considered "good" or "bad." All strategies give to a "good" recipient and do not give to a "bad" recipient. Gene 1 determines whether a current recipient who gave to his own recipient whose score was "good" when he was in the role of a donor is considered

Table 10.1 Four Genes That Assign the Score to Potential Recipients

		Second-Order Information: Current Recipient's Previous Recipient's Score	
		"Good"	"Bad"
First-order information: Current recipient's behavior toward the previous recipient	Gave	Gene 1: good or bad	Gene 2: good or bad
	Did not give	Gene 3: good or bad	Gene 4: good or bad

---

[4] There are other studies that also consider one's own score (e.g., Panchanathan & Boyd, 2003; Ohtsuki & Iwasa, 2004; Brandt & Sigmund, 2004). For simplicity, however, in this chapter we consider only two types of information.

"good" or "bad." Gene 2 determines whether a current recipient who gave to his own recipient whose score was "bad" when he was in the role of a donor is considered "good" or "bad." Gene 3 determines whether a current recipient who did not give to his own recipient whose score was "good" when he was in the role of a donor is considered "good" or "bad." Gene 4 determines whether a current recipient who did not give to his own recipient whose score was "bad" when he was in the role of a donor is considered "good" or "bad." Table 1 shows that there are 16 (2^4) possible strategies. Among all 16 possible strategies, GGGG represents ALL-C. ALL-C considers everybody "good" regardless of their behavior and, thus, gives to everybody. Likewise, BBBB represents ALL-D.

Definition of "Goodness"

The first solution that Nowak and Sigmund (1998a, b) proposed was the image scoring strategy. Although notation like Table 10.1 did not exist at that time, we can write the image scoring strategy as GGBB. Thus, it uses only first-order information. The individuals who adopt the image scoring strategy define the score of the other individual as follows. Initially (i.e., at the beginning of each generation), the individuals assume that everyone is "good." Afterwards, they assign "good" only to those who gave to another individual when being in the role of the donor the last time and assign "bad" to those who did not give to another individual when being in the role of the donor the last time. The strategy employed here can be considered a variation of the TFT strategy.

Although its simplicity is attractive, subsequent studies have shown that the image scoring strategy cannot maintain generalized exchange because the individuals who adopt this strategy sometimes hurt one another. Individuals employing the image scoring strategy only cooperate with others who gave to another individual when they were in the role of a donor the last time. However, defecting on an individual who did not give to another individual when being in the role of a donor the last time earns a reputation of "bad" from other individuals adopting the same strategy, which leads to further defections. Consequently, the expected payoff of the image scoring strategy is less than that observed for individuals adopting ALL-C, who always give and, therefore, can never be perceived as "bad." As a result, the proportion of ALL-C increases until, eventually, the population is susceptible to invasion by ALL-D, at which point generalized exchange collapses entirely.[5]

In order to overcome this weakness, Leimar and Hammerstein (2001) and Panchanathan and Boyd (2003) proposed the standing strategy,[6] represented by GGBG.[7] Following Sugden's (1986) notion, an individual who employs the standing

---

[5] See Leimar and Hammerstein (2001) and Panchanathan and Boyd (2003) for details.

[6] Panchanathan and Boyd (2003) called this strategy "RDISC."

[7] Actually, the definition of the standing strategy is more complicated than this description. For simplicity, however, we use this simple description here.

strategy defines the score of the other individuals as follows. Suppose individual A employs the standing strategy. If individual B gave to a recipient, individual A assigns B "good" just like the image scoring strategy would. However, if individual B did not give to a recipient, A's assignment depends on the reputation of B's recipient. If B did not give to a recipient whose score was "good," A considers B's behavior unjustified and assigns B "bad." However, if B did not give to a recipient whose score was "bad," A considers B's behavior justified and continues to assign B "good." Since the standing strategy distinguishes justifiable from unjustifiable defection and, unlike the image scoring strategy, assigns "good" to the former, individuals adopting the standing strategy are not considered "bad" from the viewpoint of other standing individuals when they punish ALL-D individuals. Therefore, an individual who employs the standing strategy does not lose opportunities to receive benefits from other individuals who also employ the standing strategy. This feature makes the standing strategy sustainable and makes generalized exchange possible.

Although these studies made significant contributions, none systematically examined all possible strategy combinations. At the time the image scoring strategy was proposed, things were quite simple. Since only first-order information (whether the current recipient gave last time) was considered, there could be only four strategies. However, things became more complicated once second-order information was introduced with the standing strategy. Using evolutionary computer simulations, Takahashi and Mashima (2003) examined all 16 (2^4) strategies and showed that the strict discriminator strategy (SDISC), represented as GBBB, is the solution that makes generalized exchange possible. An individual who employs SDISC assigns "good" only to those who gave to a "good" recipient. There is a distinct contrast between the standing strategy and SDISC. The standing strategy distinguishes justifiable from unjustifiable defection, while SDISC distinguishes justifiable from unjustifiable giving. Therefore, while the standing strategy regards giving to "bad" as equal to giving to "good," SDISC punishes those who give indiscriminately.

Certain versions of the standing strategy require another piece of information. An individual's behavior toward his recipient may depend on whether his own score is "good" or "bad." Taking the individual's score into consideration, there are a total of 256 (2^8) possible strategies. Ohtsuki and Iwasa (2004) examined all of these strategies and showed that only eight are evolutionarily stable and can achieve high levels of generalized exchange. They concluded that the notion of goodness should include three criteria: (1) giving to "good" individuals should be "good"; (2) not giving to "good" ones should be "bad"; and (3) not giving to "bad" ones should be "good." Thus, these three criteria are more consistent with the standing strategy than with SDISC. In fact, SDISC was not included in the leading eight, and many strategies in the leading eight failed to maintain indirect reciprocity in Takahashi and Mashima's (2003) simulation.

Takahashi and Mashima (2006) employed a combination of mathematical analysis and computer simulation and showed that when there was a possibility of perception error, the standing strategy could not maintain generalized exchange. Following Leimar and Hammerstein (2001), Takahashi and Mashima (2003) calculated the probability of misperception for each individual independently, thereby making disparate opinions of the same individual possible, some assigning the individual as "good" and some as "bad," even if all individuals adopt the same strategy. In this sense, errors in perception are subjective. Conversely, Ohtsuki and Iwasa (2004, 2006) considered perception errors to be objective. In this case, the probability of misperception is calculated once for all individuals in the population. Either everyone misperceives an individual's behavior, or everyone perceives it accurately. In other words, the notion that perception errors are objective means that there is a consensus on other people's behavior among all individuals, while the notion that perception errors are subjective means that there may not be a consensus.

Takahashi and Mashima (2006) argued that whether or not a mistake is shared among all individuals could have a potentially serious implication. Suppose perception errors are subjective. Suppose, at one point, individual X, who adopts the standing strategy and is regarded as "good" by other individuals, misperceives individual A's behavior and assigns "bad" while the other individuals, who also adopt the standing strategy, perceive A's behavior correctly and assign them as "good." Then, sometime later, X is matched with A. Since X believes that A is "bad," X does not give to A. Then, the other individuals who adopt the standing strategy assign X "bad" since they regard A as "good." This cycle of misperception can go on and on, and the individuals who adopt the standing strategy may hurt one another in the process. However, this cycle does not matter to ALL-C individuals because perception errors are irrelevant to them. Therefore, it is possible for ALL-C individuals to evolve, and eventually ALL-D individuals take over the population. Such a cycle does not occur when perception errors are objective since each individual's score is shared among all individuals. That is why the leading eight strategies could maintain generalized exchange in Ohtsuki and Iwasa (2004), where it was assumed that perception errors are objective. In the case of SDISC, whether perception errors are objective or subjective does not matter much because SDISC regards ALL-C individuals as "bad" by definition. Since this makes the expected payoff difference between ALL-C individuals and SDISC individuals significant, whether or not perception errors are subjective does not affect the evolutionary dynamics of a population with SDISC.[8]

Finally, using a paradigm known as *selective play* (Yamagishi & Hayashi, 1996), Mashima and Takahashi (2005b) reached the same conclusion as Takahashi and Mashima (2006). In their opinion, selective play is preferable to the standard paradigm of random matching because it is more similar to human social networks. It is more natural for individuals to actively select their desirable recipient if they know the scores of all the members, and there is no a priori reason for individuals to be forced to interact with randomly matched recipients. This is particularly important when we consider the SDISC strategy. SDISC regards a recipient who was previously matched with a "bad" person as "bad." In other words, from

---

[8] It is true that SDISC was not included in the leading eight in Ohtsuki and Iwasa (2004). However, this is not because SDISC performs worse than All-C or All-D. Actually, SDISC can make up an equilibrium, but the average giving rate among the whole population in that equilibrium is not high enough because the number of other individuals whom SDISC regard as "good" decreases over time.

SDISC's viewpoint, once an individual is matched with a "bad" recipient, there is nothing this individual can do to earn a good reputation. Whether he gives or he defects makes no difference. Either way, SDISC regards this individual as "bad." This seems unnecessarily strict. However, this only occurs with random matching. If individuals select their own recipient from the population, they can select "good" people and avoid "bad" ones. This is more consistent with our daily life. We do not necessarily punish bad people. It is much easier and more prevalent to shun them. Mashima and Takahashi (2005b) conducted a new set of simulations using the "selective play" setting and showed that two strategies, SDISC (GBBB) and GBBG, would maintain generalized exchange. The important point is that both strategies regard giving to "bad" as "bad." The difference between these two strategies lies in the fourth gene, which determines the behavior toward a recipient who did not give to anybody when he was in the role of a donor because there was no "good" individual in a population. The results showed that the fourth gene matters little in the selective play environment. Since it is almost always possible for a donor to find at least one desirable recipient from a population in the selective play environment, the fourth gene matters little. Thus, both SDISC and GBBG are equally successful under these conditions.

Summary of the Theoretical Background

To summarize, there is currently a debate over whether or not the definition of "goodness" should include individuals who give to "bad." Ohtsuki and Iwasa (2004, 2006) argued that it should. From their perspective, they feel it is more important to distinguish justifiable from unjustifiable defection and to assign a label of "good" to the former. Conversely, Mashima and Takahashi (2005a, b) and Takahashi and Mashima (2006) argued that it should not. Their argument that giving to "bad" is "bad" runs parallel to the position popularly held in the social dilemmas literature. In an n-person prisoner's dilemma situation, individuals who punish free riders alter the incentive structure so that free riding is no longer the dominant strategy. However, in the event that sanctioning is costly, other problems may emerge. For instance, what would be the incentive for each individual to absorb a significant cost in order to sanction free riders? It is better for each individual to encourage other individuals to sanction free riders. This second-order free-rider problem must be solved before we can address the problem of a first-order social dilemma. Otherwise, there are an infinite number of problems to consider (i.e., third-order free-rider problem, fourth-order free-rider problem, and so on). One of the solutions is that those who sanction first-order free riders should also sanction second-order free riders (Yamagishi and Takahashi, 1994). This means that those who do not sanction free riders should be punished, even if they cooperated in the original social dilemma. Thus, failure to sanction should be regarded as "bad." If we modify the well-known saying "the enemy of my enemy is my friend" to fit this principle, it would be "the enemy's friend is an enemy, too."

An Empirical Study

In the second part of this chapter, we will empirically examine how people actually use information and whether they do, in fact, regard giving to "bad" as "bad." Only a few empirical studies have examined how generalized exchange emerges (e.g., Bolton et al., 2005; Milinski et al., 2001; Wedekind & Milinski, 2000), with mixed results. First of all, it is still not clear whether people actually use second-order information given that it requires a greater level of cognitive complexity and effort. Second, even if people actually use second-order information, there is no satisfactory result that can resolve the debate explained above. Therefore, this chapter is our first attempt to provide empirical data regarding how people would behave in generalized exchange settings. As a first step, we conducted a vignette study in order to discover how people regard others in situations of generalized exchange by systematically varying two types of information. A very brief report of preliminary results appeared in Mashima and Takahashi (2005b). In this chapter, the results are reported in more detail.

The main aim of the study was to investigate (1) whether respondents use second-order information in their judgments and (2) if so, whether they distinguish justifiable from unjustifiable giving. More concretely, we focused on whether and to what degree respondents evaluate a person who gave to "good" (T1) and a person who gave to "bad" (T2) differently. According to Mashima and Takahashi (2005a) and Takahashi and Mashima (2006), T2 should be evaluated less positively than T1. Conversely, according to Panchanathan and Boyd (2003) and Ohtsuki and Iwasa (2004), T1 and T2 should be evaluated similarly.

Method

We prepared six scenarios of generalized exchange. Respondents read one of the six scenarios and then indicated their impression of the target person described in the scenario. Each scenario consisted of four situations, and each situation described whether the target person gave or didn't give to potential recipients, who were either "good" or "bad." In other words, respondents gave their impressions of four types of target person, each corresponding to a cell in Table 10.1. Thus, the design is a scenario (between subjects: six types) × situation (within subjects: four types) factorial design. Respondents were 282 undergraduate students at Hokkaido University in Japan.

We used scenarios of selective play generalized exchange. Selective play was chosen over random matching because it is considered to be a more natural environment for respondents to evaluate targets. In each situation, there were three persons, T, L, and M, who were faced with a generalized exchange setting. T is the target person whom respondents evaluated. Scenarios described how T behaved when T was in the role of a donor. L and M were T's potential recipients. Thus, T either gave his resources to L or M or did not give to anybody. First-order information was systematically varied by describing what T did to L or M and second-order information by describing L's and M's reputation scores. This produced four types of target person (T1–T4), each corresponding to a cell in Table 10.2. Situation 1 described a target who gave to a "good" person (T1), situation 2 described someone who gave to a "bad" person (T2), situation 3 described a person who did not give to a "good" person (T3), and situation 4 described someone who did not give to a "bad" person (T4).

In the first three situations, L was a "good" person who usually gave his resources to others, while M was a "bad" person who usually did not give to others. In situation 1, respondents were told that T1 gave his resources to L. Thus, T1 was considered a giver to "good." In situation 2, respondents were told that T1 gave his resources to M. In this situation, T2 was considered a giver to "bad." In situation 3, respondents were told that T3 did not give his resources to anybody. In this situation, T3 was considered a non-giver to "good." In situation 4, as in situation 3, respondents were told that T4 did not give his resources to anybody. However, in this situation, contrary to the other situations, both L and M were "bad" people who usually did not give to others. Thus, T4 was considered a non-giver to "bad."

Each respondent read one of six scenarios. Each scenario included a set of four situations. An example of situation 1 presented in the ostracism 1 scenario is shown below.

> You are living in a village where people earn their living by agriculture. All people usually help each other when they do farm work. It is tremendously hard (almost impossible) to do farm work without other people's help. Therefore, if one was ostracized by other people (i.e., other people don't give any help to him), he would have huge difficulties to earn his living. One day, person T heard that person L and person M want to do farm work that needs a lot of labor during the next weekend. The other villagers have their hands full, and T is the only one who can provide help. Since helping farm work requires a lot of time and effort during the entire weekend, T cannot help both L and M: T can help only one of the two. Person L is not ostracized in the village, because he always helps others do farm work when he can. Person M is ostracized because he doesn't help others do farm work even if he can. T went to help L.

The ostracism 2 scenario was basically the same as the ostracism 1 scenario except that the word "ostracism" was omitted. The PC scenario described a situation in which students help one another because they are required to learn the use of a particular software package in order to complete a project for each of their classes. The short paper scenario described a situation in which students help one another

Table 10.2 Four Types of Target Person in Scenarios

		Second-Order Information: Current Recipient's Previous Recipient's Score	
		"Good"	"Bad"
First-order information: Current recipient's behavior toward the previous recipient	Gave	T1: giving to good	T2: giving to bad
	Did not give	T3: not-giving to good	T4: not-giving to bad

because they are required to turn in a short paper after every lab class. The souvenir scenario described a situation in which neighbors go on a trip abroad and return with souvenirs for each other. The ticket scenario described a situation in which students exchange rare tickets for concerts and performances.

The main dependent variables were the evaluations provided for each of the four targets (T1–T4) on various dimensions. Respondents were asked to evaluate the target person on 21 dimensions immediately after they read the description of each situation. Since there were four situations, they repeated the evaluations four times. All items were measured on a 7-point scale. Then, respondents were asked to indicate what they would do if they were in the role of a donor and T1–T4 were potential recipients. They indicated their willingness to give resources to each of the targets separately on a 7-point scale (1: do not want to give at all; 7: want to give very much). Finally, they indicated their expectation about how they would be treated by others if they had given to each of the targets on three items.

Results

Evaluations

There were 21 items that measured impressions of the target person and 3 items that measured respondents' expectations about how they would be treated by others if they gave to that target person. A factor analysis of these 21 items was conducted for each scenario, revealing 3 factors that were common among all 6 scenarios. We constructed three scales based on these factors, selecting those items that had high loadings on each factor consistently across all scenarios. The first scale, labeled "generousness," was composed of five items measuring the extent to which the target was "generous," "self-interested," "nice," "kind," and "strict."[9] The second scale, labeled "social appropriateness," was composed of seven items measuring the extent to which the target's behavior was "appropriate," "unjust," and "exasperating," the extent to which the target was "fair," "wise," "trustworthy," and the probability that "the target will be ostracized."[10] The third scale, labeled "social order," was composed of four items measuring the extent to which the target was concerned with "social order," "reputation," "relationships with others," and "group harmony."[11] We also constructed an "expectation of positive treatment by others scale" with the three items measuring the respondents' expectations that "respondents would be evaluated with a good impression," "be appreciated," and "be ostracized" by other people if they gave resources to the

---

[9] "Self-interested" and "strict" are reverse-coded.

[10] "Unjust," "exasperate," and the extent that "the target will be ostracized" are reverse-coded.

[11] Among the 21 items, "I am well affected toward T," "T is thoughtful," "T can make a coup with other people in our society," "T's behavior is emotional," and "T was willing to do that" were not included in the three scales.

target.[12] Reliability coefficients for the constructed scales in each of the six scenarios are shown in Table 10.3.

Reliability was high in every scenario as well as in the combined data with the exception of the "expectation of positive treatment by others" scale in the PC and short paper scenarios. Thus, in the following analysis, we use these four scales to examine how people regard each of the four targets. For the simplicity of presentation, we use the combined data in the main text. Means and standard deviations for the four scales for each target across scenarios are presented in Table 10.4. Appendix A displays means and standard deviations of each scale in each situation in each scenario and the results of one-way ANOVAs and Scheffé post-hoc tests for each scenario.

One-way ANOVAs showed that the effect of situation was highly significant on all scales. This was followed by Scheffé post-hoc tests reported in the right column in Table 10.4. For the generousness scale, T2 was evaluated as the most generous person, followed by T1, T4, and T3. Therefore, we conclude that T2 was evaluated more positively than T1 in terms of generousness. However, quite different patterns were observed for the other three scales. For the social appropriateness scale, T1 and T4 were evaluated as more socially appropriate than T2 and T3, and T2 was evaluated as the least socially appropriate person. For the social order scale, T1 was evaluated as the person who cared the most about social order, followed by T4, T2, and T3. For the expectation of positive treatment by others scale, giving to T1 was associated with the highest positive treatment. Further, respondents expected to receive more positive treatment from others for giving to T4 than to T3.

The results of the generousness scale mean that T2 was evaluated as more "generous and kind" when compared to T1. At first glance, this result seems to contradict Takahashi and Mashima's (2006) theoretical argument. However, such a pattern was observed only for this scale. Quite different patterns were observed for the remaining scales. T2 was evaluated as the least socially appropriate person and as the person who does not respect social order or group harmony. Further, if respondents were to give to T2, they expected to be treated less positively by other people than they would if they were to give to T1. It is worth mentioning that the magnitude of the difference between T1 and

Table 10.3 Reliabilities of Constructed Scales in Six Scenarios

Scale	No. of Items in the Scale	Ostracism 1	Ostracism 2	PC	Short Paper	Souvenir	Ticket	Combined
Generousness	5	0.87	0.81	0.83	0.79	0.81	0.78	0.82
Social appropriateness	7	0.87	0.88	0.86	0.84	0.88	0.88	0.87
Social order	4	0.90	0.84	0.84	0.79	0.85	0.86	0.86
Expectation of positive treatment by others	3	0.83	0.80	0.42	0.44	0.64	0.75	0.69

---

[12] "They would be ostracized" is reverse-coded.

T2 was substantial. The T1 average was more than one standard deviation higher than the T2 average. Thus, in sum, T2 was evaluated as a generous but socially undesirable person. The fact that T2 was regarded more negatively than T1 overall is consistent with Takahashi and Mashima's (2006) theoretical argument.

Behavioral Intention

Respondents were also asked to indicate on a 7-point scale their willingness to give to the target. Means and standard deviations of the willingness to give in each situation in the combined data are also shown in Table 10.4. The effect of situation was highly significant in a one-way ANOVA, $F(3, 843) = 75.10$, $p < 0.0001$. Table 10.4 shows the results of the Scheffé post-hoc tests. Regarding the difference between T1 and T2, respondents were less willing to give resources to T2 than they were to T1. This is also consistent with Takahashi and Mashima's (2006) theoretical argument. T2 would receive fewer resources compared to T1.

Table 10.4 Means and Standard Deviations (Within Parentheses) of the Four Scales in Each Situation, and the Results of One-Way ANOVA and Scheffé Post-Hoc Tests

	T1	T2	T3	T4	F-Value	Scheffé
Generousness	4.20 (0.66)	4.70 (0.87)	3.27 (0.87)	3.51 (0.61)	204.31 ***	T2 > T1, T2 > T3, T2 > T4, T1 > T3, T1 > T4, T4 > T3
Social appropriateness	4.91 (0.76)	3.99 (0.91)	4.28 (1.12)	4.81 (0.75)	70.48 ***	T1 > T2, T1 > T3, T4 > T2, T4 > T3, T3 > T2
Social order	4.83 (0.81)	3.76 (0.86)	3.36 (1.11)	4.07 (0.91)	136.95 ***	T1 > T2, T1 > T3, T1 > T4, T4 > T2, T4 > T3, T2 > T3
Expectation of positive treatment by others	5.10 (0.98)	4.24 (1.04)	4.06 (1.00)	4.41 (0.86)	85.75 ***	T1 > T2, T1 > T3, T1 > T4, T4 > T3
Willingness to give	4.85 (1.53)	4.16 (1.59)	3.45 (1.52)	3.98 (1.49)	75.10 ***	T1 > T2, T1 > T3, T1 > T4, T2 > T3, T4 > T3

*$p < 0.05$.
**$p < 0.01$.
***$p < 0.001$.

Discussion

In the first part of this chapter, we reviewed theoretical arguments that have been developed to explain the emergence and maintenance of generalized exchange. Currently, researchers are trying to determine whether regarding giving to "bad" as "bad" is necessary for the maintenance of generalized exchange. In the second part, we described our first attempt to examine people's evaluations and willingness to give to various targets in generalized exchange settings. The results of the vignette study were clear-cut. First, given that T1 and T2 were evaluated differently, it would appear that people do consider second-order information. Second, a person who gave to "bad" was evaluated as generous but was evaluated negatively on many other aspects. This kind of person was evaluated as a socially undesirable person (i.e., one who is socially inappropriate, who disregards social order, and who should not be helped). Furthermore, respondents were less willing to give their resources to a person who gave to "bad" than they were to give to a person who gave to "good." This is consistent with Takahashi and Mashima's (2006) theoretical argument, which stipulates that generalized exchange can only be maintained if individuals who give to "bad" are punished in some way. This is also consistent with social dilemma research, which has discovered that punishing those who do not punish free riders is necessary to achieve mutual cooperation. In sum, the conclusion of this chapter is that regarding "the enemy's friend as an enemy, too" is necessary for the emergence of generalized exchange.

However, it is too early to conclude that such a pattern is observed in generalized exchange settings in real life. What we have demonstrated is only the results of a vignette study asking respondents about their impressions and intended behavior toward hypothetical targets in hypothetical situations. While these self-reports are an important first step, obviously we need to conduct laboratory experiments to examine how people act when they are faced with actual generalized exchange.

Another important issue is the mechanism behind the behavioral tendency that makes generalized exchange possible. Is it evolutionarily determined? Is it a result of rational calculation? Or, is it a heuristic? Also, is there any variation across cultures or societies? Although there is no decisive evidence, we would like to speculate that people possess a heuristic to deal with situations of generalized exchange since these situations can be quite complicated. It should be very difficult to calculate the expected payoff that corresponds to behavior every time a decision is made. However, although it might be true that such a heuristic is hard-wired, there is no reason why this must be so. Heuristics can be acquired through either natural selection or socialization. Nevertheless, since theoretical arguments suggest that a single mechanism makes generalized exchange possible, presently, we believe that such a heuristic is universal, spanning both culture and society. However, we suspect that the cues that make such a heuristic operate might be different across societies. Each society may have certain generalized exchange settings that are unique. Then, it is likely that people in a given society are sensitive to those settings they have grown accustomed to. Therefore, people in different societies may react to different cues. This may be why we observed interaction effects between the scenarios and the situations on three of the four scales (see Appendix A). It may be the case that some scenarios exhibit more or stronger cues of generalized exchange for our Japanese sample. However, this study cannot answer what these cues are. Investigating the cues would be a fruitful topic for future research.

In conclusion, the strategies considered so far to account for the emergence and maintenance of indirect reciprocity all share the same quality: Individuals must decide whether or not to give based on their recipients' past behavior. Although the criteria each strategy uses to determine who to give to are different, all of the strategies share one feature: give to "good." In this sense, Hardin (1982) was right. Indiscriminate altruism (i.e., ALL-C in generalized exchange) cannot exist. Only discriminating altruism exists.

Appendix A

Table A1 Means and Standard Deviations (Within Parentheses) of the Generousness Scale in Each Situation in Each Scenario, and the Results of One-Way ANOVA and Scheffé Test

	No. of cases	T1	T2	T3	T4	F-Value	Scheffé
Ostracism 1	46	3.91 (0.45)	5.28 (0.87)	3.23 (0.93)	3.20 (0.61)	$F(3, 135) =$ 71.28, $p < 0.0001$	T2 > T1, T1 > T3, T1 > T4, T2 > T3, T2 > T4
Ostracism 2	47	4.00 (0.58)	4.56 (0.88)	3.18 (0.87)	3.43 (0.57)	$F(3, 137) =$ 28.29, $p < 0.0001$	T2 > T1, T1 > T3, T1 > T4, T2 > T3, T2 > T4
PC	45	4.28 (0.66)	4.62 (0.72)	3.11 (0.96)	3.52 (0.64)	$F(3, 132) =$ 43.62, $p < 0.0001$	T1 > T3, T1 > T4, T2 > T3, T2 > T4
Short paper	49	4.33 (0.56)	4.88 (0.78)	3.38 (0.78)	3.62 (0.56)	$F(3, 144) =$ 47.90, $p < 0.0001$	T2 > T1, T1 > T3, T1 > T4, T2 > T3, T2 > T4
Souvenir	47	4.09 (0.79)	4.42 (0.98)	3.53 (0.87)	3.76 (0.55)	$F(3, 138) =$ 10.68, $p < 0.0001$	T1 > T3, T2 > T3, T2 > T4
Ticket	48	4.55 (0.68)	4.47 (0.71)	3.20 (0.77)	3.51 (0.61)	$F(3, 141) =$ 54.96, $p < 0.0001$	T1 > T3, T1 > T4, T2 > T3, T2 > T4

Table A2 Means and Standard Deviations (Within Parentheses) of the Social Appropriateness Scale in Each Situation in Each Scenario, and the Results of One-Way ANOVA and Scheffé Post-Hoc Test

	No. of Cases	T1	T2	T3	T4	F-Value	Scheffé
Ostracism 1	46	5.01 (0.73)	4.10 (0.86)	3.89 (1.18)	4.76 (0.72)	$F(3, 135) = 16.14$, $p < 0.0001$	T1 > T2, T1 > T3, T4 > T2, T4 > T3
Ostracism 2	47	5.10 (0.75)	3.92 (0.80)	3.59 (1.04)	4.51 (0.62)	$F(3, 137) = 27.58$, $p < 0.0001$	T1 > T2, T1 > T3, T1 > T4, T4 > T2, T4 > T3
PC	45	4.89 (0.62)	4.03 (0.89)	4.10 (1.11)	4.66 (0.59)	$F(3, 132) = 12.09$, $p < 0.0001$	T1 > T2, T1 > T3, T4 > T2, T4 > T3
Short paper	49	4.85 (0.63)	4.08 (0.96)	4.46 (0.99)	4.75 (0.76)	$F(3, 144) = 9.23$, $p < 0.0001$	T1 > T2, T4 > T2
Souvenir	47	4.68 (0.95)	3.99 (1.01)	4.74 (0.88)	5.18 (0.71)	$F(3, 138) = 16.67$, $p < 0.0001$	T1 > T2, T4 > T1, T3 > T2, T4 > T2
Ticket	48	4.91 (0.80)	3.82 (0.95)	4.86 (1.02)	5.01 (0.88)	$F(3, 141) = 22.06$, $p < 0.0001$	T1 > T2, T3 > T2, T4 > T2

Table A3 Means and Standard Deviations (Within Parentheses) of the Social Order Scale in Each Situation in Each Scenario, and the Results of One-Way ANOVA and Scheffé Post-Hoc Test

	No. of Cases	T1	T2	T3	T4	F-Value	Scheffé
Ostracism 1	46	5.40 (0.65)	3.55 (0.76)	3.13 (1.02)	4.77 (0.98)	$F(3, 135) = 67.86$, $p < 0.0001$	T1 > T2, T1 > T3, T1 > T4, T4 > T2, T4 > T3
Ostracism 2	47	4.98 (0.58)	3.71 (0.75)	3.12 (1.17)	4.09 (0.80)	$F(3, 137) = 41.79$, $p < 0.0001$	T1 > T2, T1 > T3, T1 > T4, T2 > T3, T4 > T3
PC	45	4.43 (0.83)	3.82 (0.85)	3.18 (1.11)	3.61 (0.71)	$F(3, 132) = 17.05$, $p < 0.0001$	T1 > T2, T1 > T3, T1 > T4, T2 > T3
Short paper	49	4.55 (0.65)	3.86 (0.82)	3.39 (0.83)	3.82 (0.85)	$F(3, 144) = 18.83$, $p < 0.0001$	T1 > T2, T1 > T3, T1 > T4, T2 > T3
Souvenir	47	4.65 (0.85)	3.97 (0.89)	3.79 (1.18)	4.07 (0.82)	$F(3, 138) = 9.07$, $p < 0.0001$	T1 > T2, T1 > T3, T1 > T4
Ticket	48	4.95 (0.86)	3.67 (1.01)	3.54 (1.22)	4.08 (0.87)	$F(3, 141) = 21.33$, $p < 0.0001$	T1 > T2, T1 > T3, T1 > T4

Table A4 Means and Standard Deviations (Within Parentheses) of the Expectation of Positive Treatment by Others Scale in Each Situation in Each Scenario, and the Results of One-Way ANOVA and Scheffé Post-Hoc Test

	No. of Cases	T1	T2	T3	T4	F-Value	Scheffé
Ostracism 1	46	5.38 (1.16)	4.17 (1.18)	3.65 (1.21)	4.27 (0.85)	$F(3, 135) =$ 22.59, $p < 0.0001$	T1 > T2, T1 > T3, T1 > T4, T4 > T3
Ostracism 2	47	5.23 (0.89)	4.18 (1.11)	3.81 (1.06)	4.37 (0.92)	$F(3, 138) =$ 21.65, $p < 0.0001$	T1 > T2, T1 > T3, T1 > T4, T4 > T3
PC	45	4.93 (0.83)	4.32 (0.89)	4.24 (0.90)	4.54 (0.74)	$F(3, 132) =$ 11.97, $p < 0.0001$	T1 > T2, T1 > T3, T1 > T4
Short paper	49	4.95 (0.71)	4.37 (0.95)	4.29 (0.67)	4.41 (0.69)	$F(3, 144) =$ 12.68, $p < 0.0001$	T1 > T2, T1 > T3, T1 > T4
Souvenir	47	4.89 (1.05)	4.32 (1.04)	4.35 (0.86)	4.49 (0.87)	$F(3, 138) = 6.43,$ $p < 0.001$	T1 > T2, T1 > T3
Ticket	48	5.25 (1.12)	4.07 (1.05)	4.01 (1.09)	4.36 (1.08)	$F(3, 141) =$ 17.31, $p < 0.0001$	T1 > T2, T1 > T3, T1 > T4

Table A5 Means and Standard Deviations (Within Parentheses) of the Willingness to Give in Each Situation in Each Scenario, and the Results of One-Way ANOVA and Scheffé Post-Hoc Test

	No. of Cases	T1	T2	T3	T4	F-Value	Scheffé
Ostracism 1	46	5.04 (1.44)	4.74 (1.60)	3.43 (1.50)	4.20 (1.17)	$F(3, 135) = 13.86,$ $p < 0.0001$	T1 > T3, T1 > T4, T2 > T3, T4 > T3
Ostracism 2	47	5.30 (1.35)	4.53 (1.49)	3.51 (1.53)	4.32 (1.37)	$F(3, 138) = 19.48,$ $p < 0.0001$	T1 > T2, T1 > T3, T1 > T4, T2 > T3, T4 > T3
PC	45	5.00 (1.30)	4.20 (1.38)	3.67 (1.54)	4.20 (1.38)	$F(3, 132) = 12.20,$ $p < 0.0001$	T1 > T2, T1 > T3, T1 > T4
Short paper	49	4.82 (1.44)	4.20 (1.54)	3.65 (1.60)	3.67 (1.45)	$F(3, 144) = 16.58,$ $p < 0.0001$	T1 > T2, T1 > T3, T1 > T4, T2 > T3
Souvenir	47	4.34 (1.68)	3.77 (1.70)	3.30 (1.47)	3.83 (1.70)	$F(3, 138) = 7.12,$ $p < 0.001$	T1 > T3
Ticket	48	4.60 (1.76)	3.52 (1.56)	3.13 (1.50)	3.67 (1.71)	$F(3, 141) = 14.29,$ $p < 0.0001$	T1 > T2, T1 > T3, T1 > T4

References

Axelrod, R. (1984). *The Evolution of Cooperation*. New York: Basic Books.

Axelrod, R. (1986). An evolutionary approach to norms. *American Political Science Review, 80*, 1095–1111.

Bolton, G. E., Katok, E., Ockenfels, A. (2005). Cooperation among strangers with limited information about reputation. *Journal of Public Economics, 89*, 1457–1468.

Brandt, H., Sigmund, K. (2004). The logic of reprobation: Assessment and action rules for indirect reciprocation. *Journal of Theoretical Biology, 231*, 475–486.

Hamilton, W. D. (1964). The genetic theory of social behavior. I and II. *Journal of Theoretical Biology, 7*, 1–52.

Hardin, G. (1982). Discriminating altruisms. *Zygon, 17*, 163–186.

Leimar, O., Hammerstein, P. (2001). Evolution of cooperation through indirect reciprocity. *Proceedings of the Royal Society of London Series B: Biological Sciences, 268*, 745–753.

Mashima, R., Takahashi, N. (2005a). The emergence of indirect reciprocity: Evolutionary foundation of altruistic behavior based on "strict discriminator." *The Japanese Journal of Psychology, 46*, 436–444 (in Japanese).

Mashima, R., Takahashi, N. (2005b). Is the enemy's friend an enemy too?: Theoretical and empirical approach toward the effect of second-order information on indirect reciprocity. *Sociological Theory and Methods, 20*, 177–195 (in Japanese).

Milinski, M., Semmann, D., Bakker, T. C. M., Krambeck, H. (2001). Cooperation through indirect reciprocity: image scoring or standing strategy? *Proceedings of the Royal Society of London Series B: Biological Sciences, 268*, 2495–2501.

Nowak, M. A., Sigmund, K. (1998a). Evolution of indirect reciprocity by image scoring. *Nature, 393*, 573–577.

Nowak, M. A., Sigmund, K. (1998b). The dynamics of indirect reciprocity. *Journal of Theoretical Biology, 194*, 561–574.

Ohtsuki, H., Iwasa, Y. (2004). How should we define goodness?: Reputation dynamics in indirect reciprocity. *Journal of Theoretical Biology, 231*, 107–120.

Ohtsuki, H., Iwasa, Y. (2006). The leading eight: Social norms that can maintain cooperation by indirect reciprocity. *Journal of Theoretical Biology, 239*, 435–444.

Oskamp, S. (1971). Effects of programmed strategies on cooperation in the prisoner's dilemma and other mixed-motive games. *Journal of Conflict Resolution, 15*, 225–229.

Panchanathan, K., Boyd, R. (2003). A tale of two defectors: The importance of standing in the evolution of indirect reciprocity. *Journal of Theoretical Biology, 224*, 115–126.

Sugden, R. (1986). *The Economics of Rights, Co-operation and Welfare*. Oxford: Basil Blackwell.

Takagi, E. (1996). The generalized exchange perspective on the evolution of altruism. In W. B. G. Liebrand & D. M. Messick (eds.), *Frontiers in Social Dilemmas Research* (pp. 311–336). Berlin: Springer-Verlag.

Takahashi, N. (2000). The emergence of generalized exchange. *American Journal of Sociology, 105*, 1105–1134.

Takahashi, N., Mashima, R. (2003). The emergence of indirect reciprocity: Is the standing strategy the answer? (COE Working Paper No. 29). Hokkaido, Japan: Hokkaido University, The Center for the Study of Cultural and Ecological Foundations of the Mind.

Takahashi, N., Mashima, R. (2006). The importance of subjectivity in perceptual errors on the emergence of indirect reciprocity. *Journal of Theoretical Biology, 243*, 418–436.

Takahashi, N., Yamagishi, T. (1996). Social relational foundations of altruistic behavior. *Japanese Journal of Experimental Social Psychology, 36*, 1–11 (in Japanese).

Trivers, R. (1971). The evolution of reciprocal altruism. *Quarterly Review of Biology, 46*, 35–57.

Wedekind, C., Milinski, M. (2000). Cooperation through image scoring in humans. *Science, 288*, 850–852.

Wilson, W. (1971). Reciprocation and other techniques for inducing cooperation in the prisoner's dilemma game. *Journal of Conflict Resolution, 15,* 167–195.

Yamagishi, T. (1995). Social dilemmas. In K. S. Cook, G. Fine & J. House (eds.), *Sociological Perspectives on Social Psychology* (pp. 311–335). Boston: Allyn and Bacon.

Yamagishi, T., Hayashi, N. (1996). Selective play: Social embeddedness of social dilemmas. In W. B. G. Liebrand & D. M. Messick (eds.), *Frontiers in Social Dilemmas Research* (pp. 363–384). Berlin: Springer-Verlag.

Yamagishi, T., Takahashi, N. (1994). Evolution of norms without meta-norms. In U. Schulz, W. Albers & U. Mueller (eds.), *Social Dilemmas and Cooperation* (pp. 311–326). Berlin: Springer-Verlag.

Chapter 11
The Herdsman and the *Sheep*, *Mouton*, or *Kivsa*?

The Influence of Group Culture on Cooperation in Social Dilemmas

Shirli Kopelman

Does culture influence decision making in a global economy? Without doubt, culture influences the cuisine we prefer and whether we are likely to order and enjoy a rack of lamb smothered in a Southwestern U.S.-style barbeque sauce and a cold beer, lamb stew à la Provençale with a glass of red wine, or lamb marinated in fresh herbs and served over rice along with hot mint tea. Even in an era of fusion restaurants and widespread globalization, culture may influence how decision makers manage both local and global resources in situations that risk the *tragedy of the commons*—the classic example being the decision of a herdsman grazing sheep[1] on a common pasture whether to cooperate or defect (G. Hardin, 1968). That is, the cultural context provides insights into the problem of cooperation. We may learn how to effectively manage resources in social dilemma settings (for a review, see Dawes, 1980; Messick & Brewer, 1983; Kopelman et al., 2002), by studying solutions that arise in distinct cultural settings (e.g., McCay, 2002; Ahn et al., 2004). Furthermore, even if a global management culture may be emerging, this by no means indicates homogeneity of group-level culture. Unique subcultures continue to emerge on an organizational and institutional level in which the effect of group-level factors such as cultural values and norms is critical to understanding behavior of decision makers (e.g., Gelfand & Brett, 2004; Markus & Kitayama, 1991). Therefore, it is important to incorporate culture into both the theoretical frameworks and the empirical research on cooperation in social dilemmas.

In general, social dilemmas can be defined as situations "… in which individual rationality leads to collective irrationality. That is, individually reasonable behavior leads to a situation in which everyone is worse off than they might have been otherwise" (Kollock, 1998, p. 183). For example, common dilemmas emerge when decision makers all have access to a common resource, but no one has the right to exclude others and thus they are likely to collectively take for themselves more than would be sustainable. These are situations in which collective non-cooperation leads to a serious threat of depletion of future resources (C. D. Hardin & Higgins, 1996; Van Lange et al., 1992). Likewise, in public-good dilemmas, given that people have

---

[1] Sheep in French is *mouton* and in Hebrew *kivsa* (French and Hebrew translations of English were arbitrarily referred to in the title to represent unique cultures in different parts of the world).

A. Biel et al. (eds.), *New Issues and Paradigms in Research on Social Dilemmas.*
© Springer 2008

free access to a collective good reduces the incentive to contribute voluntarily to the provision of that good. If there are many free riders in a population relative to the number of contributors, public goods disappear, because contributors, noting they are being taken advantage of, withdraw their support (Ostrom, 2000). Social psychologists, anthropologists, economists, sociologists, and political scientists alike have demonstrated great interest in understanding when people make cooperative choices rather than selfish choices, why people make the choices they do, what the factors are that influence cooperation in a social dilemma, and the interventions that are effective in eliciting more socially advantageous behavior (e.g., Agrawal, 2002; Dawes, 1980; Kollock, 1998; Komorita & Parks, 1996; Ledyard, 1995; Messick & Brewer, 1983; Van Lange et al., 1992; Kopelman et al., 2002).

There are two prevailing theoretical frameworks to decision making in social dilemmas: the expected utility (EU) model and the rational choice model (Ledyard, 1995; Luce & Raiffa, 1957; Pruitt & Kimmel, 1977). These models presume vigilant, calculating decision makers who assess choice environments with care, determine the probable utility (i.e., payoff) associated with each possible choice, and then choose to maximize their EU. The appropriateness framework, an alternative theoretical approach to decision making in social dilemmas, suggests that people making decisions ask themselves (explicitly or implicitly): "What does a person like me do in a situation like this?" (March, 1994; Messick, 1999; Weber et al., 2004). This question identifies three significant factors: (1) the identity of the individual making the decision; (2) the recognition and definition of the kind of situation encountered; and (3) the application of rules or heuristics in guiding behavioral choice. In contrast with the EU and the rational choice models, the appropriateness framework accommodates the inherently social nature of social dilemmas and the role of rule- and heuristic-based processing.

This chapter suggests a broader interpretation of the appropriateness framework in decision making that includes group culture and therefore may offer a better understanding of cooperation in social dilemmas. While the general constructs of the appropriateness framework—identity, rules, and recognition—could be universally applied, it is not self-evident where the group and its culture fit into the appropriateness model. For example, a narrow interpretation of identity as a self-focused atomistic entity is characteristic of some, but not all, cultures. Thus, the question "What does a person like me" may overemphasize the self over the group. Where does the group fit in? Is an individual perceived to be a separate entity from the group? What if there is more than one group? Is the group part of the situation? Rules and recognition of the situation—"... *do* in a *situation* like this?"—also might have substantially different implications, depending on a group's culture. In fact there may be more than one group culture to consider, if a social dilemma occurs in an intercultural setting. If most people in some cultures are likely to answer the three factors (identity, recognition, and rules) differently than most people in other cultures, then adding a cultural lens to the appropriateness framework may provide a better understanding of cooperation in social dilemmas. The three appropriateness factors—the identity of the individual making the decision, recognition and definition of the kind of situation encountered, and the application of rules or heuristics in guiding behavioral choice—are interrelated in all cultures. And yet, defining them as distinct constructs proves theoretically illuminating. Currently, the effect of culture—a group-level variable—is implied and embedded in identity, recognition of the situation, and applied rules. A model is not proposed here that diminishes the contribution of teasing apart these three factors, but rather a model that also encompasses group culture as a distinct fourth construct.

Culture and Appropriateness Framework

Embedding a group-cultural–level identity in the appropriateness framework of decision making in social dilemmas provides a more encompassing theoretical model of factors that influence individual cooperation. Culture, in the decision-making literature, is defined as a mental model shared by at least two people (Deutsch, 1973), which influences what people believe is important (values) and what they consider to be appropriate behavior (norms) (Hofstede, 1980; Schwartz, 1994). It is not surprising that the appropriateness framework has ignored group culture given that the empirical literature on social dilemmas has developed in what has been described as a cultural "vacuum" (Brett & Kopelman, 2004).

An expansive experimental literature in social psychology and experimental economics has treated an array of psychological factors that influence individual cooperation (e.g., Kopelman et al., 2002). These factors include the study of individual and situational independent variables in give-some (public-good dilemmas) and take-some games (common dilemmas), two-person and multiperson prisoner's dilemmas in the laboratory, as well as field experiments. Despite this plethora of research, the effect of group culture per se on choice in social dilemmas has not been widely studied; and, indeed, the paucity of studies that focus on group culture as a predictive variable is noteworthy, especially as the impact of culture has received increasing attention in the social and cognitive psychology literature (e.g., Markus & Kitayama, 1991).

The role of cultural values and norms in the decision of whether to cooperate or defect in social dilemma situations has been explored by only a few studies, but mostly has been treated as a control variable or an empirical artifact of data collection in different countries, rather than as a theoretical construct (Brett & Kopelman, 2004). Culture can be treated not only as a psychological construct, but also on an institutional level, including a society's characteristic laws and social structures, such as schools and government agencies, which monitor and sanction cooperation. According to research in social psychology and experimental economics, group culture plays a central role in how people think, feel, and behave in resource allocation settings (Gelfand & Dyer, 2000; Lytle et al., 1995). In this literature, culture is usually treated as a group-level psychological construct that influences decision making. Thus, group culture influences the emergence of identity, how people perceive situations, and what behavioral rules they apply.

Culture and Identity

Identity is a complex, multifaceted factor in the appropriateness framework. Often social scientists associate identity only with personality factors, and clearly, people do differ along personality dimensions such as self-monitoring (Snyder & Gangestad, 1986) or locus of control (Lefcourt, 1982). However, they also differ in other ways, such as their social value orientations (Messick & McClintock, 1968), the nature of their personal histories (Bettenhausen & Murnighan, 1985, 1991; Forgas, 1982), and personal experiences. Identity also encompasses social identity (Brewer, 1991; Taylor & Moghaddam, 1994; Turner et al., 1987) and cultural influences (Moghaddam et al., 1993). Identity is, therefore, an umbrella concept that includes all the idiosyncratic factors that individuals bring with them into a social situation. The term identity, then, includes the consideration of socially defined roles and the various idiosyncratic traits (Weber et al., 2004) and confounds these with cultural identity (i.e., shared group-level identity).

One of the most commonly studied effects of group culture in social psychology is the influence it has on the concept of the self. It is reflected by the cultural value of individualism versus collectivism (Hofstede, 1980; Schwartz, 1994). Decision makers from individualist cultures (e.g., United States) think of themselves independently of the social groups to which they belong and make decisions with little concern for social imperatives to consider the interests of others (Markus & Kitayama, 1991). Thus, what is valued in individualistic societies is self-interest. In a social dilemma setting, this leads to main effect predictions that individualistic decision makers will be less likely to cooperate but will enact individual profit-maximizing behavior. In contrast, collectivist cultures value group interests. People self-construe in terms of social group membership and are more likely to think in terms of "we" than in terms of "I." These individuals make distinctions between ingroups of which they are members and with whom they cooperate and outgroups of which they are not members and with which they compete (Triandis, 1989). In fact, comparative cross-cultural research documents that decision makers from collective cultures are more cooperative than individualists in social dilemmas. For example, in contrast to decision makers from the United States (an individualistic culture), decision makers from collectivist cultures such as Vietnam (Parks & Vu, 1994), Japan (Wade-Benzoni et al., 2002), and China (Brett, 2001; Hemesath & Pomponio, 1998) are more cooperative. The social imperatives in a collective society motivate decision makers to place group interests before individual interests, and therefore they are more likely to cooperate in social dilemmas.

Another widely studied identity factor is the effect of social motives. Social motives, or people's goals for resource allocation in socially interdependent situations (also called social value orientations), influence cooperative choice in social dilemmas (e.g., Kramer et al., 1986; Parks, 1994; Roch & Samuelson, 1997). Prosocial decision makers (whose social motive is to maximize joint gains) make more cooperative choices in social dilemmas than proself decision makers (motivated to maximize own and or own relative to other's gain). Some research suggests that social motives are at least in part a function of the social environment in which decision makers grow up (Van Lange et al., 1997), and therefore they may be influenced by group culture. A common theoretical assumption is that decision makers from collectivist cultures will be more likely to be prosocial, whereas those from individualistic cultures are proself. For example, a study of managers in an executive MBA program reports proportionately more proself decision makers from individualist cultures like the United States and Israel and more prosocial decision makers from Germany (where economic and political ideology reflects collective values) and Hong Kong (where social values are collective) (Kopelman, 1999). Although social motives are related to cultural values, they are not synonymous (Gärling, 1999; Probst et al., 1999), possibly because cultural values are broader constructs than social motives. Social motives are an individual-level variable, whereas culture is a group-level variable and thus, although they interact, they are distinct constructs.

Culture and Recognition of the Situation

To act, people must answer the question: "What kind of situation is this?" (Messick, 1999, p. 13). Answering this question defines and classifies the situation and hinges on recognition, on matching features of the situation to features of other situations that are already (at least partly) understood. Recognition, therefore, is an act of categorization according to event prototypes—"coherent and interrelated sets of characteristics concerning the sort of person who typically features in the event, the typical explanation for the event and so on" (Lalljee et al., 1992, p. 153). The definition of the situation suggests a choice set and is part of the appropriateness framework. The choice set includes questions such as: Is this a cooperative situation or a competitive situation? Is this a group task or an individual task? Is this a game or a problem to be solved? Is this a one-shot dilemma or an iterated dilemma? Is this a dilemma that demands an anonymous or a public choice? The definition of the situation should answer at least some of these questions. The definition of the situation informs the person about the norms, expectations, rules, learned behaviors, skills, and possible strategies that are relevant. It should be, therefore, the proximal mediator of behavioral choice (Weber et al., 2004). Some situational categorizations will yield a constrained list of possible behaviors, while others may be more ambiguous and consequently elicit a broad array of possible behaviors (e.g., Forgas, 1982). The recognition question encompasses yet additional factors—the understanding of a situation within its social and cultural context.

Group culture provides insight into the different solutions that groups evolve to manage socially interdependent situations. Culture is a socially shared knowledge structure, or schema, giving meaning to incoming stimuli and channeling outgoing reactions (Triandis, 1972). In this respect, cultural values (what is important) and norms (what is appropriate) provide the members of a cultural group with schemas, or templates, for interpreting a situation (Fiske & Taylor, 1991). Situational factors that influence social dilemmas include features of the task structure itself (the decision structure and the social structure) and the perception of the task (Kopelman et al., 2002). The decision structure includes factors like the payoff structure and the amount and type of uncertainty involved in the resource. The social structure includes factors such as the power and status of the individuals or organizations, the size of the group, and the ability of people to communicate with one another. Perceptual factors include perceived causes of shortages, or the way cooperation is framed.

One cultural value likely to influence recognition of the social structure of the social dilemma is whether individuals have a tendency to assume hierarchy among group members. The cultural value of hierarchy versus egalitarianism reflects the extent to which individuals focus on social status and power (Hofstede, 1980; Schwartz, 1994). Hierarchy refers to the importance placed on ascribed hierarchical roles in structuring interactions and allocating resources. In egalitarian cultures, status differences are de-emphasized, and power distances are less salient in social interactions and economic exchange. In hierarchical cultures, social status implies social power, so lower-status individuals are expected to defer to higher-status individuals (Leung, 1997). Hierarchy versus egalitarianism may lead to cultural differences in how people react to and view appointing a leader to aid in achieving goals in social dilemmas. There is a large literature identifying the conditions under which group members (in the United States, which is an egalitarian culture) are willing to appoint leaders. This research suggests that groups will opt for a leader when they have failed to manage a resource efficiently and inequalities in harvesting outcomes emerge, and followers will endorse leaders who use fair procedures while maintaining the common resource (Wilke et al., 1986; Wit & Wilke, 1988; Wit et al., 1989). Because there is greater deference to authority in hierarchical than egalitarian cultures (Brett, 2001), decision makers from hierarchical cultures may be more willing to turn control of the resource over to a leader, even before trying self-control, than decision makers from egalitarian cultures. Decision makers from hierarchical cultures also may have more confidence that their leaders will protect the interests of the group as a whole than decision makers from egalitarian cultures where interest groups lobby successfully for special treatment from government authorities.

Culture may also influence how individuals recognize and react to inter-versus intragroup situations. An intergroup paradigm of social dilemmas is set up such that the goal of doing the best for yourself is achieved by cooperating with ingroups and competing with outgroups (Bornstein, 1992; Bornstein & Ben-Yossef, 1994). The task structure differs from the regular intragroup paradigm because it has an intergroup competitive element that increases cooperation with the ingroup. Decision makers in all cultures studied to date were responsive to this task structure, competing with ingroup members in the single-group context and twice as likely to cooperate with them in the intergroup context (Bornstein, 1992; Bornstein & Ben-Yossef, 1994; Bornstein et al., 1994). However, the intergroup effect may be moderated by culture.

In general, collectivists distinguish between ingroup and outgroup members more strongly than individualists (Triandis, 1989), cooperating with ingroup members and competing with outgroup members. Collectivists not only may make clearer distinctions between in- and outgroups than individualists, but they also may define in- and outgroups differently. Both factors may lead collectivists to make rather different decisions in intergroup situations. Furthermore, culturally based assumptions of hierarchy versus egalitarianism may come into play. When studied along with the cultural value of individualism versus collectivism, four categories are defined as follows (e.g., Triandis & Gelfand, 1998): (1) vertical individualists (high on hierarchy and high on individualism); (2) horizontal individualists (low on hierarchy and high on individualism); (3) vertical collectivists (high on hierarchy and low on individualism); and (4) horizontal collectivists (low on hierarchy and low on individualism). Probst and her colleagues (1999) contrasted the single-group decision-making context with an intergroup context in cross-cultural settings. They found that decision makers from individualist and hierarchical cultures (vertical individualists) were more likely to cooperate, similarly to decision makers in the Bornstein intergroup paradigm games. They were significantly less cooperative in the single-group context than in the intergroup context where ingroup cooperation served to maximize their own individual payoffs. In contrast, vertical collectivists acted differently in the intergroup context. They cooperated with their three-person ingroup less in the intergroup context than in the single-group context, perhaps because they viewed the entire set of six people as an ingroup with whom to cooperate. They saw that cooperating across intergroup boundaries maximized for the six as a whole, even though such behavior would not maximize for them personally. Probst et al. (1999) suggested that the vertical collectivists, whose defining characteristic relates to sacrificing own interests for the interests of the group, redefined the "group."

Culture and Rules

Rules simplify behavioral choices by narrowing options in social dilemmas. Utility maximization (especially in narrow economic terms) is only one of many possible decision rules that may apply in the appropriateness framework (Weber et al., 2004). The category of rules that may influence behavior in social dilemmas includes not only explicit and codified guidelines for behavior (e.g., codes of ethics or laws), but also the less visible and explicit influence of social heuristics (e.g., "women and children first"; Allison & Messick, 1990) and habitual rituals [e.g., the equal division of resources (Messick, 1993) or equity norms (Adams, 1963)]. These may all be influenced by cultural norms.

Cultural norms are rules of appropriate social interaction behavior—what one "ought" to do in a given situation. Norms are relevant to choice in social dilemmas because "they provide a means of controlling behavior without entailing the costs, uncertainties, resistances, conflicts and power losses involved in the unrestrained, ad hoc use of interpersonal power" (Thibaut & Kelley, 1959, p. 147). Thus, cultural norms influence what rules decision makers are likely to adopt. Given a specific situation, culturally appropriate scripts or sequences of appropriate social action may be adopted (Shank & Abelson, 1977).

Communities develop rather different solutions for resource allocation problems in social dilemmas because of cultural variation in what groups consider fair. Experimental research shows that norm formation occurs quite rapidly in groups (Bettenhausen & Murnighan, 1985) and then settles in to sustain group behavior over time. Cultural differences may become more pronounced over time. This appears to happen because cultural norms become elaborated. For example, definitions of who may use the resource can become refined, and rights may be passed down from generation to generation (Ostrom, 1990).

What is perceived to be fair in one culture may not be in another (Leung, 1997). In an ultimatum bargaining setting, the amount considered fair to Israeli and Japanese decision makers was different from the amount considered to be fair in U.S. and Yugoslavian cultures (Roth, Prasnikar, Okuno-Fujiwara & Shamir, 1991). When asked to make fair divisions of a good (usually money or candy), Chinese and Japanese decision makers typically distribute it more evenly than those from Australia or the United States (Kashima et al., 1988; Leung & Bond, 1984; Mann et al., 1985). Similarly, a contextual model confirmed an interaction between group culture and power on claiming resources in a simulated social dilemma (Kopelman, 2003). In a common dilemma where parties had different economic power (asymmetric dilemma), managers from different cultural groups—vertical individualists (Israeli), vertical collectivists (Hong Kong Chinese), horizontal individualists (American), and horizontal collectivists (German)—seem to have applied different decision rules based on culturally appropriate fairness norms. Relative to managers from the United States and Germany, Israeli managers were more likely to follow an individually rational decision-making approach taking more resources in a high versus low economic power condition (following an equity rule), whereas decisions of Hong Kong Chinese managers reflected a collective rationality approach, forgoing individual profits by taking fewer resources in a high economic power condition (following an inverse equity rule). The influence of group culture was partially mediated by egocentric perceptions of fairness (Kopelman, 2003). Thus, culture influences the rules engaged in social dilemmas.

Discussion

This review of the appropriateness framework suggests that group culture influences all three current factors: identity, rules, and recognition of the situation. The identity of the individual making the decision, application of rules or heuristics in guiding behavioral choice, and recognition and definition of the kind of situation encountered could all be influenced by group culture. Whereas culture permeates these decision factors, it holds an important enough influence to be treated as a fourth factor. March's (1994) question: "What does a *person* like me *do* in a *situation* like this?" overemphasizes the self and ignores the group. Group-level values and norms, that is, group culture, significantly impact cooperation in social dilemmas and decision making at large. This chapter suggests a broader conceptualization of the appropriateness framework would take group culture into consideration and rephrase March's question to: "What does a *person* like me (identity) *do* (rules) in a *situation* like this (recognition) given this *culture* (group)?"

Theorizing the application of culture in the decision-making process in resolving social dilemmas has implications for both researchers and practitioners. To better understand decision making, future empirical research will need to examine the effect of group culture on social dilemmas within a contextual framework. A contextual approach to group culture stresses the importance of examining the interactions between group culture and individual difference measures or situational factors, such that culture is a necessary but not a sufficient determinant of decision making (Gelfand & Dyer, 2000). In a social dilemma setting, this translates into studying the interaction among group culture, identity, recognition, and rules. Although this chapter has focused on social dilemmas, implications are not limited to the decision-making process in such interdependent settings and maybe generalized to decision making in any social context. Better understanding of the influence of group culture on the decision-making process can help practitioners interpret different patterns of observed behavior, as well as design appropriate interventions for global resource management.

References

Adams, J. S. (1963). Toward an understanding of inequity. *Journal of Abnormal and Social Psychology, 62*, 335–343.

Agrawal, A. (2002). Common Resources and Institutional Sustainability. In E. Ostrom, T. Dietz, N. Dolsak, P. C. Stern, S. Sonich, & E. U. Weber (eds.), The drama of the commons (pp. 41–85). Washington DC: National Academy Press.

Ahn, T. K., Janssen, M. A., Ostrom, E. (2004). Signals, symbols, and human cooperation. In R. Sussman & A. Chapman (eds.) *The Origins and Nature of Sociality* (pp. 122–139). Hawthorne, NY: Aldine de Gruyter.

Allison, S. T., Messick, D. M. (1990). Social decision heuristics in the use of shared resources. *Journal of Behavioral Decision Making, 3*, 195–204.

Bettenhausen, K. L., Murnighan, J. K. (1985). The emergence of norms in competitive decision-making groups. *Administrative Science Quarterly, 30*, 350–372.

Bettenhausen, K. L., Murnighan, J. K. (1991). The development of an intragroup norm and the effects of interpersonal and structural challenges. *Administrative Science Quarterly, 36*, 20–35.

Bornstein, G. (1992). The free-rider problem in intergroup conflicts over step-level and continuous public goods. *Journal of Personality and Social Psychology, 62*, 597–606.

Bornstein, G., Ben-Yossef, M. (1994). Cooperation in intergroup and single-group social dilemmas. *Journal of Experimental Social Psychology, 30*, 52–67.

Bornstein, G., Erev, I., Goren, H. (1994). The effect of repeated play in the IPG and IPD team games. *Journal of Conflict Resolution, 38*, 690–707.

Brett, J. M. (2001). *Negotiating Globally*. San Francisco: Jossey-Bass.

Brett, J. M., Kopelman, S. (2004). Culture and social dilemmas. In G. Michelle & J. M. Brett (eds.), *Negotiation and Culture: Research Perspectives* (pp. 395–411). Stanford, CA: Stanford University Press.

Brewer, M. B. (1991). The social self: On being the same and different at the same time. *Personality and Social Psychology Bulletin, 17*, 475–482.

Dawes, R. M. (1980). Social dilemmas. *Annual Review of Psychology, 31*, 169–193.

Deutsch, M. (1973). *The Resolution of Conflict*. New Haven, CT: Yale University Press.

Fiske, S. T., Taylor, S. E. (1991). Social cognition (2nd ed.). New York: McGraw-Hill.

Forgas, J. P. (1982). Episode cognition: Internal representations of interaction routines. In L. Berkowitz (ed.), *Advances in Experimental Social Psychology* (Vol. 15, pp. 59–103). New York: Academic Press.

Gelfand, M. J., Brett, J. M. (2004). The Handbook of Negotiation and Culture. Stanford, California: Stanford University Press.

Gelfand, M. J., Dyer, N. (2000). A cultural perspective on negotiation: Progress, pitfalls, and prospects. *Applied Psychology, 49*, 62–99.

Gärling, T. (1999). Value priorities, social value orientations and cooperation in social dilemmas. *British Journal of Social Psychology, 38*, 397–408.

Hardin, C. D., Higgins, E. T. (1996). Shared reality: How social verification makes the subjective objective. In R. M. Sorrentino & H. E. Tory (eds.), *Handbook of Motivation and Cognition* (Vol. 3, pp. 28–84). New York: Guilford Press.

Hardin, G. (1968). The tragedy of the commons. *Science, 162*, 1243–1248.

Hemesath, M., Pomponio, X. (1998). Cooperation and culture: Students from China and the United States in a prisoner's dilemma. *The Journal of Comparative Social Science, 32*, 171–184.

Hofstede, G. (1980). *Culture's Consequences: International Differences in Work-Related Values*. Newbury Park, CA: Sage.

Kashima, Y., Siegal, M., Tanaka, K., Isaka, H. (1988). Universalism in lay conceptions of distributive justice: A cross-cultural examination. *International Journal of Psychology, 23*, 51–64.

Kollock, P. (1998). Social dilemmas: The anatomy of cooperation. *Annual Review of Sociology, 24*, 183–214.

Kopelman, S. (1999). Social motives and reciprocity in negotiations: Implications for cross-cultural settings. DRRC Working Paper #271.

Kopelman, S. (2003). Culture and power asymmetry in resource negotiations: Implications for self-interested behavior in social dilemmas. Unpublished dissertation, Northwestern University, Evanston, IL.

Kopelman, S., Weber, J. M., Messick, D. M. (2002). Factors influencing cooperation in commons dilemmas: A review of experimental psychological research. In E. Ostrom, T. Dietz, N. Dolsak, P. C. Stern, S. Sonich & E. U. Weber (eds.), *The Drama of the Commons* (pp. 113–156). Washington, DC: National Academy Press.

Kramer, R. M., McClintock, C. G., Messick, D. M. (1986). Social values and cooperative response to a simulated resource conservation crisis. *Journal of Personality, 54*, 576–592.

Lalljee, M., Lamb, R., Abelson, R. P. (1992). The role of event prototypes in categorization and explanation. In W. Stroebe & M. Hewstone (eds.), *European Review of Social Psychology* (Vol. 3, pp. 153–182). Oxford: John Wiley & Sons.

Ledyard, J. (1995). Public goods: A survey of experimental research. In J. Kagel & A. Roth (eds.), *Handbook of Experimental Economics* (pp. 111–194). Princeton, NJ: Princeton University Press.

Lefcourt, H. M. (1982). *Locus of Control: Current Trends in Theory and Research* (2nd ed.). Hillsdale, NJ: Erlbaum.

Leung, K. (1997). Negotiation and reward allocations across cultures. In P. C. Earley & M. Erez (eds.), *New Perspectives on International Industrial/Organizational Psychology* (pp. 640–675). San Francisco: New Lexington Press.

Leung, K., Bond, M. H. (1984). The impact of cultural collectivism on reward allocation. *Journal of Personality and Social Psychology, 47*, 793–804.

Luce, R. D., Raiffa, H. (1957). *Games and Decisions: Introduction and Critical Survey*. New York: Wiley.

Lytle, A. M., Brett, J. M., Barsness, Z. I., Tinsley, C. H., Janssens, M. (1995). A paradigm for confirmatory cross-cultural research in organizational behavior. In L. L. Cummings & B. M. Staw (eds.), *Research in Organizational Behavior* (Vol. 17, pp. 167–214). Greenwich, CT: JAI Press.

Mann, L., Radford, M., Kanagawa, C. (1985). Cross-cultural differences in children's use of decision rules: A comparison between Japan and Australia. *Journal of Personality and Social Psychology, 49*, 1557–1564.

March, J. (1994). *A Primer on Decision Making: How Decisions Happen.* New York: Free Press.

Markus, H. R., Kitayama, S. (1991). Culture and the self: Implications for cognition, emotion, and motivation. *Psychological Review, 98,* 224–253.

McCay, B. J. (2002). Emergence of institutions for the commons: Contexts, situations, and events. In E. Ostrom, T. Dietz, N. Dolsak, P. C. Stern, S. Sonich, & E. U. Weber (eds.), The drama of the commons (pp. 361–402). Washington DC: National Academy Press.

Messick, D. M. (1993). Equality as a decision heuristic. In B. A. Mellers & B. Jonathan (eds.), *Psychological Perspectives on Justice: Theory and Applications* (pp. 11–31). New York: Cambridge University Press.

Messick, D. M. (1999). Alternative logics for decision making in social settings. *Journal of Economic Behavior and Organization, 39*(1), 11–28.

Messick, D. M., McClintock, C. G. (1968). Motivational bases of choice in experimental games. *Journal of Experimental Social Psychology, 4,* 1–25.

Moghaddam, F. M., Taylor, D. M., Wright, S. C. (1993). *Social Psychology in Cross-Cultural Perspective.* New York: W. H. Freeman and Company.

Ostrom, E. (1990). *Governing the Commons: The Evolution of Institutions for Collective Action.* New York: Cambridge University Press.

Ostrom, E. (2000). Collective action and the evolution of social norms. *Journal of Economic Perspectives, 14,* 137–158.

Parks, C. D. (1994). The predictive ability of social values in resource dilemmas and public goods games. *Personality and Social Psychology Bulletin, 20,* 431–438.

Parks, C. D., Vu, A. D. (1994). Social dilemma behavior of individuals from highly individualist and collectivist cultures. *Journal of Conflict Resolution, 38,* 708–718.

Probst, T., Carnevale, P. J., Triandis, H. C. (1999). Cultural values in intergroup and single-group social dilemmas. *Organizational Behavior and Human Decision Processes, 77,* 171–191.

Pruitt, D. G., Kimmel, M. J. (1977). Twenty years of experimental gaming: Critique, synthesis, and suggestions for the future. *Annual Review of Psychology, 28,* 363–392.

Roch, S. G., Samuelson, C. D. (1997). Effects of environmental uncertainty and social value orientation in resource dilemmas. *Organizational Behavior and Human Decision Processes, 70,* 221–235.

Roth, A. E., Prasnikar, Okuno-Fujiwara, Shamir. (1991). Bargaining and Market Behavior in Jerusalem, Ljubljana, Pittsburgh, and Tokyo: An Experimental Study. American Economic Review, 81(5), 1068–95.

Schwartz, S. H. (1994). Beyond individualism/collectivism: New cultural dimensions of values. In U. Kim, H. C. Triandis, & G. Yoon (eds.), *Individualism and Collectivism:* 85–117. London: Sage.

Shank, R. C., Abelson, R. P. (1977). *Scripts, Plans, Goals and Understanding: An Inquiry into Human Knowledge Structures.* Hillsdale, NJ: Erlbaum.

Snyder, M., Gangestad, S. (1986). On the nature of self-monitoring: Matters of assessment, matters of validity. *Journal of Personality and Social Psychology, 51,* 125–139.

Taylor, D. M., Modhaddam, F. M. (1994). *Theories of Intergroup Relations* (2nd ed.). London: Praeger.

Thibaut, J. W., Kelley, H. H. (1959). *The Social Psychology of Groups.* New York: Wiley.

Triandis, H. C. (1972). *The Analysis of Subjective Culture.* New York: Wiley.

Triandis, H. C. (1989). Cross-cultural studies of individualism and collectivism. In J. Berman (ed.), *Nebraska Symposium on Motivation* (pp. 41–133). Lincoln: University of Nebraska Press.

Triandis, H. C., Gelfand, M. J. (1998). Converging measurement of horizontal and vertical individualism and collectivism. *Journal of Personality and Social Psychology, 74,* 118–128.

Turner, J. C., Hogg, M. A., Oakes, P. J., Reicher, S. D., Wetherell, M. S. (1987). *Rediscovering the Social Group: A Self-Categorization Theory.* Oxford: Blackwell.

Van Lange, P., De Bruin, E. M. N., Otten, W., Joireman, J. A. (1997). Development of prosocial, individualistic, and competitive orientations: Theory and preliminary evidence. *Journal of Personality and Social Psychology, 73,* 733–746.

Van Lange, P., Liebrand, W., Messick, D. M., Wilke, H. A. (1992). Social dilemmas: The state of the art introduction and literature review. In W. B. G. Liebrand, D. M. Messick & H. A. Wilke (eds.), *Social Dilemmas: Theoretical Issues and Research Findings* (pp. 3–28). New York: Pergamon Press.

Wade-Benzoni, K. A., Okumura, T., Brett, J. M., Moore, D. A., Tenbrunsel, A. E., Bazerman, M. H. (2002). Cognitions and behavior in asymmetric social dilemmas: A comparison of two cultures. *Journal of Applied Psychology, 87*, 87–95.

Weber, J. M., Kopelman, S., Messick, D. M. (2004). A conceptual review of decision making in social dilemmas: Applying a logic of appropriateness. *Personality and Social Psychology Review, 8*, 281–307.

Wilke, H. A., de Boer, K. L., Liebrand, W. B. (1986). Standards of justice and quality of power in a social dilemma situation. *British Journal of Social Psychology, 25*, 57–65.

Wit, A., Wilke, H. (1988). Subordinates' endorsement of an allocating leader in a commons dilemma: An equity theoretical approach. *Journal of Economic Psychology, 9*, 151–168.

Wit, A., Wilke, H. A., Van Dijk, E. (1989). Attribution of leadership in a resource management situation. *European Journal of Social Psychology, 19*, 327–338.

Chapter 12
Will Lessons from Small-Scale Social Dilemmas Scale Up?

Michael McGinnis and Elinor Ostrom

Scholars have found that when groups are relatively small, engage in face-to-face communication, and build norms of trust and reciprocity, they are able to agree on a strategy to solve social dilemmas and carry through on their agreements (Franzen 1994; Ostrom et al., 1994; Sandell & Stern 1998). A key question for global governance, then, is whether mechanisms exist to enable resource users and others facing social dilemmas to scale up to a larger unit where face-to-face communication with all participants is impossible. Although individuals who are able to engage in face-to-face discussion can use informal agreements and sanctioning to solve very challenging social dilemmas, one cannot realistically think about solving large-scale social dilemmas without some organization (or network of organizations) that takes on the challenge of devising rules, monitoring, and enforcing those rules.

Many contemporary environmental problems are larger than most nation-states. A question is repeatedly posed as to whether it is actually possible to scale up to undertake regulation of global environmental problems such as global warming. The actions of millions of people affect the amount of CO_2 admitted into the atmosphere. This affects the protection that is offered to the earth by the atmosphere. Everyone has an impact. If everyone were to reduce CO_2 admissions over time, the threat of global warming would become much less. While everyone would be better off if everyone contributed to correcting the amount of carbon admitted into the atmosphere, any one individual or corporate actor would be better off if others took on this task while they continued their normal activities. Since there is not a single governmental unit established for regulating the use of the atmosphere and many other large-scale resources, some scholars have felt that social dilemmas at these scales were impossible to solve.

In this chapter, we ask whether the design principles that have been proposed as ways of solving small- and medium-sized dilemmas related to use of resources are applicable at a larger scale. Obviously, these principles do not scale up automatically. On the other hand, more hope exists regarding the feasibility of scaling up than is sometimes expressed in the literature (Ostrom et al., 1999).[1] We analyze the problem

---

[1] Several scholars have, for example, posed design principles similar to those we discuss in this chapter for coping with the governance of online virtual communities (see Goodwin 1994; Kollock 1997).

A. Biel et al. (eds.), *New Issues and Paradigms in Research on Social Dilemmas.*

of scaling up solutions to social dilemma problems. We focus primarily on common pool resources where everyone's use potentially subtracts from the benefits available to others. Without some regularized boundary rules and use rules, as well as means of monitoring, sanctioning, and resolving disputes, there are major challenges in keeping individuals from adversely affecting these resources. Before addressing the design principles, let us first address the problem of matching institutions to the type of goods involved.

Matching Institutions to Physical Worlds

The World of Private Goods

When individuals engage in transactions related to private goods, matching rules to physical worlds is relatively simple. Goods are considered to be "private goods" when

- all aspects of the goods and services that individuals produce, distribute, buy, and sell can be excluded from actors who would like to use them (or, alternatively, others can avoid having externalities of a process dumped on them), and
- any good consumed by one individual is unavailable for consumption by others (Ostrom & Ostrom, 1977).

Rule configurations that generate an open, competitive market are optimally efficient when used in relation to private goods (De Alessi, 1993). Unfortunately, only a limited number of the goods and services used by individuals possess the attributes of private goods. As soon as the goods involved do not have these nice characteristics, it can be shown that various aspects of "market failure" occur.

The World of Common Pool Resources

Common pool resources (CPRs) possess only one of the characteristics of private goods, namely, the second one listed above. CPRs are defined to be natural or man-made resources in which (1) exclusion is nontrivial (but not necessarily impossible) and (2) yield is subtractable (Walker et al., 1991). CPRs share the attribute of non-exclusion with another broad class of problems that are referred to as public goods (Ostrom & Ostrom, 1977). Without non-market institutions of a wide variety of structures involving diverse forms of social capital, public goods are underprovided and common pool resources are exhausted (Uzawa, 2005). The second attribute of CPRs, which is shared with private goods but not with public goods, is the subtractability of the yield (Samuelson, 1954). Another term frequently used in economics literature to describe this attribute is *rivalness of consumption*.

Let us illustrate the importance of subtractability with examples drawn from research on groundwater basins, irrigation systems, fisheries, forests, grazing lands, computer systems, airport facilities, bridges, and other natural or man-made resources that generate an extractable yield. All of these are resources that make available a flow of resource units over time. Examples of resource and resource units include (1) tons of fish harvested from fishing grounds, (2) the quantity of water pumped out of a groundwater basin, and (3) processing time in a shared computer facility. The fish caught by one boat owner are not available to anyone else. Nor is the water withdrawn by a groundwater pumper or the CPUs used by one faculty member. The facilities or resources producing these units are, however, jointly used by multiple individual or corporate actors.

When a few users first use renewable CPRs, what one person uses does not appear to subtract from what is available for others. At low-use patterns, the abundance of units relative to demand masks the subtractability. In some resources, such as fisheries, initial withdrawals may actually increase the amount jointly available. Fish compete for food resources, and harvesting some fish allows other fish to survive their competitive race to find food. If there are no rules in place to limit the use of a CPR, and if the resource unit that can be withdrawn is valuable, then the structure of the situation leads users to invest more and more in harvesting activities. After a threshold has been reached, each individual's investment and harvesting activities adversely affect everyone else using the same resource.

Without rules to allocate resource units, users competing with one another for ever-scarcer units may engage in destructive races against one another, and their actions may destroy the very resource that is generating valuable yield for them. Garrett Hardin (1968) captured a key aspect of the problem of an open-access CPR in his now-classic use of the phrase "Tragedy of the Commons."[2] Aristotle recognized a similar dilemma when he wrote, "For that which is common to the greatest number has the least care bestowed upon it" (1942, Book II, Sec. 3). What Hardin did not understand was the capacity of the individuals involved in many such tragedies to have sufficient insight into the problems that they faced to restructure their own rules and change the incentives they faced.

Where a resource produces a single, valuable resource unit with a high level of predictability known to all participants (or, where storage facilities, such as dams, enhance predictability), it is possible to devise marketable rights or other simple allocation rules that enable individuals to make efficient long-term use of the resource (Hurwicz, 1973; Clark, 1980). Blomquist (1992) demonstrated the enhanced efficiency achieved in groundwater systems when marketable rights to the flow are

---

[2] Hardin (1978) also contributed to the contemporary presumption that there were only two solutions to this kind of problem. The "only" alternatives that he posed for solving tragic overuse was what he called "a private enterprise system," on the one hand, or "socialism" on the other (p. 310). He proposed that change would need to be instituted with whatever force was needed. In other words, "if ruin is to be avoided in a crowded world, people must be responsive to a coercive force outside their individual psyches, a 'Leviathan' to use Hobbes's term" (p. 314). Contrary to many casual, contemporary descriptions, the English commons was not an open access CPR (see Dahlman, 1980). For a vigorous re-evaluation, see Feeny et al. (1990).

perfected. Fishery economists, drawing on the influential work of Gordon (1954) and Schaefer (1957), have developed important conceptual models of a predictable single-species fishery where excessive harvesting is efficiently curbed by devising a transferable quota system (Scott, 1979, 1982). The same institution, however, is not at all efficient nor effective when applied to multispecies fisheries with complex interdependencies (Townsend, 1986; Townsend & Wilson, 1987). Devising an efficient, effective, and equitable transferable quota system for a multispecies fishery is problematic (see Copes, 1986; Wilson, 2002). Many global CPR problems also involve complex interactions among many interrelated processes and are unlikely to be solved with extremely simple institutional arrangements (see McGinnis & Ostrom, 1992).

Prior Research on Robust CPR Institutions

Prior research has included an intensive analysis of field settings where (1) resource users have devised, monitored, and followed their own rules to control the use of a CPR and (2) the resource systems, as well as the institutions, have survived for long periods of time. The robust CPR institutions originally studied included grazing and forest CPR institutions in Switzerland and Japan, and irrigation systems in Spain and the Philippine Islands (see Ostrom, 1990, 2005). Since then, many more cases of robust CPR institutions have been studied and the theory extended to more complex cases (see Tang, 1992; Lam, 1998; Acheson, 2003; Weinstein, 2000; Anderies et al., 2004; Jones, 2003).

In CPR institutions that have survived for long periods of time, operational rules-in-use have not necessarily remained fixed since they were first initiated. All of these environmental settings are complex and variable over time. In such settings, it would be difficult to get "the operational rules right" on the first try, or even after several tries. These institutions are "robust" or in "institutional equilibrium" in the sense defined by Shepsle. Shepsle (1989, p. 143) regards "an institution as 'essentially' in equilibrium if changes transpired according to an *ex ante* plan (and hence part of the original institution) for institutional change." In these cases, the participants designed basic operational rules, created organizations to undertake the operational management of their CPRs, and modified the rules-in-use over time in light of past experience according to their own collective-choice and constitutional rules.

In earlier work, we have developed two types of explanations for long-term changes in resource regimes. The first type of explanation has focused on why some institutions are robust in the Shepsle sense and others are not. Why do some architectural structures of institutional-choice processes survive for very long periods in dynamically changing situations while other institutional arrangements fail the test of time?

The second type of explanation has focused on the factors most likely to affect the design and subsequent reform of these institutional-choice processes themselves (Ostrom, 1990, Ch. 6). In particular, we must understand those factors that affect the cost-benefit calculations of those who design institutions so that we may better understand processes in which new rules are selected. To a great extent, this second type of explanation presumes that at least some partial answers have already been provided to the first set of questions. For if institutional designers are to have any hope of crafting long-lasting institutional arrangements, then they must have some basic understanding of the factors that determine long-term success or failure.

A key insight of the CPR literature is that small communities around the world have exhibited an intuitive understanding of the principles behind building robust institutions for resource management, or at least an ability to react to emerging problems in a sustainable manner. As policy analysts, we take it to be our task to refine these implicit principles in order to provide a sounder basis for institutional design in other contexts. Of course, since partisan struggles and many factors other than long-term viability are typically involved in any collective process of institutional design, analysts also need to have a solid understanding of cultural and political dynamics as well as organizational theory.

In this chapter, we focus on the first type of explanation, specifically the applicability of research on CPR regimes for the long-term sustainability and effectiveness of international regimes related to global change. We ask what lessons can be drawn from research on robust CPR institutions that help us understand the conditions under which international institutions will support robust regimes. We are confident that significant principles do indeed apply across these dramatically different scales, as long as due care is taken in the process of extrapolating from one institutional context to another.

In explaining why some CPR institutions are robust and others are fragile, we found that we could not develop a coherent explanation that focused on the *detail* of the specific rules used by robust CPR institutions. While the particular rules that are used within each setting cannot be the basis for an explanation for the institutional robustness and sustainability across these CPRs, part of the explanation for their success is based on the fact that the particular rules differ. By differing, particular rules take into account specific attributes of the related physical systems, cultural views of the world, and the economic and political relationships that exist in the setting. Without different rules, users could not take advantage of the positive features of a local CPR or avoid potential pitfalls that could occur in one setting but not others. *Given the diversity of the settings, one should not expect to be able to discover a single best formulation or set of optimal mechanisms.*

Instead of similar specific rules, there are similar design principles that are generally present in most of the robust CPR institutions. By "design principle" is meant an essential element or condition that helps to account for the success of these institutions in sustaining the CPRs and gaining the compliance of generation after generation of participants to the rules-in-use.[3] Focusing on underlying principles

---

[3] We do not think it is possible to elucidate necessary AND sufficient principles for enduring institutions as it takes a fundamental willingness of the individuals involved to make any institution work. No set of logical conditions are sufficient to ensure that all sets of individuals are willing and able to make an institution characterized by such conditions work.

rather than specific mechanisms may enable us to learn lessons from a wide diversity of small field settings that have relevance to the design of robust international regimes.[4] The design principles of robust CPR institutions were identified as

1. **Clearly defined boundaries.** Individuals or households who have rights to withdraw resource units from the CPR must be clearly defined, as must the boundaries of the CPR itself.
2. **Congruence between appropriation and provision rules and local conditions.** Appropriation rules restricting time, place, technology, and/or quantity of resource units are related to local conditions and to provision rules requiring labor, materials, and/or money.
3. **Collective-choice arrangements.** Most individuals affected by operational rules can participate in modifying operational rules.
4. **Monitoring.** Monitors, who actively audit CPR conditions and participant behavior, are accountable to the participants or are the participants.
5. **Graduated sanctions.** Participants who violate operational rules are likely to be assessed graduated sanctions (depending on the seriousness and context of the offense) by other participants, by officials accountable to these participants, or by both.
6. **Conflict-resolution mechanisms.** Participants and their officials have rapid access to low-cost local arenas to resolve conflicts among participants or between participants and officials.
7. **Minimal recognition of rights to organize.** The rights of participants to devise their own institutions are not challenged by external governmental authorities.
8. **Nested enterprises.** Appropriation, provision, monitoring, enforcement, conflict-resolution, and governance activities are organized in multiple layers of nested enterprises.

These eight principles have been stated in slightly different forms over the course of a still-evolving research program on the robust management of common pool resources. The second principle, in particular, encompasses related concerns that can be stated with different emphases. The rules in question must be "congruent" both with the biophysical dynamics that underlie the replenishment of the resource and with the culturally shaped expectations of the participants in that resource regime. Rewards to individual participants must be related in some fashion to the degree of extractive effort exerted by that individual, and yet that person's contribution to the collective maintenance of the resource regime should also play some role in the allocation process. If community norms underlie the system in question, then norms of egalitarianism may come into play, requiring that some minimal level of benefit be conveyed even to those unable to participate fully in either individual appropriation or collective maintenance. In more diverse communities, participants from divergent cultures may still cooperate on practical matters of direct importance to their own livelihood. Participants may advocate contrasting bases for

---

[4] These principles are drawn from Ostrom (1990) and are explained in more detail therein.

equity, but any regime, to be viable in the long term, must strike an acceptable balance among these contending senses of equity. Each of the eight design principles listed above can be satisfied in diverse ways, and the critical feature is whether or not all principles are manifested in ways that complement each other.

The Global Relevance of Research on Local CPR Regimes

Several reasons underlie our thinking that lessons learned from past research on small-scale CPRs can be usefully applied to the problems of dealing with resource management and governance at the international level. Three reasons are particularly important:

1. The analytical structure of some global problems shares similar features with the analytical structure of many local CPRs.
2. Concepts and tools devised for the analysis of local CPRs provide a solid foundation for building theories and models appropriate for application at a global level.
3. Many global problems (e.g., deforestation) are themselves the result of inadequate solutions at a micro level of a complementary and interactive commons problem.

To the extent that global commons dilemmas share analytical attributes with smaller-scale CPRs, the theoretical and empirical lessons learned from studying micro-level phenomena may "scale up" so that direct lessons may be learned (see Buck, 1998). Analyzing complex patterns of interaction in the simplest possible example of the structure (the biologist's strategy) may enable the analyst to understand the way things work in the simplest exemplar without being overwhelmed by the sheer complexity of the problem (Kirch, 1997). To the extent that work at a micro level does not easily scale up, it still may be the case that key variables are identified in micro-level theories and models. Starting with the work at this level may save considerable time as contrasted to an effort to move to the global level directly. Even though it is impossible to completely decompose global problems into entirely discrete subproblems, working upwards may enable solutions to be reached faster than starting from the global and working downwards—at least for some subset of problems (see Ashby, 1960; Polanyi, 1951).

As an example of a global problem rooted in inadequate local arrangements, consider the contribution of deforestation to global climatic change (Cruz, 1991; Lele, 2002). Deforestation may be the result of conversion from lower-valued to higher-valued uses of particular forest products. It may also be the result of either (1) ill-defined property rights where the transaction costs of gaining clear property rights (whether strictly private or communal) are very high or (2) the creation of a concession economy as the foundation for resource mobilization by national government officials (for their government as well as for themselves). Problems like deforestation will deteriorate still further until more effective institutional arrangements can be devised at the local level (Hayes & Ostrom, 2005). Given the varieties of physical environments that exist within even one country, no single set of rules related to the use of forests will create appropriate incentive systems for all individuals whose decisions affect the regeneration of forests over time (Lambin et al., 2001).

Another major point of similarity is the shared concern for finding means to cooperate despite the absence (or disinterest) of a higher level of political authority. Research on international regimes has emphasized the ability of governments to cooperate in an environment of "anarchy," defined as the absence of any central authority at the global level (Young, 1989, 1999). Since many of the micro settings where individuals have jointly devised their own institutions have existed far from the purview of national, regional, or local government officials, the design of these institutions and their enforcement have not always depended on the presence of a "State." Many of the self-organized institutions devised in these micro settings are not dependent upon enforcement of their rules by external officials. Indeed, enforcement by the users themselves is an essential aspect of sustainability (Gibson et al., 2005). Further, since many of these micro institutions are neither a market nor a state, we may gain insight to alternative international institutions from studying these micro institutions.

On the other hand, we are cautious about casual analogies. We fully recognize that there are substantial differences in the range of actors involved in many global problems. In many micro studies, the actors involved are individuals whose own livelihood depends strongly on solutions to use a resource system more efficiently over time. In many local commons around the world, individuals do devise for themselves rather ingenious institutional arrangements that have enabled them to make productive use of fragile resource systems over long periods of time. Even then, there are many "tragedies of the commons" in these situations where individuals interact directly with one another.

Once we move to the problem of the global commons, in addition to the millions of individuals who make choices, we add many corporate actors who are designated as the agents for complex publics. Understanding the behavior of agents is more complex, yet similar decision models apply to agents as well as individuals acting on their own behalf. Indeed, the extensive body of research on agent–principal relations (Moe, 1984; Miller, 1992) provides a key link in our chain of argument. No matter how complex a formal organization may become, some individual or identifiable set of individuals is ultimately responsible for implementing any decision or action taken in the name of that organization. Understanding the incentives facing the relevant agents is a critical step in any application of institutional analysis.

For example, since corporations and national governments can reasonably be expected to exist for long periods of time, at least some of their agents face compelling incentives to establish predictable rules of behavior that reduce future levels of uncertainty (Keohane, 1984). Still other agents will seek ways to take advantage of that regularity, to shirk their responsibilities or otherwise exploit their position of authority for personal or partisan gain.

As noted above, forestry management may not be sustainable unless local citizens whose livelihood is directly affected by the continued viability of the relevant resources are involved in the monitoring process. Any effort to rely solely on the monitoring efforts of government officials runs the risk that the official will face contrasting incentives to shirk on that responsibility. When we move to the global level, none of the design principles can operate effectively if the incentives of the relevant agents are poorly aligned. An issue that we emphasize below is the extent to which the nature of these collective-action organizations affects the patterns of monitoring and sanctioning that can realistically be expected to occur in any global regime.

In the next section, we begin the process of speculating about how the CPR design principles should be transformed to be relevant for regimes created at the international level to cope with global commons issues, such as climate change due to the increased greenhouse gases present in the stratosphere.

Dilemmas of Extending Design Principles to the Global Scale

There are many reasons to question whether the same principles of institutional design that have proven so effective for sustainable community-based management of common pool resources can be easily generalized for application to regimes at larger scales. In this section, we examine these issues in some detail, with particular attention to the potential applicability of these design principles to the management of global commons and to global environmental regimes in general.

We discuss these concerns under two categories. First, the design principles are inductive generalizations from a set of case studies on CPR regimes with a shared set of characteristics. Thus, their relevance is limited by the extent to which these characteristics differ from aspects of global environment or commons management regimes. Second, the particular institutional arrangements that underlie successful community management may not even be available for use at the global scale.

For this second part of our analysis, we draw upon a more extensive evaluation of the complementary strengths and weaknesses of organizations and processes within the private, public, voluntary, and community sectors (see Lichbach, 1996; Hanisch & McGinnis, 2005). Community-based organizations are grounded in specific processes that should not be expected to operate in a similar manner at the global level. As a consequence, organizations from other sectors may be required to serve as replacements for the functions fulfilled in smaller-scale, community-based management regimes. But this is simply a reshuffling of responsibilities. For even community-based management regimes can be successfully sustained only in the context of supportive institutional arrangements in the private, public, and voluntary sectors. To replicate the successful management of CPRs at higher scales, institutional designers must craft an innovative recombination of private, public, voluntary, and community-based organizations that can, to the extent feasible, mimic the dynamic processes summarized in the design principles as laid out above.

Limits to Direct Generalization

A large and diverse set of case studies was examined in the process through which these design principles were identified (see cases cited in Ostrom, 1990; Ostrom et al., 1994). Still, the following generalizations are appropriate:

1. Most cases were small in scale, although some did consist of multiple small-scale regimes working together under similar principles or nested into larger organizations.
2. Most cases involved resources located in physical locations remote from population centers or capital cities.
3. In most cases, management of the particular type of resource was not a matter of intense political contention at the national or provincial level.
4. Most cases involved peoples whose lives and livelihoods were directly dependent on continued access to the resource being managed.
5. Although there were often disparities in resource access or wealth among the participants in a given regime, these disparities were not extreme in magnitude.
6. Some cases involved homogeneous communities, but many included participants from diverse ethnic, cultural, linguistic, or religious traditions.
7. Nearly all cases involved resource users who had, over decades or even centuries, developed intimate levels of knowledge of the local distribution of the resource and its variability over time and space. This local knowledge was communicated across generations by informal mechanisms.
8. Most communities were relatively poor, at least in the sense of having limited access to easily transferable economic capital. On the other hand, most of these same communities enjoyed substantial endowments of social capital.

In sum, the design principles developed from studies of robust CPR institutions extrapolate from the experience of mostly small (but not necessarily ethnically homogeneous) communities isolated from centers of national power or economic prosperity facing highly salient and well-understood problems of resource management. Economic disparities existed, but not to an extent that undermined a common sense of community. This is not to say, of course, that no sources of conflict remained within these communities. Conflicts inevitably arose, but long-term, sustainable regimes include processes by which disputes can be managed without excessive violence.

By definition, the first generalization from the successful cases—that most cases were small in scale—cannot apply to global regimes. It is not immediately obvious how many other characteristics remain relevant. Indeed, different types of regimes will violate different combinations of these characteristics. Informally, one might conclude that the principles should be more relevant for extension to cases that match more of the generalizations listed above. Yet, even this guideline proves of limited utility.

Consider, for example, the large number of functionally specific international regimes that have developed in such technical areas as communication and transportation (Zacher, 1996). Given the low political profile assigned to such matters in normal circumstances, these functional regimes are just as isolated from political controversies as many of the local CPR regimes upon which the design principles are based. Furthermore, such regimes tend to be dominated by technical experts for whom that topic is especially salient, since it constitutes the basis of their own professional careers. The number of such experts may be large relative to small-scale regimes, and yet most professions have developed mechanisms for coordination and professionalization across national boundaries. In this sense, technical regimes are dominated by "epistemic communities" of like-minded experts (Haas, 1989). For members of an epistemic community, the operations of monitoring, sanctioning, and dispute resolution may well operate pretty much as specified in the design principles.

Yet, there is much more to global regimes than technical questions. Most environmental regimes, for example, touch upon sensitive issues of politics and economic interests. Typically, sharply contrasting world views energize activists on all sides of the issue, and deep divisions exist in terms of access to resources or political power (Young, 1994). When few if any of the characteristics listed above remain relevant, analysts should be especially cautious in any effort to extend the design principles.

An additional complication is illustrated by the history of the evolving regime on the management of whales, which is still based on the 1946 International Convention for the Regulation of Whaling (Stoett, 1997; Friedheim, 2001). Originally, this treaty-based regime was established by a small number of governments of countries intensely involved in the harvesting of whales throughout the world's oceans. In effect, then, the International Whaling Commission (IWC) was a voluntary club of major whaling nations. At that time, it was not a particularly controversial sector of the political economy, nor did it prove to be a particularly successful management scheme (Andresen, 2002). With the rise of environmental consciousness, the situation changed dramatically. Activists came to see whales as intelligent creatures that should not be hunted and consumed (Chopra & D'Amato, 1991). As political controversies mounted, more and more IWC members downgraded their interest in whaling as traditionally practiced and came to prefer additional limitations. After all, substitutes have been found for nearly all products originally garnered from the harvesting of whales,[5] with the exception of whale meat for human consumption.

Although moratoriums on commercial whaling have been declared, they have been peppered with exceptions that allow the practice to continue in different forms. Japan, where some consumers retain a taste for whale meat, and Norway, with an economic interest in commercial whaling, feared being perpetually outvoted within the IWC. In response, the IWC was expanded to include non-whaling countries, whose votes were presumed to have been exchanged for generous provision

---

[5] Nadelmann (1990) stresses the importance of finding substitutes for products if there is to be any hope of establishing a global prohibition regime. But, as Nadelmann argued, supportive changes are required in the political and administrative realms as well as the economic.

of economic assistance from IWC members supporting the continued hunting of whales. Opponents were not averse to similar stratagems, and this practice of selectively allowing some non-whaling states into the regime while keeping others out has become a source of continuing controversy. Even more controversy has been generated by the actions of Greenpeace and other organizations deeply committed to the prohibition of commercial whaling, under any pretenses. This regime has yet to become fully integrated within the broader system of global management centered around agencies of the United Nations, but the logical progression of these controversies might well result in that outcome (Friedheim, 2001; Burns & Gillespie, 2003).

This example demonstrates the limited usefulness of any exercise in counting the number of ways in which particular cases deviate from the characteristics of the set of cases upon which the design principles were constructed. For as a situation moves away from a club-like arrangement to become more of a matter of high politics, about the only thing that can be concluded is that these design principles may not be so obviously relevant. However, as long as the participants remain sufficiently clever to cope with this increased complexity by adopting new rules, this regime may still remain viable. In the next section, we move to an alternative approach that provides a sounder basis for the evaluation of alternative policy responses.

Cross-Sectoral Foundations of Institutional Design

The design principles summarize the observed patterns generated by an underlying dynamic process of collective management. In nearly all cases, aspects of community-based organization were critical. That is, participants had built upon the unique advantages of community-based forms of organizing in their construction and maintenance of these resource regimes. In this section, we move to consider more explicitly the nature of these *institutions*, rather than the underlying *resources*.

For this analysis, we draw upon a generalization of standard evaluations of the relative strengths and weaknesses of private, public, and voluntary modes of organization. Justifications of government intervention as a response to the perceived failures of markets have been recognized as a classic insight of standard theories of public policy (Weimer & Vining, 1989; Bickers & Williams, 2001). More generally, markets require a supportive institutional environment in order to fully realize their well-known efficiencies in the production, distribution, and consumption of private goods. Secure property rights, a system of dispute resolution, a common currency, and other public goods are more effectively provided by public organizations. An additional supplement to pure market forces is provided by the existence of nonprofit producers, especially of goods for which quality information is difficult to obtain before purchase. For such products, the option of purchasing it from an organization with a reputation for motivations beyond base profit can be especially attractive. Other voluntary associations make useful contributions to the smooth operation of markets, notably in the area of voluntary codes of good conduct and other forms of socialization and self-regulation by professional associations. Furthermore, community values can set effective limits against the expansion of market exchange into undesired or sensitive areas of human interaction, notably drugs and prostitution. Conversely, if markets are allowed a totally free reign, then anything and anybody can become a commodity.

In sum, markets operate best if they are situated within a supportive context of public and voluntary organizations. In similar fashion, free markets facilitate the smooth operation of processes grounded in the public or voluntary sector (see Lichbach, 1996; Hanisch & McGinnis, 2005). By this same line of argument, since the design principles identified by Ostrom (1990) reflect the smooth operation of institutions of community-based organizations, this operation can only be ensured if supportive contributions are made from private, public, and voluntary organizations.

For purposes of comparison with the familiar private, public, and voluntary sectors, we introduce the term "community-based sector." For analytical purposes, we distinguish between voluntary associations and community-based organizations by presuming that members of the latter face a high cost of exit. That is, any member of a community is assumed to be tied to other members by a large number of social linkages, and these linkages can serve as a basis for social capital and for social sanctioning of inappropriate behavior. Community-based organizations build upon the extensive array of interpersonal relationships that constitute a community. Voluntary associations similarly create social capital, but of a less intimate and perhaps more ephemeral nature.

In general, community organizations have several advantages over organizations from other sectors. Close-knit relationships may be essential to providing individual members with a sense of belonging, a sense of ultimate meaning for their actions, and a grounding of their personal sense of identity. Social pressure for conformity to norms can be especially powerful, particularly in close-knit communities. Members of communities have access to many forms of social capital, especially protection in times of particular distress. Communities are effective in the transmission of culture from one generation to the next. Finally, the traditions of long-lasting communities embody an essential body of local knowledge upon which effective management regimes are built.

All five of these generic strengths of community-based organizations (a sense of belonging, social pressure for conformity, access to social capital, transmission of culture, and local knowledge) are directly or indirectly manifested in the dynamic operation of the design principles. Resource appropriators are cognizant of their joint membership in a community with clear boundaries and commonly understood values and strategies. Of particular importance is the low cost and high effectiveness of monitoring and sanctioning within close-knit communities. Members often draw upon broader shared values for norms regulating participation and the resolution of disputes, although it is sometimes possible to restrict attention to only those values directly implicated in managing the particular resources in question.

Yet, as suggested above, it is not sufficient to consider the positive aspects of any one sector in isolation from the others.[6] Community-based organizations also suffer from generic weaknesses or even failures that must be compensated for by the complementary strengths of other sectors. Community pressure can, for example, stifle innovation and freeze into place local tyrannies or other existing inequities and injustices. Access to markets can act to offset this disincentive for innovation. On the other hand, community organizations with a shared interest in sustaining profitable enterprises can implement new practices remarkably quickly, in the right circumstances. Access to a broader legal system of remedies can offset any tendency for marginalization or victimization of those negatively affected by a community's actions. However, as noted in the design principles themselves, the most direct contribution of government to their smooth operation lies in the area of recognizing the rights of communities or user groups to organize for their own common interest. In fact, the nesting of local regimes within broader supportive systems speaks directly to the necessary embedding of community-based organizations within a broader cross-sectoral system of multilevel governance.

Institutional Adjustments Needed in Scaling Up Sustainable Regimes

We are now in the position to examine the consequences of expanding regimes beyond the local scales at which communities operate best. Complications can arise with respect to each of the design principles, and yet specific institutional responses can be devised to deal with each of these complications. It is worth noting that in *The Federalist* and in related documents, the framers of the American constitution engaged in a similar process of institutional extension. They were building upon principles of democratic rule or republican governance that had thus far only worked for relatively small-scale polities (Ostrom, 2007). They endeavored to devise a set of institutional arrangements that might enable a republican form of government to operate successfully at a continental scale (Keohane, 2001, makes a similar argument). We draw inspiration from their successes, as well as from the subsequent realization of limitations inherent in their own design, as we humbly offer our evaluation of the ways in which successful schemes of community-based resources management might be extended to a global scale.

For purposes of clarity, we discuss each of the design principles in detail. First, let us examine "clearly defined boundaries." Boundaries do typically become more

---

[6] Our insistence on the mutually supportive and complementary contributions of organizations from four sectors was inspired by the four categories that Lichbach (1996) used to organize the interdisciplinary literature on alternative resolutions of dilemmas of collective action. However, organizations in our sectors of the public economy do not correspond exactly to Lichbach's categories of exchange, contract, community, and hierarchy. In addition, we are much more explicit about the need for networking among organizations of different types.

diffuse and dynamic at higher scales. Yet, this is precisely why a larger-scale regime is required. Boundaries between relatively isolatable activities or resources are the very foundation of effective organization, at all scales of analysis (Simon, 1981). If the dynamic operation of a resource cannot be partitioned into smaller chunks, then it is necessary to devise a management scheme at a higher, more appropriate scale. The important thing remains that all the essential actors are included within the scope of the management scheme. In other words, the challenge in moving to a larger scale lies not primarily in the increasingly diffuse nature of the boundaries but rather with the need to craft a management scheme that can cope with resources that happen to have diffuse boundaries and effects.

This concern with potentially diffuse boundaries nicely segues into the second design principle, which requires that the rules-in-use must be at least minimally congruent with (1) biophysical dynamics and (2) the perceived values of participants regarding equity and related concerns. Note that this does not require that all participants in a robust regime must share all cultural values in common, for if that were necessary, perhaps no cooperation could ever be achieved. Instead, it is only necessary that participants share a commitment to resolving what they realize to be a common problem. It is this shared problem definition that constructs the boundaries by which the membership of the regime is defined, and their perceptions in turn shape the breadth of the biophysical factors to be evaluated under this regime.

As we noted earlier, the second design principle highlights the critical importance of the local knowledge upon which sustainable resource regimes invariably rest. Rules-in-use must be congruent with the actual operation of the physical and biological processes by which that resource is generated and utilized. Fortunately, the participants' knowledge of these processes need not be complete in any scientific sense, not as long as they can draw upon long records of practical experience. At larger scales, it becomes imperative to move beyond traditional forms of knowledge to explicitly incorporate scientific knowledge that has been generated by a more systematic process of analysis. Too often, scientific expertise remains as an imperfect substitute for local knowledge, especially in its tendency toward broad generalizations rather than allowing for a full accounting of local variation. However, recent developments in multidisciplinary research have strengthened scientists' appreciation for the contextual nature of knowledge (Ebbin, 2002; Wilson, 2002). To the extent that scientific research findings are more precise and contextualized, the more useful they can be in supporting sustainable resource regimes.

As we discussed when we first listed these principles, another aspect of this second principle concerns equity, in the sense that the rules must be arrayed so that the benefit derived by individual appropriators is commensurate with that appropriator's exertion of individual effort or contribution toward the collective goal. This criterion is most easily satisfied when a community's value system helps participants coordinate on a particular standard of evaluation. This turns out to be an especially problematic criterion for global regimes. For at that level, participants have at their disposal a virtually endless array of alternative bases for the distribution of benefits. Should benefits be distributed according to effort or equally to all? If the latter, should all organizational members receive the same benefit, even if they vary widely in the size of their membership? Similarly, should levels of fair contributions be determined on the basis of wealth, or should unique contributions be rewarded? Disputes of this type lie at the heart of endless discourses within organizations composed of polities of diverse sizes, resources, capabilities, and other characteristics. Heikkila and Gerlak (2005) provide an excellent analysis of the challenge of forming large-scale collaborative resource management institutions even within a single country. Their analysis can usefully be extended to international collaborations.

To be sustainable, the members must arrive at some consensus on distributional principles. The details of the distribution scheme matter less than the legitimacy with which it is perceived by the members (Chayes & Chayes, 1995). Furthermore, there must be some mechanism to revise contribution or distribution schemes to take into account new developments or demographic or political changes. As our earlier discussion of the whaling regime suggests, the perceived nature of the collective-action problem may shift over time, and may indeed be contentious at times, but in any robust regime the rules-in-use must effectively adjust to these changing perceptions. In sum, an effective regime must have procedures in place that facilitate revision of its own rules of procedure.

The third principle deals with the participation of relevant actors in the design and management of processes of collective choice with a given regime. Although the relevant actors are now large corporations or other collective entities rather than individual farmers or fishermen, the sheer number of key actors is not necessarily larger in absolute magnitude for larger-scale regimes. The critical factor instead is that the replacement of individual actors by collective ones generates several complications. Participation must be via the agents of these organizations, rather than by individuals acting solely in their own interests. Participation via representatives is at best an imperfect substitute for direct participation, and yet for regimes beyond minimal scale such a compromise is inevitable.

Especially important is the extent to which the interests of these agents have been aligned with the interests of their constituent members. Prospects for effective representation of constituent interests are greatly facilitated when the member organizations reflect meaningful communities of interest. That is, a sense of shared community of values between members and agents helps mitigate (but never entirely overcomes) enduring dilemmas of relations between principals and agents. Thus, not only must the full array of organizations, that include as members the relevant stakeholders, fully participate in the design and implementation of management schemes, these organizations themselves must be so arranged that the agents can honestly represent the interests of their own stakeholders.

This additional aspect of the third design principle proves to be especially problematic at the global level, for the agents of sovereign states are by no means always directly accountable to their constituents. For an international functional regime to be effective, the relevant agents must share some common understanding among themselves, even if this same understanding is not more widely shared among their respective publics. However, now that globalization has facilitated the easy mobilization of dissatisfied publics by transnational advocacy coalitions, purely technical regimes are unlikely to remain isolated from political upheaval. For this reason, global regimes are most likely to remain effective when agents of participating organizations are accountable to those stakeholders principally concerned with a given resource or environmental condition. Some autocratic rulers may serve as good custodians of their country's general interest in a healthy environment or sustainable revenue stream from resource extraction, but such success is highly dependent on the personal views of the person who happens to be in power. In the long term, democratic regimes are much preferred because of their easier reformability.

We now move to the conceptual core of the dynamic foundation for these principles of institutional design, namely, the fourth and fifth principles related to monitoring and sanctioning that must occur on a regular basis in any viable regime. Here is where the movement away from small-scale community organizations has its most dramatic impact. No longer is it possible to rely primarily upon social sanctions to magnify the effects of the initially low levels of sanctioning called for in the design principles. Nor can members rely on naturally close interactions to mutually monitor each other's behavior. Instead, specialized mechanisms must be set up for monitoring and sanctioning (Chayes & Chayes, 1995; Young, 2002). For this purpose, careful study of small-scale resource regimes can prove very useful, since effective regimes often include systems of monitoring and sanctioning so sophisticated that they can serve as exemplars of sound strategic design (see models in McGinnis, 2000).

In monitoring rules set for global regimes, technological solutions including satellite-imaging technology, when feasible, can be effective (Ostrom et al., 1999). For those regimes that deal with potentially sensitive issues, the participation of non-profit, non-governmental organizations may be especially useful. Environmental NGOs, for example, can derive substantial benefits from exposing violations by governments or corporations that might result in major damage to the environment. Even though they are rarely included as official signatories to the treaty underlying a regime, NGOs often make essential contributions to the monitoring of subsequent outcomes.

Sanctioning is also an area in which NGOs can play essential roles, by responsibly besmirching the reputations of governments or corporations that violate previous agreements. These same organizations play critical roles in publicizing the detrimental consequences of activities allowed under the current regime, and in mobilizing support for significant reform.

The corporate nature of the actors in global regimes generates an important complication in the area of sanctioning. The reason why graduated sanctions are so helpful in community-based systems is that even low levels of sanctions can effectively convey a signal to the rule violator about the potentially high costs of continuing to violate that community's norms. Precisely because of the high salience attached to membership in that community can the threat of prohibitive costs easily be made credible. At the same time, by being small they give the perpetrator time to change behavior before potentially irreparable damage causes an escalation in tension.

It is not clear that graduated sanctions work so well when applied to collective actors. Indeed, this necessity of sanctioning leaders as individuals rather than simply as corporate agents was recognized as a critical innovation in the American system of constitutional order. At the international level, there have been remarkable recent developments in the extent to which former leaders are held accountable for human rights abuses committed during their time in office (Rudolph, 2001).

One especially promising, recent innovation concerns targeted sanctions in which individual leaders are prevented from traveling to certain countries because of their actions while in power (Cortright & Lopez, 2002). To this point, such sanctions have been reserved for individual leaders suspected to have committed heinous war crimes or human rights abuses. It is generally more difficult to assign responsibility to the individuals responsible for particularly egregious instances of environmental damage, for example. Even so, the level of public outrage can be intense. Perhaps environmental watchdog organizations could, in conjunction with transnational news media, informally enforce a similar form of sanction on leaders of state agencies or multinational corporations, one that would restrict their ability to continue to participate in that area of work. Of course, this policy tool should not be applied when it cannot be expected to be effective (Tostensen & Bull, 2002), and extension of the principle of graduated sanctions to support global regimes may be the one design principle that needs the most creative implementation. For the most part, those who suffer from violations of the rules embedded in global resource regimes will have to pursue compensation through legal means.

When it comes to the easy access to dispute-resolution mechanisms required in the sixth design principle, the global system is actually closer to satisfying this criterion than most observers realize. In recent decades, there has been a dramatic but underappreciated extension in the network of international forums at which disputes of particular kinds can be discussed and resolved (Koremenos et al., 2004; Orrego Vicuña, 2004). Only one of these forums, the dispute mechanism within the World Trade Organization (WTO), ever generates news that is widely covered in the media (Petersmann, 1997). Other more specialized forums remain relatively unknown (Collier & Lowe, 1999). Even more importantly, corporations from different countries routinely include in their contracts a provision for reference to certain members of an extensive albeit informal network of international commercial arbitration. This system of private international law has been in place for many years and is constantly being supplemented by new forms of quasi-public international law (Mattli, 2001). In sum, there is already a rather elaborate network of global governance in place (Reinicke, 1998).

The final two design principles—recognition of the rights to organize and nesting of enterprises—refer to the overarching context within which any particular regime must operate. Attention is directed to the nesting of procedures within governance systems at a higher scale of aggregation, which in turn must convey a meaningful recognition of the rights of smaller groups to self-organize and establish their own rules. There is, of course, no fully fledged system of governance in place at the global level, but, as just discussed, there are many other mechanisms available for use in particular types of disputes. In the absence of global authority, smaller groups have acted upon their inherent right to self-organize. Indeed, any of the major functional regimes are grounded on exactly this basis. As discussed earlier, in the IWC a club of whaling nations came together to formulate their own system of rules. What has changed in recent years is a decreased legitimacy for any such collective actions taken outside of the context of the United Nations (see Gillespie, 2002). Virtually all international organizations by now have some affiliation of one kind or another with one or more of the many agencies affiliated with the UN system, and those outside the system experience pressure to conform. Even so, nothing prevents smaller bodies of states or other organizations from forming new club-type organizations to cooperate for their own collective benefit. The option of forming new units of self-governance remains an essential part of polycentric governance.

In sum, any extension of the design principles of sustainable CPR management to the global scale highlights the complementary strengths offered by organizations located in the private, public, voluntary, and community sectors. It is not just a matter of nesting local arrangements within a supportive institutional context at the national and international levels. Equally important is nesting political institutions within supportive and complementary institutions from other sectors.

A Continuing Need for Creativity

We have endeavored to provide a balanced analysis of the prospects for the extension of successful principles of resource management from local communities to the world as a whole. We strove to articulate a position between the extremes of presuming that this extension is either automatic or impossible. What we do acknowledge to be impossible is any effort to duplicate, at the global level, exactly the same processes or institutional structures through which community-based management operates. Instead, a creative recombination of institutional components from the private, public, and voluntary sectors is needed to cobble together a mutually reinforcing system of governance appropriate for each particular set of policy problems. Such cross-sectoral networks will prove easier to construct in some issue areas than in others, but in no instance should this prove to be an impossible task. Institutional designers need to take advantage of the opportunities made available to them by the strengths of pre-existing organizations and by the boundless human capacity for institutional innovation.

Our final point is to emphasize that analysts of global regimes need to cast their nets more widely than the formal public sector. Any effort to craft governance regimes that rely entirely upon national governments or intergovernmental treaties is certain to fail. International treaties and the organizations they construct can play important, even pivotal roles in the establishment of new global regimes of cooperative management, and yet private, voluntary, and even community-like organizations each add their own unique contributions to the mix.

Acknowledgments Support from the Ford Foundation, the MacArthur Foundation, and The Kroc Institute for International Peace Studies, University of Notre Dame, is deeply appreciated. We also thank Daniel Eek for useful suggestions and Patty Lezotte for her excellent editing.

References

Acheson, J. (2003). *Capturing the Commons: Devising Institutions to Manage the Maine Lobster Industry.* Hanover, NH: University Press of New England.

Anderies, J. M., Janssen, M., Ostrom, E. (2004). A framework to analyze the robustness of social-ecological systems from an institutional perspective. *Ecology and Society, 9*(1), 18.

Andresen, S. (2002). The International Whaling Commission (IWC): More failure than success? In: E. L. Miles, A. Underhal, S. Andresen, J. Wettestad, J. Birger Skjær Seth & E. M. Carlin (eds.), *Environmental Regime Effectiveness: Confronting Theory with Evidence* (pp. 379–403). Cambridge, MA: MIT Press.

Aristotle (1942). *Politics.* Trans. B. Jowett. New York: Modern Library.

Ashby, W. R. (1960). *Design for a Brain: The Origin of Adaptive Behavior* (2nd ed.). New York: John Wiley.

Bickers, K., Williams, J. T. (2001). *Public Policy Analysis: A Political Economy Approach.* Boston: Houghton Mifflin.

Blomquist, W. (1992). *Dividing the Waters: Governing Groundwater in Southern California.* San Francisco: ICS Press.

Buck, S. J. (1998). *The Global Commons: An Introduction.* Washington, DC: Island Press.

Burns, W. C. B., Gillespie, A. (eds.) (2003). *The Future of Cetaceans in a Changing World.* Ardsley, NY: Transnational Publishers.

Chayes, A., Chayes, A. H. (1995). *The New Sovereignty: Compliance with International Regulatory Agreements.* Cambridge, MA: Harvard University Press.

Chopra, S. K., D'Amato, A. (1991). Whales: Their emerging right to life. *American Journal of International Law, 85*(1), 21–62.

Clark, C. W. (1980). Restricted access to common-property fishery resources: A game-theoretic analysis. In P.-T. Liu (ed.), *Dynamic Optimization and Mathematical Economics* (pp. 117–132). New York: Plenum Press.

Collier, J. G., Lowe, V. (1999). *The Settlement of Disputes in International Law: Institutions and Procedures.* New York: Oxford University Press.

Copes, P. (1986). A critical review of the individual quota as a device in fisheries management. *Land Economics, 62*(3), 278–291.

Cortright, D., Lopez, G. A. (eds.) (2002). *Smart Sanctions: Targeting Economic Statecraft.* Lanham, MD: Rowman & Littlefield.

Cruz, M. C. (1991). Population pressure, deforestation, and common property institutions: An overview. Paper presented at the Second Annual Meeting of the International Association for the Study of Common Property (IASCP), Winnipeg, September 26–29.

Dahlman, C. J. (1980). *The Open Field System and Beyond: A Property Rights Analysis of an Economic Institution.* Cambridge: Cambridge University Press.

De Alessi, L. (1993). How markets alleviate scarcity. In V. Ostrom, D. Feeny & H. Picht (eds.), *Rethinking Institutional Analysis and Development: Issues, Alternatives, and Choices* (pp. 339–376). San Francisco: ICS Press.

Ebbin, S. A. (2002). Enhanced fit through institutional interplay in the Pacific Northwest salmon co-management regime. *Marine Policy, 26*, 253–259.

Feeny, D., Berkes, F., McCay, B. J., Acheson, J. M. (1990). The tragedy of the commons: Twenty-two years later. *Human Ecology, 18*(1), 1–19.

Franzen, A. (1994). Group size effects in social dilemmas: A review of the experimental literature and some new results for one-shot N-PD games. In U. Schulz, W. Albers & U. Mueller (eds.), *Social Dilemmas and Cooperation* (pp. 117–145). Berlin: Springer-Verlag.

Friedheim, R. (ed.) (2001). *Toward a Sustainable Whaling Regime*. Seattle: University of Washington Press; Edmonton: Canadian Circumpolar Institute Press.

Gibson, C., Williams, J., Ostrom, E. (2005). Local enforcement and better forests. *World Development, 33*(2), 273–284.

Gillespie, A. (2002). Forum shopping in international environmental law: The IWC, CITES, and the management of Cetaceans. *Ocean Development & International Law, 33*(1), 17–56.

Goodwin, M. (1994). Nine principles for making virtual communities work. *Wired, 2*(6) (June), 72–73.

Gordon, H. S. (1954). The economic theory of a common property resource: The fishery. *Journal of Political Economy, 62* (April), 124–142.

Haas, P. M. (1989). Do regimes matter? Epistemic communities and Mediterranean pollution control. *International Organization, 43*, 378–403.

Hanisch, M., McGinnis, M. (2005). Analyzing problems of polycentric governance in the growing EU. Paper presented at Workshop on Analyzing Problems of Polycentric Governance in the Growing EU, Humboldt University, Berlin, June 16–17, 2005. http://www.indiana.edu/~workshop/papers/intro_berlin.pdf.

Hardin, G. (1968). The tragedy of the commons. *Science, 162*, 1243–1248.

Hardin, G. (1978). Political requirements for preserving our common heritage. In H. P. Bokaw (ed.), *Wildlife and America* (pp. 310–317). Washington, DC: Council on Environmental Quality.

Hayes, T., Ostrom, E. (2005). Conserving the world's forests: Are protected areas the only way? *Indiana Law Review, 38*(3), 595–619.

Heikkila, T., Gerlak, A. K. (2005). The formation of large-scale collaborative resource management institutions: Clarifying the roles of stakeholders, science, and institutions. *Policy Studies Journal, 33*(4), 583–612.

Hurwicz, L. (1973). The design of mechanisms for resource allocation. *American Economic Review, 63*(2), 1–30.

Jones, E. C. (2003). Building on Ostrom's "the rudiments of a theory of the origins, survival, and performance of common-property institutions." *Journal of Ecological Anthropology, 7*, 65–72.

Keohane, R. O. (1984). *After Hegemony*. Princeton, NJ: Princeton University Press.

Keohane, R. O. (2001). Governance in a partially globalized world. *American Political Science Review, 95*(1), 1–13.

Kirch, P. V. (1997). Microcosmic histories: Island perspectives on "global" change. *American Anthropologist, 99*(1), 30–42.

Kollock, P. (1997). Design principles for online communities. In *The Internet and Society: Harvard Conference Proceedings*. Cambridge, MA: O'Reilly & Associates.

Koremenos, B., Lipson, C., Snidal, D. (eds.) (2004). *The Rational Design of International Institutions*. New York: Cambridge University Press.

Lam, W. F. (1998). *Governing Irrigation Systems in Nepal: Institutions, Infrastructure, and Collective Action*. Oakland, CA: ICS Press.

Lambin, E. F., et al. (2001). The causes of land-use and land-cover change: Moving beyond the myths. *Global Environmental Change, 11*, 261–269.

Lele, U. (ed.) (2002). *Managing a Global Resource: Challenges of Forest Conservation and Development. World Bank Series on Evaluation and Development, vol. 5*. New Brunswick, NJ: Transaction Publishers.

Lichbach, M. I. (1996). *The Cooperator's Dilemma*. Ann Arbor: University of Michigan Press.

Mattli, W. (2001). Private litigation in a global economy: From litigation to arbitration. *International Organization, 55*(4) (October), 919–947.

McGinnis, M. (ed.) (2000). *Polycentric Games and Institutions: Readings from the Workshop in Political Theory and Policy Analysis*. Ann Arbor: University of Michigan Press.

McGinnis, M., Ostrom, E. (1992). Institutional analysis and global climate change: Design principles for robust international regimes. In M. Rice, J. Snow & H. Jacobson (eds.), *Global Climate Change: Social and Economic Research Issues*. Proceedings of a conference held at Argonne National Laboratory, Chicago, IL, pp. 45–85.

Miller, G. J. (1992). *Managerial Dilemmas: The Political Economy of Hierarchy*. New York: Cambridge University Press.

Moe, T. M. (1984). The new economics of organization. *American Journal of Political Science, 28*, 739–777.

Nadelmann, E. A. (1990). Global prohibition regimes: The evolution of norms in international society. *International Organization, 44*, 479–526.

Orrego Vicuña, F. (2004). *International Dispute Settlement in an Evolving Global Society: Constitutionalization, Accessibility, Privatization*. New York: Cambridge University Press.

Ostrom, E. (1990). *Governing the Commons: The Evolution of Institutions for Collective Action*. New York: Cambridge University Press.

Ostrom, E. (2005). *Understanding Institutional Diversity*. Princeton, NJ: Princeton University Press.

Ostrom, E., Burger, J., Field, C., Norgaard, R., Policansky, D. (1999). Revisiting the commons: Local lessons, global challenges. *Science, 283*, 278–282.

Ostrom, E., Gardner, R., Walker, J. M. (1994). *Rules, Games, and Common-Pool Resources*. Ann Arbor: University of Michigan Press.

Ostrom, E., Ostrom, V. (1977). Public goods and public choices. In E. S. Savas (ed.), *Alternatives for Delivering Public Services: Toward Improved Performance* (pp. 7–49). Boulder, CO: Westview Press.

Ostrom, V. (2007). *The Political Theory of a Compound Republic: Designing the American Experiment* (3rd ed.). Lanham, MD: Lexington Books.

Petersmann, E.-U. (1997). *The GATT/WTO Dispute Settlement System: International Law, International Organizations, and Dispute Settlement*. London and Boston: Kluwer Law International.

Polanyi, M. (1951). *The Logic of Liberty: Reflections and Rejoinders*. Chicago: University of Chicago Press.

Reinicke, W. H. (1998). *Global Public Policy: Governing Without Government?* Washington, DC: Brookings Institution Press.

Rudolph, C. (2001). Constructing an atrocities regime: The politics of war crimes tribunals. *International Organization, 55*(3) (September), 655–691.

Samuelson, P. (1954). The pure theory of public expenditure. *Review of Economics and Statistics, 36*, 387–389.

Sandell, R., Stern, C. (1998). Group size and the logic of collective action: A network analysis of a Swedish temperance movement 1896–1937. *Rationality and Society, 10*(3), 327–345.

Schaefer, M. (1957). Some considerations of population dynamics and economics in relation to the management of the commercial marine fisheries. *Journal of the Fisheries Research Board of Canada, 14*, 669–681.

Scott, A. (1979). Development of economic theory of fisheries regulation. *Journal of the Fisheries Board of Canada, 36*, 725–740.

Scott, A. (1982). Regulation and the location of jurisdictional powers: The fishery. *Osgoode Hall Law Journal, 20*, 780–805.

Shepsle, K. A. (1989). Studying institutions: Some lessons from the rational choice approach. *Journal of Theoretical Politics, 1*, 131–149.

Simon, H. A. (1981). *The Sciences of the Artificial* (2nd ed.). Cambridge, MA: MIT Press.

Stoett, P. J. (1997). *The International Politics of Whaling*. Vancouver: University of British Columbia Press.

Tang, S. Y. (1992). *Institutions and Collective Action: Self-Governance in Irrigation*. San Francisco: ICS Press.

Tostensen, A., Bull, B. (2002). Are smart sanctions feasible? *World Politics, 54*(3) (April), 373–403.

Townsend, R. E. (1986). A critique of models of the American lobster fishery. *Journal of Environmental Economics and Management, 13*, 277–291.

Townsend, R. E., Wilson, J. (1987). An economic view of the 'tragedy of the commons'. In B. J. McCay & J. M. Acheson (eds.), *The Question of the Commons: The Culture and Ecology of Communal Resources* (pp. 311–326). Tucson: University of Arizona Press.

Uzawa, H. (2005). *Economic Analysis of Social Common Capital*. Cambridge: Cambridge University Press.

Walker, J. M., Gardner, R., Ostrom, E. (1991). Rent dissipation and balanced deviation disequilibrium in common-pool resources: Experimental evidence. In R. Selten (ed.), *Game Equilibrium Models II: Methods, Morals, and Markets* (pp. 337–367). Berlin: Springer-Verlag.

Weimer, D. L., Vining, A. R. (1989). *Policy Analysis: Concepts and Practice*. Englewood Cliffs, NJ: Prentice Hall.

Weinstein, M. S. (2000). Pieces of the puzzle: Solutions for community-based fisheries management from native Canadians, Japanese cooperatives, and common property researchers. *Georgetown International Environmental Law Review, 12*(2), 375–412.

Wilson, J. A. (2002). Scientific uncertainty, complex systems, and the design of common-pool institutions. In E. Ostrom, T. Dietz, N. Dolšak, P. C. Stern, S. Stonich & E. Weber (eds.), *The Drama of the Commons* (pp. 327–329). Washington, DC: National Academy Press.

Young, O. R. (1989). The politics of international regime formation: Managing natural resources and the environment. *International Organization, 43*, 349–375.

Young, O. R. (1994). *International Governance: Protecting the Environment in a Stateless Society*. Ithaca, NY: Cornell University Press.

Young, O. R. (ed.) (1999). *The Effectiveness of International Environmental Regimes: Causal Connections and Behavioral Mechanisms*. Cambridge, MA: MIT Press.

Young, O. R. (2002). Institutional interplay: The environmental consequences of cross-scale interactions. In E. Ostrom, T. Dietz, N. Dolšak, P. C. Stern, S. Stonich & E. Weber (eds.), *The Drama of the Commons* (pp. 263–292). Washington, DC: National Academy Press.

Zacher, M. W., with Sutton, B. A. (1996). *Governing Global Networks: International Regimes for Transportation and Communications*. New York: Cambridge University Press.

Chapter 13
Effect of Information Structure in a Step-Level Public-Good Dilemma Under a Real-Time Protocol

Chi Sing Ngan and Wing Tung Au

A public good (PG) is a commodity or service made available to all members of a group. It has the property of non-rivalry that multiple people can simultaneously consume the same unit of the good. It also has the property of non-excludability that it is not possible (or very costly) to exclude people who do not pay from consuming the good (Davis & Holt, 1993). Public-good provision typically depends on the voluntary contribution by group members. Once provided, all can enjoy the benefits of the PG, regardless of whether or not they contributed. In the typical case that the marginal return on the PG is not sufficient to induce voluntary contribution, there is a strong temptation to free-ride (not contribute) in the hope that others will contribute sufficiently. A key classification of public-good dilemmas is the relationship between the level of contributions and the level of provision of the public good (Kollock, 1998). Discrete good, also known as step-level good, can only be provided in its entirety; it is not practical to provide in a lesser amount (Komorita & Parks, 1994). An example is a bridge, which will only be built if voluntary contributions are enough to cover the whole cost. On the contrary, continuous goods can be provided at any level, determined by the rate or amount of contribution. There is not a minimum amount of contribution before it can function. This study examines a step-level public-good dilemma.

Protocols of Play

Protocol of play specifies the sequence of moves, as well as the information structure under which the play takes place. Previous experimental research on the public-good dilemma mainly focused on the simultaneous protocol of play, in which all participants are asked to make a decision simultaneously with equal amount of information known. Recently, several studies have implemented a sequential protocol of play in which decisions are made one after the other in a prespecified known order (Chen et al., 1996; Erev & Rapoport, 1990). This protocol enables players to capture different information such as their position in the sequence and the number of preceding players who have contributed. In practice, the position assigned in the sequence is common knowledge. Before making

A. Biel et al. (eds.), *New Issues and Paradigms in Research on Social Dilemmas.*
© Springer 2008

decisions, a player is also given information regarding group size, provision point, and choices made of preceding members, all of which have proven to be crucial factors for a cooperative choice.

Erev and Rapoport (1990) revealed that simultaneous protocol of play, where decisions are made privately and anonymously, is significantly less effective in solving dilemmas than the sequential protocol, where decisions are made sequentially with complete information about previous decisions in the sequence. Their results showed that although a sequential contribution mechanism (M = 45%) did not enhance the percentage of contributors more than a simultaneous contribution mechanism (M = 43%), the provision of public good in a sequential contribution protocol (M = 67%) was significantly higher than in a simultaneous contribution mechanism (M = 14%).

In fact, it was pointed out by Taylor (1987) that a central feature of the n-person chicken game is the existence of an incentive for players to attempt to bind themselves irrevocably to non-cooperation. This is intended to compel some of the remaining players to cooperate and attain the provision without contributing themselves. Such an irrevocable binding to non-cooperation, which "forces" other group members to cooperate, is only possible when the protocol is sequential rather than simultaneous.

Real-Time Protocol

Simultaneous and sequential protocols to a certain extent simulate some real-life social dilemma situations. However, these types of protocols are unrealistic in the sense that people's positions of making decisions are assigned in advance. In real-life settings, people also decide when to declare a decision. Some people may decide earlier than others in order to take up the leading role or create a conformity atmosphere by influencing those who have not yet made up their minds. On the other hand, some may choose to delay their decisions until enough information has been collected to reduce social uncertainty. In fact, it is more ecologically valid when players are not assigned a fixed position and decide for themselves at an appropriate time to make decisions. Researchers have labeled this protocol of play a "real-time protocol" (Dorsey, 1992; Goren et al., 2003, 2004; Kurzban et al., 2001) in which information regarding other players' decisions is instantaneously updated. Goren, Kurzban, and colleagues have studied the real-time protocol on public-good dilemmas. They identified a robust effect across different studies that cooperation can be enhanced by asking people to make irrecoverable commitments, i.e., people can increase, but not decrease, their contribution to the public good over time. Goren et al. (2004) have also found that the real-time protocol induced more cooperation than a simultaneous protocol of play.

A variant of the real-time protocol of play is a "periodical update" version where other players' information is updated periodically. An experimental study on this protocol was conducted on a common resource pool dilemma (Au & Ngai, 2003). There were several rounds within each game, and participants could choose when to make their harvest (once) in any of the rounds. In contrast with a sequential protocol of play, they found that resource provision was less efficient under the periodical-update variant of the real-time protocol. Participants' "rush" to make their harvest in the first round depleted the pool of resources rapidly, whereas in the sequential protocol only one person could make a harvest in each round.

Information Structure

An important factor that affects contribution behavior is the structure of information given. In Erev and Rapoport (1990), individuals in a five-person group were informed only of the number of preceding cooperators or defectors, without knowing their sequential positions to make decisions. They found that information about preceding defectors was significantly more effective than information about preceding cooperators in the likelihood of providing a public good. In fact, the sequential protocol remains equally effective when all information is disclosed or restricted to the number of previous non-cooperative choices.

Among the groups having information on previous cooperation decisions, only 40% of the choices were cooperative, which did not differ from the simultaneous protocol situation. An interesting phenomenon is that whereas the first cooperative choice increased the likelihood of a second cooperative decision to 67%, the second cooperative choice decreased the likelihood of the third (which is the critical) cooperative decision to 21%. A possible alternative explanation is that people cooperate, at least in part, in order to influence others to do the same. However, if this goal is not achieved, few people continue to cooperate.

It is expected that a similar pattern will be obtained in our study under the real-time protocol. Knowing previous non-cooperative choices (DefectInfo) will be equally effective with the condition in which information about all previous decisions is disclosed (FullInfo) in terms of contribution rate and public-good provision. This will in turn be more effective than knowing previous cooperative choices (CoopInfo), whereas no information about others' decisions (NoInfo) will be the least effective.

Criticality

An important factor that affects cooperation rates is a member's criticality. Rapoport (1988) proposed that a person is in a critical situation *if and only* if his or her contribution is required to provide the PG. Such a condition can also be described as a necessary (only if) and sufficient (if) condition. For example, consider a five-person, step-level public-good game where three people's contributions are required to provide a public good. A person's contribution is both necessary and sufficient if, among the four other people in the group, two have decided to contribute whereas two have decided not to contribute. Underlying this definition is the assumption that criticality is an "all or none" phenomenon, i.e., the contribution is either critical or non-critical to the provision of a PG. However, a person may perceive varying degrees of criticality in the provision of the PG. Perceived criticality is the extent to which a person believes that his or her contribution affects the provision of the PG. Perceived criticality has been shown to be effective in inducing cooperation through enhancing a sense of social responsibility (De Cremer & Van Dijk, 2002). Experimental studies demonstrating the effect of criticality are abundant, but sometimes they were being conducted under the name of "efficacy" (Au, 2004; Au et al., 1998; Chen et al., 1996; De Cremer & van Dijk, 2002; Kerr, 1989, 1992; Rapoport, 1988). In short, (perceived) criticality enhances cooperation.

The Logic of Critical Mass

The theory of "critical mass" was proposed by Oliver, Marwell, and their associates (Oliver et al., 1985; Oliver & Marwell, 1988). It addresses a fundamental problem of collective action based on solving the two jaws of "social trap" (Platt, 1973). The first problem is a free-rider problem, where an individual member of the group can benefit even if she does not contribute. The second one is an efficacy problem, in which a person may not benefit even if the person does contribute. However, the Oliver–Marwell experiments showed that collective action can successfully be mobilized through direct appeals to a common interest. Although public goods are not non-excludable, there is also "jointness of supply" that the benefits of a public good do not decrease with the size of the group that consumes them. An important implication is that when free riders are not a burden on those who contribute, a small subset or "critical mass" of "highly resourceful and interested members" can patronize a much larger group without worrying that the benefits to other people will diminish their own (Oliver & Marwell, 1988). The concentration of interests and resources solves the efficacy problem by "small, isolated contributions," which "explains why most action comes from a relatively small number of participants who make such big contributions to the cause that they know they can make a difference" (Oliver & Marwell, 1988, p. 7). In sum, the theory of critical mass demonstrates that investments in public goods could be highly cost-effective no matter how many non-contributors there are.

According to Macy (1990), social learning theory can explain how adaptive actors might learn to avoid self-defeating competition despite the risk that socially responsible behavior may be exploited by others. The model assumes that symbiotic behavior emerges in response to the signals generated through social interaction. If the leverage obtained by symbiotic behavior and the interest in the outcomes are sufficiently strong, critical mass will be achieved regardless of the size of the group and dispersion of resources. Therefore, the key to escape from social traps is the capacity to respond decisively to social sanctions and cues. This study examines how public-good provision may be facilitated by a real-time protocol with a possible emergence of a critical mass under different information structure conditions.

Method

Participants

One hundred and sixty-eight undergraduate students at the Chinese University of Hong Kong participated in the experiment, which lasted for one and a half hours. They were recruited by open advertisements on campus. Each participant who completed the experiment received HK$75 (~US$10) for their participation, with a chance to win an extra bonus of up to $240 (~US$30) depending on their performance.

Design

The task was a seven-person, step-level public-good dilemma. There were four protocols of play: (a) a full-information (FullInfo) protocol, in which participants were updated with the number of people choosing the Joint and Personal accounts; (b) a no-information (NoInfo) protocol, in which participants did not know others' decisions; (c) a cooperation-information (CoopInfo) protocol, in which participants were updated with the number of people who chose the Joint account (but they did not know the number of people who chose the Personal account), and (d) a defection-information condition (DefectInfo), in which participants were updated with the number of people who chose the Personal account (but they did not know the number of people who chose the Joint account). Participants in each session played two of the four protocols; the order of these two protocols was counterbalanced to eliminate an order effect.

Procedure

In each experimental session, 14 participants arrived at the computer laboratory individually and were assigned to sit in front of a networked personal computer. Participants first signed an informed consent to participate in an individual and group decision-making experiment. They would receive a basic experiment fee of HK$75 with a chance to earn an extra bonus up to HK$240 depending on their performance. With printed instructions on hand, participants were instructed that

(1) each person would be part of a seven-person group to play an investment game for multiple trials, (2) group membership changed randomly on each trial, (3) the two groups of seven persons were independent of each other, and the two groups or any two persons were not cooperating nor competing with each other, (4) at the beginning of each trial, each participant would be given an endowment of HK$20 (~US$2.56), (5) they could invest (contribute) all of their endowment into either of the two accounts: a Personal account or a Joint account, (6) if four or more participants invested in the Joint account, each of the seven persons would receive a bonus of HK$100 (~US$12.82), regardless of whether or not a person had contributed to the Joint account, (7) if fewer than four persons invested in the Joint account, there would be no bonus, and those who chose the Joint account would receive nothing, (8) a person who invested in the Personal account would get his HK$20 back, in addition to any bonus given out by the Joint account, (9) they would have 45 seconds to make their decisions on the computer on each trial, (10) they were not allowed to change their choices once they had submitted their decisions, (11) the investment decision would be made privately and anonymously, (12) at the end of each trial, participants would know how many people had chosen the Joint and Personal account, respectively, and their payoffs on that trial, (13) at the end of the experiment, 2 of 14 participants would be selected randomly to receive monetary payoffs based on their results on two randomly selected trials.

After the instructions, participants completed a short quiz on the computer about the rules and procedures of the investment game. Correct answers with explanations were presented after they had answered each question to ensure that participants fully understood the task. Participants also played two practice trials before the actual game started. On each trial, there was a timer counting down from 45 seconds on the computer screen to indicate the remaining time to make a decision. Participants indicated their decisions by clicking one of two radio buttons for the Joint or Personal account, followed by clicking a "submit" button. They could submit their choices any time during the 45-second interval. If they did not submit their choices within 45 seconds, the choice as indicated by the "clicked" radio button would be taken as their final decision. Depending on the experimental condition, the computer screen would update instantaneously the number of participants in their own seven-person group who chose (1) the Joint account (CoopInfo condition), (2) the Personal account (DefectInfo condition), and (3) both the Joint account and the Personal account (FullInfo condition). No information was displayed in the NoInfo condition. The investment decision and the time of submitting the decision were recorded. At the end of each trial, participants were presented feedback about the total number of people invested in the Joint and Personal accounts, whether the extra bonus was given, and their payoff on that trial.

Participants played the investment game under two experimental conditions for 20 games each. After finishing both sets of investment games, participants answered two open-ended questions on the reasons behind their choices and the timing of their decisions. At the end of the experiment, the experimenter randomly selected two persons to receive the bonus and paid each participant individually. Participants were then debriefed, thanked, and dismissed.

Results

Contribution Rate

The overall contribution rate across the four experimental conditions was 35%. Contribution rates in the FullInfo, CoopInfo, DefectInfo, and NoInfo conditions were 40%, 44%, 23%, and 34%, respectively, as shown in Table 13.1. A one-way ANOVA found that contribution rates differed significantly among the four experimental conditions, $F(3, 11) = 4.03$, $p < 0.05$. A post-hoc Tukey HSD test showed that contribution rates between the FullInfo (M = 40%) and CoopInfo (M = 44%) conditions were not significantly different. The contribution rate in the DefectInfo condition (M = 23%) was significantly smaller than that in the NoInfo condition (M = 34%), which was also significantly smaller than those in the FullInfo and CoopInfo conditions. In summary, people contributed more in the FullInfo and CoopInfo conditions, and they contributed less in the NoInfo condition and much less in the DefectInfo condition.

Public-Good Provision

The overall public-good provision rate across the four experimental conditions was 33%. Provision rates in the FullInfo, CoopInfo, DefectInfo, and NoInfo conditions were 46%, 52%, 9%, and 23%, respectively, as shown in Table 13.1. A one-way ANOVA found that public-good provision rates differed significantly among the four experimental conditions, $F(3, 11) = 10.79$, $p < 0.05$). A post-hoc Tukey HSD test showed that contribution rates between the FullInfo (M = 46%) and CoopInfo (M = 52%) conditions were not significantly different.

Table 13.1 Mean Individual Contribution Rates and Mean Public-Good Provision Rates (Standard Deviation in Parentheses) Across Experimental Conditions

Information Condition	Mean Individual Contribution Rate	Mean Public-Good Provision Rate
Full	0.40 (0.22)	0.46 (0.50)
No	0.34 (0.29)	0.23 (0.42)
Cooperation	0.44 (0.24)	0.52 (0.50)
Defection	0.23 (0.22)	0.09 (0.29)

The public-good provision rate in the DefectInfo condition (M = 9%) was significantly smaller than that in the NoInfo condition (M = 23%), which was also significantly smaller than those in the FullInfo and CoopInfo conditions. In summary, the public good was provided more often in the FullInfo and CoopInfo conditions, less often in the NoInfo condition, and much less often in the DefectInfo condition

Timing of the Decisions

In order to examine the pattern of decision submission across time, each trial of 45 seconds was divided into 15 time blocks; each represents a period of 3 seconds. It was found that participants tended to submit their investment decisions at the beginning of the trials when information about previous choices was not available (NoInfo condition). This is illustrated in Table 13.2 and Figure 13.1, where 47.6% of the decisions were made within time block 1 (from 0 to 3 seconds after a trial started) in the NoInfo condition. In the FullInfo, CoopInfo, and DefectInfo conditions, where information of part or all previously made choices was revealed and updated, the decision submission pattern was reversed. As shown in Table 13.2 and Figure 13.1, around 12–15% of the decisions were made in time block 1, and the number of decisions dropped in subsequent time blocks until time block 15. Decisions recorded in time block 15 accounted for about one-third of the overall number of decisions. While 30.1% choices were made in the last time block in the FullInfo condition,

Table 13.2 The Number of Decisions Made (with Percentage) across Experimental Conditions

Time Block	Number of Decisions Made			
	No Information	Full Information	Cooperation Information	Defection Information
1	812 (48.3%)	215 (13.5%)	196 (11.7%)	239 (15.2%)
2	309 (18.4%)	100 (6.3%)	87 (5.2%)	98 (6.2%)
3	127 (7.6%)	74 (4.6%)	52 (3.1%)	61 (3.9%)
4	75 (4.5%)	44 (2.8%)	45 (2.7%)	55 (3.5%)
5	43 (2.6%)	58 (3.6%)	49 (2.9%)	47 (3.0%)
6	41 (2.4%)	60 (3.8%)	51 (3.0%)	41 (2.6%)
7	28 (1.7%)	59 (3.7%)	61 (3.6%)	31 (2.0%)
8	21 (1.2%)	62 (3.9%)	41 (2.4%)	28 (1.8%)
9	22 (1.3%)	68 (4.3%)	54 (3.2%)	33 (2.1%)
10	24 (1.4%)	54 (3.4%)	57 (3.4%)	32 (2.0%)
11	17 (1.0%)	75 (4.7%)	42 (2.5%)	38 (2.4%)
12	26 (1.5%)	70 (4.4%)	66 (3.9%)	38 (2.4%)
13	14 (0.8%)	70 (4.4%)	85 (5.1%)	43 (2.7%)
14	20 (1.2%)	106 (6.6%)	132 (7.9%)	88 (5.6%)
15	101 (6.0%)	481 (30.1%)	662 (39.4%)	696 (44.4%)

A time block represents a period of 3 seconds in each trial.

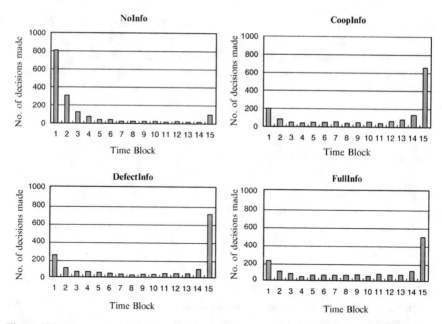

Figure 13.1 The number of decisions made against time across experimental conditions. *Note.* A time-block represents a period of 3 seconds in each trial. NoInfo = No Information Condition, FullInfo = Full-Information Condition, CoopInfo = Cooperation Information Condition, & DefectInfo = Defection Information Condition

there were even more decisions made in the last time block in the CoopInfo and DefectInfo conditions (39.4% and 44.4%, respectively). More participants waited until the last seconds to decide when information was partially available.

Discussion

Four information structures under the real-time protocol of play were examined in the present study. In a cooperation-information structure, group members are being informed of others' contribution decisions. This is perhaps the most typical method for people to express their contribution decisions. An instantiation of this procedure is a sign-up sheet that is posted in a common area where people who are interested to volunteer in a charitable event can write their names. Everyone can see who has decided to volunteer. However, not until the end of the sign-up period we will know for sure that not-yet-signing-up is an indication of whether people are still making up their minds or have decided not to volunteer. This "sign-up" procedure can easily be modified to implement a defection-information structure by having people put down their names to indicate *not* volunteering. The default option is thus "volunteering" unless indicated otherwise. A full-information structure can also similarly be implemented. Instead of marking one's names on the response sheet, people have to indicate with a "yes" or "no" decision next to their names on the sign-up sheet. During the sign-up period, everyone will then know the decisions of all people who have already decided. Yet another type of sign-up procedure can be making a direct contact with the charitable event's organizer to indicate one's voluntary decision—no one knows each other's decisions. This is an instantiation of the no-information structure. We contrasted these four information structures in this study and found that some procedures were more effective in inducing cooperation than others.

The present results replicated previous findings that providing people with full information regarding other's cooperation and non-cooperation decisions (the FullInfo condition) is significantly more effective in solving a public-good dilemma game than withholding all this information (the NoInfo condition). Nevertheless, findings on the CoopInfo and DefectInfo conditions contradicted results reported by Erev and Rapoport (1990). Erev and Rapoport used a sequential protocol in which participants made decisions one by one. They found that the DefectInfo condition, which revealed only the number of people choosing defection, was the most effective in providing the public good, whereas the CoopInfo information, in which only the number of people choosing cooperation was known, was the least effective. However, our present experiment using the real-time protocol found the opposite pattern—the CoopInfo condition was the most effective (and as equally effective as the FullInfo condition), whereas the DefectInfo condition was the least effective.

Effectiveness of the Real-Time Protocol

A distinctive feature of the real-time protocol is that a person has to decide *when* to make a decision. Some participants prefer making a decision early. Perhaps they are certain of their choices, or perhaps they want to take up a leading role to influence the decisions of the others. Responses from the post-experimental questionnaires reflected that some people did have a stronger tendency to take up the leading role while others were more willing to act as followers. Some players who submitted their cooperation decisions early during the trial period reported that, "I was just guiding other group members to simulate the choices I have made," or "I believe other players would not contribute unless they saw some other members have made cooperation decisions." Some other players, however, claimed that they intended to be the second or third among the seven-person group to contribute or they would contribute once the first cooperator appeared. According to the Learning Theory, people model behaviors of others within their social network. Note that in the CoopInfo and FullInfo conditions, the number of cooperation choices was available. The increasing number of people choosing cooperation might have created (a false impression of) a cooperative norm that people in the group were indeed cooperative. In the DefectInfo condition, however, only the number of people choosing defections was visible. Knowing the number of people defecting should reveal to others that their contributions are critical and force them to contribute in order to provide the public good. However, our participants did not seem to behave rationally and did not expect others to behave rationally as well. People seemed to have been adversely affected by the defecting norm, and they followed with defection. Seeing that other people were defecting, the remaining people may also have chosen defection to purposely deny the public-good provision. This phenomenon can be seen from the following results: On the one hand, the contribution rate within time blocks 1 to 3 in the CoopInfo condition was 65%, which was higher than the mean contribution rate across the 15 time blocks (M = 44%). It shows that there were people creating a cooperation norm. On the other hand, the contribution rate within time blocks 1 to 3 in the DefectInfo condition was 18%, which was lower than the mean contribution rate across the 15 time blocks (M = 23%). This shows that a defecting norm was "set up" at the beginning of the game.

The protocol of play here seems to affect how people interpret early defective decisions. In a standard sequential protocol of play, as in Erev and Rapoport's (1990) experiment, it is considered rational to defect, according to backward induction, if you were assigned early positions in the sequence. The motivation of defection is attributed externally. However, in a real-time protocol, players make a conscious decision to be the first one to defect. This gives others a more personal attribution to the temptation to free-ride. Others are more likely to regard them as greedy rather than rational to defect. Sometimes, due to a fundamental attribution bias, the bad impression given to early defective movers is exaggerated. Using the concept of tolerance of free riding by Chen and Bachrach (2001), which is defined as "the extent to which group members are willing to continue cooperation after observing other members' defection behavior," we suggest that the real-time protocol decreases members' level of tolerance compared with a traditional sequential protocol with assigned positions. Participants' open-ended responses also supported this idea. For example, one player expressed that he lost confidence in other group members when they followed early defective behaviors instead of being compelled to cooperate in the DefectInfo condition. Another player also felt that group members were selfish, they distrusted one another, and they did not understand the logic of how to obtain the collective interest. Due to these negative perceptions of early defectors, the DefectInfo condition became the least effective information structure in a step-level public-good dilemma under the real-time protocol.

Criticality

In Erev and Rapoport's (1990) study, criticality played a major role in decision making. They found that in a necessary and sufficient criticality situation, the contribution rate reached 93%. The contribution rate of a necessary criticality situation was 91%, while the contribution rate of a sufficient criticality situation was 21%. In the present study, when the numbers of cooperators and defectors both reached three in the FullInfo condition, a necessary and sufficient criticality situation occurred.

The contribution rate in the situation was found to be 79%. In the DefectInfo condition, when the number of defectors reached three, the contribution of the remaining members became necessarily critical because one more defection would deny public-good provision—the contribution rate reduced to only 21% in this case. In the CoopInfo condition, when the number of cooperators reached three, the situation became sufficiently critical—the contribution rate was 43%. This again contradicts Erev and Rapoport's results—we found that sufficient criticality induced more contribution than necessary criticality.

It is a clear reflection of greed to choose to defect in a sufficiently critical situation, which is the case when the number of cooperation decisions was equal to three in the CoopInfo condition. The pattern of decisions made under this situation was indicated

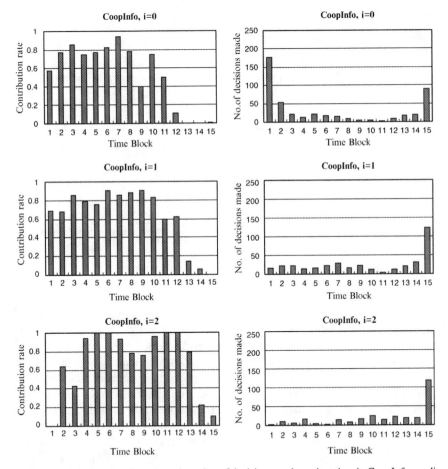

Figure 13.2 The contribution rate and number of decisions made against time in CoopInfo condition with different number of previous cooperation choices
Note. The left panel shows the contribution rate and the right panel shows the number of decisions made against time. The notation *i* represents the number of previous cooperation choices when decisions were made.

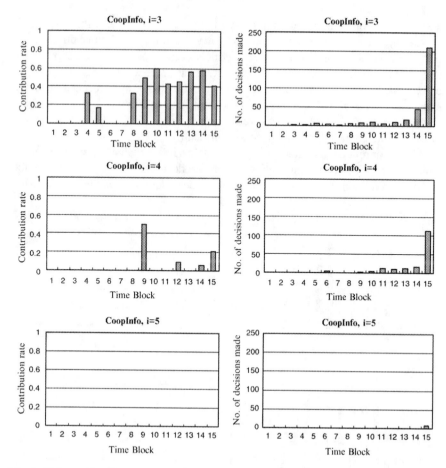

Figure 13.2 (continued)

in the fourth row of Figure 13.2. The left panel shows the *contribution rate* against time, and the right panel shows the *number of decisions* made against time. The different rows (using the notation *i*) in Figure 13.2 represent the number of previous cooperation decisions at the time when the decisions were made. The relatively low contribution rate (M = 43%) in this instance suggested that sufficient criticality is not particularly effective in promoting contribution. Contrast that with the fourth row in Figure 13.3, which shows the decision pattern in a necessary criticality situation. In this situation, if a person chooses not to contribute, the public good will never be provided; however, it does not guarantee a public good even though a person has indeed contributed. The low contribution rate (M = 21%) in this case is a result of fear and mistrust. People might become jealous when they see people who defect in the early part of the game are finally able to obtain the public good at the end. A rational individual should have waited until the last moment in this situation to check whether there were more defection choices before responding to this critical moment. However, 38% of the decisions in the necessary critical situation were made before the last moment of the trial (i.e., between 1–44 seconds) when the number of defectors was equal to 3, among whom only 9% of the decisions were cooperation. This demonstrates a high mistrust between group members when the defection rate was high at the beginning. People tended to believe in equality rules and punish defectors by following the defection norm. Those defectors may fear punishment from other members and thus keep on fulfilling individual interests in the remaining trials.

Irrational Decision-Making Behaviors

It is interesting to note that, in the FullInfo and CoopInfo conditions in which the numbers of cooperation decisions were known, some participants still contributed

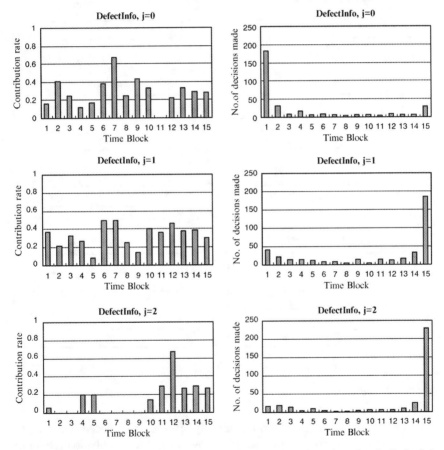

Figure 13.3 The contribution rate and number of decisions made against time in DefectInfo condition with different number of previous non-cooperation choices.
Note. The left panel shows the contribution rate and the right panel shows the number of decisions made against time. The notation *j* represents the number of previous non-cooperation choices when decisions were made

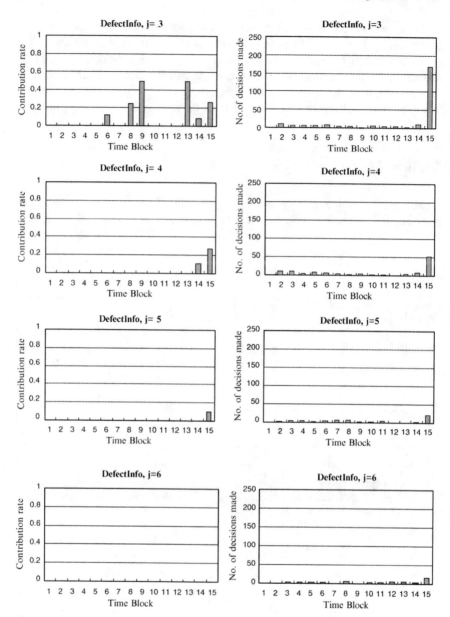

Figure 13.3 (continued)

when the number of contributions had already reached or exceeded four (i.e., the public good is obtained for sure). Results showed that the contribution rate in the CoopInfo condition when the number of previous cooperators was equal to 4 was 15% ($N = 177$). Among these 27 appearances of irrational behaviors, 20 were made during the last second of the game. A possible explanation is that the players had insufficient time to change their choices, as the time between when they realized such a situation existed and the end of game was too short, say, only a few seconds. This may also reflect that those players considered an equal distribution of resources more important than satisfying personal interests.

The Management of Time in the Real-Time Protocol

The management of time in decision making is a special feature in the real-time protocol. Figure 1 already shows that choices of submission pattern with time roughly formed a U-shaped curve—high in the beginning and at the end while low in the middle of the trials. In the NoInfo condition where decisions made by other group members were not known, nearly half of the total decisions were made within the first time block of the game. It indicates that participants required very little time before they made up their minds when there was no information as reference. In conditions with full or partial information, participants tended to use time to "buy" extra information in order to make a more informed decision, and they made their decisions until the later part of the game, as illustrated in Table 2 and Figure 1. Responses from the post-experimental questionnaire supported this observation. For instance, "I would wait until the end of trial before submitting a decision to ensure to obtain the greatest payoff," or "I would rather keep my decision undisclosed to prevent it from influencing other players." In general, it seems more secure to take others' behaviors as references before making one's own decision.

Acknowledgment This research was supported in part by the Direct Grant for Research (Project code 2020506) at the Chinese University of Hong Kong.

References

Au, W. T. (2004). Criticality and environmental uncertainty in step-level public goods dilemmas. *Group Dynamics, 8,* 40–61.

Au, W. T., Chen, X. P., Komorita, S. S. (1998). A probabilistic model of criticality in a sequential public good dilemma. *Organizational Behavior and Human Decision Process, 75,* 274–293.

Au, W. T., Ngai, M. Y. (2003). Effects of group size uncertainty and protocol of play in a common pool resource dilemma. *Group Processes and Intergroup Relations, 6,* 265–283.

Barry, B., Hardin, R. (1982). *Rational Man and Irrational Society?* Beverly Hills, CA: Sage.

Budescu, D. V., Au, W. T., Chen, X. P. (1997). Effect of protocol of play and social orientation on behavior in sequential resource dilemmas. *Organizational Behavior and Human Decision Processes, 65*(3), 179–193.

Budescu, D. V., Suleiman, R., Rapoport, A. (1995). Positional order and group size effects in resource dilemma with uncertain resources. *Organizational Behavior and Human Decision Processes, 61,* 225–238.

Chen, X. P., Au, W. T., Komorita, S. S. (1996). Sequential choice in a step-level public goods dilemma: The effects of criticality and uncertainty. *Organizational Behavior and Human Decision Processes, 69,* 179–193.

Chen, X. P., Bachrach, D. G. (2001). Tolerance of free-riding: The effects of defection size, defection pattern and social orientation in a repeated public goods dilemma. Manuscript submitted for publication.

Cornes, R., Sandler, T. (1996). *The Theory of Externalities, Public Goods, and Club Goods.* Cambridge: Cambridge University Press.

Davis, D. D., Holt, C. A. (1993): Experimental Economics, NJ: Princeton University Press.

Dawes, R. M. (1975). Formal models of dilemmas in social decision-making. In M. F. Kaplan & S. Schwartz (eds.), *Human Judgment and Decision Processes.* New York: Academic Press.

De Cremer, D., Van Dijk, E. (2002). Perceived criticality and contributions in public good dilemmas: A matter of feeling responsible to all? *Group Processes and Intergroup Relations, 5,* 319–332.

Deutsch, M. (1958). The effect of motivational orientation upon trust and suspicion. *Human Relations, 13,* 123–139.

Dorsey, R. E. (1992). The voluntary contributions mechanism with real time revisions. *Public Choice, 73,* 261–282.

Erev, I., Rapoport, A. (1990). Provision of step-level public goods: The sequential contribution mechanism. *Journal of Conflict Resolution, 34,* 401–425.

Goren, H., Kurzban, R., Rapoport, A. (2003). Social loafing vs. social enhancement: Public good provisioning in real time with irrevocable commitments. *Organizational Behavior and Human Decision Processes, 90,* 277–290.

Goren, H., Rapoport, A., Kurzban, R. (2004). Revocable commitments to public goods provision under the real-time protocol of play. *Journal of Behavioral Decision Making, 17,* 17–37.

Hardin, G. (1968). The tragedy of the commons. *Science, 162,* 1243–1248.

Kerr, N. L. (1989). Illusions of efficacy: The effects of group size on perceived efficacy in social dilemmas. *Journal of Experimental Social Psychology, 25,* 287–313.

Kerr, N. L. (1992). Efficacy as a causal and moderating variable in social dilemmas. In W. Liebrand, D. Messick & H. Wilke, (eds.), *A Social Psychological Approach to Social Dilemmas.* New York: Pergamon Press.

Kollock, P. (1998). Social dilemmas: The anatomy of cooperation. *Annual Review of Sociology, 24,* 183–214.

Komorita, S. S., Parks, C. D. (1994). *Social Dilemmas.* Madison, WI: Brown & Benchmark.

Kurzban, R., McCabe, K., Smith, V. L., Wilson, B. J. (2001). Incremental commitment and reciprocity in a real-time public goods game. *Personality and Social Psychology Bulletin, 27,* 1662–1673.

Liebrand, W. B. G. (1984). The effect of social motives, communication, and group size on behavior in an N-person multi-stage mixed-motive game. *European Journal of Social Psychology, 14,* 239–264.

Liebrand, W. B. G., McClintock, C. G. (1988). The ring measure of social values: A computerized procedure for assessing individual differences in information processing and social value orientation. *European Journal of Personality, 2,* 217–230.

Macy, M. W. (1990). Learning theory and the logic of critical mass. *American Sociological Review, 55,* 809–826.

Marwell, G., Ames, R. (1981). Economists free ride, does anyone else? Experiments on the provision of public goods, IV. *Journal of Public Economics, 15,* 295–310.

McClintock, C. G. (1972). Social motivation—A set of propositions. *Behavioral Science, 17,* 438–454.

McClintock, C. G. (1988). Evolution, systems of interdependence, and social values. *Behavioral Science, 33,* 59–76.

Oliver, P. E., Marwell, G. (1988). The paradox of group size in collective action: A theory of the critical mass, III. *American Sociological Review, 53,* 1–8.

Oliver, P. E., Marwell, G., Teixeira, R. (1985). A theory of the critical mass, I.: Interdependence, group heterogeneity, and the production of collective goods. *American Journal of Sociology, 91,* 522–556.

Olson, M. (1965). *The Logic of Collective Action*. Cambridge, MA: Harvard University Press.

Parks, C. D. (1994). The predictive ability of social values in resources dilemmas and public goods games. *Personality and Social Psychology Bulletin, 20,* 431–438.

Platt, J. (1973). Social traps. *American Psychologist, 28,* 641–651.

Rapoport, A. (1988). Provision of step-level public goods: Effects of inequality in resources. *Journal of Personality and Social Psychology, 45,* 432–440.

Roch, S. G., Samuelson, C. D. (1997). Effects of environmental uncertainty and social value orientation in resource dilemmas. *Organizational Behavior and Human Decision Processes, 70,* 221–235.

Schelling, T. C. (1973). Hockey helmets, concealed weapons, and daylight saving: Binary choices with externalities. *Journal of Conflict Resolution, 17,* 381–428.

Taylor, M. (1987). *The Possibility of Cooperation*. Cambridge: Cambridge University Press.

Chapter 14
Toward an Analysis of Cooperation and Fairness That Includes Concepts of Cooperative Game Theory

Axel Ostmann and Holger Meinhardt

Cooperation and Fairness

In a situation that can be classified as a social dilemma, people involved ought to consider how to overcome the problem of hurting common interests when acting upon individualistic standards; one has to question how to realize gains through cooperation. Human history provides a multitude of examples demonstrating institutional solutions for social dilemmas. Some of these examples have both attained success and survived for a long time (cf. Ostrom, 1990).

With respect to the (material) incentive structure, we can distinguish between two different kinds of institutions: first, institutions that change incentives (e.g., introduction of control and sanctions, introduction of binding contracts, etc.); and second, institutions that do not change incentives. Communication belongs to the second. In this chapter, we deal with such a situation. People may talk to each other before deciding on their (individual and hidden) actions.

Some economists label such communication "cheap talk." Even if a negotiation takes place and an agreement is reached, people are not bound to fulfill the agreement by acting accordingly. Drawing on the theory of pure individual rationality, actions are assumed to be determined only by individual incentives and not by the previous discussion of the possible prospects by reaching an agreement. In contrast, there is multiple evidence from field and laboratory studies that agreements are successfully established even in the absence of institutions guaranteeing the fulfillment of these agreements (Dawes et al., 1977; Ostrom, 1998; Sally, 1995).

Since we deal with non-binding agreements (called "agreements" from here on), the results may not conform to the agreements when people have carried out their decisions. This might be caused by the fact that people have deviated from the once-agreed-upon outcome in pursuing their own interests. Thus, the question of compliance becomes crucial: Under which conditions can we expect compliance, and in which conditions will the agreement be implemented? The extent of compliance may depend on both the incentive structure and the course of negotiation.

A popular hypothesis states that people reduce compliance if they feel they are treated unfairly. If this holds true, it becomes an important issue to examine the

A. Biel et al. (eds.), *New Issues and Paradigms in Research on Social Dilemmas.*
© Springer 2008

explanatory power of fairness in such conditions. In these settings that do not allow for communication, most scholars use the notion of "fairness" in a rather narrow sense. They use models incorporating fairness into the (personal) utility function, that is, outcomes are evaluated in a "fair way" by reflecting not only the own utility but also the others' utilities up to some degree. One may call this a social value orientation.[1] By the assumption that humans act as if they maximize a utility function after determining the personal utility function, it would be possible to predict how the people will decide. In the following, we do not base the notion of fairness on utility functions. Moreover, we interpret fairness as a (public) standard and not as the private property of an individual.

In its everyday use, the word "fairness" is somewhat misty in its content. Without a doubt, acting fairly is seen as opposed to such social actions that devalue, debase, or exploit the opponent. In our view, fairness establishes a standard, a norm, and rules guaranteeing the comprehensive and non-discriminatory respect and recognition of the other as partner, with autonomous rights and needs. An impressive example of the success of this, for its time innovative idea in non-discriminatory terms, is the humanism-inspired conduct of the Dutch in Far East trade. In about 1650, the General Instructions of the East Indian Company recommended: "to look to the wishes of the ... (other) nation and to please it in everything ... only modest, humble, polite, and friendly individuals should be sent out there" (quoted in Krug, 1998, p. 21). Such attitudes, indeed, paid off. For example, the Dutch were the only ones allowed to remain in Japan during the isolationist period of the Tokugawa-shogunate (1640–1854) (cf. Krug, 1998).

Fairness refers to non-discriminatory and upright standards that even apply in situations with unequal partners. Imagine a situation in which there are a rich and powerful individual and a poor one. Equality rules would hurt the rich, and the extensive use of power would hurt the poor—it hurts their feelings, harms their individual rights, and does them material damage. Fairness rules establish respectful behavior and a solution that can be freely accepted from both sides— say a fair compromise.

Fairness standards include that the compromise should be reached by fair means and that fraud is excluded. If partners agree on fair play, they may agree to disagree, but they will not accept a proposal they intend to obstruct. Beyond fair play, not only a selfish motive but also the feeling of being treated unfairly may cause obstruction.

In social dilemmas, there is a strong motive for trying to reach a fair compromise. Put formally, since in our context the non-cooperative solutions lack efficiency, subjects usually correct their fate by arranging to reach or at least to approach some welfare optimum. When talking with each other, welfare optima can

---

[1] The concept of "social value orientation" is discussed and examined in many studies. Starting with Deutsch (1958), it has been recognized that individuals systematically differ in the kind of accounting gains for themselves and for other people. An overview of the findings was given in Liebrand et al. (1992). In this book, the concept plays a major role in Chapter 2.

become a target for agreements, even if there will be no binding contract. Indeed, commons observed in the field often allow for communication by providing meetings of the members. It is more than natural that these meetings are also used for reflection of the state and process of the commons and for strategy coordination as well as for conflict resolution. These issues are not taken into account if the situation is modeled and analyzed taking a purely non-cooperative approach.

In the more formalized settings examined in experiments, the bargain for agreements on future action becomes a central task. Nevertheless, such settings traditionally are analyzed by means of non-cooperative game theory. By the hypothesis of "cheap talk," it is erroneously assumed that in the absence of binding contracts only non-cooperative concepts are to be considered.

In communication not only proposals and claims can be exchanged, but also arguments that support a demand and may motivate the opponent to move. The exchange of proposals and arguments creates a common virtual world beyond the basic relations found in reality. If the partners agree on a specific compromise as being justified and binding, then they engage in a situation in which compliance is not a problem.

Since most settings are symmetrical with respect to actors, all single-point solutions of cooperative game theory prescribe the unique symmetric welfare optimum as cooperative solution. Equality and fairness solutions coincide, and both an explicit cooperative analysis and fairness considerations seem to be unnecessary. Things change if we turn to asymmetric settings. Then, concepts from cooperative game theory as well as fairness concepts gain more power.

In order to advance the understanding of results in social dilemmas that allow for communication, we propose to add constructs of cooperative game theory to our toolkit. We will proceed as follows.

Before discussing the theoretical framework, we introduce some notation. Next, specific games are defined; solution concepts and properties of these games are reported. As examples, two games that have been used in experiments by Hackett et al. (1994) are analyzed. After deriving fairness solutions from cooperative game theory, their experimental data are reconsidered.

Games

A large part of experiments on social dilemmas is based on a normal form game $(N, (A_i)_{i \in N}, (U_i)_{i \in N})$ (see Ostmann, 2002b). A normal form game is specified by the components shown in Table 14.1.

Every individual $i \in N$ can decide on real-valued actions $x_i \in A_i$. The action causes private cost $c_i(x_i)$ and contributes to a joint action s resulting in a joint product $f(s)$. The product is distributed between the individuals. Let $s = \Sigma\{x_j : j \in N\}$. Then $y_i = s - x_i$ denotes the sum of all contributions but individual i's. Denoting the

Table 14.1 Elements of Non-cooperative Games

N	$A_i; i \in N$	$U = (U_i)_{i \in N}$
Players' set	Action spaces	Payoff functions

share of the joint product of individual i by q_i, we can write the private payoff U_i to individual i as

$$U_i(x_1, x_2, \ldots, x_n) = u_i(x_i, y_i) = -c_i(x_i) + q_i\, f(s).$$

Note that according to this formula, the payoff only depends on y_i and not on how this amount is distributed among the partners of individual i.

The following well-known setups belong to this class of normal form games: In the generalized prisoner's dilemma, shares are equal, say $q_i = 1$, and cost and production are linear. Often action spaces are binary ($x_i \in \{0,1\}$), but there are also generalizations to larger action spaces. Formally, the generalized prisoners' dilemma is equivalent to a public-good game with linear cost and linear production. There are also public-good settings with quadratic concave production (e.g., Keser, 1996).

In the Bloomington CPR-setups (cf. Ostrom et al., 1994), cost functions are linear and the production functions are quadratic and concave. Shares are proportional to actions (say $q_i = x_i/s$), a property that is essential for common dilemmas.

Our theoretical results are valid for a large class of games (Meinhardt, 2002; Driessen & Meinhardt, 2005a; 2005b). The reanalysis of empirical results is only done for two example games of the Bloomington type. This is why in the following we restrict our attention to common dilemmas as reported by the Bloomington group. Their standard experimental commons use a repeated game framework. Our attention is concentrated on a setup enriched by explicit communication breaks (cf. Ostrom & Walker, 1989). Moreover, we are going to deal with the asymmetric setup examined by Hackett et al. (1994).

The most popular (static) solution concept of the theory of non-cooperative games is the Nash equilibrium. It can be characterized as "the individually best reply to itself." This characterization can be interpreted by relying on the following stability property: Once known and propagated, no individual has an incentive to deviate from it. Defined more precisely, a strategy combination $x = (x_i)_{i \in N}$ is a Nash equilibrium if, for all $i \in N$, the action x_i maximizes i's payoff if the partners' actions $(x_j)_{j \neq i}$ are fixed. Since in our case the payoff only depends on total amounts, we can speak of a best reply to y_i or can state that a best reply is a maximizer of the function $u_i(., y_i)$. Denoting the set of best replies by $b(y_i)$, a Nash equilibrium fulfills

$$(x_i, y_i) \in (b(y_i), y_i) \text{ for all players } i.$$

For the class of normal form games under consideration ("Bloomington CPR-setups"), it has been shown that there is a unique Nash equilibrium. Moreover, as typical for social dilemmas, the Nash equilibrium is inefficient (in other words, Pareto-suboptimal), that is, it makes every individual worse off compared to some other possible outcomes. But such better outcomes can only be reached by a joint strategy. Whereas an individual i can only decide on the strategy x_i, a group S of individuals can coordinate their choices and can choose a joint strategy vector $(x_i)_{i \in S}$.

Such joint strategies may enhance payoffs. Let us call every subset S of N a coalition, and the subset $N - S$ its opposition. The grand coalition provides optimum (Pareto-optimal) results. In case the coalition is smaller than the grand coalition, the opposition has substantial influence on the result via y_S, and the result may be suboptimal.

For getting a simple formalism allowing for the derivation of commons dilemma games, we replace the above notation by functions called $u = u_S$ that map two numbers x and y to a payoff $u(x,y)$. If we fix a coalition S, then x is the sum of actions chosen by the coalition, y is the sum of the actions chosen by its opposition, and $u(x,y)$ is the joint payoff to coalition S. Note that the payoff does not depend on how the actions are distributed internally. However, u is dependent on S via $q_S = \Sigma \{q_i ; i \in N\}$. We can interpret the functions u_S and u_{N-S} as payoff functions of a two-person game with the players S and $N - S$. Moreover, u_S is independent of how actions are split within the coalition and how actions are distributed within the opposition.

A cooperative game (N,v) specifies values of a joint payoff $v(S)$ for each coalition S (see Table 14.2). If we derive the game from a normal form game, then there are different ways for values to be determined. In the following, we focus on the so-called alpha and beta games (or characteristic functions) as introduced by von Neumann and Morgenstern (1944) and further developed especially by Aumann (cf. Aumann, 1961).

Table 14.2 Elements of Cooperative Games

N	$S; S \subseteq N$	$S \rightarrow v(S)$
Players' set	Coalitions	Value

The corresponding alpha values and beta values refer to different types of argumentation in a stylized bargaining process.

Say coalition S will choose the joint action x; then the poorest result they can get is the payoff min $u(x,y)$. Choosing a joint action x that maximizes this expression, we get a value that coalition S can guarantee to itself. This value is called the alpha value. By using alpha values, the so-called alpha game is derived. The alpha value specifies what a coalition can guarantee to itself, formally:

$$v_\alpha(S) = \max_x \min_y u(x,y).$$

The above formula states that a particular coalition is taking into account the worst case the opposition can cause to its joint payoff. Thus, the alpha value is derived from a prudent or pessimistic perception of how much payment a coalition can guarantee to itself. This is done by also including the joint strategies of the opposition that cause the worst impact on their joint payoff, a situation that might be disastrous for the members of the opposition, when they are really carried out. Assuming a worst-case scenario, the value $v_\alpha(S)$ represents a bottom line for claims in a bargaining process to achieve an agreement. A coalition can justify this bottom line by referring to the fact that the coalition can distribute $v_\alpha(S)$ among its members without relying on the cooperation of the opponents. Clearly, the higher the alpha value, the stronger the bargaining position. A higher share compared to what a coalition can guarantee to itself might only be achievable by cooperation with members of the opposition.

If it is known that the opposition chooses action y, then the coalition may choose its best reply (analogously to the individual best replies discussed in the context of Nash equilibrium) and would get max $u(x,y)$. Choosing an action y that minimizes this expression, we get a value that coalition S cannot be prevented from. Whatever the opposition tries to do, the coalition may get at least this value. This is the way the beta value and the beta game are defined. The beta value specifies what a coalition cannot be prevented from; formally,

$$v_\beta(S) = \min_y \max_x u(x,y).$$

In contrast to the alpha value, the beta value is derived from an optimistic perception of how much payment a coalition can get. It cannot be prevented from a certain payoff, because it may choose the best reply.

Due to the fact that the opposition is able to react on the joint strategy chosen by the opposition and then choose its best reply, the potential bargaining position is stronger than under the alpha case. That means that the beta value is equal to or greater than the alpha value, that is, $v_\alpha(S) \leq v_\beta(S)$. The (open) interval between alpha and beta values is called a determinant gap. The size of this gap opens an extra place for bargaining. A non-empty determinant gap may disturb the bargaining process by setting an incentive to react passively and to wait for the joint action of the opponents: Waiting and reacting pays extra.

Now let us consider in what way the communication added to the common dilemma influences how we can interpret the alpha and beta values. The form of communication added in the experiments conducted, for instance, by Ostrom et al. (1994) and by Hackett et al. (1994) was face-to-face within the whole group. In such settings, an explicit bargaining can take place, exchanging claims and arguments, discussing joint strategies for the whole group or for a part of the group. Moreover, an individual or a larger coalition can announce what it plans to do. In such a situation, the virtuality of reaction that underpins the idea of beta arguments has vanished. This means that in the course of negotiation, the opponents have to carry out their actual response by reacting on the move of the proposer rather than doing it virtually as in the case of beta arguments, where it is just enough to perform a thought experiment to be sure about one's own bargaining position. It is evident that not all possible arguments will be stated, but it is enough that individuals find the favorable ones that serve their own interests.

If alpha and beta games differ, then solution concepts may deliver competing distinct solutions. In such a case, we can expect that some bargaining difficulties will appear, since an agreement that belongs to a solution relying on alpha arguments may be destabilized by beta arguments. Notice that this is due to the following relationship between the alpha and beta argument: $v_\alpha(S) \leq v_\beta(S)$. Hence, switching between the modes of argument may sharpen the conflict. The stability of an agreement may be questioned, or break-offs may even happen. But fortunately, as Ostmann (1994) proved, common pool games (and public-good games) are clear games (cf. Jentzsch, 1964); in this case, the alpha and the beta values coincide, that is, $v_\alpha(S) = v_\beta(S)$.

Since alpha and beta games coincide, we can use the standard theory on solutions of cooperative games. The usual application of this theory deals with settings in which the individuals are (directly) informed about the value of every coalition and have the task to negotiate for contracts in which the coalition of signing parties agrees on how to distribute the value of the coalition between the partners. It is assumed that there will be free face-to-face communication (see Selten, 1972, for a complete set of standard conditions). Moreover, the fulfillment of the contracts is guaranteed due to "binding agreements."

When applying the theory on solutions of cooperative games to social dilemma setups, we face two main differences to the usual settings. We label them as "hidden cooperative game" and "non-binding contracts." We dealt with the latter in the first part of this chapter, arguing that with the introduction of (direct) communication in a situation, in which significant gains can be realized through cooperation, argumentation can create a virtual reality in which a fair compromise helps to establish compliance. The second deviation from the usual setting is that subjects are not informed about the cooperative game directly. Rather, they get information on what combination of individual actions will end in which results. The structure describing the gains through cooperation is hidden; thus, we call it a "hidden cooperative game." But even when the basic structure of the cooperative game is not obvious, it is nevertheless still adequate to base the analysis of experimental outcomes on hidden properties, since humans are led not only by the forces they have considered and calculated in mind, but also by non-visible forces set from outside, which restrict or extend their range of opportunities. In our view, it is primarily an empirical question if hidden structure influences or even determines results. This view may be called a descriptive approach. Nevertheless, after demonstrating significant effects, how this influence is produced is an important question. Here some "normative theory" (and the usual interpretation of a game-theoretical solution is normative) may help.

Core and Convexity

An important concept for evaluating payoff vectors $z = (z_1, ..., z_n)$ in the light of coalitional values is called excess. Setting $z(S) = \Sigma\{z_i; i \in S\}$, the excess $e(S,z)$ of z for a coalition S is given by

$$e(S,z) = v(S) - z(S).$$

Members of S can argue that no proposed efficient distribution z is acceptable if the coalition S gets less than $v(S)$. From the viewpoint that $v(S)$ is a sure gain, a lower gain can be seen as a loss. The smaller the excess for a particular coalition at a proposed efficient payoff distribution, the better off the coalition will be.

Now, the core is the set of payoff vectors such that no coalition suffers a loss, which means the excess for a coalition S is non-negative. The core is defined as the set of efficient payoff vectors z that is coalitionally rational. Formally, the core is specified by

$$v(S) \leq z(S) \text{ for all coalitions } S,$$

or in another form, as

$$e(S,z) \leq 0 \text{ for all coalitions } S.$$

For a core allocation, no coalition can be better off by blocking an agreement. Large-scale cooperation is more preferable than acting independently; the incentive to merge economic activities into a monopoly is weak.

In contrast to settings with binding agreements, claims based on the coalitional values cannot be enforced by actions. Nevertheless, as long as such claims are accepted as justified during the negotiation, it would be inappropriate to exclude them from the analysis. If actors negotiate in order to overcome the threat of inefficiency (induced by the dilemma situation), the goal of the negotiation can be assumed to be as efficient a result as possible. The alpha and beta games provide arguments and claims actors can exchange when they have the opportunity to freely communicate with each other in order to coordinate their strategies, in the case of binding agreements as well as in the non-binding case.

Of course, if agents decide to specify a non-binding contract, some of them may decide sooner or later to deviate from the committed payoff distribution. Observe that a non-empty core opens the room for commitments. An agreement in the grand coalition that specifies an element of the core lies in the interest of every agent. During a stylized bargaining process, a core allocation is stable in the sense that no subgroup of actors can argue against it by referring to a larger value: It cannot be improved upon.

During the bargaining process, actors may refer to values of coalitions without making binding contracts to establish the values. They refer to virtual values, merely possible actions; nevertheless, these arguments are not "cheap talk." Scholars who assume that tools of cooperative game theory are not adequate if contracts are not binding face the problem of explaining why coalitional values should be accepted in the absence of a binding commitment. Such a view would imply that it is completely useless to rely on the core concept even in standard settings.[2] How compliance is reached is not described in game-theoretical terms. In the case of binding agreements, usually substantial legal sanctions are assumed to enforce the agreement. The existence of forces that produce compliance in the case of non-binding agreements cannot be denied.

---

[2] For a comprehensive and more formal discussion of binding and non-binding agreements, we refer the reader to Ichiishi (1993).

Games may exhibit an empty core, which makes multilateral cooperation more complicated, if not impossible. In such a situation, it is much harder to stabilize a proposal. However, for common dilemma games, the core can be expected to be large. This can be derived from the convexity property of such games, since it is well-known (Shapley, 1971) that convex games exhibit a fully dimensional core. A game is convex if

$$v(S \cup \{i\}) - v(S) \leq v(S \cup \{i,j\}) - v(S \cup \{j\}) \text{ for all pairs } \{i,j\} \text{ and all } S \subseteq N - \{i,j\}.$$

The convexity property means that values added by one individual increase with the size of the coalition to which it is added. By using the definition $\partial_i v(S) := v(S \cup \{i\}) - v(S)$, one may also write the convexity property as $\partial_j \partial_i v(S) \leq 0$ for all pairs $\{i,j\}$ and all $S \subseteq N - \{i,j\}$. In Meinhardt (1999), it is proven that common dilemma games are convex games.

The notion of convexity states the principle that the incentives of a particular individual for joining a coalition increases as the coalition size expands, or equivalently, that the value added by an individual increases with the coalition to which the individual is merged. Due to the overproportional benefits that will be generated by convex games, the joining of economic activities in larger units like a cartel or monopoly is profitable (Driessen & Meinhardt, 2005a, b). For common dilemma situations, the convexity property can be understood such that appropriators have a strong incentive to reorganize the exploitation of the common property by a monolithic organization. Doing so will produce the largest profits to the overall player coalition, the grand coalition.

We can conclude that rational subjects have a strong incentive to extricate themselves from the common dilemma and to treat the common property with care in contrast to the usual non-cooperative game-theoretical prediction that it will be overharvested or even destroyed. Moreover, due to the largeness of the core, a non-binding agreement that belongs to the core remains stable given a small perturbation in the underlying parameter space. The core remains non-empty and the incentive for mutual cooperation remains valid, since the non-binding agreement point is still a core element and cannot be blocked by any coalition. No justified objection can be found against the agreed-upon payoff distribution.

Let us stress the fact that according to experimental research on cooperative games based on a normal form game, the properties of clearness and convexity make easier agreements as well as stability. The first point, agreements, is caused by the availability of attractive proposals, namely elements of the core. The latter, the stability, can be explained from the experience made in the negotiation that waiting or reaction does not pay extra.

Example Games

In this section we consider games that are based on the same individual cost function and the same joint production function, namely $c(x) = 5x$ and $f(s) = s(33 - 0.25s)$. Both functions are used in the asymmetric common dilemma situation Hackett et al.

(1994) deal with, a slight change with respect to the symmetric standard setting (Ostrom et al., 1994).

In the following, we will discuss three games, one with three players, called CP3, and the other two with eight players, called HSW1 and HSW2, referring to the two experimental games in Hackett et al. (1994). The games specified in Table 14.3 differ in endowment data (the total endowment is fixed). Moreover, for CP3 we make things simple by dealing with a small strategy space. There are two types of players in HSW1, which, according to their endowment, are called "poor" and "rich," respectively. In HSW2 the formerly rich are split into two pairs of very rich and moderately rich, and the formerly poor into two pairs of very poor and moderately poor.

Table 14.3 Endowments and Strategy Spaces

Games	CP3	HSW1	HSW2
Endowments	(20,40,60)	(8,8,8,8,24,24,24,24)	(8,8,12,12,20,20,24,24)
Total	120	120	120
Strategies	Three per person	Continuous	Continuous

The CP3 Game

The individual strategy space of the CP3 game consists of the following investments in the common:

N	Investing nothing
H	Investing half of the endowment
A	Investing all of the endowment

The following convention is used for arranging the payoff data of the normal form game:

Player 1 (endowment 20) chooses between rows
Player 2 (endowment 40) chooses between columns
Player 3 (endowment 60) chooses between matrices

In table 14.4 the entries are payoffs to player 1, player 2, and player 3, respectively.

By evaluation of the best replies, we can detect the equilibrium *(A,A,H)* associated with a total payoff of 495. The maximal total payoff of 780 can be produced via *(H,H,H)*, *(N,N,A)*, and *(A,A,N)*. Defining the efficiency of a strategy combination by its total payoff divided by the maximum total payoff, the equilibrium shows an efficiency of about 63%.

Table 14.4 Normal Form and Nash Equilibrium

Matrix 1 (N)

	Column 1 (N)			Column 2 (H)			Column 3 (A)		
Row 1 (N)	0	0	0	0	460	0	0	720	0
Row 2 (H)	255	0	0	205	410	0	155	620	0
Row 3 (A)	460	0	0	360	360	0	260	520	0

Matrix 2 (H)

	Column 1 (N)			Column 2 (H)			Column 3 (A)	
Row 1 (N)	0	0	615	0	310	465	0	420
Row 2 (H)	180	0	540	130	260	390	80	320
Row 3 (A)	310	0	465	210	210	315	110	220

Matrix 3 (A)

	Column 1 (N)			Column 2 (H)			Column 3 (A)		
Row 1 (N)	0	0	780	0	160	480	0	120	180
Row 2 (H)	105	0	630	55	110	330	5	20	30
Row 3 (A)	160	0	480	60	60	180	−40	−80	−120

The values $v(\{i\})$ of the one-person coalitions $\{i\}$ can be easily calculated by evaluating $\min\{u_i(x_i, y_i); y_i\}$. For example, for $i=1$, we get the numbers 0 (for $x_1 = N$), 5 (for $x_1 = H$), −40 (for $x_1 = A$), and finally the value $v(\{1\}) = 5$. Correspondingly, we get $v(\{2\}) = 60$ and $v(\{3\}) = 165$. A similar calculation establishes $v(\{1,2\}) = 165$, $v(\{1,3\}) = 320$, $v(\{2,3\}) = 525$. The value of the grand coalition $v(\{1,2,3\})$ equals a maximum total payoff of 780.

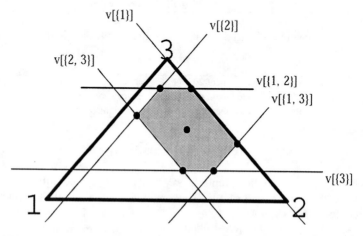

Figure 14.1 Graphical representation of the cooperative game, its core, and its kernel

In Figure 14.1, the triangle 1-2-3 represents the payoff vectors lying between the three vertices (780,0,0), (0,780,0), and (0,0,780), points at which a single player gets all of $v(N)$. The six lines correspond to the equations $\Sigma \{x_i; i \in S\} = v(S)$. The shaded area represents the core. The point in its middle is the kernel.

The HSW1 and HSW2 Games

The strategy spaces of the corresponding non-cooperative games are given by the intervals $[0, e_i]$, whereas the symbol e_i denotes the endowment of player i. Players are said to be of the same type if they have the same endowment. The profile of a coalition is the vector-numbering members of each type (ordered by decreasing endowments). For example, the profile of the coalition of all poorest players is (0, 4) in HSW1 and (0, 0, 0, 2) in HSW2. If coalitions show the same profile, then the same value is assigned to them. By evaluating the formulas for the value of a coalition, we can summarize the result for the HSW1 game in Table 14.5:

Note that the extreme four-person coalitions with profile (0, 4) and (4, 0) get 16 and 400, respectively. The latter value is much larger than 256, the coalitions' payoff in equilibrium, two-thirds of the total equilibrium payoff.

For the HSW2 game, there are $3^5 = 243$ different profiles. We summarize the results of the calculations for all profiles in a similar table as for HSW1. This is done by joining the two poorer types on the one side and the two richer types on the other

Table 14.5 HSW1 Coalitional Values for Different Profiles

Number of rich players	Number of Poor Players				
	0	1	2	3	4
0	0	0	0	4	16
1	4	16	36	64	100
2	64	100	144	196	256
3	196	256	324	400	484
4	400	484	576	676	784

Table 14.6 HSW2 Coalitional Values for Different Pseudo-Profiles

Number of rich players	Number of poor Players				
	0	1	2	3	4
0	0	0	0–4	9–16	36
1	1–4	9–25	25–64	64–100	121–144
2	36–64	64–121	100–196	196–256	256–324
3	144–169	196–256	256–361	361–441	484–529
4	324	400–441	484–576	625–676	784

side. Correspondingly, we get crude pseudo-profiles. Consequently, some entries in Table 14.6 show intervals to which the value of a corresponding coalition belongs.

In both underlying non-cooperative games, the Nash equilibrium proscribes that the four poor individuals are restricted by their endowment. Raising the diversity has lowered the equilibrium payoff. Coalitions having a majority of rich members tend to gain less in HSW2 than in HSW1. Coalitions having a majority of poor members tend to gain more in HSW2 than in HSW1.

Fairness Solutions

In the previous discussion, we have introduced the core concept that specifies all efficient and coalitionally rational payoff distributions. We argued that agreements in the core are favorable outcomes that are self-enforcing. Agreements might be reached by exchanging claims and arguments in some bargaining process. But up to now we cannot judge if an agreed-upon core allocation is really a fair outcome.

If subjects are concerned only about their own favorable outcomes, it is relatively simple to decide on the approval or disapproval of some proposal. It is sufficient to judge if this proposal will give them a higher share compared to outcomes they can achieve in various coalitions to which they can belong. No information about the payoffs of the opponents is really needed to judge if this has improved one's own situation or not. In contrast, if subjects are also concerned about some fairness standards, then in order to judge the fairness of a proposal, one needs information on one's own payoff share and the payoff shares of the opponent. Cooperative game theory provides more than one fairness standard. In the following, we only deal with the two best known: the Shapley value and the kernel.

The **Shapley value** assigns a payoff vector to every game. We can classify this payoff vector as a (1) fairness solution of the game by referring either to a set of principles or by a simple rule of distributive justice. The four principles (axioms) are as follows:

Efficiency	The solution should distribute the maximal total payoff.
Symmetry	Any two players who contributes the same should obtain the same payoff.
Dummy player	Any player who contributes nothing to any coalition should obtain his value.
Additivity	Adding the solution of two games produces the solution of the sum of these games (in this sense the solution is invariant against an arbitrary decomposition of the game).

The Shapley value Φ is the unique function that maps game v to the **n**-vector $(\Phi_i(v))_{i \in N}$ and satisfies these principles.

It is easy to show that the Shapley value can be characterized by the following simple rule of distributive justice: Every player should receive his mean contribution to the coalitional values (Rosenmüller, 1981). We get the mean value added by considering the $n!$ different orderings in which the players may appear one after another. There are $(n - s - 1)!s!$ orderings in which a coalition S is assembled and a specific player i comes next. Setting $\pi(S) = (n - 1 - s)!s!/n!$, the Shapley value is given by the following formula:

$$\Phi_i(v) = \Sigma \ \{\pi(S) \ \partial_i v(S) \ ; \ S{\subset}N, \ i{\in} N\}.$$

The weight $\pi(S)$ can be interpreted as the probability that S is already assembled; and in this sense the Shapley value is a vector of mean contributions. Both the axiomatic properties of the Shapley value and its probabilistic interpretation as mean contribution embody its attractiveness as a fairness standard.

Another prominent fairness solution concept in cooperative game theory is the kernel (Davis & Maschler, 1965). The kernel has the advantage that it solves a stylized bargaining process, in which the figure of argumentation is a pairwise equilibrium procedure where each pair of individuals involved exchange best alternatives against each other to claim (reject) a higher (lower) share from the opponent. In this pairwise bargaining procedure, an individual refers to the largest loss or smallest gain as a member of a coalition without counting on the cooperation of her opponent. The maximal loss or smallest gain an individual i will receive without relying on the collaboration of opponent j in some coalition S if z were realized is given by

$$s_{ij}(z) = \max\{e(S, z); \ i \in S \ \text{and} \ j \notin S\}.$$

The kernel is defined as the set of efficient payoff vectors, which balances the maximal "losses" between pairs of individuals; formally:[3]

$$K(v) = \{z{\in} R^n; \ s_{ij}(z) = s_{ji}(z) \ \text{for all i}, \ j{\in} N, \ i \neq j\}.$$

If the largest loss of an agent is greater than the largest loss of its opponent, a proposal is refused as being unfair. An individual can use the coalitions to whom he or she belongs as best alternatives to propose that the opponent should lower his or her claim. By balancing the maximal losses between pairs of individuals, the kernel solution can be considered as a fair compromise. In cases such as ours, where the core is not empty, the largest losses are negative and thus the pairs

---

[3] The usual definition is a little bit more complex, because one of the consequences of simply equalizing the maximal losses between pairs of individuals can be that an individual i gets less than its value $v(\{i\})$. This would certainly violate individual rationality. One of the appealing properties of convex games is that we need not care about individual rationality; each agent will get at least her individual rational payoff.

compare their smallest gains in order to equalize them. Moreover, the games we are dealing with are convex games. In Maschler et al. (1972, 1979), it was shown that for convex games the kernel is a singleton and belongs to the core.

Since the kernel is a singleton, it coincides with another prominent fairness solution discussed in cooperative game theory: the nucleolus. The nucleolus is defined as the set of efficient payoff vectors that minimize "losses" of coalitions simultaneously. For symmetric games, the kernel solution is trivial, because it assigns $v(N)/n$ to each player. For asymmetric games, like ours, the task of computing the kernel solution is more difficult. Trying to solve the system of nonlinear equations given in the definition of the kernel is hopeless. Accordingly, the calculations for the kernel (especially of the second example game) must be done by solving a sequence of quadratic functions (cf. Meinhardt, 2006b) or by a computer.[4]

Finally, reaching an agreement to split the benefits from mutual cooperation when heterogeneities in the endowments and cost structure, together with some fairness standards, must be considered can be easily solved by relying on the Shapley value or kernel/nucleolus. Both solution concepts are elements of the core, and no justified objection can be presented with respect to these distribution rules.

Applying the above fairness standards to our example games and comparing the solutions to the respective Nash equilibria, we learn that all individuals are remarkably better off than in Nash equilibrium. Moreover, differences between the two different fairness standards are small or even vanish.

Note that for the CP3 game, the fairness solutions nucleolus, kernel, and Shapley value coincide; we get the vector (130, 260, 390) and the proportions 1:2:3. Due to the restricted strategy space of this game, the Nash equilibrium proscribes that only the rich have to carry the burden of reduction (Table 14.7).

Table 14.8 shows the shares the different types of players can collect according to the three standards (note that the types have the same multiplicity, namely 1, 4, and 2, respectively).

Table 14.7 Solutions for the Example Games

	CP3	HSW1	HSW2
Kernel/nucleolus	(130,260,390)	(54,…,54,142,…,142)	(216,216,318,318,511,511, 523,523)/4
Shapley value	(130,260,390)	(348,…,348,1024,…,1024)/7	(1389,1389,2073,2073,342 1,3421,4093,4093)/28
Nash equilibrium	(110,220,165)	(32,32,32,32,64,64,64,64)	(720,720,720,720,1296, 1296,1296,1296)/25

---

[4] The algorithms to compute the kernel of the game are described in Meinhardt (2006a, b), while the corresponding computer program can be downloaded from http://library.wolfram.com/infocenter/MathSource/5709/.

Table 14.8 Share per Type for the Example Games

	CP3 (3 types)	HSW1 (2 types)	HSW2 (4 types)
Kernel/nucleolus	(0.167, 0.333, 0.500)	(0.276, 0.724)	(0.138, 0.203, 0.326, 0.334)
Shapley value	(0.167, 0.333, 0.500)	(0.254, 0.746)	(0.127, 0.189, 0.312, 0.373)
Nash equilibrium	(0.222, 0.444, 0.333)	(0.333, 0.667)	(0.178, 0.178, 0.322, 0.322)

Experimental Results Reconsidered

The HSW1 data set contains the strategy vectors for eight (independent) trials in groups consisting of eight persons. In each trial, the group met for 10 rounds. Since half of the eight trials are carried out under the condition that the rich positions had been auctioned, we can speak of two different conditions. The HSW2 data set contains 3 trials (8 persons per group, 10 rounds). The authors speak of a third condition, the "complex" condition (using the more complex game). In total, we get 80 and 30 payoff vectors. Hackett et al. (1994) reported that in three trials the members of the group agreed on a rotation scheme. In this case, it is evident that observations are not independent.

Efficiency and Compliance

Experiments with cooperatively played normal-form games, unrestricted communication, and binding agreements were reported by Michener and his group (see Ostmann, 2002a). They demonstrated that participants prefer to agree to a beta-core solution. A larger study with cooperatively played normal-form games, unrestricted communication, and mainly non-binding agreements was reported in Ostmann (1988, 2002a). The set of games studied also includes games with an empty beta core (Moulin, 1981, speaks of "competition for the second move"). For games with a non-empty beta core, a comparison of "binding agreements" with "non-binding agreements" shows that the percentage of break-offs in the "binding" environment nearly translates to the percentage of no agreement or no compliance in the "non-binding" environment.

Let us define the (degree of) **efficiency** of a payoff vector by its total payoff divided by maximum total payoff. Then the points on the Pareto frontier (this includes the core and the Shapley value) get 100% efficiency. The Nash equilibria imply an efficiency of 49% and 45%, respectively. As in the setups mentioned above, we expect that agreements will be nearly efficient. Nearly all efficiency losses will be due to lack of compliance. Moreover, agreements within the beta core are nearly always confirmed by action. Table 14.9 reports the efficiencies of the results for the 4 + 4 + 3 trials based on the HSW1 and HSW2 games.

Efficiencies are remarkably lower for the HSW2 games. In all three trials, a partial lack of agreement and compliance was observed. The two low-efficiency groups of the HSW1 setup are due to the fact that in one group an agreement was

Table 14.9 Efficiency Data

Game	HSW1	HSW1	HSW2
Condition	Standard	Auction	Complex
Efficiencies (in %)	83, 97, 98, 99	91, 97, 98, 99	86, 87, 89
Mean efficiency (in %)	94	96	87

never reached (the 84% case) and in the other a rotation scheme was agreed upon, but there was no compliance (the 91% case).

According to the studies mentioned above, one may expect that agreements will be confirmed if located in the core. But as we will see, no agreement is hitting the core. For the HSW1 game (only two types), failure to reach an agreement is concentrated to one trial (a failure rate of 10%). Defection is concentrated to the other low-efficiency trial where a rotation scheme was used (an individual defection rate of 6.4%).

For the second HSW2 game (four types), the efficiency is reduced to the level that was reached in the other experiment in cases of defection. Compared to the first experiment, the failure rate triples (30%) and the individual defection rate doubles (12.9%). Two of the three trials use rotation schemes that may invite defection.

Geometric Localization of Results

The failure to hit the core can be interpreted as a deviation from "*homo oeconomicus* rationality." In all of the experiments that support the beta-core expectation, the individual strategy set consisted of three options as in the above CP3 game (cf. Michener et al., 1981, 1984). Consequently, it was not possible to interpolate between strategies in order to redistribute profits fairly, as is possible in games with continuous strategy spaces. In most experimental social dilemma setups, strategy spaces are not continuous, but larger integer intervals are, which can be seen as an approximation.

The following two graphs (Figures 14.2 and 14.3) show the 80 observations of joint payoffs of the rich by the joint payoffs of the poor as realized using the first game and the corresponding 30 observations using the second game. The declining line represents maximum total payoff (it is called the Pareto frontier). The triangle is generated by the three reference points: Nash equilibrium (lower left), best equal payoffs (upper left), and the kernel/nucleolus (at right). The other two lines show equal proportions and proportions according to endowments, respectively. All the points far away from the line between the equality payoff vector and the nucleolus are results not based on an agreement or results that originate from broken agreements.

For the second game, we get a similar picture, the same explanation of points outside the triangle, and points that are remarkably inefficient. Not all of the points are situated within the borders of the triangle. This happens in nearly all cases in which agreements prescribe some rotation scheme. A further analysis based on the

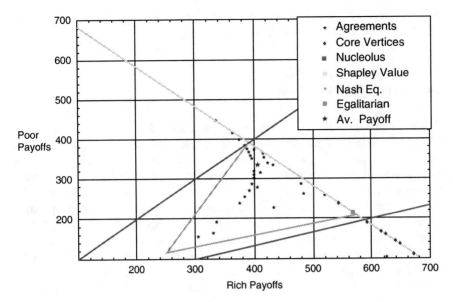

Figure 14.2 HSW1 payoff data

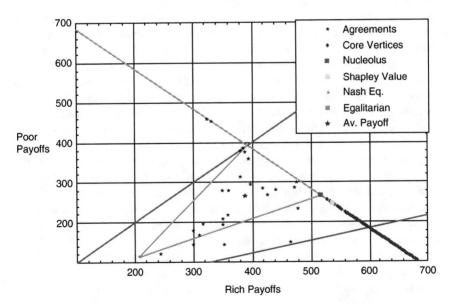

Figure 14.3 HSW2 payoff data

distances between the payoff vectors and the three vertices of the triangle can be found in Ostmann and Meinhardt (2007).

Summary and Discussion

Empirical data referring to social dilemmas that allow for communication but not for binding contracts usually show that people can reach better results than explained by (purely individually) "rational actor" theories. These results are in line with the many results from experimental games. Nevertheless, in mainstream economics these facts have not really been accepted up to now. According to the "purely rational" theories, it would be appropriate to use models of non-cooperative game theory, which prescribe results at equilibria or approaching such equilibria (in case learning processes are assumed) even in cases when these equilibria are suboptimal. In most cases, people do better than what equilibrium behavior prescribes with respect to both agreements and compliance to agreements. In order to explain these facts, we added tools from cooperative game theory to the non-cooperative game-theoretical analysis. The application of these tools was justified by the type of arguments that can be set up during negotiation and by possible standards of fairness.

The main result of the cooperative game-theoretical analysis is that common dilemma games are clear and convex, two properties favorable for stable and efficient solutions. For clear games, the two main paths for deriving coalitional values coincide: Arguing by reacting to what others announce establishes no advantage if it is compared with what one can guarantee to oneself without referring to what others will do. For clear games there are no competing standards for coalitional claims. Moreover, the games are convex. This property has important consequences. First, claims based on coalitional values can simultaneously be fulfilled, i.e., the core of these games is not empty. This property also means that it is favorable to end up with an agreement in the grand coalition. Second, with respect to the fairness solutions "kernel" and "Shapley value," both are elements of the core. Finally, the "kernel" consists of a unique payoff vector (the "nucleolus"). To summarize: For the analyzed example games, CP3, HSW1, and HSW2, attractive normative solutions for the participants are available, that is, the kernel and the Shapley value.

Discussing experiments of the Michener group (Michener & Potter, 1981), Kahan and Rapoport (1981) argued that in more complex situations, it is not enough to deal with alpha and beta games. Beside the classical alpha and beta concepts, another kind of argumentation is found in the literature that represents a sophisticated way to justify somewhat larger claims (known as s-types introduced by Moulin, 1981, 1988, for 2-person games and as gamma values for n-person games; see Ostmann, 1988, 1994). Here, a coalition announces an action and invites its opposition to choose its best reply (in economics, elements of this argumentation are found under the notion of "Stackelberg solutions"). It was shown that for the class of common pool games, the resulting coalitional values are too large to be fulfilled simultaneously (say, the gamma core is empty; as proven in Meinhardt, 2002). Ostmann (1988) argued that participants may judge a type of argumentation as invalid if they detect that this type makes it impossible to find a solution. Thus, in our context, we do not consider the class of gamma games according to its empty core.

Confronting experimental results with the fairness solutions, we found that participants had compromised among the Nash equilibrium, the egalitarian standard, and the fairness standard. We interpret this observation as follows:

- People set the goal that communication is used to solve the dilemma and to establish solutions better than equilibrium.
- In order to reach compliance, people have to activate some standard of behavior that motivates opponents to accept the agreement as result.
- Whereas the egalitarian standard clearly favors the poor, power-oriented standards favor the rich. Although we expected fairness standards (like the ones we used) to be "neutral" and a convincing choice, the data showed that people compromise between equality and (such) fairness. In the presence of an egalitarian norm in order to "buy" compliance, it may be necessary to make results more equal.

In some cases, subjects do not succeed in establishing an agreement in the grand coalition. In these cases, a smaller coalition may agree upon a joint strategy while other individuals may disagree. Despite the fact that such a coalitional solution is not favorable from the normative view, since it is not Pareto efficient, it is nevertheless of great practical importance. Coalitions can also be formed if some outsiders try to block an agreement (remember Kyoto and Den Haag). Schmitt et al. (2000) examined a setup where only incomplete agreements could be made. In this setup, the individual investment into the joint production was framed as appropriation; thus, cooperation is accomplished by agreeing to a certain reduction policy. They found that outsiders may respond strategically to reductions in appropriation by the coalition and that insiders (i.e., members of the coalition) may deviate from the agreement if overappropriation can be blamed on outsiders.

Up to now we have not had much experience with asymmetric common dilemma games that allow for communication. Here, in contrast to settings without communication, opponents can draw on the coalitional properties of the game structure studied in cooperative game theory. In order to identify how people make use of these properties and how their actual solutions are related to the formal game structure, many more experimental results are needed. So the above interpretation may only serve as a first step in an analysis that no longer excludes tools from cooperative game theory when dealing with negotiations. Further theoretical and experimental research dealing with asymmetric commons is needed.

References

Aumann, R. J. (1961). A survey on cooperative games without side payments. In M. Shubik (ed.), *Essays in Mathematical Economics in Honor of Oskar Morgenstern* (pp. 3–27). Princeton, NJ: Princeton University Press.

Davis, M., Maschler, M. (1965). The kernel of a cooperative game. *Naval Research Logistics Quarterly*, 12, 223–265.

Dawes, R. M., McTavish, J., Shaklee, H. (1977). Behavior, communication, and assumptions about other people's behavior in a commons dilemma situation. *Journal of Personality and Social Psychology*, 35, 1–11.

Deutsch, M. (1958). Trust and suspicion. *Journal of Conflict Resolution*, 2, 265–279.

Driessen, T., Meinhardt, H. (2005a). Convexity of oligopoly games without transferable technologies. *Mathematical Social Sciences*, 50, 102–126.

Driessen, T., Meinhardt, H. (2005b). On the supermodularity of oligopoly games. Discussion paper, University of Karlsruhe, Karlsruhe, Germany.

Hackett, S., Schlager, E., Walker, J. (1994). The role of communication in resolving commons dilemmas: Experimental evidence with heterogeneous appropriators. *Journal of Environmental Economics and Management*, 27, 99–126.

Ichiishi, T. (1993). *The Cooperative Nature of the Firm*. Cambridge: Cambridge University Press.

Jentzsch, G. (1964). Some thoughts on the theory of cooperative games. *Annals of Mathematical Studies*, 52, 407–442.

Kahan, J. P., Rapoport, A. (1981). Matrix experiments and theories of n-person games. *Journal of Conflict Resolution*, 25, 725–732.

Keser, C. (1996). Voluntary contributions to a public good when partial contribution is a dominant strategy. *Economic Letters*, 50, 359–366.

Krug, B. (1998). *On Mores, Manners, and Marginal Utility*. Delft: Eburon.

Liebrand, W., Messick, D. M., Wilke, H. (eds.) (1992). *Social Dilemmas: Theoretical Issues and Research Findings*. Oxford: Pergamon.

Maschler, M., Peleg, B., Shapley, L. (1972). The kernel and bargaining set for convex games. *International Journal of Game Theory*, 1, 73–93.

Maschler, M., Peleg, B., Shapley, L. S. (1979). Geometric properties of the kernel, nucleolus, and related solution concepts. *Mathematics of Operations Research*, 4, 303–338.

Meinhardt, H. (1999). Common pool games are convex games. *Journal of Public Economic Theory*, 2, 247–270.

Meinhardt, H. (2002). Cooperative decision making in common pool situations. *Lecture Notes in Economics and Mathematical Systems*, Vol. 17. Heidelberg: Springer.

Meinhardt, H. (2006a). An LP approach to compute the pre-kernel for cooperative games. *Computers and Operation Research*, 33, 535–557.

Meinhardt, H. (2006b). A dual pre-kernel representation based on the Fenchel–Moreau conjugation of the characteristic function. Mimeo.

Meinhardt, H., Ostmann, A. (1999). Resolving commons dilemmas by cooperative games. Disc. Paper 10, Institute for Statistics and Economic Theory, University Karlsruhe, Karlsruhe, Germany.

Michener, H. A., Potter, K. (1981). Generalizability of tests in n-person side-payment games. *Journal of Conflict Resolution*, 25, 733–749.

Michener, H. A., Dettman, D. C., Choi, Y. C. (1984). The beta-core solution in cooperative non-sidepayment n-person games. *Advances in Group Processes*, 1, 145–181.

Michener, H. A., Ekman, J. M., Dettman, D. C. (1986). Predictive superiority of the beta-characteristic function in non-sidepayment N-person games. *Theory and Decision*, 21, 99–128.

Moulin, H. (1981). Deterrence and cooperation. *European Economic Review*, 15, 179–193.

Moulin, H. (1986). *Game Theory for the Social Sciences*. New York: NYU Press.

Moulin, H. (1988). *Axioms of Cooperative Decision Making*. Cambridge: Cambridge University Press.

Ostmann, A. (1988). Limits of rational behavior in cooperatively played normal form games. In R. Tietz, W. Albers & R. Selten (eds.), *Bounded Rational Behavior in Experimental Games and Markets*. Lecture Notes in Economics and Mathematical Systems (Vol. 314, pp. 317–332). Berlin: Springer.

Ostmann, A. (2002a). Coalitions in multilateral negotiations. Aspirations, agreements, outcomes. In F. Bolle & M. Lehmann-Waffenschmidt (eds.), *Surveys in Experimental Economics* (pp.139–158). Heidelberg: Physica.

Ostmann, A. (2002b). Cooperation in environmental commons. In F. Bolle & M. Lehmann-Waffenschmidt (eds.), *Surveys in Experimental Economics* (pp.31–58). Heidelberg: Physica.

Ostmann, A., Meinhardt, H. (2007). Non-binding agreements and fairness in commons dilemma games. Forthcoming in *Central European Journal of Operation Research*.

Ostrom, E. (1990). *Governing the Commons (The Evolution of Institutions for Collective Action)*. Cambridge: Cambridge University Press.

Ostrom, E. (1998). A behavioral approach to the rational choice theory of collective action. *American Political Science Review*, 92, 1–22.

Ostrom, E., Gardner, R., Walker, J. (1994). *Rules, Games and Common Pool Resources*. Ann Arbor.: University of Michigan Press.

Ostrom, E., Walker, J. M. (1989). Communication in a commons: Cooperation without external enforcement. Bloomington, IN: Workshop on Political Theory and Political Analysis.

Ostrom, E., Walker, J., Gardner, R. (1992). Covenants with and without a Sword: Self-governance is possible. *American Political Science Review*, 86, 404–417.

Rosenmüller, J. (1981). *The Theory of Games and Markets*. Amsterdam.

Sally, D. (1995). Conversation and cooperation in social dilemmas. *Rationality and Society*, 7, 58–92.

Schmitt, P. M., Swope, K. J., Walker, J. (2000). Collective action with incomplete commitment: Experimental evidence. *Southern European Journal*, 66, 829–854.

Selten, R. (1972). Equal share analysis of characteristic function experiments. In H. Sauermann (ed.), *Beiträge zur experimentellen Wirtschaftsforschung* (Vol. 3; pp. 130–165). Tübingen: Mohr.

Shapley, L. S. (1971). Cores of convex games. *International Journal of Game Theory*, 1, 11–26.

von Neumann, J., Morgenstern, O. (1944). *Theory of Games and Economic Behavior*. Princeton, NJ: Princeton University Press.

Chapter 15
Using Genetic Algorithms for Simulation of Social Dilemmas

Ilan Fischer

Introduction

Studying social dilemmas and their underlying behavioral, cognitive, and evolutionary constructs is a more complicated challenge than most laboratory experiments or empirical data collection methods can meet. In contrast to those behaviors observed in a well defined laboratory setting, naturally occurring social dilemmas have a high level of complexity, interdependencies, and many non-linear links. Over the last three decades, several attempts have been made to study intricate social interactions by using computer simulations. A well-known study conducted by Robert Axelrod (1980a, b, 1981, 1984) examined the evolution of cooperation among agents who played a repeated prisoner's dilemma game in a heterogeneous population. This seminal work inspired many more studies in diverse social science domains (see, for example, Latane & Novak's (1997) study of attitude change, Fischer & Suleiman's (1997) study of the evolution of intergroup cooperation, or Axelrod's (1986) and Saam & Harrer's (1999) studies on the influence of social norms).

Indeed, computer simulations provide a controllable and convenient setting for testing the interaction between behavioral patterns and environmental conditions. In this way, the function and structure of individuals, the rules of engagement, and the harshness of the environment can be manipulated and monitored. But how should one capture the cognitive function of simulated human individuals or decide which characteristics are representative of their behavior? Axelrod's influential work used an original approach, asking human experts to generate strategies, and then proceeding to simulate their interaction with each other. This approach combined the complexity of human cognition and the controllable environment of the simulation.

While Axelrod's procedure proved to be highly successful, its success was dependent on the pre-simulation selection and cognitive effort of the individuals who contributed its inputs. Nevertheless, naturally occurring social dilemmas cannot always be seeded with a composition of potent and pre-defined strategies.

A. Biel et al. (eds.), *New Issues and Paradigms in Research on Social Dilemmas.*

Genetic Algorithms

Social structure is a complex configuration that emerges from the simultaneous function and reasoning of its members. It reflects learning and adaptations, but it also relates to concealed goals and motives that are often not fully understood by the actors themselves. In many cases it is not easy to explain why some patterns exist, and how their existence influences the entire population. Such highly complex environments require a special simulation approach that is capable of representing complex structures of a multifaceted population, allowing it to develop under controlled manipulations, and yet imposes as few constraints as possible on the underlying cognitive processing of the simulated individuals. Since in many cases these cognitions are unknown, individuals may only be represented in terms of their phenotypes, or revealed traits.

Such an approach can be derived from the Darwinian principle of evolution and modeled by evolutionary computations that simulate continuously developing populations that are subjected to environmental pressures. During the simulation process, the fitness of individuals in the population is evaluated according to a fitness function, which determines their survival and forms the basis for building a new generation. This process is repeated as long as there is enough variation remaining in the population for changes to occur from one generation to the next. Among the several computational models that have been studied (for an overview, see Dasgupta & Michalewicz, 1997), we focus upon the class known as genetic algorithms (GAs), due to its qualities, listed in the next section.

Since their development in the 1960s by Holland (1975), GAs have proven effective in searching large and complex solution spaces and in solving non-linear problems (see, for example, Gorrini & Dorigo, 1996). Instead of progressing from point to point like other techniques, GAs search from one set of problem solutions to another. This feature allows them to escape local optima, to be dependent on relative rather than absolute fitness, and to function without global system-level knowledge (Chattoe, 1998). GAs process coded linear sequences (vectors) of binary or higher-order numbers resembling the information structure of a chromosome.

A typical GA is described by the following stages: (1) the *initialization* of a population of vectors; (2) the transformation and *recombination* of vectors according to specific evolutionary operands; and (3) the evaluation and selection of individual vectors according to a *fitness function*. A typical GA will also induce some random changes denoted as mutations. This is an important characteristic since it accounts for the emergence of new patterns not available in the existing data set. If the mutation rate is low, the negative influence of random noise may be easily removed by the evaluation function, which in most cases would assign the mutated vectors a low rank and eliminate them from the data set (Fischer & Sullivan, 2007).

While both recombination and evaluation processes shape the data set, the former controls the flexibility of change, whereas the latter reflects the pressures of the environment. For instance, the recombination of two vectors may be subjected to the constraint that the new link will comprise only ascending values. Thus, the recombination of the first vector (1, 1, 1, 1) with a second vector (2, 2, 2, 2) is acceptable, although the opposite is not. The evaluation stage may favor other types of combination; it may rate vectors with descending values as better than vectors with ascending ones and thus cancel the changes induced by the recombination process.

Figure 15.1 depicts a generic GA, showing the initialization of the vector set (1); the generation of a new vector (3, 4) by recombining two randomly selected vectors (2); the function of the mutation process (5); and the evaluation of each vector by the selection function (6). The values assigned to each vector serve as a selection mechanism (7) accounting for the survival of the higher-ranking vectors and the removal of the lower-ranking ones.

It is important to emphasize that the converged data pattern (also referred to as a forecast or solution) does not represent a global truth value. Its qualities are derived from the constraints embedded in the recombination stage and the fitness function. In this sense, a solution is simply a data structure that corresponds to the constraints embedded in the GA.

Figure 15.2 depicts an evolutionary development of a simple GA operating on a vector set of 500 individuals (rows) with 6 possible elements (depicted as 6 distinct colors or shades of grey) distributed along a sequence of 490 possible locations. The (initially defined) fitness function is programmed to favor a pre-defined color distribution and thus grants vectors that exhibit such color distributions a higher fitness level. Panel a depicts an initial random distribution of the colored vectors (rows), panel b shows the same population after several hundred generations, and panel c shows the converged set. The convergence along the evolutionary pass is easily observed, as more colored columns pop out (since similar vectors have identical

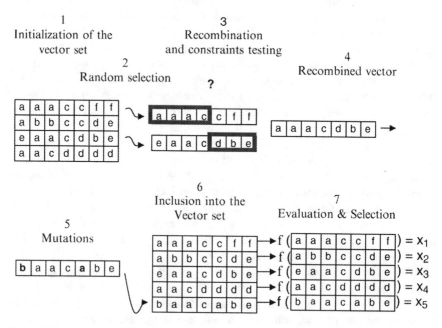

Figure 15.1 Seven stages of a genetic algorithm

Figure 15.2 Three phases of a genetic algorithm

color distributions). Clearly, the similarity of the vector set increases along the evolutionary pass, until all vectors have very similar structures. This implies that the development of successful patterns is rather global and simultaneous. Once convergence occurs, the survival of individuals depends on their ability to interact with *mutants* and *copies of themselves*, which exhibit only small differences from one another.

To apply GAs to the study of social dilemmas, one needs to identify the representative variables, which capture both the individual's and the societal perspectives. Fischer and Sullivan (2007) have suggested using time-use diaries for this purpose.

Time-use diary data are derived from surveys in which respondents record their activities throughout the day as a continuous sequence of coded digits, representing different activities. A typical time-use report of a 24-hour period comprises a sequential set of activities such as sleep, personal care, paid work, leisure activities, some unpaid work, and more personal care and sleep. While the precise nature of the activities may change from day to day, the overall pattern repeats itself, characterizing the individual's biological and psychological constraints as well as the social and economic environments.

At the macro level, time-use data provide important information on the way in which time is divided between production and consumption activities within a society (Gershuny, 2000; Robinson, 1997), while at the micro level information is provided about how individuals divide their time between paid and unpaid work, or the amount and use of leisure time (Gershuny & Sullivan, 1998). As in a classical social dilemma construct, societies are better off if more individuals use their time to produce (increasing the amount of paid work). On the other hand, individuals prefer to reduce the time spent on paid work and increase consumption and leisure activities.

At the macro level, patterns of time use are continuously developing data that reflect the pressures and constraints that shaped a particular population in its past, and at the same time delineate a novel starting point for future evolutionary developments. They therefore furnish us with a both suitable and highly relevant source for modeling purposes. Existing data show that changes in patterns of time use occur over time (for instance, there has been a general trend toward shorter working hours and longer durations of leisure), but there is little knowledge in regard of the developmental processes that underpin such changes. Observations of empirical time-use patterns reveal the consequences of several factors such as personal habits, social norms and preferences, economic and cultural constraints, as well as various adaptation pressures. Hence, it is a good candidate for a genetic algorithm-based simulation that is capable of modeling both the stabilizing forces, such as norms, habits, physiological and psychological constraints, and external pressures that attempt to impose new behavioral patterns.

While Fischer and Sullivan (2007) showed that this approach is capable of causing a random data set to evolve into a converged social structure that has many resemblances to actual populations, here I use the "GA-based time-use simulation" to model the products of a social dilemma. I show how individual preferences (with regard to personal care and leisure activities) merge with a centrally imposed policy of increased production (translated into a pressure to increase time spent in paid work activities). The emergence of a new population is the result of the selection of individuals that are capable of satisfying both their personal preferences and the societal constraints. Next, I describe the characteristics of the Fischer and Sullivan (2007) time-use GA-based simulation

Simulation

The simulation is based on the above-mentioned GA structure. However, it is designed for the purpose of modeling actual populations. Hence, it incorporates various constraints, sampled and extracted from empirically observed human behavior.

Initialization of the Vector Populations

This involved the initialization of a population, represented by a vector set $V_t = (x_1, x_2, ..., x_{nt})$, where x_1 to x_n denote a set of values corresponding to specific activities, n denotes the time intervals (measured in quarter-hour intervals), and t denotes the iterations of the model (thus representing the duration of the evolutionary development of the examined vector population). In this way, each vector represents one individual, described according to his or her activities through the time span of one week.

Transformation and Recombination of Individual Patterns

At this stage, pairs of vectors are randomly chosen, split, and recombined at several randomly chosen sites, to produce two newly structured vectors. Following this crossover, an additional mutation process randomly alters some of the activity codes of the vectors. The more crossovers allowed, the stronger the impact the recombination stage will have. To define recombination rules that reflect the empirically observed behavior of an actual population, Fischer and Sullivan (2007) used the 1987 British time-use data set. The probabilistic recombination rules have been calculated from the distribution of activities across time and the observed transition probabilities between adjacent activities (calculated separately for weekdays and weekends). They comprise (1) a set of time-dependent probabilities reflecting both human physiology and empirically observed behavior for each of the six activities along the diurnal cycle (e.g., sleeping during the night has a higher probability than sleeping during the day), (2) two sets of probabilities p_i (j = 1, 2, ..., 35, 36) and q_j (j = 1, 2, ..., 215, 216) reflecting the duration and transition between activities. The first-order (p_i) and second-order (q_j) probabilities reflect the conditional probability of a particular activity following another specific activity, and the conditional probability of a particular activity following a sequence of two previous activities, respectively (e.g., paid work preceded by outdoor leisure, and paid work preceded by paid work preceded by outdoor leisure). To transfer and maintain these dependencies in the next vector generation, two random numbers r_2 ($0 \le r_2 \le 1$) and r_3 ($0 \le r_3 \le 1$) were computer-generated, and the new recombination was approved only if each of the dependencies had a higher value than the thresholds provided by the random number with which it was compared. Following the recombination and generation of new vectors, a certain percentage of vectors (0.05% in this study) undergo mutations, which randomly alter some of their activity codes and help the simulated population to develop and to improve beyond local maxima. It is expected that a non-adaptive mutation will be deselected by the following evaluation stage, and hence be removed from future vector sets.

Evaluation and Selection of a Sampled Subgroup

The evaluation function ranks the vector's components. Vectors that comply better with the constraints obtain higher ratings and thus have a better chance of being included in the next generation, while vectors complying to a lesser degree with the specified constraints have a lower chance of survival. This evaluation forms the selection mechanism of the model; it can be manifested by a discrete function assigning only the values of 0 (expire) and 1 (survive) to each vector, or by a continuous scale allowing to assign and compare relative fitness values.

The simulation program uses the following simple polynomial comprising six time-use categories as the evaluation function:

$$F = \sum_{i=1}^{6} \beta_i \times f_i \times (\sum TU_i),$$

where F denotes the overall fitness of a particular vector, and $\Sigma\ TU_i$ denotes the sum of the time intervals spent on each of the six different time-use categories (1 = personal care, 2 = paid work, 3 = domestic work, 4 = outdoor leisure, 5 = indoor leisure, 6 = non-definable activities occurring in empirically sampled data). β (i = 1, ..., 6) denotes weights representing the strength of the contribution of each activity to the overall fitness. Systematically varying the β weights allows one to experiment with different environments comprising various time-use preferences. For instance, assigning relatively high β values to personal care will increase the overall amount of this activity and reduce the amount of the other activities in the simulated vector set. The functions f_1 to f_6 allow for the possibility of including additional non-linear relationships between the variables.

Note that the evaluation and selection stage allows complementary models to be represented, where the higher weights assigned to some activities are compensated by reduced weights of other activities. Nevertheless, it also allows conflicting interests such as those of a social dilemma to be represented. Such non-complementary models may simultaneously attempt to maximize leisure and personal care as well as paid work. Such a model is the parallel of a social dilemma where one social system accounts for both individuals' preferences and centrally imposed constraints, as demonstrated in the next section.

A Time-Use Social Dilemma

To show the effectiveness of the simulation for studying social dilemmas, we simulate three scenarios. First, we simulate only the societal, or centrally imposed, perspective; we then integrate both the individual's and the societal perspectives; and, finally, we experiment with some parameters.

We assume that a policy maker wishes to increase production and hence amplifies the pressure on paid work (either by reducing taxes or by increasing salaries). He may believe that implementing the new policy will render the population a more productive society. Figure 15.3 shows a converged vector set (after 15,000 iterations) evolved from a randomly distributed vector set (see Figure 15.2a) and evolutionary dynamics comprising (1) the constraints embedded in the recombination stage and (2) a selection function that assigns a β value of 0.8 units to every paid work activity and 0 to all five other activities. While the emerging forecast seems to comply with the policy maker's intensions, it almost completely ignores the individual's perspectives (except for using the empirical recombination constraints that account for the remaining diurnal cycles of work and personal care).

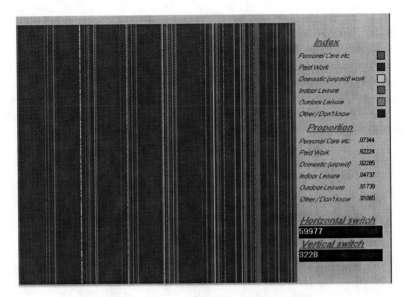

Figure 15.3 A converged time-use vector set, after 15,000 iterations, shaped by a selection function with the following β weights: personal care—0, indoor leisure—0, outdoor leisure—0, domestic work—0, paid work—0.8; and using recombination constraints estimated from the 1987 British time-use data set. The indices of horizontal and vertical switches indicate the sum of the alternations between different activities within (horizontal) and across (vertical) vectors. A small number of horizontal switches indicates the emergence of long, single-activity strings, and a small number of vertical switches indicates increasing similarity between individuals and hence the convergence of the data

To predict the actual outcome of the "increased-production" policy, we add individual preferences into the evaluation function. We use a set of satisfaction ratings collected in Britain (Sullivan, 1996) that represent the satisfaction individuals associated with various activities. Transforming the ratings into proportional selection weights and adding the increased weight to paid work, we obtain the following set of selection weights for personal care, indoor leisure, outdoor leisure, domestic work, and paid work: 0.8, 0.83, 0.91, 0.61, 0.8 (= 0.61 actual satisfaction rate with the policy amplification of 0.19), respectively. Clearly, individuals prefer to spend time on outdoor and indoor leisure activities or on their personal care, rather than working. These preferences contradict the policy of increased production, and hence turn into a non-compensational model or a typical social dilemma structure.

Figure 15.4 shows five stages in the emerging time-use vector set, sampled while developing toward its converged form. The outcome after 15,000 iterations is considerably different from that depicted in Figure 15.3. It shows less than 10% of time being given to paid work and would have probably been regarded as a failure of the increased production policy. However, since this outcome is only a simulation result, the policy maker can further experiment with the increased production policy and observe its expected outcome under various parameters. For example, we continue to increase the weights of paid work to 0.84 and 0.86 (Figures 15.5 and 15.6, respectively) and observe the new converged vector sets, or forecasts. Surprisingly, these relatively minor changes give rise to 22% and 28% of time being spent on paid work activities.

Naturally, the simulation itself cannot decide whether the required selection pressure put on paid work is a feasible policy. Some policies may be too harsh to materialize. In these cases, the simulation can help in preventing policy makers from setting too ambitious goals.

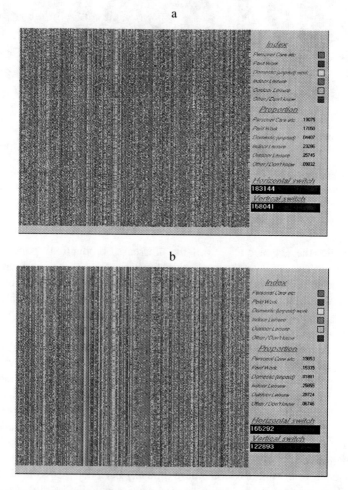

Figure 15.4 Five snap shots along the convergence of a time-use vector set after 3,000, 6,000, 8,000, 11,000, and 15,000 iterations, shaped by a selection function with the following β weights: personal care—0.8, indoor leisure—0.83, outdoor leisure—0.91, domestic work—0.61, paid work—0.8; and using recombination constraints estimated from the 1987 British time-use data set

c

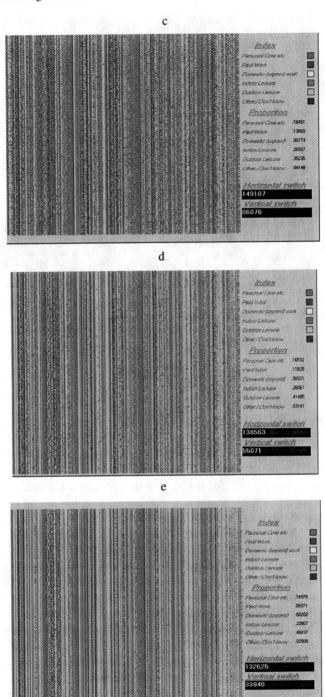

d

e

Figure 15.4 (continued)

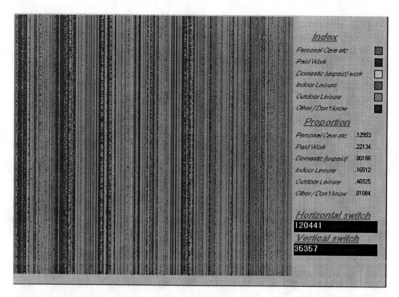

Figure 15.5 A converged time-use vector set, after 15,000 iterations, shaped by a selection function with the following β weights: personal care—0.8, indoor leisure—0.83, outdoor leisure—0.91, domestic work—0.61, paid work—0.86; and using recombination constraints estimated from the 1987 British time-use data set

Conclusions

Studying and predicting the outcomes of a social dilemma are complicated tasks that go beyond the understanding of its underlying structure. In real life, individuals are trying to optimize several goals that are interconnected and affected in different manners by governmental or other centrally imposed policies. The involved processes function long before their products become visible and change the social structure. In this chapter, I was trying to show that genetic algorithm-based simulations are vehicles for reproducing social processes and studying their long-term impacts. The qualities of the genetic algorithm that allow it to function on the basis of relative, rather than absolute, fitness and without having to define individuals' cognitions and intentions seem to provide both social scientists and policy makers with a relatively simple platform for examining and predicting social change.

Clearly, such simulations need to undergo reliability and validity examination. While the reliability of a simulated model can be established by its almost unlimited replications, assessing its validity is a more intricate process, which requires long-term empirical data collection that can be compared with the simulation's predictions. For most social issues, it is highly unlikely that such data are available in sufficient detail to enable the validation of the simulation tool. Nevertheless, in spite of this and other limitations, genetic algorithms enable us to experiment with the complexity of social variables and outline a predicted course of expected changes. In many cases where

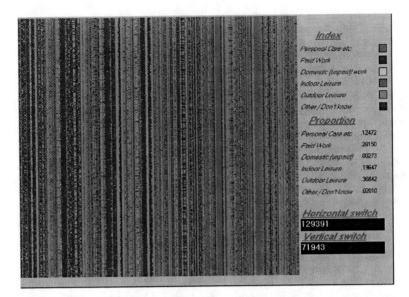

Figure 15.6 Five snap shots along the convergence of a time-use vector set after 3,000, 6,000, 8,000, 11,000, and 15,000 iterations, shaped by a selection function with the following β weights: personal care—0.8, indoor leisure—0.83, outdoor leisure—0.91, domestic work—0.61, paid work—0.86; and using recombination constraints estimated from the 1987 British time-use data set

data are missing and experiments are impossible to conduct, simulations are the only tools for studying social forces and attempting to forecast their development. For example, in our simulation, the effect of putting more weight on paid work was not reflected in an equivalent increase in the time individuals spent working. The behavioral norms embedded in the recombination rules together with the attempt of individuals to pursue their private goals hindered the imposed policy from having the expected consequences. Still, a small additional increase of the weights assigned to paid work almost tripled its impact. These non-linear interactions mirror the complexity and the interdependent nature of actual social dilemmas.

Acknowledgments This research was supported by the Israel Science Foundation funded by the Academy of Sciences and Humanities.

References

Axelrod, R. (1980a). Effective choice in the prisoner's dilemma. *Journal of Conflict Resolution,* *24*, 3–25.

Axelrod, R. (1980b). More effective choice in the prisoner's dilemma. *Journal of Conflict Resolution, 24*, 379–403.

Axelrod, R. (1981). The emergence of cooperation among egoists. *American Political Science Review, 75*, 306–318.

Axelrod, R. (1984). *The Evolution of Cooperation*. New York: Basic Books.

Axelrod, R. (1986). An evolutionary approach to norms. *American Political Science Review, 80,* 1095–1111.

Chattoe, E. (1998). Just how (un)realistic are evolutionary algorithms as representations of social processes? *Journal of Artificial Societies and Social Simulations, 1*(3). http:/www.soc.surrey. ac.uk/JASSS/1/3/2.html.

Dasgupta, D., Michalewicz, Z. (1997). Evolutionary algorithms—An overview. In D. Dasgupta & Z. Michalewicz (eds.), *Evolutionary Algorithms in Engineering Applications* (pp. 3–28). Berlin: Springer-Verlag.

Fischer, I., Suleiman, R. (1997). The emergence of cooperation in a simulated intergroup conflict. *Journal of Conflict Resolution, 41,* 483–508.

Fischer, I., Sullivan, O. (2007). Evolutionary modeling of time-use vectors. *Journal of Economic Behavior and Organization*.

Gershuny, J. (2000). *Changing Times*. Oxford: Oxford University Press.

Gershuny, J., Sullivan, O. (1998). Sociological uses of time-use diary data. *European Sociological Review, 14,* 69–85.

Gorrini, V., Dorigo, M. (1996). An application of evolutionary algorithms to the scheduling of robotic operations In J. M. Alliot, E. Lutton, E. Ronald & M. Schoenauer (eds.), *Artificial Evolution*. New York: Anchor Books.

Holland, J. (1975). *Adaptation in Natural and Artificial Systems*. Ann Arbor: University of Michigan Press.

Latane, B., Nowak, A. (1997). Self-organizing social systems: Necessary and sufficient conditions for the emergence of consolidation, clustering, and continuing diversity. In G. Barnett & F. Boster (eds.), *Progress in Communication Sciences: Persuasion* (Vol. 13, pp. 43–74). Norwood, NJ: Ablex.

Robinson, J. P (1997). *Time for Life: The Surprising Ways Americans Use Their Time*. Philadelphia: Pennsylvania State University Press.

Saam, N. J., Harrer, A. (1999). Simulating norms, social inequality, and functional change in artificial societies. *Journal of Artificial Societies and Social Simulation, 2*(1). http://www.soc.surrey.ac.uk/JASSS/2/1/2.html.

Sullivan, O. (1996). The enjoyment of activities: Do couples affect each others' well-being? *Social Indicators Research, 38,* 81–102.

Chapter 16
Toward a Comprehensive Model of Social Dilemmas

Robert Gifford

I am honored to have been asked to write a concluding chapter for this valuable book, which represents the cutting edge of research in an area that may be called, without exaggeration I believe, "a matter of life and death" (Gifford, 2002b). This collection of authors certainly represents the most sophisticated thinking in the domain of social dilemmas, and therefore the challenge of attempting to sensibly comment on, summarize, or synthesize their collectively magnificent and manifold thoughts is a special one.

Before I leave the theme that this research area is crucially important and the well-earned flattery, I feel compelled to rant—at the risk of alienating some authors and readers—about the use of certain terms in this literature. Presumably because research on social dilemmas developed in part from game theory, some researchers and authors continue to use the terms "players" and "games" to describe the participants and paradigms in their studies. The use of these terms may well suggest, to academics from other areas of science, to students, to the general public, to funding agencies, and to research participants that the topic is not serious, that social dilemmas and decisions made in studies of them may be treated lightly, and that winning is the goal; why else do people "play games"? Therefore, let us retire these terms, given that our studies pertain to important global issues. Many alternative terms are available for use: participants, decision makers, contributors, paradigms, procedures, and micro worlds are among the possibilities.

The Problem, and the Nay-Sayers

I will briefly restate the central issues in resource dilemmas and public-goods problems, that is, more generally, in social dilemmas. Each person and each group in this world curates a stream of natural resources that have been transformed into usable goods. Whenever we use a vehicle for transport, turn on a light, buy clothing, read a book, or even eat a carrot, natural resources have been transformed into products that are consumed and, usually but not always, one or more undesirable products (e.g., garbage, smoke, greenhouse gases, excess fertilizers, or toxic chemicals) are added to the environment. Of course, we need to consume some of these transformed natural resources to survive. Just as clearly, some persons consume far more than others and usually find it easy to justify their consumption.

A. Biel et al. (eds.), *New Issues and Paradigms in Research on Social Dilemmas.*
© Springer 2008

Mindfully or not, individuals and groups use resources along a continuum that ranges from pure community or environmental interest to pure self-interest. Public-goods problems are, in many ways, similar. Individuals and groups decide whether to support common goals and projects. They donate (or not).

In either case, decisions are made, decisions that constitute the management of resources. Whether those decisions reflect the taking or the giving of resources, decision makers face social dilemmas in which their personal interest appears to conflict with the common interest. Certainly, much management is done by governments, corporations, and other organizations, but individuals are faced with their own management problems. To varying degrees, they monitor their personal use of resources, observe the effects that their usage or donations have on the environment, and are aware of the choices made by other individuals.

Not everyone agrees that self-interest and the community interest *are* in conflict. Adam Smith (1776) asserted that acting in one's self-interest benefits humankind, and more recent writers such as the economist Julian Simon (1980) and the political scientist Bjorn Lomborg (2001) agree. Simon closed his book with an explicit restatement of Smith's famous dictum. Lomborg claims a conversion experience, from being a Greenpeace supporter to believing in something close to the Smith–Simon viewpoint. These economists believe that environmental problems are exaggerated. In contrast, William Lloyd (1837/1968) long ago pointed out that when natural resources are finite, widespread self-interest must eventually have fatal, rather than beneficial, consequences. The Simonites prefer to believe that in a functional sense, resources probably are not finite.

Public-goods problems appear to be less controversial in that no one denies that if enough contributors do not appear, the public good will not be realized. No one denies that there *are* public-goods problems. However, Simon (1980) argued that a greater population will produce more humans, from which one may expect more contributors to the public good, including very rich ones like Andrew Carnegie and Bill Gates, and that these greater numbers and wealthy persons will always step to the fore, in Smithian invisible-hand fashion, to save the day.

Simon and other nay-sayers do admit that real problems exist, at least in the short term, but have faith that in the long term, all will be well, primarily based on their contention that so far in history everything *is* getting better, at least for *this* species. Perhaps one way of resolving what seem to be irreconcilable differences between these optimistic economists and many authors in this book is to believe that environmentalists *are* the invisible hands that are guiding society toward salvation from environmental disaster. If so, the ideas described in this book are essential.

Toward a Comprehensive Model

And so, to business. For about three decades before the conference that forms the basis of this volume, social scientists have investigated influences on the decisions made by individuals in *n*-person dilemmas (cf. Dawes, 1973), which developed into studies of decisions about how to use the transformed natural resources that come within their reach, and decisions about whether to contribute to the common good. For the most part, individual studies have focused on one or a few influences. A number of earlier reviews, chapters, and books have, usually in narrative fashion, summarized these influences (e.g., Dawes, 1980; Gifford, 2002a, Chapter 14; Komorita & Parks, 1994; Liebrand et al., 1992; Schroeder, 1995; Shulz et al., 1994; Suleiman et al., 2004).

For the last several years, I have set myself the goal of integrating these many influences on and outcomes of social dilemmas into a coherent and comprehensive model (Gifford, 2002a, 2005). The value of models is that they postulate relations among key influences and help to represent complex systems in understandable ways. They can stimulate investigation of the properties of the system and suggest predictions of future outcomes. Initially, I considered that influences on cooperation could be grouped into those associated with the resource itself (its abundance, its regeneration rate, etc.), the individual decision makers (their values and experience, for example), relations among decision makers (trust and communication, for example), and the structure of the dilemma (the rules that govern harvesting) (Gifford, 1987). Since then, the model has been expanding and relations among these categories of influence have been described and investigated. In a meta-analysis Donald Hine and I conducted (1991), about 30 different influences could be identified. This gradually led to the attempt to create a comprehensive model, mainly so I could comprehend this plethora of factors in a more organized way.

The antecedent influences on dilemma decisions may be grouped into five major categories, as shown in Figure 16.1: geophysical, governance, interpersonal, decision-maker, and dilemma-awareness influences on decision making. The sixth category concerns the various strategies that decision makers actually employ. Finally, two kinds of outcomes form categories seven and eight: those for the decision maker and those for the environment (including the resource itself, the environment in general, and for other people in the community). The model is meant to apply to both main forms of social dilemmas, resource and public goods.

The eight categories require brief introductions. First, the harvesting of resources, often in their original, pre-transformed form, is affected by important non-human factors such as the elusiveness of the resource itself (e.g., wild game), extraction difficulties (e.g., mining for gold, squeezing oil from tar sands), weather (e.g., fishing in a storm), the scarcity of the resource (e.g., finding water during a drought), or uncertainty about the amount of the resource (e.g., estimates of remaining oil reserves). These *geophysical influences* are non-human, but they cannot be ignored as important factors in a comprehensive model that describes the human consumption of resources, and sometimes whether contributions are made to the public good (disasters may reduce local donations and increase donations from afar, for example). Resources may decline for different reasons, and this affects cooperation. Generally, more harvesting occurs when a resource is abundant than when it is scarce, but this difference is magnified when the cause of depletion is natural rather than when it is human (Rutte et al., 1987). If decision makers think that other *people* are depleting the resource, they want to take more too, but if *nature* is depleting the resource, we are more willing to restrain our harvests. Donations to charities decline when the annual goal is met.

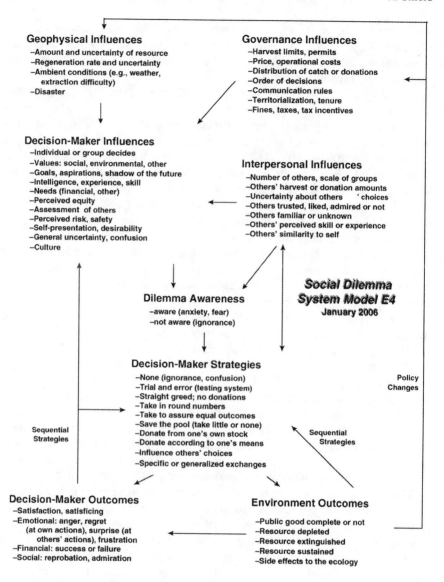

Figure 16.1 The proposed general model of social dilemmas

Second, resource harvesting and contributions to public goods are rarely, perhaps never, entirely free of constraints, and so a variety of legislated, market, and customary rules are applied to harvesting and donating (not that the rules are always followed; in the everyday world, regulations are influences, not absolute determinants). Among these *governance influences* (or "rules and regulations") are harvest limits, prices, tax incentives for giving, the creation of harvest territories, legal entitlements, organizational pressure to donate, guidelines for fair use, penalties for overuse, and regulations or customs concerning communication (e.g., of harvest amounts, mandated communication by and among the decision makers, etc.). It must be noted that some social dilemmas are managed well; in some places, hunted wildlife such as ducks and deer are managed relatively well by systems of permits, seasons, and hunting rules. Some local fisheries are well-managed through local customs (Leal, 1998). Some public goods work very well. We can and should learn from these examples of successful management, but there are many social dilemmas that are *not* working, too.

Third, decision makers are influenced by other decision makers. Mutual trust, conformity, competition, kinship or friendship ties, and the nature of informal (non-mandated) communication are some of these *interpersonal influences*. Non-decision makers, such as family members or observers who are not decision makers, may well also exert some interpersonal influence. Those others do not even have to be personally known; when decision makers know that strangers have attitudes identical to their own, they cooperate more (Smith et al., 1988).

Fourth, each decision maker has a set of motivations, cognitions, abilities, mission statements, experience, values, skills, experience, resources (e.g., financial, tools, information, and assistants), aspirations, intelligence, need, and perceptions of equity or social comparison that influences harvesting. All these factors are located within the decision maker, and so this category is called *decision-maker influences*.

Fifth, we have noticed in our studies, and anecdotal evidence from the everyday world strongly suggests, that not every decision maker who is, objectively, in a social dilemma realizes that. A campaign to donate blood may not have reached some persons; some fishers have never heard of resource dilemmas, even in some vernacular form. Yet other decision makers experience the dilemma to various degrees, from mild concern or amusement (the latter perhaps most often among participants who have been told they are "playing a game") to acute concern or even psychological distress. Thus, the model includes *dilemma awareness*, the degree to which being in a dilemma is experienced *as* a dilemma, as a crucial influence on cooperation. Although dilemma awareness is important, it is often overlooked because experimenters usually make the dilemma clearly salient to their participants.

Sixth, as a presumed consequence of all the five previous categories of influence, decision makers adopt some strategy, or a series of strategies. These *decision-maker strategies* include such classic plans as "getting what you can," "saving the environment," and "taking what others take." However, from our qualitative studies, we have also learned that some decision makers employ the "strategy" of doing nothing that seems particularly strategic, such as "trying out the system" (e.g., Hine & Gifford, 1997).

Less obvious, perhaps, but certainly real, is the class of social dilemma strategies that might be called *reverse decisions*: for example, when harvesters donate resources back to the pool, as when a lumber company finances a tree-planting project, or someone removes a resource from a public good, for example, embezzling money from a charity. One study supported the notion that when donations are possible, the resource depletes less quickly (Naseth, 1990), and others demonstrate that theft does occur (Edney & Bell, 1984).

Decision makers sometimes surprise: Although some are greedy, others are altruistic and do not even wait for an authority to tell them they can donate (cf. tree-planting as a donation practice imposed on logging companies). One of the most touching moments in my own research career occurred when a 4-year-old girl in one study saw that the resources (walnuts that could be traded later for cookies) were quickly disappearing from the bowl that held them. The other 4-year-olds were in sheer greed mode. This girl looked at the bowl, looked at her own stash, looked at me, and then put some of her own walnuts back into the bowl.

Sometimes participants harvest according to needs or goals that are only dimly related to the dilemma. For example, we once interviewed decision makers after each season in a fishing simulation and were told by one that she took a few extra fish because she imagined that some guests were coming to dinner that day (Gifford, 1994). This may have been idiosyncratic, but one wonders how many decision makers base their choices on rationales that are far from the neatly postulated IV-based decision making that researchers assume is occurring. Almost all social dilemma experiments apply a set of conditions to the participants and then measure objective differences in cooperative behavior. Such a strategy ignores the thinking processes engaged in by participants as they face the dilemma.

Therefore, it is important to examine the "online" thinking processes of group members as they grapple with the dilemma (Hine & Gifford, 1997). One way to do this is grounded theory analysis (e.g., Strauss & Corbin, 1990). Such qualitative approaches, or at least interviews of decision makers, could be employed more often than the extant literature suggests that they are being used now. We need to "get inside the heads" of decision makers. The results, in some instances, can be startling.

Whatever strategies or non-strategies are used by individual decision makers, they have immensely important consequences, particularly once they are aggregated. These consequences may be divided into those for the decision makers and those for resource, the environment, and the community. The seventh category, *decision-maker outcomes,* ranges from becoming wealthy, to breaking even, to losing everything. In resource dilemmas, this is the familiar range of consequences; in public-goods situations, the decision maker may receive tax breaks and social recognition for contributing, receive the benefits of free-riding if others successfully support the public good, or personally suffer a loss because the good was not established.

The eighth category includes *environmental outcomes,* ranging from extinction to sustainability to an increase in abundance in the resource in question (as when an endangered species is rescued by a successful conservation program or, in public-goods contexts, the failure or success of the project or organization). They also include epiphenomenal outcomes for the environment: For resource dilemmas, reductions in a resource of interest often have some ecological consequence for other flora, fauna, or non-living yet important components of the ecosystem, and for public goods, this might be unemployment for staff and the economic loss to the community. Community outcomes represent the consequences for those who do not make decisions but must live with the consequences of those decisions. For example, when a species is extinguished, most people did not directly kill it, but they will never see a live example of that animal or plant again. On the positive side, when organ donation campaigns are successful, someone who may not have made a decision either way about donating organs may benefit from others' decisions by receiving a donated organ. All of us who move into a community that has established public goods, whether by being born into it or through immigration, benefit without having contributed as a decision maker.

Such a listing of influence and outcome categories is fairly straightforward. Postulating links *among* them is both more interesting and more challenging. For example, some decision makers' strategy is geared toward sending a message to other decision makers; the explicit message of some participants in our resource dilemma studies has been, for example, "Look, I am taking a sustainable amount and I want you to do the same." Hence, a causal link exists between *decision-maker strategies* and *interpersonal influences*. At the larger social scale, consequences for resources (*environmental outcomes*) often are reflected in changes in policies or regulations (*governance influences*). These hypothesized links between categories, and the conditions under which influence occurs or does not occur, represent the heuristic value of the model. The reader may easily postulate other links among the model's categories.

The objective of this chapter is to identify how the ideas presented earlier in this volume complement and supplement this developing model. Figure 16.1 represents some updates from its predecessor (Gifford, 2002b) based on insights I was privileged to glean from the chapters in this volume.

Complementary and Supplementary Ideas

In reviewing the contributions to this symposium, the foregoing chapters, one may see how each supplements the model, or finds a place in it. For example, Ngan and Au (Chapter 13) describe the somewhat neglected influence called "protocol of play" (Budescu et al., 1997). As Ngan and Au note, the information that each person possesses when making a decision is "determined by the various institutional arrangements that control the nature of the interactions" between the individuals and their access to the resource. When participants were assigned a place in the harvest sequence requests, Budescu et al. (1997) found, was greatest by the first decision maker and least by the final decision maker. Ngan and Au and others are therefore sensitive to the second category in the model, *governance influences*. Thus, protocol of play affects *decision-maker strategies*, that is, the actual pattern of resource choices made by those in the dilemma.

Decision makers are only new to a dilemma once. Much more often, one presumes, decision makers have made decisions more than once, and therefore have some experience with choices in social dilemmas. What is "the effect of having a common history on decision making in social dilemmas" (van Dijk et al., Chapter 4)? Experience is one of many decision-maker characteristics that reflects the fourth of the the model's categories, *decision-maker influences*. The effect of experience on defection versus cooperation is also affected, as van Dijk et al. point out, by other personal characteristics, such as social values, as well as by factors from the other main categories of influence, including trust (from the *interpersonal influence* category) and structural factors (from the *governance influence* category). Clearly, no "simple and sovereign" theory (George, cited in Allport, 1954) can explain decisions made in social dilemmas: The truth is multi-determined and lies in interactions within and between influences. That decision-maker experience plays an important role also shows the impact of feedback loops. In the model, *decision-maker outcomes* are proposed to affect *decision-maker influences* and the *decision-maker strategies* of participants. Illustrative of an interaction between *decision-maker influences* and *governance influences* is the finding that men and women as a whole cooperate about equally, but men cooperate more—and women do not—when group members trust one another and can communicate with each other (Moore et al., 1987).

Another good example of this is provided by the work of Eek and Gärling (Chapter 2, this volume). Social values (*decision-maker influences*) generally are thought to be associated with cooperative choices in resource dilemmas. One school of thought is that cooperation is actualized by the participant's goals or aspirations (another *decision-maker influence*) that result in maximized outcomes for self and other (*decision-maker outcomes*). However, Eek and Gärling convincingly make the case that a different goal—equal outcomes for all decision makers—often is more influential than the joint maximization goal. Thus, choices presumably are a function of social values *and* goals, rather than social values *or* goals.

Decision makers usually are investigated in this literature as individuals, but in the everyday world, decisions are sometimes, perhaps usually, made by groups such as boards of directors or government committees. Recognizing this, Bornstein (Chapter 3) examines how individuals and two kinds of groups make decisions, and which kinds of strategic decision making they employ. Groups may be largely unified in their goals and decisions, or not cooperative. Kazemi and Eek (Chapter 6) also demonstrate the importance of considering the group as a decision maker. Group goals (as well as individual goals) can affect the decisions made in a social dilemma. Clearly, given the ecological validity of the group as a decision maker, this is an important direction for research to take. The model's *decision-maker influences* category obviously must include groups as well as individuals as the decision makers. Its *decision-maker strategies* category includes several popular strategies used by decision makers, and a link is necessary from that category to the *interpersonal influences* category, thereby postulating that strategies used by decision makers will influence such within-group factors as trust, admiration, and perceived similarity to self.

The sense of fairness and justice, and the procedures designed to achieve these goals, are an essential part of public-goods and resource dilemmas. Probably every researcher in the area, and certainly I, has heard at least figurative and sometimes literal cries of revenge or anguish from participants who found the actions of others reprehensible. Therefore, justice-related issues cannot be ignored in social dilemma contexts. In their game-theoretical analyses of social dilemmas, Ostmann and Meinhardt (Chapter 14) show how fairness considerations can be modeled.

By introducing bargaining concepts, they point out that communication and non-binding agreements among rational actors are likely to increase the wealth for all involved parties. Schroeder et al. (Chapter 9) consider four justice systems: distributive, procedural, restorative, and retributive. Justice systems may be imposed from above (*governance influences*), or agreed-upon by decision makers (*interpersonal influences*) but then implemented *as* rules and regulations, thus creating a link between those two categories.

Quite a number of studies have investigated the implications for cooperation in social dilemmas as a function of rules for distribution, governance, or justice. Schroeder et al. believe that procedural justice systems will be more stable and cooperation-inducing than distributive justice systems, and they explicitly argue that although such systems are best created through communication and agreements among those most affected (the decision makers), they should become instituted as structural (i.e., rules and regulations) solutions to the eternal problem of transgressions in the commons.

Another essential element of the social dilemma is trust (or the lack of it). When decision makers remove less of the resource than they could have, or donors make a sizable contribution, many of them are trusting in a norm of fairness and reciprocity that, unfortunately, is not always shared by other decision makers. For example, laboratory studies show that stealing from others in the commons is frequent (Edney & Bell, 1984). Another factor, a sense of community or group identity, is important (Dawes & Messick, 2000) and can provide a positive glow in the dilemma. Apparently, not much is required to create enough group identity to improve cooperation. In one study, the only difference between "high-identity" and "low-identity" participants was that the high-identity participants came to the lab and received their instructions together, yet the high-identity harvesters cooperated more (Samuelson & Hannula, 2001). When harvesters think of themselves more as individuals than as group members, they overharvest more (Tindall & O'Connor, 1987).

As an example of how decision-maker influences are affected by geophysical influences, Brann and Foddy (1987) showed that less trusting participants harvested at about the same rate regardless of how fast the resource disappeared, but more trusting participants harvested more when the resource was depleting slowly and less when the resource was rapidly disappearing. Thus, trusting harvesters seem to be sensitive to the rate of resource depletion, but distrusting harvesters seem not to be. Foddy and Dawes (Chapter 5) report that trust is greater for others who are believed to be part of one's own group, even if the decision maker knows little or nothing else beyond membership about the other decision maker. This much seems intuitive enough; one expects others on one's team or work unit (usually!) or one's religious faith to be more cooperative than others who are not. Trust within groups clearly is part of the *interpersonal influences* category.

Groups, however, can be constituted at multiple levels. At the largest scale, do citizens of a given country trust others citizens of the country more than citizens of other countries? At the smallest scale, would they trust members of their own family more than others? What of the mid-range? Do players on a team trust other players in the same sport (even those not on the same team, but similar only in that they play the same game) more than those who do not play the sport? The issue of group *scale* and trust may need further research.

Uncertainty can be a factor in every part of the model, from uncertainty about geophysical influences to uncertainty about quantitative and qualitative outcomes. For example, if a fisher takes several tonnes of fish from a lake, it would not be difficult to measure the weight or number of fish taken. However, uncertainty about the effect of this harvest on the lake's ecology or whether the fisher was wrong to take the fish is not easily decided. In sum, certainty may exist *only* in the laboratory. For that reason, ecological validity in this area demands more studies of uncertainty in all the categories of the model.

McGinnis and Ostrom (Chapter 12) approach the problem of common resources from a political science perspective and quite naturally ask whether the often optimistic results obtained by social scientists who work at the small-group level would apply at larger scales. Of course, this question has been haunting psychologists for many years (e.g., Edney, 1981), particularly when many studies show a decline in cooperation as the size of the harvesting group grows, even in fairly small groups (by societal standards) of 3 versus 7 (e.g., Sato, 1989). Nearly every study of group size has found that behavior in resource management tends increasingly toward self-interest as group size increases. Cooperation declines both as the number of decision makers rises and as the number of groups *within* a commons with a constant total membership rises (Komorita & Lapworth, 1982).

There are some good reasons for this. First, as group size increases, the harm from any one participant's greed is spread thinner among the other participants: no single other decision maker is badly hurt. Second, violations of sustainability or failures to donate are often less visible to others in larger groups. Third, in large groups, the effect of the harm done to other decision makers often is less visible to the violator (Edney, 1981); it is easier to inflict pain if one does not have to watch the victim experience pain. Fourth, negative feedback or sanctions to violators or free riders are increasingly difficult to manage in larger groups.

Obviously, McGinnis and Ostrom's ideas complement the *governance influence* portion of the model, but they greatly expand the nature of that element of the model by describing eight "design elements" that institutions and governments would have to implement to facilitate sustainable resource management. Some of these, for example, clearly defined boundaries, echo ideas and findings from small-scale studies, in which the term "territorialization" usually is used. Although monitoring is another element of the model drawn from small-scale studies, McGinnis and Ostrom correctly point out that outside the laboratory this monitoring of harvest practices and consequences often requires high-tech "eyes" such as satellite cameras, as opposed to proximate human scanning. Others of their design elements also reflect small-scale model elements, such as the use of sanctions for violators and the rights of participants to set and change the rules.

Yet other design elements (e.g., conflict-resolution mechanisms at the local level) are implied in some small-scale investigations by the opportunity to communicate (or not) among decision makers, but rarely implemented in experiments as a manipulated factor. McGinnis and Ostrom add to the familiar list of factors that promote cooperation in the commons with their notion of nested enterprises, that is, *layers* of governance: Most small-scale studies include no more than one level of governance, and often governance does not appear at all as a factor in small-scale studies.

In general, McGinnis and Ostrom's chapter is a valuable reminder of the generalizability problem that small-scale researchers face, yet once one translates the eight design elements into language that is familiar to, for example, psychologists who work in this area, some elements become familiar. This is reassuring; if the design elements associated with sustainable resource management at the societal or global level were completely unanticipated by small-scale theorists, the prospects for progress would be frighteningly daunting. However, identifying the design elements and noting that many are similar to those known to small-scale researchers is not the same thing as enabling the design elements in the real world. The tremendous challenge of implementing the eight design elements remains.

After becoming familiar with work such as that of McGinnis and Ostrom's at the political science level, some researchers or theorists may fear that what is found in small-group research lacks credibility. What can we really learn from a resource simulation in which three or six people manage a common resource pool in a laboratory, when political scientists and economists are studying real situations, such as international whaling or water use in the Middle East? The answers are systematic control of factors and experimental realism. The ability to systematically vary the conditions under which participants manage resources permits small-scale researchers to test theories in scientifically pure ways. The results do need to be cross-checked at the larger scale, where experimental control is impossible, but without experimental control, one can never be sure whether a given factor is influential or not.

Many small-scale studies have demonstrated the mundane realism of laboratory micro worlds. Even small payoffs can produce behavior that *seems* quite similar to that which could be expected in a real, valuable, limited commons. In one study in which participants could win no more than $10.50, participants were so caught up in the dilemma that defectors were sworn at, and unrequited cooperators cried, stormed out of the room, and told defectors they "would have to live with their decisions for the rest of their lives" (Dawes et al., 1977). Other researchers with similarly small payoffs have reported equally strong responses. Some participants have threatened ("jokingly") to beat up defectors, to destroy their reputations, and even to kill them (Bonacich, 1976)! In my own lab, subjects have said such things as "You greedy pig!" and "You die!" and "I could have smashed some heads" (Tindall & O'Connor, 1987).

Thus, despite the lack of field investigations, the research using simulations of commons dilemmas may have reasonable validity. Of course, the small- and large-scale dynamics of social dilemmas are directly connected: The crucial aspect of micro-level resource management is that it sums up across thousands or millions of decision makers to the macro level in mysterious, irrational, yet all-important ways.

Exchange, by its very nature, implies at least two parties who give and receive. Exchange is not a necessary part of social dilemmas, in the sense that some decision makers may see the situation solely as an opportunity to take (in resource dilemmas) or to avoid contributing (in public-goods problems), without consideration of others. Not to see social dilemmas as inherent exchanges may represent a primitive viewpoint, but one that does, unfortunately, exist. Once exchange begins, however, strategy, in benign or malign forms, follows closely. Mashima and Takahashi (Chapter 10) consider the nature of social exchange, in particular generalized exchanges, in which one does not donate directly to another. In public-goods problems, some decision makers may wish to direct their donations to specific *kinds* of organizations, without being so restrictive as to specify a particular recipient.

For example, where I live, an omnibus charity exists in which management hopes that donors will donate to a general fund that the organizers can parcel out according to some rational or need-based manner. However, the charity recognizes that some donors prefer that their money goes to certain recipient groups and that other donors wish to be sure that their money does *not* go to certain other groups. For this reason, and to maximize its total donations, the omnibus charity allows donors to target their donations. In terms of the model, these considerations clearly fall into the *decision-maker strategies* category and certainly relate to the link labeled strategic influence, which points back at the *interpersonal influences* category.

In Chapter 8, Samid and Suleiman examine a variety of strategies that an authority might use to elicit cooperation. The authors' assumption is that some coercion is necessary, and they explore the forms and limits of coercion that might best bring about a beneficial balance of exchanges. In this sense, Samid and Suleiman link the *governance influence* and *decision-maker strategies* categories and usefully supplement the model through their observation that authorities as well as decision makers engage in strategic efforts.

Decision makers in the real world do not have equal economic or political power. Kopelman (Chapter 11) explores these power differentials, as well as their cultural backdrops. This reference to differences in resources reflects the model's *decision-maker influences* category; that decision makers are products of different cultural traditions also does so.

In their chapter (7) on sanctions in social dilemmas, Shinada and Yamagishi masterfully review the history of research inspired by Hobbes's *Leviathan*. The obvious goal of sanctioning those who harvest too much or fail to contribute to the common good is to influence that malfeasant. Overlooked in that simplistic view is the interest of others in the dilemma, onlookers who wish to cooperate (e.g., Yamagishi, 1986). The "indirect effect" of sanctioning is to assure, or reassure, these would-be cooperators that it is safe to cooperate. But how strong is that effect, given that direct sanctioning of the non-cooperator seems strong and salient? Apparently, the indirect effect is about as strong as the direct effect (Eek et al., 2002; Yamagishi et al., 2005). In terms of the proposed model, sanctions clearly belong to the governance influences category. The "added value" for the model is the knowledge that the indirect effects of sanctions affect decision-maker influences, by changing a participant's assessment of others, and perhaps of the governance process itself.

In Chapter 14, Fischer sets out to demonstrate that genetic algorithm-based simulations are fit vehicles for reproducing social processes in social dilemmas and studying their long-term effects. Although he uses a very different paradigm from that employed to develop the current model, Fischer shares with it the goal of achieving a macro-scale image of social dilemmas. Beginning from the Axelrod (1984) perspective on group competition, Fischer develops a rationale for using time-use diaries and decision-maker goals to explain the eventual outcome of dilemmas with different sets of parameters. For this writer, Fischer's chapter doubly highlights the complexity of the problem confronting social dilemma researchers: seeing the same "elephant" with very different disciplinary eyes, and seeing how very complex the elephant really is.

The chapters in this book have touched on, reinforced, and supplemented the model, for which I am grateful. Certainly, it is more sophisticated than it was without the insights provided in this book. Its several influence categories, each with numerous individual factors, illustrate the complex causal and interactive dynamics that affect cooperation or the lack of it in social dilemma. In addition to these multiple causes, we have proposed that over the course of a commons dilemma, different influences are strongest at different times (Gifford & Hine, 1997). This is reflected in the "sequential strategy" note in the model. Nevertheless, however helpful a comprehensive model might be for visualizing the big picture in social dilemmas, the challenge for all of us is to find ways to encourage those influences that promote cooperation and sustainability.

References

Allport, G. W. (1954). The historical background of modern social psychology. In G. Lindzey (ed.), *Handbook of Social Psychology* (Vol. 1, pp. 3–56). Reading, MA: Addison-Wesley.

Axelrod, R. (1984) *The Evolution of Cooperation*. New York: Basic Books.

Bonacich, P. (1976). Secrecy and solidarity. *Sociometry, 39,* 200–208.

Brann, P., Foddy, M. (1987). Trust and the consumption of a deteriorating common resource. *Journal of Conflict Resolution, 31,* 615–630.

Budescu, D. V., Au, W. T., Chen, X. P. (1997). Effect of protocol of play and social orientation on behavior in sequential resource dilemmas. *Experimental Behavior and Human Decision Processes, 65,* 179–193.

Dawes, R. M. (1973). The commons dilemma game: An N-person mixed motive game with a dominating strategy for defection. *ORI Research Bulletin, 13,* 1–12.

Dawes, R. M. (1980). Social dilemmas. *Annual Review of Psychology, 31,* 169–193.

Dawes, R. M., McTavish, J., Shaklee, H. (1977). Behavior communication and assumptions about other people's behavior in a common dilemma situation. *Journal of Personality and Social Psychology, 35,* 1–11.

Dawes, R. M., Messick, D. M. (2000). Social dilemmas. *International Journal of Psychology, 35,* 111–116.

Edney, J. J. (1981). Paradoxes on the commons: Scarcity and the problem of equality. *Journal of Community Psychology, 9,* 3–34.

Edney, J. J. (1984). Rationality and social justice. *Human Relations, 37,* 163–180.

Edney, J. J., Bell, P. A. (1984). Sharing scarce resources: Group-outcome orientation, external disaster, and stealing in a simulated commons. *Small Group Behavior, 15,* 87–108.

Eek, D., Loukopoulos, P., Fujii, S., Gärling, T. (2002). Spill-over effects of intermittent costs for defection in social dilemmas. *European Journal of Social Psychology, 32,* 801–813.

Gifford, R. (1987). *Environmental Psychology: Principles and Practice* (1st ed.). Newton, MA: Allyn and Bacon.

Gifford, R. (1994). A community study of the commons dilemma. Unpublished study, Department of Psychology, University of Victoria.

Gifford, R. (2002a). *Environmental Psychology: Principles and Practice* (3rd ed.). Colville, WA: Optimal Books.

Gifford, R. (2002b). Resource management: A matter of life and death. Keynote address to the International Association of Applied Psychology, Singapore.

Gifford, R. (2005). Resource dilemmas: A perspective from environmental psychology. Keynote address to the Nordic Environmental Social Science Conference, Gothenburg, June 2005.

Gifford, R., Hine, D. W. (1997).Toward cooperation in commons dilemmas. *Canadian Journal of Behavioural Sciences, 29*, 167–179.

Hine, D. W., Gifford, R. (1991). The commons dilemma: A quantitative review. Canadian Psychological Association annual meetings, Calgary, June.

Hine, D. W., Gifford, R. (1997). What harvesters really think about in commons dilemma simulations: A grounded theory analysis. *Canadian Journal of Behavioural Sciences, 29*, 180–194.

Hardin, G. (1968). The tragedy of the commons. *Science, 162*, 1243–1248.

Komorita, S. S., Lapworth, C. W. (1982). Cooperative choice among individuals versus groups in an N-person dilemma situation. *Journal of Personality and Social Psychology, 42*, 487–496.

Komorita, S. S., Parks, C. D. (1994). *Social Dilemmas*. Madison, WI: Brown & Benchmark.

Leal, D. R. (1998). Community-run fisheries: Avoiding the "tragedy of the commons." *Pollution and Environment: A Journal of Interdisciplinary Studies, 19*, 225–245.

Liebrand, W., Messick, D. M., Wilke, H. (eds.) (1992). *Social Dilemmas: Theoretical Issues and Research Findings*. Oxford: Pergamon.

Lloyd, W. F. (1837/1968). *Lectures on Population, Value, Poor Laws and Rent*. New York: August M. Kelley.

Lomborg, B. (2001). *The Skeptical Environmentalist: Measuring the Real State of the World*. New York: Cambridge.

Messick, D. M., Wilke, H., Liebrand, W. B. G. (eds.), *Social Dilemmas: Theoretical Issues and Research Findings*. Oxford: Pergamon.

Moore, S. F., Shaffer, L. S., Pollak, E. L., Taylor-Lemeke, P. (1987). The effects of interpersonal trust and prior commons problem experience on commons management. *Journal of Social Psychology, 127*, 19–29.

Naseth, G. J. (1990). The effects of warning of impending resource depletion, resource control and environmental attitudes on behavior in a social dilemma. *Dissertation Abstracts International, 51(3-B)*, 1549.

Rutte, C. G., Wilke, H. A., Messick, D. M. (1987). Scarcity or abundance caused by people or the environment as determinants of behavior in the resource dilemma. *Journal of Experimental Social Psychology, 23*, 208–216.

Samuelson, C. D., Hannula, K. A. (2001). Group identity and environmental uncertainty in a sequential resource dilemma. Unpublished manuscript, Department of Psychology, Texas A&M University.

Sato, K. (1989). Trust and feedback in a social dilemma. *Japanese Journal of Experimental Social Psychology, 29*, 123–128.

Schroeder, D. A. (ed.) (1995). *Social Dilemmas: Perspectives on Individuals and Groups*. Westport, CT: Praeger.

Shulz, U., Albers, W., Mueller, U. (eds.) (1994). *Social Dilemmas and Cooperation*. Berlin: Springer-Verlag.

Simon, J. (1980). *The Ultimate Resource*. Princeton, NJ: Princeton University Press.

Smith, A. (1776). *An Inquiry into the Nature and Causes of the Wealth of Nations*. London: Methuen.

Smith, J. M., Bell, P. A., Fusco, M. E. (1988). The influence of attraction on a simulated commons dilemma. *Journal of General Psychology, 115*, 277–283.

Strauss, A., Corbin, J. (1990). *Basics of Qualitative Research: Grounded Theory Procedures and Techniques*. Newbury Park, CA: Sage.

Suleiman, R., Budescu, D., Fischer, I., Messick, D. (eds.) (2004). *Contemporary Approaches to Social Dilemma Research*. Cambridge: Cambridge University Press.

Tindall, D. B., O'Connor, B. (June 1987). Attitudes, social identity, social values, and behavior in a commons dilemma. Presentation at the Canadian Psychological Association Conference, Vancouver, BC.

Yamagishi, T. (1986). The provision of a sanctioning system as a public good. *Journal of Personality and Social Psychology, 51*, 110–116.

Yamagishi, T., Shinada, M., Kasahara, M. (July 2005). Direct and indirect effects of punishment in social dilemmas. Paper presented at the 11th International Conference of Social Dilemma, Krakow, Poland.

INDEX

Printed in the United States
92169LV00003B/106-144/A

9 780387 725956